# FEDERAL RULES

## OF

# EVIDENCE

## IN A NUTSHELL

### SIXTH EDITION

By

MICHAEL H. GRAHAM
Professor of Law
University of Miami

**THOMSON**

**WEST**

Mat #40147597

To
My Wife, Jeannette Graham

\*

# PREFACE TO SIXTH EDITION

The last twenty-eight years have seen the Federal Rules of Evidence assume their rightful place of importance alongside the Federal Rules of Civil Procedure and the Federal Rules of Criminal Procedure. Not only do the Federal Rules of Evidence govern proceedings in the federal court, forty-one states have promulgated rules of evidence modeled on the Federal Rules. While evidence courses in law school in the mid nineteen seventies taught the common law of evidence employing the Federal Rules of Evidence to highlight and contrast, today's students of the law of evidence study principally the Federal Rules of Evidence with often only passing reference to common law antecedents. Even closer to home is the relationship of the Federal Rules of Evidence to the multistate bar examination.

The structure of this Nutshell, Sixth Edition, is to present each rule of the Federal Rules of Evidence in the order in which it appears in the Federal Rules followed by commentary explaining and exploring the concepts underlying the particular rule. Commentary sections also discuss the relationship between rules so that a complete picture may be obtained. The Nutshell has been revised to reflect amendments to the Federal Rules of Evidence going into effect up to and including December 1, 2003, as well as judicial interpretations of the rules culled from thousands of citations to the Federal Rules of Evidence appearing since publication of the Fifth Edition. Overall literally tens of thousands of citations in reported federal decisions have been examined in the process of the creation of the Nutshell.

Generally speaking, consistent with the nature of a Nutshell, the commentary sections are crisp and to the point. However with respect to the definition of hearsay and exploration of the most commonly encountered exceptions more exhaustive treatment is provided. The importance of hearsay to the course in evidence and its complexity warrant the additional attention. The same holds true with respect to several other areas as well such as expert witness testimony and the operation of the confrontation clause.

The Federal Rules of Evidence address the area of privilege in Article V in a single rule, Rule 501, which requires that privileges "shall be governed by the principles of the common law as they may be interpreted by the courts of the United States in light of reason and experience." To further assist the student, the common law privileges of lawyer-client and husband-wife are discussed along with the general question of waiver. Similarly, while the Federal Rules of Evidence do not address presumptions in criminal cases or burdens of proof specifically in either civil or criminal cases, these matters are explored in considerable detail in conjunction with the discussion of presumptions in civil cases, Article III of the Federal Rules of Evidence.

Certain areas of the law of evidence are best understood in the context of concrete illustrations. To this end illustrations are provided with respect to the definition of hearsay, the operation of presumptions in civil cases, the collateral-noncollateral distinction, expert witness reasonable reliance, prior consistent statements, the business record hearsay exception and the Original Writing Rule.

This Nutshell on the Federal Rules of Evidence contains very few citations for two reasons. First, as an aid to student understanding of the law of evidence, citations to numerous authorities are not only not helpful but serve to destroy the natural flow of the commentary sections. Second, the text of the commentary sections of this Nutshell tracks very closely the text of Graham, Handbook of Federal Evidence (5th ed., West 2001), a four volume handbook for trial attorneys and judges. Students desiring authorities in support of stated propositions are referred to the exhaustive footnotes contained in the Handbook.

It is sincerely hoped that the discussion of the Federal Rules of Evidence contained in this Nutshell will assist the student in coming to grips with the law of evidence and at the same time make the task both easier and more enjoyable.

MICHAEL H. GRAHAM

March, 2003

\*

# SUMMARY OUTLINE

*

# OUTLINE

## ARTICLE II.   JUDICIAL NOTICE

## ARTICLE III. [BURDENS OF PROOF AND] PRESUMPTIONS IN CIVIL [AND CRIMINAL] ACTIONS AND PROCEEDINGS

## ARTICLE IV.  RELEVANCY AND ITS LIMITS

# OUTLINE

## OUTLINE

## OUTLINE

## ARTICLE VII.   OPINIONS AND EXPERT TESTIMONY

## ARTICLE VIII.　HEARSAY

# OUTLINE

# OUTLINE

# OUTLINE

## ARTICLE IX. AUTHENTICATION AND IDENTIFICATION

## OUTLINE

## ARTICLE X. CONTENTS OF WRITINGS, RECORDINGS, AND PHOTOGRAPHS

# OUTLINE

## ARTICLE XI.  MISCELLANEOUS RULES

## OUTLINE

\*

# TABLE OF CASES

\*

# FEDERAL RULES
OF
# EVIDENCE
## IN A NUTSHELL
SIXTH EDITION

*

# ARTICLE I

# GENERAL PROVISIONS

*Table of Rules*

## Rule 101.

## SCOPE

These rules govern proceedings in the courts of the United States and before the United States bankruptcy judges and United States magistrate judges, to the extent and with the exceptions stated in Rule 1101.

## § 101.1  Scope of Rules

Rule 101 follows the pattern set by Rule 1 of each of the Federal Rules of Civil Procedure, Federal Rules of Criminal Procedure, and Federal Rules of Appellate Procedure in making a broad general statement as to the scope of the Federal Rules of Evidence. The rule also refers to Rule 1101 where the exceptions to coverage are specified in detail.

## Rule 102.

# PURPOSE AND CONSTRUCTION

**These rules shall be construed to secure fairness in administration, elimination of unjustifiable expense and delay, and promotion of growth and development of the law of evidence to the end that the truth may be ascertained and proceedings justly determined.**

## § 102.1  Purpose and Construction

Rule 102 presents a generalized statement of purpose and construction comparable to Rule 1 of the Federal Rules of Civil Procedure and Rule 2 of the Federal Rules of Criminal Procedure. Perhaps the most significant aspect of the rule is its recognition that the Federal Rules of Evidence do not and cannot deal in specific terms with all situations that may arise. In this context, Rule 102 negates the common law rule that statutes and rules in derogation of the common law are to be strictly construed. In its place Rule 102 directs that the court shall exercise its discretion to promote the ascertainment of truth in the proceeding at hand. In addition the rule encourages the exercise of discretion in favor of promotion of growth and development of the law of evidence including reasoning by analogy to cover new or unanticipated situations.

## Rule 103.

## RULINGS ON EVIDENCE

(a) **Effect of Erroneous Ruling.** Error may not be predicated upon a ruling which admits or excludes evidence unless a substantial right of the party is affected, and

(1) **Objection.** In case the ruling is one admitting evidence, a timely objection or motion to strike appears of record, stating the specific ground of objection, if the specific ground was not apparent from the context; or

(2) **Offer of Proof.** In case the ruling is one excluding evidence, the substance of the evidence was made known to the court by offer or was apparent from the context within which questions were asked.

Once the court makes a definitive ruling on the record admitting or excluding evidence, either at or before trial, a party need not renew an objection or offer of proof to preserve a claim of error for appeal.

(b) **Record of Offer and Ruling.** The court may add any other or further statement which shows the character of the evidence, the form in which it was offered, the objection made, and the ruling thereon. It may direct the making of an offer in question and answer form.

**(c) Hearing of Jury.** In jury cases, proceedings shall be conducted, to the extent practicable, so as to prevent inadmissible evidence from being suggested to the jury by any means, such as making statements or offers of proof or asking questions in the hearing of the jury.

**(d) Plain Error.** Nothing in this rule precludes taking notice of plain error affecting substantial rights although they were not brought to the attention of the court.

## § 103.1   Rule 103(a): Reversible and Harmless Error; An Overview

The function of reviewing courts is to correct errors committed by trial courts. As indicated in Rule 103(a), a trial court is not generally regarded as committing error in the admission or exclusion of evidence unless the error and the specific ground therefor comes to the attention of the court, and the court nevertheless persists. The policy is designed to afford the court an intelligent basis of decision and to enable the opponent to take possible corrective steps. Moreover, a mere technical violation of a rule of evidence properly brought to the court's attention is not a sufficient basis for reversal. For error to result in reversal the appellate court must also find that the admission or exclusion affected a substantial right of a party, Rule 103(a). Thus for error to be reversible error it must first be error and second such error must affect a substantial right.

**Error on appeal.** The United States Supreme Court has opined that all evidentiary rulings are reviewed under the abuse of discretion standard. Unfortunately the abuse of discretion standard was itself not defined.

Some decisions view the review of evidentiary rulings as composing three independent determinations. To the extent the trial courts determination turns on an interpretation of a rule of evidence, i.e., a mistake of law, the review is plenary, frequently called de novo. Where the trial court has made a factual finding, the standard of review is clearly erroneous. Under this standard a finding of fact will be reversed only if it is completely devoid of a credible evidentiary basis or bears no rational relationship to the evidence in support. Application of a rule of evidence to the facts, is reviewed applying the abuse of discretion standard. Reversal will occur only if the ruling is manifestly erroneous, i.e., the trial court commits a clear error of judgment. Sometimes these three determinations employing three different standards of review are stated to be component parts of the abuse of discretion standard while on other occasions, in spite of the United States Supreme Courts pronouncements, the three determinations are stated to be independent. The fact that abuse of discretion is often stated to include three elements, one of which is demonstrated abuse of discretion obviously adds to the confusion. Complicating the matter still further, when a constitutional challenge to the evidence is interposed, the United States Supreme Court has indicated that the appropriate standard of review is plenary. Maybe the labeling of different issues as governed on appeal by different standards is at least on occasion a lot to do about nothing.

**Substantial right.** A substantial right is affected by error that had a "material affect" upon or "substantially swayed" the deliberations of the jury. Error not affecting a substantial right is often characterized as harmless. Rule 103(a) did not change the law with respect to either harmless error or reversible error.

*Per se* **rule of reversal.** Under certain circumstances, an appellate court will reverse a judgment because of an error committed at trial in the absence of a finding that a substantial right of a party was affected. Such *per se* rules are fashioned when the risk of affecting a party's substantial rights is unusually high, but proof of such prejudice may be difficult to establish, when an important social policy will be served by a prophylactic rule, when a more definite standard is required to guide official conduct in future cases, or when case-by-case analysis places an unjustifiable burden on limited judicial resources. To illustrate, there are a limited number of constitutional rights that are so basic to a fair trial that their infraction can never be treated as harmless, for example, complete lack of counsel, a biased trial judge, or a coerced confession, but not, for example, violation of the confrontation clause. Constitutional rights the violation of which requires reversal automatically are said to be "structural."

A formal exception need not be taken in order to make any ruling or action of the court reviewable.

In making or responding to objections with respect to the admission or exclusion of evidence, it is of course improper for counsel to invoke any statements solely for the purpose of inflaming, prejudicing or merely addressing the jury. The making of such speeches for the benefit of the jury may constitute reversible error. Accordingly, Rule 103(c) provides that in jury cases proceedings shall be conducted to the extent practicable so as to prevent inadmissible evidence from being suggested to the jury by any means.

Trial counsel should not permit the immediate objective of convincing the trier of fact to obscure the importance of making a proper record for possible review. Thus if the ruling is one admitting evidence, a timely objection or motion to strike must appear of record stating the specific ground of objection, if the specific ground is not apparent from the context, Rule 103(a)(1). On the other hand if the ruling is one excluding evidence, the substance of the evidence must be made known to the court by offer unless the substance of the evidence is apparent from the context within which the questions are asked, Rule 103(a)(2). In either event, the court may add any other or further statement which shows the character of the evidence, the form in which it was offered, the objection made, and the ruling thereon. It may also direct the making of an offer in question and answer form, Rule 103(b).

Error by the trial court concerning the admission or exclusion of evidence not brought to the attention of the court may nevertheless be considered by the appellate court if the error constitutes plain error affecting a substantial right, Rule 103(d).

## § 103.2　Rule 103(a)(1): Error in Admitting; Objection, Presentation and Waiver

Failure to make a timely and proper objection at trial to the admissibility of evidence constitutes a bar to raising the issue on appeal unless plain error exists. Similarly the admission of evidence cannot be assigned as error if an objection was made but not ruled upon, if ruling was reserved but never made, or if the objection is withdrawn at any time. Generally speaking a failure to object to earlier like evidence on the same point does not preclude objection when such additional evidence is offered. To be effective on review, the objection must state the specific ground relied upon for exclusion, unless the ground is so obvious from the context that it must have been apparent, Rule 103(a)(1). No particular words need be employed in making an objection. Whether the particular words used at the trial court adequately stated the specific ground of objection being raised on appeal must be evaluated in light of the purposes of the rule to bring the objection to the trial court's attention so that the matter may be ruled upon and to assure that the opponent be advised of what is objectionable so that it may be corrected. If only a portion of an item offered in evidence is objectionable, the objection must be directed specifically to that segment. A proper objection by one party preserves the question for review on appeal when raised by a coparty aligned in interest.

A specific objection which is overruled constitutes a waiver of all grounds not stated, or in other words one ground cannot be urged below and another on appeal. A specific objection erroneously overruled will be sustained on appeal if another ground for admissibility is asserted on appeal which if raised at trial would not itself have been subject to objection. If a specific objection is erroneously sustained, the action of the trial court in excluding evidence will be upheld on appeal if the ruling excluding the evidence was proper for some other reason and if with respect to the proper reason the objection could not have been obviated.

A general objection such as "I object, the evidence is irrelevant, immaterial, incompetent, and inadmissible" is not availing on appeal unless the offered evidence is not admissible for any purpose. Thus the general objection raises only the objection that the evidence fails to meet the test of relevancy specified in Rule 401. Following an overruled general objection, specific grounds other than relevancy may not be raised for the first time on appeal. If a general objection is sustained, where the proper ground for sustaining the objection can only be raised by a specific objection (a ground other than relevancy), the decision will be upheld on appeal only if it would be useless to reverse the case because counsel would be sure to use the correct specific objection if the case was retried to exclude what already was excluded and the specific objection could not be obviated. The party offering the evidence may discover the specific ground relied upon by the court by asking the court to state or have opposing counsel state the basis of the ruling. Once the specific ground is discovered, it is possible that the objection may then be obviated.

A party who has objected and obtained a ruling clearly indicating the attitude of the court to the admissibility of the evidence is not required to repeat the objection each time such evidence is offered whether during the examination of the same witness or another witness. Where the court has clearly ruled, repetition of the objection serves only to waste time and prejudice the objecting party in the eyes of the jury. A request for a continuing objection to the line of inquiry and a statement on the record when such evidence is again offered (which need not be made in the presence of the jury) that the earlier objection still applies, offers counsel additional protection especially where the attitude of the court to the introduction of such evidence may be less than perfectly clear. In the absence of a continuing objection, a failure to object to similar evidence waives any claim that the evidence actually admitted was admitted erroneously.

With respect to evidence which is objectionable but as to which no objection has been made, the jury may

consider the evidence for whatever probative value it
may in their judgment possess.

## § 103.3   Rule 103(a)(1): Error in Admitting; Time of Objecting; Motion to Strike; Curative Instructions

Objection to evidence must be made as soon as the
ground for objection becomes apparent, usually after the
question has been propounded but before the answer is
given. Sometimes the ground for objection is not apparent or available until after the evidence has been given
and in that event a motion to strike is appropriate. For
example, a proper question may evoke an inadmissible
answer such as hearsay; the witness may blurt out the
answer before an objection can reasonably be interposed;
evidence may become immaterial through dismissal of
the pertinent count of the complaint; evidence may not
be produced to connect up evidence admitted subject to
being connected up; or cross-examination may establish
that the direct testimony was based upon hearsay. Failure to move promptly to strike objectionable evidence
once the objection becomes apparent waives the objection.

If evidence is stricken, an instruction to the jury to
disregard it should be given on request. The sufficiency
of such a curative instruction must be determined under
all the circumstances. The human mind is not a slate,
from which can be wiped out, at the will and instruction
of another, ideas and thoughts written thereon. Nevertheless, the giving of a curative instruction is considered
sufficient in all but the most aggravated situations, and a
mistrial need not be declared.

## § 103.4  Error in Admitting: Waiver of Right to Object by Other Than Failure to Make; Door Opening

Waiver of the right to object may also occur in ways other than by failure to make an objection or move to strike. Thus a party introducing evidence of a particular kind as to a fact of consequence cannot later complain as to its admission and frequently will not be heard to complain as to the opposing party thereafter offering evidence relating to the same subject matter in rebuttal. This principle, often referred to as "opening the door," "curative admissibility," or "invited error," is compatible with Rule 103(a)(1). This aspect of waiver does not extend broadly to rules of evidence. Thus a party offering hearsay evidence, for example, would not waive the right thereafter to object to any hearsay whatever but only to hearsay offered to rebut.

If a party who has objected to inadmissible evidence produces evidence of the same fact from his own witness or goes beyond assuming the existence of such evidence to the extent of affirmatively relying upon it, he waives his objection. However, the party may cross-examine the witness presenting the evidence objected to concerning the matter and offer evidence to explain or rebut without it constituting a waiver of his objection. On the other hand, anticipatory disclosure on direct examination or otherwise of evidence definitively ruled admissible in advance of or earlier at the trial on a motion in limine, Rule 103(a), waives the right to assert error on appeal; the opposing party must be given the choice of whether or not to actually offer the evidence at trial.

The failure of the opposing party to object is of no consequence if the evidence offered is relevant and otherwise admissible. Whether admitting proof of irrelevant or otherwise inadmissible facts without objection opens the door to rebuttal evidence finds no clear answer in the decisions. Some cases take the view that the party offering the original evidence cannot complain if the trial judge accepts the boundaries of the controversy set by the litigant and permits not only cross-examination and redirect examination but also the admission of rebuttal evidence. Other cases sustain the trial court in precluding cross-examination and/or in excluding rebuttal evidence, pointing out that an adequate remedy was available by way of objection to the original evidence or that the doctrine of "opening the door", designed to prevent unfairness, should not be permitted to be used to inject prejudice. Admissibility ultimately turns on a balancing of the need to attack the inference raised against the risk of prejudice that would be posed by cross-examination and/or the introduction of the rebutting evidence, Rule 403. However the cases permitting and those denying cross-examination and/or the admission of rebuttal evidence under the foregoing standard, including those instances involving a criminal defendant's overly broad assertion of lack of prior criminal activity or prior involvement with such things as weapons or drugs, are not easily reconciled.

Inadmissible matters brought out on cross-examination cannot be used by the cross-examiner to open the door to otherwise inadmissible rebuttal evidence. It is proper, however, for the cross-examiner to inquire as to matters within the scope of the accused's direct examination and then impeach such answers with previously excluded inconsistent statements of the witness and illegally seized evidence.

Objections not raised at the first trial of a case may be urged at a later trial and are not waived, even though the later trial is one de novo on appeal or on remand. A contrary result should be reached if the objection is based on the confidential nature of information which was disclosed without objection at the earlier trial since confidentiality cannot be restored.

## § 103.5 Error in Admitting: Nonjury and Chancery Cases

In nonjury cases, it is assumed that in reaching a decision the trial judge disregarded evidence admitted improperly over objection if the record contains sufficient competent evidence to sustain the result. The effect of the assumption is to prevent a substantial right of the party from being affected under Rule 103(a). The assumption may be rebutted by a showing to the contrary. Possible methods of making the requisite showing include statements from the bench and statements contained in specific findings of facts either prepared separately or as part of an opinion or memorandum of decision. If the court improperly excludes evidence which ought to have been received, its ruling will be subject to the same standard applied in jury trials.

In nonjury cases courts frequently avoid the risk of error by following the practice of simply responding to an objection with the statement that the evidence will be admitted with the objection "considered as going to the weight of the evidence." The court then carefully avoids including evidence so admitted in detailing evidence forming the basis of decision. The same objective is also accomplished by the court reserving ruling on admissibility and then if pressed admitting but not relying upon the evidence.

## § 103.6  Rule 103(a)(2) and (b): Error in Excluding; Offer of Proof

Just as the objection is the key to saving for review any error in admitting evidence, the offer of proof is the key to saving error in excluding evidence. The purpose of the offer of proof is to disclose the nature of offered evidence to which objection is interposed not only for the information of the trial judge in the hope that the court will correct its alleged error but also to enable the reviewing court to determine whether the exclusion was erroneous and if so whether it affected a substantial right. While the circumstances and the question itself may sufficiently indicate the purpose and substance of the evidence sought, Rule 103(a)(2), the making of an offer is the safer course. Unless excused because apparent from the context, failure to make an offer of proof precludes raising the question on appeal, Rule 103(a)(2). A proper offer of proof by one party preserves the question for review on appeal when raised by a co-party aligned in interest.

Questions with respect to offers of proof usually arise with respect to evidence excluded during direct examination of a friendly witness. Sometimes, however, similar questions arise when evidence is excluded upon cross-examination or direct examination of an adverse witness. Under such circumstances, an offer of proof is frequently unnecessary in that the substance of the evidence being excluded is apparent from the context, Rule 103(a)(2). This may occur where a particular answer to a leading question permits, and examining counsel obviously expects, an answer favorable to his client. The substance of excluded evidence may also be sufficiently apparent as well where the cross-examiner expects an unfavorable response and obviously intends to pursue a given line of inquiry. If the substance of the cross-examiner's intended examination is not apparent to the court, an offer of proof can be made outside the witness' presence.

Sometimes, however, on cross-examination or direct of an adverse witness not only is the substance of the evidence excluded not apparent, it can not be anticipated even by examining counsel. Under such circumstances, there is authority creating an additional exception to the requirement of an offer on the theory that the examination being exploratory, counsel is not in a position to know what the witness could or would testify to if permitted to do so. However since such a difficulty is overcome by the taking of the offer of proof in question and answer form outside the presence of the jury, combining a liberal interpretation of when the substance of the evidence is apparent from the context with a requirement of an offer of proof on cross-examination or direct of an adverse witness when substance is not apparent seems preferable to recognizing an exception to the requirement of an offer of proof not contained in Rule 103.

When an offer of proof as to excluded evidence is required under Rule 103(a)(2), an offer is sufficient if counsel makes known to the court outside the hearing of the jury, Rule 103(c), with particularity the substance of the witness or witnesses anticipated answers even if the witness or witnesses are not actually produced, provided no question is raised as to his ability to produce each witness or of a witness testifying as represented. Under Rule 103(b), the court in its discretion may permit or direct counsel to make an offer of proof in question and answer form. The taking of the offer in question and answer form resolves all doubts as to the content of the proposed testimony. Cross-examination of the witness on the offered testimony may also be permitted in the

discretion of the court as may be the offering of contradictory evidence or comment on the offer by counsel to
pinpoint areas of controversy. If the evidence excluded
consists of a document authenticated in the record or by
offer of proof, a sufficient offer of proof is made by
requesting the reporter to insert the exhibit in the record. The purpose of the offered evidence, if not readily
apparent, should be stated. The court may add a statement showing the character of the offered evidence, the
form in which offered, the objection and ruling, Rule
103(b). A reviewing court will consider the propriety of
an exclusionary ruling only in light of the stated purpose
and legal basis for the offer actually made.

Although trial courts are required to permit counsel to
make an offer of proof, an extremely hostile attitude on
the part of the trial judge to the offer will excuse the
making of an offer.

Sustaining an objection to an offer which contains
admissible as well as inadmissible matter is not error.
Excluding for a wrong reason is not error if there is in
fact a valid reason which could not be obviated in the
trial court. Impropriety in the form of the question,
being correctable, does not fall in the latter category.

Offers of proof need not be repeated where the court
has clearly indicated at trial that certain evidence will
not be received. However, if the court postpones ruling
on the question, or indicates that the offer may later be
accepted, the offer must be renewed at the appropriate
time.

## § 103.7   Rule 103(c): Hearing of Jury; Motions in Limine

To the extent practicable, proceedings are to be conducted so as to prevent inadmissible evidence from being

suggested to the jury by any means, Rule 103(c). Objectionable questions propounded to the witness, the making of statements by counsel, and offers of proof in the hearing of the jury are provided as illustrations in Rule 103(c). The jury may be excused, the court and counsel may retire to chambers, or counsel may approach the bench, as means of preventing the question, statement or offer from coming to the jury's attention. If the jury is to be excused, the offer will frequently be made after the witness' testimony has been concluded.

Another alternative, and one increasing in popularity, is to seek a ruling as to the admissibility of evidence in advance of trial, a process frequently referred to as a motion in limine. A motion in limine not only shields the trier of fact from inadmissible evidence being presented in their presence as well as the unfair prejudice that may arise from the mere asking of a question and the making of an objection, it also affords a basis for advance planning of trial strategy. A motion in limine may be made either during pretrial or at trial in advance of the presentation of evidence. The court has considerable discretion to rule or refuse to rule upon the motion prior to the actual offer of the evidence at trial. Frequently a pretrial ruling would be inappropriate in light of the necessity to determine the admissibility of the evidence in relation to various factors which themselves would surface only at trial.

Rule 103(a) provides that "once the court makes a definitive ruling on the record admitting or excluding evidence, either at or before trial, a party need not renew an objection or offer of proof to preserve a claim of error for appeal." Conversely, a ruling made by the court which is not "definitive" does not preserve error for appeal; the losing party is required to either renew the objection or make an offer of proof at trial. Such rulings are sometimes referred to as "provisional" or "tentative". The same requirement of objection or offer of proof to preserve error for appeal is of course imposed where the court reserves its ruling. The Advisory Committee's Note advises that the rule "imposes the obligation on [losing] counsel to clarify whether an in limine or other evidentiary ruling is definitive when there is doubt on that point."

Even where the court's ruling is "definitive", nothing in Rule 103(a) prohibits the court from revisiting its decision when the evidence is actually to be offered at trial. Moreover, anticipatory disclosure on direct examination or otherwise of evidence definitively ruled admissible in advance of or earlier at trial on a motion in limine, for example a prior conviction, waives the right to claim error on appeal; the opposing party must be given the choice whether or not to actually offer the evidence at trial. If the court changes its ruling, an objection or offer of proof must then be made to preserve the claim of error for appeal. Similarly, evidence offered in violation of the terms of the court's initial ruling must be objected to at trial.

A definitive advance ruling is reviewed in light of the facts and circumstances before the trial court at the time of the ruling. If the relevant facts and circumstances change materially after the advance ruling has been made, those facts and circumstances cannot be relied upon on appeal unless they have been brought to the attention of the trial court by way of a renewed, and timely, objection, offer of proof, or motion to strike. Nor may the opponent claim error on appeal based upon new evidence actually adduced at trial if the objection is not renewed. Similarly, if the court decides in an advance ruling that proffered evidence is admissible subject to the eventual introduction by the proponent of a foundation for the evidence, and that foundation is never provided, the opponent cannot claim error based on the failure to establish the foundation unless the opponent calls that failure to the court's attention by a timely motion to strike or other suitable motion. Conversely, on appeal the court will consider in support of the trial court's advance ruling all evidence admitted at trial, including evidence not presented at the advance ruling hearing.

## § 103.8 Rule 103(d): Plain Error

The adversary system, based on party responsibility, is deeply engrained in our jurisprudence, particularly in the field of evidence. This belief in the efficacy of the adversary system together with considerations of judicial economy, underlie the requirement that for potentially reversible error to be considered on appeal it must first have been brought to the attention of the trial court, Rule 103(a)(1). Occasionally, however, the error committed so affects a substantial right as to induce the reviewing court to reject the result at trial in spite of the fact that since a proper objection was not made, strict adherence to the adversary system would require affirmance. This so-called doctrine of "plain error," incorporated into Rule 103(d), finds greater application in criminal cases. However, on rare occasion the circumstances of a civil case may fall within it. The infrequency with which the doctrine is generally applied precludes deliberate reliance upon it during the trial of a case.

The relationship between Rule 103(a) which defines reversible or non-harmless error as one affecting a "substantial right" and Rule 103(d) providing for the consideration on appeal of errors affecting "substantial rights" when not brought to the attention of the trial court is less than totally clear. If the term "substantial right" is given the same meaning in each rule, failure to object at trial would be inconsequential. Not surprisingly most of the attempted definitions suggest that plain error is obvious error of a somewhat more fundamental or serious nature than reversible error; plain error is error that seriously affects the fairness, integrity or public reputation of judicial proceedings. As a practical matter, however, it is still not very clear how much more serious an error must be than reversible error in order to merit plain error treatment, nor is it clear how to determine whether a given error is more serious than reversible error. Recent opinions dealing with the question of plain error often seem to reflect nothing more than the conclusion reached by the court. The current definition of plain error seems best viewed as only a general indicator of the nature of the inquiry.

## Rule 104.

## PRELIMINARY QUESTIONS

(a) **Questions of Admissibility Generally. Preliminary questions concerning the qualification of a person to be a witness, the existence of a privilege, or the admissibility of evidence shall be determined by the court, subject to the provisions of subdivision (b). In making its determination it is not bound by the rules of evidence except those with respect to privileges.**

(b) **Relevancy Conditioned on Fact. When the relevancy of evidence depends upon the fulfill-**

ment of a condition of fact, the court shall admit it upon, or subject to, the introduction of evidence sufficient to support a finding of the fulfillment of the condition.

(c) Hearing of Jury. Hearings on the admissibility of confessions shall in all cases be conducted out of the hearing of the jury. Hearings on other preliminary matters shall be so conducted when the interests of justice require, or when an accused is a witness and so requests.

(d) Testimony by Accused. The accused does not, by testifying upon a preliminary matter, become subject to cross-examination as to other issues in the case.

(e) Weight and Credibility. This rule does not limit the right of a party to introduce before the jury evidence relevant to weight or credibility.

## § 104.1  Rule 104(a) and (e): Preliminary Questions of Admissibility; Weight and Credibility

The rules of evidence are administered by the trial judge. The admissibility of evidence, the assertion of a privilege, or the qualification of a witness as an expert, often depends upon the existence of a disputed factual condition. Submitting factual issues of this kind generally to the jury, as they arise from time to time during the trial or at its conclusion, would be hopelessly confusing, as well as beyond the probable capacity of the jurors. To illustrate, with respect to the admissibility of a statement asserted to be protected from disclosure by the lawyer-client privilege, if the jurors heard the actual statement with instructions to erase it from their minds if they find it was not made knowingly in the presence of a third party, the jury would be incapable of doing so. It is something like telling a little boy to go to the corner and not think of elephants. The result would be frustration of the policy underlying the privilege. Hence pursuant to Rule 104(a) preliminary questions of fact as conditions precedent to admissibility or competency of witnesses, other than those involving relevancy conditioned on fact, Rule 104(b), are decided solely by the court.

In making its determination the court is not bound by rules of evidence except those with respect to privilege, Rule 104(a). Accordingly, affidavits or other hearsay statements may be considered in reaching its preliminary determination of admissibility. In addition, an item offered and objected to may itself be considered by the court in ruling on admissibility. Thus the content of a statement against interest, Rule 804(b)(3), may be considered in determining whether it was against interest. Similarly, evidence of personal knowledge, Rule 602, may consist of the content of the statement of the witness itself. The testimony of a witness may also be considered for example in determining whether the witness is a qualified expert.

Some of the rules which exclude relevant evidence rest upon policy considerations having no immediate connection with weight and credibility. Hence the evidence upon preliminary questions of fact, as well as the decision of such issues, is for the trial judge alone, Rule 104(a). Illustrations are determinations in miscellaneous proceedings as delineated in Rule 1101(d)(3); whether an original has been shown to be lost thereby permitting introduction of secondary evidence of its contents; incompetency of witness on technical grounds such as where witness is also a juror or banned by a Dead Man's Statute; whether a particular communication is privileged; and whether a particular witness is unavailable.

Other rules which exclude relevant evidence rest upon policy considerations intimately connected with or overlapping weight and credibility. While the court in these cases pursuant to Rule 104(a) also decides alone preliminary issues of fact, the evidence adduced thereon bears upon weight and credibility as well, and, in the event of a ruling favorable to admissibility or competency, falls within the province of the jury in determining that question. Examples are the competency of a lay witness, qualification of an expert witness, admissibility of a statement under a hearsay exception or as not hearsay, and whether a confession was voluntary. In the interest of saving time, the practice of presenting the preliminary evidence to the court and jury simultaneously seems proper, except in cases in which a ruling against admissibility would allow the jury to hear prejudicial evidence, Rules 103(c) and 104(c). While the determination as to whether the possibility of unfair prejudice requires the initial presentation of evidence be made outside the presence of the jury is usually left to the discretion of the court, Rule 104(c) provides specifically that hearings are to be conducted outside the hearing of the jury when the issue concerns the admissibility of a confession. If the confession is admitted, the accused may present his evidence again before the jury. Hearings on other preliminary matters must also be conducted outside the hearing of the jury when the accused is a witness and so requests, Rule 104(c).

Clearly the jury should not be instructed to second-guess the favorable ruling of the court on admissibility and to disregard the evidence if they find the evidence inadmissible; their function is to determine weight and credibility, not admissibility. To assist the jury any party may, of course, introduce evidence relevant to weight or credibility, Rule 104(e).

In reaching a determination pursuant to Rule 104(a) on a question of admissibility for the court alone whether that be in a criminal or a civil case, the court should apply the standard for the burden of persuasion applicable generally in civil cases of more probably true than not true.

## § 104.2 Rule 104(b): Relevancy Conditioned on Fact; Connecting Up

Where the relevancy of a particular item of evidence depends upon the existence of a preliminary or connecting fact, if determination of such conditional relevancy was made solely by the court, the function of the jury would be unduly restricted. Accordingly, pursuant to Rule 104(b) when relevancy depends upon the fulfillment of a condition of fact, such as authentication or personal knowledge, the matter is given different treatment. If relevancy depends upon facts of this kind, a prima facie showing of their existence is required as a prerequisite to admitting the evidence. Thus evidence sufficient to support a finding by a reasonable juror of the fulfillment of the condition must be introduced, Rule 104(b). In reaching a determination under Rule 104(b), the court may consider only that evidence which the jury will have before it evidence admitted under the rules of evidence. If a prima facie showing has been made, evidence in support together with contrary evidence produced by the opponent is then considered by the jury as part of the overall process of determining the facts of the case.

Where appropriate, the jury may be instructed to determine whether the evidence is relevant by deciding whether the condition is fulfilled, and to ignore or employ the evidence accordingly. Moreover, if considering all the evidence upon the issue including evidence subsequently introduced by the opponent the jury could no longer reasonably find that the condition was fulfilled, the court should instruct the jury to disregard the evidence.

Where the admissibility of evidence depends upon connecting facts, the order of proof is largely within the discretion of the trial judge. Evidence admitted upon a promise to connect it up will be excluded on a motion to strike if the appropriate connection has not been established.

## § 104.3 Rule 104(c): Hearing in Presence of Jury

It is usually within the court's discretion to determine whether the interests of justice require that the hearing of a preliminary matter pursuant to either Rule 104(a) or (b) be conducted outside the hearing of the jury, Rule 104(c). The use of the word "hearing" of the jury rather than presence clearly is designed to permit side bar conferences. In exercising its discretion, the court must weigh the potential for prejudice derived from the jury's hearing the evidence against such trial concerns as waste of time caused by taking the same testimony twice and the dislike of juries in being excluded.

Under Rule 104(c), however, when the preliminary matter concerns the admissibility of a confession, the hearing must be conducted outside the jury's hearing. Hearings on other preliminary matters must also be conducted out of the hearing of the jury where the accused is a witness and so requests. In the rare cases in

which a matter usually decided prior to trial involving a
constitutional right of the accused surfaces initially at
trial such as pretrial identification, search and seizure, or
*Miranda* warnings, the interests of justice will normally
call for identical treatment.

### § 104.4   Rule 104(d): Testimony by Accused Upon Preliminary Matter; Suppressed Evidence

An accused by testifying upon a preliminary matter,
such as a motion to suppress, does not subject himself to
cross-examination as to other issues in the case, Rule
104(d). While such testimony by the accused as to a
preliminary matter may not be used against him as
evidence in chief at trial, it may be admitted to impeach
the defendant if he testifies. Similarly, if a statement of
the defendant is suppressed, for example, because of
failure to give *Miranda* warnings or for failure to provide
him a lawyer upon request, if the statement is otherwise
shown to have been voluntarily made, the statement may
be employed to impeach. Evidence illegally seized may
also be employed for impeachment purposes.

### Rule 105.

### LIMITED ADMISSIBILITY

**When evidence which is admissible as to one
party or for one purpose but not admissible as to
another party or for another purpose is admitted,
the court, upon request, shall restrict the evidence
to its proper scope and instruct the jury accordingly.**

## § 105.1   Limited Admissibility

Evidence may be admissible as to one party or for one purpose but not admissible as to another party or for another purpose. Upon objection, the offering party has the burden of advising the court as to the party or the limited purpose for which the evidence is admissible. Under such circumstances an opposing party is entitled on request to an instruction to the jury, referred to alternatively as a limiting or cautionary instruction, restricting their use of the evidence to its proper scope, Rule 105. Counsel frequently refrain from requesting a limiting instruction in order to avoid emphasizing potentially damaging evidence or for other strategic reasons. Absent plain error, a failure to request a limiting instruction precludes raising the question on appeal. When the court believes that the giving of a limiting instruction may be required in order to avoid plain error, the court may on its own initiative give such an instruction or first inquire whether counsel desires a limiting instruction be given. Evidence admissible as to one party but not another is similarly treated.

On occasion despite the availability of a limiting instruction, the harm likely to result from improper use of the evidence by the jury nevertheless requires exclusion of the evidence. Under Rule 403 the potential harm which might result from the jury considering evidence admitted for a limited purpose or against less than all parties for a prohibited purpose or against the remaining parties, must be considered in light of the potential effectiveness of the limiting instruction in deciding whether the evidence should be excluded. If, after taking into consideration the probable effectiveness of a limiting instruction, the court determines that the "probative value is substantially outweighed by the dangers of unfair prejudice, confusion of the issues, or misleading the jury," Rule 403, the evidence will not be admitted.

In Bruton v. United States (S.Ct.1968), the Supreme Court held that the substantial risk that the jury, despite instructions to the contrary, would consider extrajudicial statements of a nontestifying codefendant as implicating the accused made introduction of such statement improper. However, a properly redacted statement of a nontestifying codefendant, not substantively admissible against the codefendant, may be introduced; the confrontation clause is not violated by the admission of a nontestifying codefendants confession with a proper limiting instruction when the confession is redacted to eliminate not only the defendants name but any reference to her existence. A properly redacted statement is one that does not facially incriminate the codefendant. A redacted statement has been held to satisfy the foregoing standard following insertion of the pronouns "we" or "they" or the indefinite pronoun such as "someone" when following such insertions the statement does not facially, without reference to other evidence, still obviously refer to and implicate the codefendant. A proper limiting instruction is, of course, required.

The effectiveness of a limiting instruction has been characterized as trying to unring a bell and as a mental gymnastic which is beyond not only the jury's powers, but anybody else's. In spite of such condemnations, as pointed out in the Advisory Committee's Note, where the risk of prejudice is not as severe as it was in *Bruton,* the common practice is to admit evidence for a limited purpose or against less than all parties and instruct the jury accordingly.

## Rule 106.

## REMAINDER OF OR RELATED WRITINGS OR RECORDED STATEMENTS

When a writing or recorded statement or part thereof is introduced by a party, an adverse party may require the introduction at that time of any other part or any other writing or recorded statement which ought in fairness to be considered contemporaneously with it.

### § 106.1 Remainder of or Related Writings and Recorded Statements Employed at Time of Introduction

When a party introduces a writing or recorded statement, or only part of a writing or recorded statement, an adverse party may require him to introduce at that time any other part or any other writing or recorded statement which in fairness ought to be considered contemporaneously, Rule 106. Recognition is thus given in Rule 106 to the principle of completeness: a writing or recorded statement or a part thereof may be so related to another that in fairness both should be considered together without regard to whether the related writing or recorded statement is or is not contained in the same document. Accordingly, Rule 106 authorizes the adverse party to require the proponent of evidence in the form of a writing or recorded statement to introduce *at the time* offered into evidence any other part or any other written or recorded statement which ought in fairness to be considered at the same time. As stated in the Advisory Committee's Note, Rule 106 "does not in any way circumscribe the right of the adversary to develop the matter on cross-examination or as part of his own case." Oral statements are not included in Rule 106.

The importance of bringing out such related material at the time of introduction is apparent. First, it avoids the danger of mistaken or misleading first impression when matters are taken out of context. Second, it avoids the inadequate remedy of requiring the adverse party to wait until a later point in the trial to repair his case. The provisions of Rule 106 apply with equal force to writings and recorded statements introduced for a limited purpose such as impeachment.

To be admitted under Rule 106, the additional part or other writing or recorded statement must relate to the same subject matter and tend to deny, explain, modify, qualify, counteract, repel, disprove, or otherwise shed light on the writing or recorded statement already received. Moreover, it is sometimes stated that such writing or recorded statement may be admitted only if otherwise admissible. However, since admissibility includes principles governing the operation of the concept of waiver of objection through "door opening", otherwise inadmissible evidence often does in fact become admissible. Ultimately, whether otherwise inadmissible evidence offered to deny, explain, modify, qualify, counteract, repel, disprove, or otherwise shed light on the part already received is admitted should depend upon whether its probative value in such regard is substantially outweighed by dangers of unfair prejudice, confusion of the issues, misleading the jury, or waste of time, Rule 403.

The party seeking admission of any other part or any other writing or recorded statement under Rule 106 must lay a sufficient foundation which consists of specification of the portion sought to be introduced and an articulation of why in fairness such portion ought to be considered contemporaneously.

## § 106.2  Remainder of Oral Statements, Writing or Recorded Statement Employed on Next Examination

With respect to other parts of writings and recorded statements or related writings and recorded statements, counsel may eschew Rule 106 and develop the matter on cross-examination or as part of his own case. Similarly, the remainder of oral statements and related oral statements may be introduced by an opposing party on his next examination of the same witness, whether cross or redirect. Of course, as with written or recorded statements, it is sometimes stated that the additional oral statements may be admitted only if otherwise admissible. Clearly the principle of completeness does not give an adverse party an unqualified right to introduce an omitted part of a conversation or related conversation otherwise inadmissible merely on the ground that the opponent has "opened the door." To the extent however that such evidence, otherwise inadmissible, tends to explain, modify, qualify or shed light on the evidence offered by the opponent, the evidence may be admitted provided its explanatory value is not substantially outweighed by dangers of unfair prejudice, confusion of the issues, misleading the jury, or waste of time, Rule 403.

Under unusual circumstances, the court may require the proponent to introduce contemporaneously other parts of oral conversations pursuant to the general authority of the court to control the mode and order of interrogating witnesses and presentation of evidence.

# ARTICLE II

# JUDICIAL NOTICE

*Table of Rules*

## Rule 201.

## JUDICIAL NOTICE OF ADJUDICATIVE FACTS

**(a) Scope of Rule. This rule governs only judicial notice of adjudicative facts.**

**(b) Kinds of Facts. A judicially noticed fact must be one not subject to reasonable dispute in that it is either (1) generally known within the territorial jurisdiction of the trial court or (2) capable of accurate and ready determination by resort to sources whose accuracy cannot reasonably be questioned.**

**(c) When Discretionary. A court may take judicial notice, whether requested or not.**

(d) **When Mandatory.** A court shall take judicial notice if requested by a party and supplied with the necessary information.

(e) **Opportunity to Be Heard.** A party is entitled upon timely request to an opportunity to be heard as to the propriety of taking judicial notice and the tenor of the matter noticed. In the absence of prior notification, the request may be made after judicial notice has been taken.

(f) **Time of Taking Notice.** Judicial notice may be taken at any stage of the proceeding.

(g) **Instructing Jury.** In a civil action or proceeding, the court shall instruct the jury to accept as conclusive any fact judicially noticed. In a criminal case, the court shall instruct the jury that it may, but is not required to, accept as conclusive any fact judicially noticed.

### § 201.1   Rule 201(a): Nature of Judicial Notice; An Overview

Judicial notice is founded on the assumption that certain factual determinations are not subject to reasonable dispute and thus may be appropriately resolved other than by the production of evidence before the trier of fact at trial. This process is known as judicial notice of an adjudicative fact. Adjudicative facts are simply the facts of the particular case the facts that normally go to the jury. Adjudicative facts are the "who did what, where, when, how and with what motive or intent." They relate to the parties, their activities, their properties, their businesses. Not only may adjudicative facts be judicially noticed which would otherwise be for the jury to determine, judicial notice of adjudicative facts may be

taken where the factual determination in question is to
be made by the court. Rule 201 deals solely with judicial
notice of adjudicative facts.

A high degree of indisputability is an essential prerequisite for adjudicative facts to be judicially noticed. In
some instances the particular fact may be beyond reasonable dispute because generally known within the territorial jurisdiction of the trial court, Rule 201(b)(1). Courts
are presumed to be no more ignorant than the public
generally, and will take judicial notice of that which is
generally known to be true. Or, if not generally known,
the matter may be beyond controversy because verifiable
from sources of such nature as to eliminate reasonable
dispute. Thus judicial notice may be taken of a fact
capable of accurate and ready determination by resort to
sources whose accuracy cannot reasonably be questioned,
Rule 201(b)(2). Propositions of generalized knowledge
from encyclopedias or other sources may not be judicially
noticed pursuant to Rule 201(b).

As a matter of practice, a request for judicial notice of
an adjudicative fact should rarely arise at trial in civil
litigation conducted by evenly matched competent counsel. Where a matter is generally known or capable of
accurate and ready determination, the matter is the
proper subject of either a stipulation or request to admit.
If counsel refuses to admit such fact, several remedies
are available including a motion in limine requesting the
court to take judicial notice. Judicial notice of an adjudicative fact occasionally arises at trial in both civil and
criminal cases under circumstances where a party either
did not or could not anticipate in advance the need to
prove a potentially judicially noticeable fact. In some
such instances resort to proof would be extremely time

consuming and expensive. In others, sufficient admissible evidence could not be produced at all within a reasonable period of time. While it appears nowhere in Rule 201, the court's willingness to take judicial notice of an adjudicative fact either before or at trial is greatly influenced by the relationship of the particular fact to the litigation at hand.

Another basis for judicial notice, not always recognized and labeled as such, is that the matter is best decided by the judge and best decided by him without the confining limitations of ordinary evidence and the rules governing its admission. Within this aspect falls the determination of applicable law as reflected in constitutional provisions, statutes, court opinions, court rules, etc. Within it also falls the factual foundations of rules of decision including social, scientific, economic and often political factors whether or not generally known or readily determinable, referred to as judicial notice of legislative facts. Both judicial notice of law and legislative facts are outside the scope of Rule 201. With respect to judicial notice of legislative facts, a high degree of indisputability is not required. From the foregoing remarks, it seems apparent that courts may be expected to apply judicial notice in a more restricted fashion when the matter involved is an adjudicative fact, one relevant only to the particular case, than when the formulation, validity, or construction of a legal rule, i.e., legislative fact, is concerned.

The precise line of demarcation between adjudicative facts and legislative facts is not always easily identified. For example, consider the determination of whether cocaine hydrochloride is a derivative of the coca leaf so as to come within the comprehensive Drug Abuse Prevention and Control Act of 1970. Is it a legislative fact in the sense of interpretation of a statute or is it adjudicative in the sense that it clearly and immediately affects the parties? What about the effect of inflation as it affects judicial salaries?

Judicial notice, adjudicative and legislative, may also be taken by any court of appellate jurisdiction even if the taking of judicial notice was refused by the trial court or not requested below, Rule 201(f).

## § 201.2 Rule 201(b)(1): Adjudicative Facts; Matters Generally Known

A court will take judicial notice of matters which are generally known in the territorial jurisdiction of the trial court and not subject to reasonable dispute. Universal knowledge is not required; generally known is sufficient, Rule 201(b)(1). For example, judicial notice has been taken that the Ohio River is navigable; that lethal voltages of electricity are present in television sets; that the Ledger is New Jersey's only statewide newspaper as well as the largest in circulation and advertising; that vast amounts of purchases are made by credit card; and of the wind factor in the San Francisco Bay Area. The foregoing illustrations provide only a flavor of the variety of facts which have been judicially noticed.

The matter judicially noticed must be determined by the court to be generally known in the territorial jurisdiction in which the court sits; it is insufficient that the judge is personally aware of the matter as an individual observer outside of court.

## § 201.3 Rule 201(b)(2): Adjudicative Facts; Accurate and Ready Determination

Although not generally known, matters may be so capable of verification by resort to sources whose accuracy cannot reasonably be questioned as to be beyond reasonable dispute and hence proper subjects of judicial notice, Rule 201(b)(2). Matters falling within this category are numerous and varied as shown by the following typical and by no means exclusive illustrations:

**Acts, records and personnel of court.** A court will take judicial notice of its own acts and records in the same case, of facts established in prior proceedings in the same case, of the authenticity of its own records of another case between the same parties, of the files of related cases in the same court, and of public records on file in the same court. In addition judicial notice will be taken of the record, pleadings or judgment of a case in another court between the same parties or involving one of the same parties, as well as of the record of another case between different parties in the same court. Judicial notice will also be taken of court personnel.

**Geographic and physical facts.** Judicial notice has been taken of physical facts such as that relating to a reservoir and of geographic distances and locations including that the Federal Correctional Institute, Tallahassee, Florida is located within the special territorial jurisdiction of the United States; that certain named streets are located in a federal enclave; that North Little Rock, Arkansas is in Pulaski County which is in the Eastern District of Arkansas; that Alaska lies west of the ninety-eighth meridian; and that Lake Bisteneau has not been navigable since construction of a dam forty years ago.

**Published compilations.** The fact that industrial statistics relevant to renegotiation are available in reliable and readily accessible sources was judicially noticed but not the specific items of comparative information because of the difficulty of identifying and making the relevant comparisons without assistance from the parties. Judicial notice has also been taken of the content of the Yellow Pages of the Providence Telephone Directory.

**Statistical facts.** Judicial notice may be taken of present discounted value tables as well as of the mean grade point average for an entering class of veterinary students as well as the results of a survey showing the customary billing rate for attorneys in Columbus, Ohio.

**Historical facts.** Earliest known records of vehicle wheels judicially noticed by reference to encyclopedia along with fact disclosed in encyclopedia of pro football that Jack Snow was drafted in the first round by the Minnesota Vikings.

**Government matters and public records.** Judicial notice has been taken of decisions and orders of the National Mediation Board issued pursuant to Board's statutory power to certify bargaining representatives; of a voter roster as published in newspapers as evidencing a designation of beneficiaries; and of appointment of a state court judge to fill a vacancy. It has also been judicially noticed from the records of the Vessel Documentation Division of the Coast Guard that an individual's vessel is enrolled and licensed; that the United States does not endeavor to procure the return to this country of defendants indicted for violation of the Selective Service laws or regulations; and that a prisoner has been moved. Judicial notice may be taken of recorded deeds, tax liens and the county general index.

**Religious facts.** The fact that dietary laws are of critical theological importance to orthodox Judaism has been judicially noticed.

**Political facts.** Judicial notice was taken that the State of Mississippi maintained a policy of segregation in its public schools and colleges and that the Klan is a white hate group, but not of the political philosophy of Lenin.

**Business facts.** Judicial notice has been taken that Citibank, N.A., is an F.D.I.C. insured bank and one of the world's largest banking institutions.

**Scientific principles and authoritative treatises.** Taking judicial notice of elementary principles of physics and other sciences is commonplace and requires no investigation. Beyond these rudimentary matters, the extent to which judicial notice will be taken of scientific principles remains largely unexplored. At the same time it is clear that the use of scientific experts produced by the parties as witnesses does not always afford a satisfactory resolution of scientific questions. The exasperation with expert witnesses is evidenced both by the existence of Rule 706 providing for court appointed experts and the Advisory Committee's comment that "the practice of shopping for experts, the venality of some experts, and the reluctance of many experts to involve themselves in litigation, have been matters of deep concern." Judicial notice has a role to play. Rule 803(18) provides for judicial notice of the reliability of learned treatises.

Judicial notice takes on particular importance in connection with the admissibility of various scientific tests, processes, instruments, etc., on behalf of the government in criminal cases. In order for the results of a test, process, instrument, etc., to be admissible, the scientific principle upon which it is based must be determined by the court to possess evidentiary reliability. Once such reliability of the scientific principle has been firmly judicially established, the validity of the scientific principle may then be judicially noticed in later actions, leaving only the application of the test, process, instrument, etc., in the case at hand in dispute. This process has occurred, for example, with respect to radar, ballistics, DNA, fingerprints, typewriting comparisons, and tests for intoxication and paternity.

## § 201.4  Judicial Notice: Ascertaining the Appropriate Law

Pleading and proof of the laws of the United States, whether embodied in statute or court decision, are neither necessary nor appropriate. Matters appearing in the Federal Register and the contents of the Code of Federal Regulation must also be judicially noticed. In addition federal courts are obligated to judicially notice the statutes and case law of the various states. However, judicial notice need not be taken of state administrative regulations, private acts, or local ordinances and unpublished federal items of the same nature. The taking of judicial notice of such items rests in the court's discretion. Determination of foreign law is governed by the provisions of Fed.R.Civ.Proc. 44.1 and Fed.R.Crim.Proc. 26.1, each of which provides both for the availability of judicial notice upon notice of intent and for the submission of evidence, including testimony.

Thus federal courts are permitted to determine domestic or foreign law on the basis of any relevant material or source, whether or not submitted by a party and whether or not admissible under the Federal Rules of Evidence. Where domestic law is involved, the court may and in some instances must judicially notice such law even though neither party offers evidence. However, where questions of foreign law are asserted, determination by the court through judicial notice can occur only if notice of intent to rely on the law of a foreign country has been provided by the party raising the issue.

## § 201.5   Judicial Notice of Legislative Facts: Factual Bases of Judicial Rules

It is familiar doctrine that a case is decided by applying the law, as determined by the court, to the facts, as determined by the trier of fact. The facts contemplated are the adjudicative facts of the particular case as developed by the conventional process of producing evidence at the trial or as judicially noticed within the rather limited categories previously discussed. Another way in which facts enter most significantly into the judicial process is in the formulation of the rules of law themselves by the courts.

Many rules of law are predicated upon factual foundations. These factual foundations are commonly constructed by the process of judicial notice. Often they consist of patterns of human behavior, assumed to exist on the basis of casual observation, experience, and anecdote, but without systematic or statistical observation. No judicial counterpart even of the legislative hearing exists. These assumptions are thus wide ranging and far reaching, without the cautious insistence upon certainty and opportunity to be heard which characterizes judicial notice of adjudicative facts. For example, the husband-wife privilege is supported by the notion that adverse testimony by a spouse of an accused in a criminal prosecution is likely to destroy a marriage; that the incentive to invent supplied by the patent law will not work in organized research because it destroys team work and cooperation; and that the test of insanity then in use was out of step with the view of society.

## § 201.6   Judicial Notice of Legislative Facts: Factual Aspects of Legislation

Facts also enter importantly into the process of making law by legislative enactment and in the treatment accorded its product by the courts.

The validity of a statute not infrequently depends upon the reasonableness of the legislature's view of the factual basis upon which it is erected. This reasonableness is commonly tested by the courts against a factual background of their own developed by the broadest kind of judicial notice. For example, a statute requiring disclosure of weight on a product label was stricken after the court judicially noticed that purchasers of bread would not confuse a ten-ounce loaf with a pound loaf. In addition judicial notice has been taken of facts concerning whether cocaine and heroin are imported or domestically grown in determining the validity of criminal statutory presumptions; of municipal methods of funding in deciding the constitutionality of the Municipal Claims Act; of the detrimental effects of segregation on Negro children; and in determining the constitutionality of a statute prohibiting the sale of contraceptives to persons under 16 that persons under sixteen do engage in sexual intercourse and that the result is often venereal disease, unwanted pregnancy, or both.

Judicial notice is also taken by the court in determining the constitutionality of legislative enactments as applied in particular cases. For example, the literature relating to the significance of dietary laws to Orthodox Jews was judicially noticed in determining entitlement to such food while in prison. In addition judicial notice has been taken that federal judges, members of Congress, and federal employees in the Executive Schedule among others comprise the class of citizens who have borne the brunt of inflation.

Finally, judicial notice also plays a significant role in the construction and application of legislation. For example, judicial notice was taken of Ohio House Bill No. 610 in an action to determine whether there was subject matter jurisdiction under Title VII of the Civil Rights Act of 1964. In addition judicial notice has been taken on a motion for a preliminary injunction by civil service employees of the Army to prevent them from being fired that Congress had already appropriated funds to pay all members of plaintiffs' class and that even one day's break in a federal employee's service will entail the loss of salary retention rights, and that cocaine hydrochloride is a derivative of the coca leaf and consequently subject to the Controlled Substance Import and Export Act.

## § 201.7  Rules 201(c)-(g): Procedural Aspects of Judicial Notice

The procedure established by Rule 201 for the taking of judicial notice of adjudicative facts conforms to accepted standards of fairness and due process. Opportunity to be heard outside the presence of the jury on the question of the propriety of taking judicial notice of an adjudicative fact and the tenor of the matter noticed is afforded all parties, Rule 201(e), whether the proposal for taking judicial notice originates with the court, Rule 201(c), or with a party. If a party is not given prior notification, request for an opportunity to be heard may be made after judicial notice has been taken, Rule 201(e). Judicial notice which may be taken at any stage of the proceeding, Rule 201(f), must be taken where the requirements of Rule 201(b) are satisfied if requested by a party and the court is supplied with the necessary information, Rule 201(d). The provisions of Fed.R.Civ.Proc. 44.1 and Fed.R.Crim.Proc. 26.1 specifying notice to the adverse party as a prerequisite to asking that judicial notice be taken of matters of foreign law, are in accord with these standards.

Consistent with the adversary theory of litigation, a party is not entitled to complain of the court's failure to take judicial notice of an adjudicative fact unless he has so requested and brought the appropriate materials to the attention of the court, Rule 201(d). Since the determination of propriety of taking judicial notice of an adjudicative fact is a matter solely for the court, rules of evidence, other than privilege, do not apply, Rule 104(a). The decision of the trial judge should be made a matter of record, thus rendering unnecessary any speculation in the reviewing court concerning the trial court's action.

If the matter is one which would fall within the province of the jury were judicial notice not taken, the court must insure that the jury is aware that the particular fact has been judicially noticed. This may be accomplished at the time judicial notice is taken as a direct result of the jury hearing counsel's request for judicial notice and the court's concurrence or by the court advising the jury specifically at that time that he has judicially noticed the particular fact. It is of course necessary for the court to instruct the jury with respect to any fact judicially noticed in advance of trial. In some situations it may be appropriate to include an instruction to the jury at the time they are formally charged as to the law to the effect that a particular fact has been judicially noticed. Whether done at the time of judicial notice, otherwise during trial, or at the formal instruction stage, in civil cases the court must advise the jury to accept as conclusive any fact judicially noticed, Rule 201(g). In criminal cases, it is even more critical that the court insure that the jury is aware that it may, but is not required to, accept as conclusive against the criminal defendant the fact judicially noticed, Rule 201(g).

If an adjudicative fact has been judicially noticed in a civil case, contrary evidence may not be placed before the jury. The opposing party is amply protected by broad provisions guaranteeing an opportunity to be heard on the propriety of the court taking judicial notice. With respect to criminal cases, Rule 201(g) apparently contemplates that contrary evidence is admissible, which of course means that evidence, if any, in support of the fact judicially noticed may also be admitted. Problems arising with respect to the court considering inadmissible evidence in determining the propriety of taking judicial notice coupled with the confusion that naturally would be expected to arise in the jury's mind when presented with judicial notice accompanied by conflicting evidence, makes resort to judicial notice in criminal cases where the opposing party is prepared to introduce contrary evidence highly undesirable.

If judicial notice is not requested at the trial court, the appellate court may, but is not required to, take judicial notice whether requested to or not. With respect to judicial notice of an adjudicative fact against a criminal defendant, it has been incorrectly suggested on the basis of jury nullification that Rule 201(g) serves to prohibit resort to judicial notice initially on appeal. Where judicial notice of an adjudicative fact is taken by an appellate court on its own motion, an issue arises as to whether the provisions of Rule 201(e) concerning an opportunity to be heard are to be applied. At this moment the question is unresolved. A similar issue arises with respect to legislative facts judicially noticed at any stage of the proceeding.

# ARTICLE III

# [BURDENS OF PROOF AND] PRESUMPTIONS IN CIVIL [AND CRIMINAL] ACTIONS AND PROCEEDINGS

*Table of Rules and Standards*

## Rule 301.

### PRESUMPTIONS IN GENERAL IN CIVIL ACTIONS AND PROCEEDINGS

In all civil actions and proceedings not otherwise provided for by Act of Congress or by these rules, a presumption imposes on the party against whom it is directed the burden of going forward with evidence to rebut or meet the presumption, but does not shift to such party the burden of proof in the sense of the risk of nonpersuasion,

**which remains throughout the trial upon the party on whom it was originally cast.**

## § 301.1 Burdens of Proof and Presumptions in Civil Cases: An Introduction

Consideration of presumptions in civil cases has been the subject of considerable scholarly debate. Rule 301 adopts the Thayer bursting bubble theory of presumptions rather than the Morgan shifting burden of persuasion theory recommended by the Advisory Committee. Thus pursuant to Rule 301, in all civil cases to the extent that federal law provides the rule of decision, the burden of persuasion shifts only if an act of Congress specifically so provides.

As employed in Rule 301, a presumption may be defined as a procedural device which requires that the existence of a fact (presumed fact) be taken as established when certain other facts (basic facts) are established unless and until a certain specified condition is fulfilled. Thus once the basic fact that gives rise to the presumption is sufficiently established, the opponent must produce evidence to rebut the presumed fact or, depending upon the nature of the fact presumed, either a verdict will be directed on the issue or the jury instructed to find in favor of the presumed fact. If evidence is introduced sufficient to support a finding contrary to the existence of the presumed fact, the presumption is rebutted and has no further function at the trial. This determination is to be made by the court and not the jury, Rule 104(a). Applying Rule 301, unless specified to the contrary by Act of Congress, a presumption has no effect on the burden of persuasion. Only the burden of producing evidence is affected by a presumption.

The disappearance of the presumption does not deprive the offered evidence of whatever probative value it otherwise has. Thus the natural inference, if any, which flows from the basic fact remains to be considered. Under certain circumstances, such natural inference may be itself sufficient to support a jury finding. Under the general provisions of Rule 301, a jury should never be instructed in terms of a presumption. However, in certain instances where demanded by the interests of justice, the jury may be instructed as to the existence of the natural inference.

Rule 301 applies in civil actions and proceedings where federal law provides the rule of decision with the exception of those statutory presumptions as to which Congress has specifically provided that the presumption shall have some other effect. In civil actions and proceedings where state law supplies the rule of decision with respect to a fact which is an element of a claim or defense, the effect of a presumption respecting such fact is determined in accordance with the state law, Rule 302.

Before proceeding with a discussion of the ramifications of adoption of the Thayer rather than the Morgan theory as the general approach to be followed with respect to presumptions in civil cases, it is first necessary to undertake an exploration of concepts collectively referred to as the burden of proof.

## § 301.2 Burden of Proof: Allocating the Elements; Burden of Pleading

In any given situation, the law recognizes certain elements as of consequence to the case. Examples of these elements in a contract dispute include offer, acceptance, consideration, payment, and in a negligence action, negligence, contributory negligence, proximate cause, and damage. Their presence or absence is properly to be considered in deciding the case. They constitute the substantive law. A plaintiff is not required to deal with every element which might conceivably affect the decision of the case. On the contrary, the elements are allocated between the parties so that plaintiff is entitled to recover if he establishes certain selected elements comprising a "claim for relief", unless defendant establishes another element called an "affirmative defense."

The cases dealing with problems of allocation do not generally disclose the fundamental reasons why a particular result is reached. Nevertheless, the following factors seem to underlie the decisions, with now one and now another being predominant, but none alone being conclusive: (1) *Caution* and *convenience* often result in the burden of proof being placed upon the party seeking change. (2) *Policy* may dictate charging one side or the other with a particular element as a means of encouraging or discouraging a given kind of litigation. An example is truth in actions for libel. Observe that policy considerations may be of prime importance in cases of complete absence of proof on the particular point, so that the allocation of the burden is decisive of the case. (3) *Fairness* may suggest placing the burden of an element upon the party within whose control the evidence lies. Thus payment and discharge in bankruptcy have long been regarded as affirmative defenses and are among those enumerated as such in Rule 8(c) of the Federal Rules of Civil Procedure. (4) *Probabilities* may be estimated and the burden placed upon the party who will benefit by a departure from the supposed norm. Payment mentioned above is illustrative.

Generally speaking in claims for relief based on statute, if an exception appears in the enacting clause, i.e., the clause creating the right sued upon, the burden is on the party invoking the statute to negative the applicability of the exception; otherwise the exception is the responsibility of the opposite party. Certain aspects of contract litigation are decided by similar mechanical tests. For example, in insurance cases plaintiff must bring himself within the general coverage of the policy; exceptions are affirmative defense. Conditions precedent are allocated to plaintiff, conditions subsequent to defendant.

One of the useful functions served by the pleadings is to settle in advance of trial, in accordance with the substantive law, not only what matters are relevant to the merits but also which party is responsible for them. Thus the complaint, the vehicle employed to satisfy plaintiff's burden of pleading, will set forth the elements of plaintiff's claim for relief, for example, in a negligence action, negligence, cause in fact, proximate cause and damage; the answer contains affirmative defenses, for example, comparative fault, and so on. The accuracy of the blue-point of the trial thus created may, however, be distorted by the workings of presumptions.

## § 301.3    Burden of Proof: Description and Nature of Responsibility; State Law Supplying Rule of Decision

In civil cases the nature of the burden imposed upon a party charged with responsibility for a particular contested element is normally threefold: (1) the burden of pleading; (2) the burden of production as to the particular matter, referred to also as the burden of going forward; and (3) the burden of persuading the trier of fact of its existence. To illustrate, in a typical contract action plaintiff will have the burdens of (1) pleading the existence of the contract, (2) producing sufficient evidence of the existence of the contract, and (3) persuading the trier of fact of the contract's existence. The defendant bears the same three burdens with regard to the affirmative defense of payment. The term burden of proof as frequently used includes both the concepts of burden of production and burden of persuasion. Analytical description is fostered and confusion avoided by separate reference to each burden.

Where state law supplies the rule of decision, the burdens of production and persuasion as to any fact which is an element of such a claim or defense are determined in accordance with state law, Rule 302.

## § 301.4  Burden of Production: Measure and Effect; Prima Facie Case

The burden of producing evidence or going forward is satisfied by evidence which, viewed in the aspect most favorable to the burdened party, is sufficient to enable the trier of fact reasonably to find the issue for him. For example, where the burden of persuasion of more probably true than not true is also imposed upon the party, the burden of producing evidence is satisfied by the introduction of evidence which, viewed in the aspect most favorable to the burdened party, is sufficient to enable the trier of fact reasonably to find that element of the claim for relief to be more probably true than not true. When the plaintiff thus burdened introduces such evidence as to each element of the claim for relief, he is said to have presented a prima facie case. Failure to satisfy the burden of producing evidence requires a decision by the court as a matter of law on the particular issue adverse to the burdened party.

In its minimum aspect, the case so made is sufficient to support, but does not require, a finding in favor of the burdened party. While the opposite party is entitled to introduce contrary evidence, he is under no compulsion to do so and may submit the issue to the trier of fact on this evidence alone. No burden of producing evidence is cast upon him. However, evidence introduced as to one or more elements of the claim for relief may be much stronger than that required to satisfy the minimum requirement. The testimony of witnesses which is not contradicted, impeached, or made inherently improbable by either internal or external circumstances, cannot arbitrarily be disregarded. Real and documentary evidence of such character may also have been introduced. Where such evidence when viewed most favorably to the opposing party nevertheless would require a reasonable jury to find that the burdened party has satisfied his burden of persuasion as to an element of the claim for relief, a burden of producing evidence is imposed on the opponent to meet it, and in the absence thereof requires the court to rule for the burdened party as to that element as a matter of law.

In most situations, however, the burdened party will satisfy his burden of producing evidence with the introduction of evidence less than sufficient to entitle him to a directed verdict as a matter of law if the opponent fails to introduce sufficient contrary evidence. However the trier of fact may conclude that the burdened party has in fact satisfied his burden of persuasion. In such instances, although neither party is aware of it, the practical effect is to shift the burden of production to the opposing party.

At times the term prima facie case has also been applied where the introduction of evidence has shifted the burden of producing evidence as a matter of law by virtue of the weight of such evidence or as a result of a presumption, as well as where the burden of production has actually shifted in the minds of the trier of fact. Clarity would be enhanced if the term prima facie case was employed solely to refer to satisfaction of the burden of production as to each element of the claim for relief or affirmative defense.

It is possible to visualize the foregoing by means of a needle diagram:

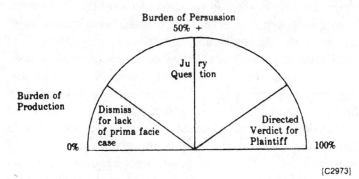

Burden of Persuasion
50% +

Ju ry
Ques tion

Burden of
Production

Dismiss
for lack
of prima facie
case

Directed
Verdict for
Plaintiff

0%                                                    100%

[C2973]

## § 301.5  Burden of Persuasion: Incidence and Measure in Civil Cases

As has been seen the burden of producing evidence may shift from party to party as the case progresses. The burden of persuasion, unlike the burden of producing evidence, never shifts as the result of the introduction of evidence. While the correctness of this general proposition cannot be doubted, it must be taken as qualified to the extent that either an act of Congress or applicable state law provides for the shifting of the burden of persuasion in connection with a presumption, Rules 301 and 302.

In the usual civil case satisfaction of the burden of persuasion requires that the trier of fact find that the existence of the proposition to be proved is more probably true than not true. The phrase seems more likely to be meaningful to juries than the term "preponderance of the evidence" with which it is frequently albeit incorrectly equated. Preponderance is simply more than the contrary evidence, not necessarily more probable than all other possibilities. Occasional references can be found in the case law to application of the burden of persuasion referred to as "clear and convincing" or a derivative thereof. This burden of persuasion, resting between more probably true than not true the general civil burden, and beyond a reasonable doubt the criminal burden of persuasion, has been applied for example with respect to citizenship as well as with respect to certain claims including fraud, mutual mistake, and the contents of a lost deed. "Clear and convincing" evidence is evidence which produces a firm belief or conviction in the mind of the fact finder that the matter is true.

## § 301.6  Presumptions in Civil Cases: Definition and Nature

A presumption is a rule of law which requires that the existence of a fact (the presumed fact) be taken as established when certain other facts (the basic facts) are established unless and until a certain specified condition is fulfilled. Both the Thayer approach adopted in Rule 301 and the Morgan approach which can be specified by statute are aimed at providing criteria for the specific condition removing the requirement that the presumed fact be taken as established.

**Thayer.** Rule 301's "bursting bubble" approach may be stated as follows:

> When the basic facts (A) are established, the presumed fact (B) must be taken as established unless and until the opponent introduces evidence sufficient to support a finding by the trier of fact of the nonexistence of the presumed fact. Upon introduction of such evidence the presumption is overcome and disappears, without regard to whether it is believed. However any inference which exists from fact A to fact B remains.

Under the Thayer "bursting bubble" approach the burden of persuasion remains throughout upon the originally burdened party. However application of the presumption shifts the burden of production to the opposing party.

**Morgan.** The Morgan approach to presumptions may be described as follows:

> When fact A is established the jury is instructed that it must find fact B unless and until the opponent persuades the jury that the nonexistence of fact B is more probably true than not true.

Pursuant to the Morgan approach, application of a presumption shifts both the burden of production and the burden of persuasion to the opposing party.

Asserting that Rule 301 "bursting bubble" accords too slight an effect to presumptions, proponents of the Morgan theory stress that presumptions rest upon the same considerations of caution, convenience, policy, fairness, and probability which govern the allocation of the elements of the case originally and are an aspect of allocation, working within the larger framework of the elements of the case. To hold that the sole effect of a presumption is that of requiring the opposite party to produce evidence sufficient to support a finding of the nonexistence of the presumed fact, wholly without regard to whether the evidence is in fact believed, is argued by those supporting the Morgan approach to ignore the wisdom which underlies presumptions. In apparent response to such contentions, Rule 301 provides that the Morgan shifting burden of persuasion approach may be adopted with respect to a particular presumption by Act of Congress or these rules.

Notice that pursuant to Rule 301 when a presumption operates against a party who already has the burden of production as to the presumed fact, the presumption has no effect. Similarly, taking the Morgan approach, a presumption operating against a party already possessing the burden of persuasion as to the presumed fact has no effect.

To illustrate the Thayer Rule 301 and Morgan approaches, assume that a plaintiff brings an action for damage suffered when his car was struck by a taxi at 3:00 a.m. In the jurisdiction where the action is brought, there is a statute in force which states that in actions against a taxi company for damages to persons or property, if it is established that the taxi involved in an accident is owned by the company, it shall be presumed that the driver was acting at the time of the accident as an agent of the taxi company. For purposes of this illustration, assume further it is uncontested that the particular taxi is owned by the defendant company.

Under the Thayer theory the burden of producing evidence is shifted to the taxi company. The taxi company must satisfy the burden of production to avoid a directed verdict. The taxi company thus must produce evidence which when viewed most favorably to the taxi company is sufficient to support a finding by a reasonable trier of fact that the nonexistence of the presumed fact is more probably true than not true, i.e., evidence demonstrating that the driver was not acting as agent of the taxi company at the time of the accident. Upon production of such evidence (for example, that the driver's shift ended at 10:00 p.m. and that the driver was returning home from a date when the accident occurred), the procedural effect of the presumption is completely extinguished, "the bubble has burst." Any natural inference from ownership to agency remains to be considered by the trier of fact.

The Morgan theory not only places the burden of production but also the burden of persuasion upon the taxi company. Not only would establishing ownership of the taxi require the taxi company to produce evidence sufficient to support a finding by a reasonable trier of fact of the nonexistence of the driver's agency, but it would also require the taxi company to persuade the trier of fact that it is more probably true than not that the driver was acting outside the scope of his employment. Thus the procedural effect of the presumption does not "burst" upon the introduction of the contrary evidence sufficient to support a finding. The procedural effect of the presumption continues and places the burden of persuasion upon the taxi company.

**Confusion in terminology.** The unhappy confusion which surrounds the subject of presumptions arises in no small degree from loose and imprecise terminology. A presumption involves a legally recognized relation between facts. A court which makes a statement such as "Courts are presumed to be no more ignorant than the public generally," has in mind a supposedly correct proposition of legal reasoning, rather than a true presumption. Or, where inquiry involves the jurisdiction of a federal court the assertion that the "presumption in every stage of a cause being that it is without * * * jurisdiction, * * * unless the contrary appears from the record," is merely an allocation of the element of jurisdiction to the plaintiff. Courts and laymen also use the term "presumed" as a synonym for an inference, in such expressions as "Dr. Livingston, I presume." Finally, when a court speaks of the "presumption" of sanity in a criminal case, it simply means that sanity does not become an element of the government's or defendant's case unless and until evidence is introduced raising the issue. The persistent use of the term "presumption" to describe these nonpresumption situations inevitably leads to difficulty in view of the natural assumption that things of the same name have the same characteristics. It is an example of what is known in the field of logic as the fallacy of the transplanted category. Even where a true presumption is involved, overall confusion of terminology breeds still further confusion.

## § 301.7 Presumptions: Inferences and Permissive Presumptions

While the words "inference" and "presumption" are sometimes used interchangeably, they by no means are synonymous. An inference is a conclusion as to the existence of a particular fact reached by considering other facts in the usual course of human reasoning. With respect to an inference, if fact A is established fact B may be deduced from fact A through reasoning and logic. An inference is thus a deduction the factfinder may in its discretion draw, but is not required to draw as a matter of law. Under certain circumstances an inference may be so strong that no other conclusion may reasonably be reached. However this is because of the compelling nature of the particular factual circumstances rather than that, as is the case with a presumption, a rule of law requires the conclusion to be drawn.

Running through the cases and the literature one finds use of the terms presumption, presumption of fact, and permissive presumption when referring to basic facts which if found permit but do not require the trier of fact in the absence of rebutting evidence to reach a certain conclusion. Since the use of the term presumption, presumption of fact, or permissive presumption under circumstances where the trier of fact is not required as a matter of law to reach a conclusion fails to meet the accepted definition of a presumption, the practice should be discontinued. Where the jury is not required by rule of law to reach a certain conclusion but may do so by reasoning and logic from fact A to fact B, reference should be made to an "inference" and not a "presumption."

## § 301.8  Presumptions: Prima Facie Evidence

The term prima facie evidence has been employed with respect to common law presumptions and by Congress in the drafting of statutes. Unfortunately the term prima facie evidence creates confusion similar to that surrounding the term prima facie case. This is not surprising since prima facie evidence is frequently used to mean evidence sufficient to satisfy the burden of production as to one element of a prima facie case or as to a fact having a lesser effect. In addition both prima facie evidence and prima facie case are used to describe situations where the burden of production shifts to an opposing party by virtue of a presumption or the weight of the evidence.

Clarity would be enhanced by employing the term prima facie case solely to indicate satisfaction of a burden of production as to all elements of the claim for relief and the term prima facie evidence as satisfying the burden of production as to a particular element of a claim for relief or a particular fact having a lesser effect. Instead of employing the term prima facie evidence to refer to a presumption, use of either "presume" or "presumption" is preferable. Where now intended to refer to a presumption, the term prima facie evidence should be treated as synonymous with the terms "presume," "presumption," "presumptive," and "presumptive evidence."

### § 301.9 Presumptions: Conclusive and Irrebuttable Presumptions

A so called presumption which cannot be rebutted by evidence is not a presumption but a rule of substantive law. Thus the effect of saying that everyone is presumed to know the law is to preclude ignorance of the law as a defense. Similarly the so-called common law presumption that a child under the age of seven is "conclusively presumed" not to have committed a felony is simply an expression of substantive law, as is the so-called presumption that when an attorney once represented a client in matters substantially related to those embraced by a subsequent case he wishes to bring against the former client he is "irrebuttably presumed" to have benefited from the confidential information. The use of the terms irrebuttable and conclusive presumption, referring solely to rules of law and not presumptions, should be discontinued as useless and confusing.

## § 301.10   Presumptions as Evidence

It was once somewhat fashionable to treat a presumption as evidence to be weighed by the jury in determining the existence of a particular fact. However it is now universally recognized that a presumption is a rule of law for the handling of evidence, not a species of evidence. It is clearly impossible to weigh a presumption as evidence on the one hand against physical objects and personal observations on the other. The presumption as evidence doctrine never had a firm foothold in the federal court.

## § 301.11   Conflicting Presumptions

Rule 301 does not address directly the situation where the court is faced with inconsistent presumptions. A solution of considerable appeal is to apply the presumption founded upon weightier considerations of social policy. If policy considerations are of equal weight, both presumptions are then disregarded. The principle was incorporated in Rule 15 of the Uniform Rules of Evidence approved in 1953 by the Commissioners on Uniform State Laws. The principal class of cases in which the problem has arisen is where rights are asserted under a second marriage but no direct evidence is available of a death or divorce terminating the first marriage before the second. Most courts say the presumption of the validity of a marriage is stronger than the presumption of continuance of life or continuance of marriage.

Another solution is to consider that the conflicting presumptions have disappeared, with the facts upon which the respective presumptions were based simply being weighed as circumstances with all the other facts that may be relevant, thus giving no effect to the presumptions. When the conflicting presumptions involved are based upon probability or upon procedural convenience but not clear considerations of social policy, this solution is a fairly practical one.

## § 301.12   Presumptions: Attack by Rebutting Basic Facts or Presumed Fact; Effect on Jury Instructions

Two methods of attack are open to the party against whom a presumption is invoked: he may introduce evidence tending to disprove the existence of the basic facts on which the presumption depends, or he may offer evidence tending to disprove the presumed fact itself.

**Basic facts.** If the attack is made solely by introducing evidence to disprove the basic facts, then the only issue of fact presented is as to their existence. This issue would be presented to the jury under an instruction outlining the result which follows success or failure in proving the basic facts. Thus the jury would be instructed under both a Rule 301 Thayer approach and a Morgan approach that if they find the existence of the basic fact they must find the existence of the presumed fact. Conversely, assuming either no or insufficient evidence supporting the presumed fact other than the basic fact has been introduced, the jury would be instructed that if they do not find the existence of basic fact, they must also find the nonexistence of the presumed fact.

**Presumed fact—Rule 301.** If a presumption is attacked by introducing evidence to disprove the existence of the presumed fact, the question arises whether the presumption continues to have any effect in the case. Pursuant to Rule 301 adopting the "bursting bubble" theory, a presumption vanishes entirely upon the introduction of evidence sufficient when viewed most favorably to its proponent to support a finding by a reasonable jury that the nonexistence of the presumed fact is more probably true than not true. The bursting bubble theory is easy to apply, since the court need only determine whether the requisite contrary evidence has been introduced. If the court finds in the affirmative, no reference is made to the presumption in instructing the jury. If the court finds in the negative, the jury is instructed to find the presumed fact if they find the basic fact to have been proved. However if the presumption is found to have been rebutted, i.e., the bubble has burst, any underlying inference remains to be considered by the trier of fact and is a potential subject for jury instruction. Such an inference instruction, where appropriate, should advise the jury that if they decide in favor of the basic facts they may but are not required to consider the logical inference existing between the basic facts and the presumed fact.

Occasionally at common law presumptions given a Thayer effect, due to perceived unusually compelling considerations of policy, were held to impose a greater burden of production upon a party attacking the presumption to burst the bubble than merely producing evidence sufficient to support a finding as to the nonexistence of the presumed fact. Thus it was said in state court decisions that the presumption that a deed was delivered to a grantee in possession of it could be overcome only by "clear and convincing" evidence; that the presumption that a child born during marriage is the offspring of the married couple could be overcome only by "clear and irrefragable" proof; and in a federal court decision that the presumption of the arrival of a letter in due course of the mails is rebutted only by "direct and positive proof of affirmative facts."

In some of these common law situations, since allocating an element of the case to a particular party along with the burden of persuasion with respect thereto rather than a presumption is in reality involved, the rule on presumptions will not apply, and the heavier burden may be appropriate. Where a true presumption is presented, since Rule 301 fails to define the burden of production imposed to "burst the bubble", one could certainly argue that an additional quantum of evidence could be required in such situations beyond that sufficient in the court's judgment to support a finding of the nonexistence of the presumed fact. Of course, similar contentions would also support the bursting of the bubble as to certain presumptions on the presentation of "some evidence" but not sufficient evidence to support a finding of the nonexistence of the presumed fact. On balance, however, the single standard sufficient to support a finding by a reasonable jury that the nonexistence of the presumed fact is more probably true than not true, is clearly preferable if the confusion perceived as to the early common law handling of presumptions is not to be reintroduced into Rule 301.

**Presumed fact—Morgan.** With respect to Morgan presumptions specified by Act of Congress or by rule, if the basic fact is established the presumed fact must be found unless and until the party opposing the existence of the presumed fact has established to the satisfaction of the trier of fact its nonexistence to be more probably true than not true. Occasionally for reasons of strong public policy, the burden of persuasion placed upon the opponent of a Morgan presumption is to establish the nonexistence of the presumed fact by clear and convincing evidence. Notice that by shifting the burden of persuasion the Morgan presumption remains in the case when contrary evidence is introduced as to the presumed fact. Where a Morgan presumption is operating the jury must be instructed with respect to the presumed fact whenever, on the evidence taken as a whole, the trier of fact may reasonably find either way with respect to the existence of the presumed fact.

## § 301.13  Presumptions: Instructing the Jury

Under Rule 301 or a Morgan presumption neither the particular presumption nor the term presumption need be nor should be mentioned to the trier of fact. However in both cases, the jury may be instructed in terms of the procedural effects of the presumption.

The Rule 301 Thayer "bursting bubble" approach to presumptions is simple for both the court and jury to apply. Consider the presumption that a letter properly addressed, with proper postage, mailed in a proper location and not returned was duly received:

(1) If the basic fact of mailing is not disputed, and if sufficient evidence as to nonreceipt to rebut is not introduced, the jury will be instructed to find receipt of the letter.

(2) If the basic fact is disputed but evidence sufficient to rebut the presumption has not been introduced, the jury would be instructed as follows: If you find it is more probably true than not true that the letter properly addressed and stamped was mailed and not returned, then you must find the letter was duly received. Conversely, if you do not find that it is more probably true than not true that the letter was properly addressed, stamped, mailed and not returned, then you must find that the letter was not received.

(3) If the presumption is rebutted by the introduction of evidence sufficient to support a finding on non-receipt of the letter, no instruction will be given with respect to the presumption for the presumption has burst. However, the court may give an inference instruction: "If you find that the letter was properly addressed, stamped, mailed, and not returned you may but are not required to infer from these facts that the letter was duly received. If you do draw such an inference, then consider the inference together with all other evidence in the case in deciding whether plaintiff has established that it was more probably true than not true that the letter was duly received." Whether an inference instruction should be given rests in the discretion of the court. The importance of the question to the trial as well as the likelihood of the jury realizing the propriety of drawing the permitted inference absent such an instruction should, of course, be considered.

In contrast to the simple jury instruction approach under Rule 301, consider the complexity associated with the recommended procedure for a Morgan presumption:

**(1) Determination on Evidence of Basic Facts.** When no evidence is introduced contrary to the existence of the presumed fact, the question of its existence depends upon the existence of the basic facts and is determined as follows:

(A) If reasonable minds would necessarily agree that the evidence renders the existence of the basic facts more probable than not, the judge shall direct the jury to find in favor of the existence of the presumed facts; or

(B) If reasonable minds would necessarily agree that the evidence does not render the existence of the basic facts more probable than not, the judge shall direct the jury to find against the existence of the presumed fact; or

(C) If reasonable minds would not necessarily agree as to whether the evidence renders the existence of the basic facts more probable than not, the judge shall submit the matter to the jury with an instruction to find in favor of the existence of the presumed fact if they find from the evidence that the existence of the basic facts is more probable than not, but otherwise to find against the existence of the presumed fact.

**(2) Determination on Evidence of Presumed Fact.** When reasonable minds would necessarily agree that the evidence renders the existence of the basic facts more probable than not, the question of the existence of the presumed fact is determined as follows:

(A) If reasonable minds would necessarily agree that the evidence renders the nonexistence of the presumed fact more probable than not, the judge shall direct the jury to find against the existence of the presumed fact; or

(B) If reasonable minds would necessarily agree that the evidence does not render the nonexistence of the presumed fact more probable than not, the judge shall direct the jury to find in favor of the presumed fact; or

(C) If reasonable minds would not necessarily agree as to whether the evidence renders the nonexistence of the presumed fact more probable than not, the judge shall submit the matter to the jury with an instruction to find in favor of the existence of the

presumed fact unless they find from the evidence
that its nonexistence is more probable than its existence, in which event they should find against its
existence.

**(3) Determination on Evidence of Both Basic
and Presumed Facts.** When evidence as to the existence of the basic facts is such that reasonable minds
would not necessarily agree whether their existence is
more probable than not and evidence as to the nonexistence of the presumed fact is such that they would not
necessarily agree that its nonexistence is more probable than not, the judge shall submit the matter to the
jury with an instruction to find in favor of the existence of the presumed fact if they find from the evidence that the existence of the basic facts is more
probable than not and unless they find the nonexistence of the presumed fact more probable than not,
otherwise to find against the existence of the presumed
fact.

The strongest single argument in favor of Rule 301
and against the Morgan approach is paragraph 3 above.
It is ventured to say that not only does such an instruction, if understood, by its very structure result in a
greater burden of persuasion being placed upon the party
opposing the presumption than if the identical burden of
persuasion had been initially placed, but that there is not
one juror in a hundred able to understand the instruction as presented at trial.

## § 301.14 Presumptions: Statutory and Common Law Illustrations

Common law and statutory presumptions and instructed inferences are numerous and varied. Only a few
selected illustrations are included:

**Official actions.** Acts of public officers in an official capacity, including judicial proceedings, are presumed to have been regularly and legally performed and all necessary prerequisites to the validity of an official act presumed to have been complied with.

**Common carriers.** A presumption exists that as between connecting carriers, the damage occurred on the line of the last carrier.

**Mailing; Fax; E–Mail.** A letter properly addressed, stamped, mailed, and not returned is presumed to have been duly delivered to the addressee. A similar presumption arises with respect to properly authenticated faxes, e-mail or similar transmissions.

**Acts of congress.** Various acts of congress create presumptions employing either the term presumption or prima facie evidence. These presumptions are wide ranging in content. Some presumptions referred to in Rule 902(10) serve to authenticate documents or copies of documents. Others extend to creating hearsay exceptions, Rule 802. Still others deal solely with factual matters.

**Uniform Commercial Code.** Under Rule 302 where the state law supplies the rule of decision, resort will frequently be had to the Uniform Commercial Code. The Uniform Commercial Code defines "presumption" and "presumed" consistently with the approach taken in Rule 301. Where the Uniform Commercial Code contemplates a shift in the burden of persuasion, it employs the term "burden of establishing" which is defined in terms equivalent to the Morgan shifting burden on persuasion approach. The Uniform Commercial Code also employs the term prima facie evidence although it is not specifically defined. It is assumed that the legislature intended that the term be employed in accordance with its preferred usage.

## Rule 302.

# APPLICABILITY OF STATE LAW IN CIVIL ACTIONS AND PROCEEDINGS

**In civil actions and proceedings, the effect of a presumption respecting a fact which is an element of a claim or defense as to which State law supplies the rule of decision is determined in accordance with State law.**

## § 302.1　Applicability of State Law in Civil Actions and Proceedings

Rule 302 recognizes that the rationale of Erie R. R. Co. v. Tompkins, (S.Ct.1938) requires that the effect of some presumptions in civil actions be governed by state law where state law provides the rule of decision. Rule 302 is however designed to restrict the applicability of state law to the area actually encompassed by *Erie*. Certain Supreme Court decisions discussing presumptions and the allocation of the burdens of production and persuasion establish that where a substantive element of a claim or defense governed by state law is at issue, such as bona fide purchase, contributory negligence, or non-accidental death of the insured, state law is to be followed with respect to allocation of the burden of production and persuasion and with respect to the question of presumptions. In such cases, state policy favoring one side or another as to the substantive element was reflected in the initial allocation of the burdens or in the creation of a presumption.

In other situations such as establishment of receipt of a mailed letter, the presumption does not reflect a consensus on state policy favoring one side or another as to a substantive element of a claim or defense. Such "tactical" presumptions, operating as to a lesser aspect of the case, serve as rules of convenience, without reference to the respective positions of the parties. Rule 302, treating such presumptions under *Erie* as rules of procedure rather than as substantive law, limits applicability of state law to situations where the presumption operates upon "a fact which is an element of a claim or defense." The rationale for this distinction is stated by McCormick, Evidence § 349 at 477 (5th ed.1999) as follows:

> Although tactical presumptions may in some instances influence the outcome of a case, their effect is no greater than that of a rule governing the admission or exclusion of a single item of evidence. As in the case of those rules, the desirability of providing a uniform procedure for federal trials through a fixed rule governing tactical presumptions outweighs any preference for increased certainty of identity of result in the state and federal courts.

In cases of doubt where the procedural versus substantive policy distinction is less than clear, it has been suggested that federal law should be applied.

Of course, for the state presumption rule to be applied, state law must supply the rule of decision, Rule 302. The concept of "rule of decision" is not equivalent in all circumstances to "diversity cases." Rule of decision was incorporated in Rule 302 to reflect that *"Erie"* applies to any claim or issue having its source in state law, regardless of the basis of federal jurisdiction, and does not apply to a federal claim or issue, even though jurisdiction is based on diversity. Thus under *Erie* it is the sources of the right relied upon and not the basis of federal jurisdiction which governs the choice of law.

### Standard 303.

## PRESUMPTIONS IN CRIMINAL CASES

### [Not enacted.]

(a) **Scope.** Except as otherwise provided by Act of Congress, in criminal cases, presumptions against an accused, recognized at common law or created by statute, including statutory provisions that certain facts are prima facie evidence of other facts or of guilt, are governed by this rule.

(b) **Submission to Jury.** The judge is not authorized to direct the jury to find a presumed fact against the accused. When the presumed fact establishes guilt or is an element of the offense or negatives a defense, the judge may submit the question of guilt or of the existence of the presumed fact to the jury, if, but only if, a reasonable juror on the evidence as a whole, including the evidence of the basic facts, could find guilt or the presumed fact beyond a reasonable doubt. When the presumed fact has a lesser effect, its existence may be submitted to the jury if the basic facts are supported by substantial evidence, or are otherwise established, unless the evidence as a whole negatives the existence of the presumed fact.

(c) **Instructing the Jury.** Whenever the existence of a presumed fact against the accused is submitted to the jury, the judge shall give an instruction that the law declares that the jury may regard the basic facts as sufficient evidence of the presumed fact but does not require it to do so. In addition, if the presumed fact establishes guilt or is an element of the offense or negatives a defense, the judge shall instruct the jury that its existence must, on all the evidence, be proved beyond a reasonable doubt.

## § 303.1 Burden of Proof in Criminal Cases: Allocating the Elements; Procedure for Allocating

Written pleadings remain at an unsophisticated level in criminal cases. An indictment or information must, of course, set forth the prima facie elements of the crime, and in this respect resembles the complaint in a civil action. As regards the accused, however, all "defenses" remain available under the general plea of not guilty. Although notice as to alibi or a defense based upon mental condition is required, the accused's entering of a plea itself serves no function of allocation. Moreover, its informational aspects go no further than to serve notice that the prosecution is put to proof of all elements of its case.

In criminal cases the pattern of allocation resembles that of civil cases to the extent that the prosecution need not in the first instance assume responsibility for every element which might bear upon the guilt of the accused. Thus in conformance with treatment accorded statutes in civil cases, the government need not initially negative an exception which is not part of the description of the offense but withdraws certain acts or persons from the operation of the statute. At this point however the resemblance to civil cases ends. For example, under federal practice with the exception of insanity the accused is hardly ever responsible for an affirmative defense in the same sense as is a defendant in a civil case.

The term "defense" is, however, used and used loosely and often misleadingly in the criminal law. Cases discuss such matters as alibi, duress, entrapment and self-defense as defenses. Yet none of these matters is a true affirmative defense in the sense of requiring the defendant to establish anything to be more probably true than not true. The maximum effect of such a so-called defense in a criminal case is to enable the accused by the presentation of sufficient evidence to impose on the prosecution responsibility for an additional element which would not otherwise be a part of the government's case. Some matters traditionally called defenses do not even have this effect but merely designate particular kinds of disproof of the state's case. As the Working Papers of the National Commission on Reform of Federal Criminal Laws point out, alibi, often described as a defense, is nothing more than a denial of the crime by reason of being elsewhere when it was committed.

There are some rarely employed statutes placing an affirmative defense in the sense of allocation of a burden of persuasion of more probably true than not true upon the defendant. For example, 15 U.S.C.A. § 792–3 which deals with public utility holding companies, and 15 U.S.C.A. § 80(a)–48, which deals with investment companies, each make willful violations of their subchapters or any rule, regulation or order thereunder criminal, but provide that "no person shall be convicted * * * for the violation of any rule, regulation or order if he proves that he had no actual knowledge of such rule, regulation, or order." Of most significance, insanity, i.e., that the accused as a result of a severe mental disease or defect was unable to appreciate the nature and quality or the wrongfulness of his acts, is now an affirmative defense as to which the defendant bears the burden of persuasion of clear and convincing evidence.

## § 303.2 Burden of Proof: Burden of Producing Evidence

The prosecution in a criminal case has the burden of going forward, of producing evidence, upon which a reasonable jury could conclude that each element of the substantive offense charged has been established beyond a reasonable doubt. If the prosecution fails to meet the burden, the court must enter a judgment of acquittal.

With the exception of insanity and those rare statutes creating a true affirmative defense placing the burden of production and persuasion upon the defendant, the only burden placed upon the accused in a criminal case is that of producing sufficient evidence as to certain so-called "defenses" such as self defense, entrapment or duress which he wishes to inject into the case. The burden of producing evidence in order to raise such a defense has been variously described as evidence that "fairly" raises the issue, slight evidence, and some evidence but more than a mere scintilla. The Model Penal Code reflects the view that evidence sufficient to raise a reasonable doubt is the appropriate standard. Any difference in the articulated standards in most cases will be without significance in view of the essential inexactness of any attempt to describe the quantity or quality of evidence with precision. Where sufficient evidence has been introduced as to the so-called defense by any party, the issue is injected into the case and the government must then prove the contrary beyond a reasonable doubt.

Whether the burden of producing or going forward with sufficient evidence has been satisfied is a question for the court in the administration of the trial, Rule 104(a); it is not a proper subject of instruction to the jury.

## § 303.3  Burden of Persuasion: Incidence, Measure and Shifting

In criminal cases the burden on the prosecution is to prove every element of the crime beyond a reasonable doubt. If the accused raises a so-called defense by introducing sufficient evidence that element is added to the case which the prosecution must prove beyond a reasonable doubt. With respect to those few federal statutes creating a true affirmative defense, the defendant bears the burden of establishing such defense to be more probably true than not true; as to insanity the defendant bears the burden of clear and convincing evidence.

The government through its criminal laws may allocate the burden of producing evidence and the burden of persuasion without running afoul of the Due Process Clause, unless in so doing it offends some principle of justice so rooted in the traditions and conscience of our people as to be ranked as fundamental. Once the government defines a crime, however, it must prove each element of the crime as defined beyond a reasonable doubt. Having defined the elements of a crime, the government may not shift the burden of persuasion to the defendant by means of a presumption. Since a verdict may not be directed against the criminal defendant as a matter of law, the burden of production similarly may not be shifted. None of the foregoing prevents the government, under appropriate circumstances, from requiring the defendant to initially produce sufficient evidence as to a defense before the government becomes required to prove the then introduced element beyond a reasonable doubt.

While attempts to elaborate upon the meaning of "reasonable doubt" have been described as unnecessary and misleading, current federal practice appears generally to favor an attempted definition.

Circumstantial evidence alone is sufficient to establish the elements of a crime. Proof of circumstances must be such that on the whole each element of the offense may be found by the trier of fact to exist beyond a reasonable doubt. Thus no greater degree of certainty is required of circumstantial evidence than direct evidence; the defendant is not entitled to an instruction that circumstantial evidence must exclude every reasonable hypothesis other than guilt.

## § 303.4 Standard 303(a), (b) and (c): Presumptions in Criminal Cases; Definition, Nature and Instructions; Constitutionality

Proposed Rule 303, now Standard 303, dealing with presumptions in criminal cases was not enacted by Congress. The Report of House Committee on the Judiciary states that rule 303 was deleted from the Federal Rules of Evidence solely on the ground that the subject of presumptions in criminal cases was then before Congress in the form of bills to revise the federal criminal code. In recognition of the fact that deleted rule 303 is useful as a statement of existing law, the proposed rule has been renumbered and presented as Standard 303.

Standard 303 covers presumptions against an accused in criminal cases and includes both those recognized at common law and those created by statute. Statutory provisions phrased in terms of "prima facie evidence," "presumptive evidence," or "presumed" are also included in Standard 303(a). Standard 303(a) provides that a presumption may have a different effect from that provided by Standard 303 if a statute so provides.

Standard 303(b) provides that if a presumed fact establishes guilt, is an element of the offense, or negatives a defense, the court may submit the question of guilt or of the existence of the presumed fact to the jury, but only if a reasonable juror on the evidence as a whole, including the evidence of the basic facts, could find guilt or the presumed fact beyond a reasonable doubt. However if the presumed fact has only a lesser effect, the question of its existence may be submitted to the jury provided the basic facts are supported by substantial evidence or are otherwise established, unless the court determines that a reasonable juror on the evidence as a whole could not find the existence of the presumed fact. Under no circumstances is the judge permitted to direct the jury to find a presumed fact against an accused.

Standard 303(c) provides that whenever the existence of a presumed fact against the accused is submitted to the jury, the court should instruct the jury that it may regard the basic facts as sufficient evidence of the presumed fact but is not required to do so. In addition, if the presumed fact establishes guilt, is an element of the offense, or negatives a defense, the court should instruct the jury that its existence on all the evidence must be proved beyond a reasonable doubt.

Notice that the foregoing description of the nature and operation of presumptions in a criminal case does not comport with the definition of presumptions in civil cases, since in criminal cases there can be no compelled finding of the presumed fact. Upon a finding as to the basic facts, the trier of fact in a criminal matter may, but is not required to, find the presumed fact, i.e., permissive rather than mandatory. Thus a presumption as employed in criminal matters corresponds to an inference in civil matters. Clarity would be fostered by reference to criminal instructed inferences rather than criminal presumptions.

The purpose of a presumption operating against the accused in a criminal case, i.e., an instructed inference, is to guide the jury by highlighting the propriety of drawing a factual inference they might otherwise be naturally less likely to draw. Reluctance on the part of the jury to draw the inference may arise simply because the jury is unaware that once having found particular facts to exist they may infer an element of the offense such as intent or knowledge. In other cases the reluctance to infer arises because the jury may be unaware absent an instruction that a particular fact naturally flows from certain other facts they have found to exist. The latter may occur, for example, with respect to the presumption that illegal importation may be inferred solely from possession of certain specified narcotic drugs by the defendant in this country. Encouragement of the trier of fact to draw the factual inference, by virtue of it being the subject of an instructed inference, is designed to assist the prosecution.

The applicability and constitutionality of Standard 303(b) must be evaluated in light of the Supreme Court decisions in County Court of Ulster v. Allen (S.Ct.1979), Sandstrom v. Montana (S.Ct.1979), and Francis v. Franklin (S.Ct.1985). As a result of these decisions it is clear, if it wasn't before, that it is never permissible to shift to the defendant the burden of persuasion to disprove an element of a crime charged by means of a presumption, and of course, that a conclusive or irrebuttable presumption operating against the criminal defendant is also unconstitutional.

Beyond these points, confusion abounds. The majority opinion in *Ulster,* implicitly rejected in part in *Sandstrom* and left unclarified in *Francis,* created out of whole cloth the dual concepts of (1) "permissive inference or presumption" and (2) "mandatory presumption":

The most common evidentiary device is the entirely permissive inference or presumption, which allows, but does not require, the trier of fact to infer the elemental fact from proof by the prosecutor of the basic one and that places no burden of any kind on the defendant. * * * When reviewing this type of device, the Court has required the party challenging it to demonstrate its invalidity as applied to him. * * * Because this permissive presumption leaves the trier of fact free to credit or reject the inference and does not shift the burden of proof, it affects the application of the "beyond a reasonable doubt" standard only if, under the facts of the case, there is no rational way the trier could make the connection permitted by the inference. For only in that situation is there any risk that an explanation of the permissible inference to a jury, or its use by a jury, has caused the presumptively rational factfinder to make an erroneous factual determination.

A mandatory presumption * * * may affect not only the strength of the "no reasonable doubt" burden but also the placement of that burden; it tells the trier that he or they *must* find the elemental fact upon proof of the basic fact, at least unless the defendant has come forward with some evidence to rebut the presumed connection between the two facts.

The term presumption as employed in *Ulster* in reference to a permissive presumption differs in effect from the term presumption as employed in civil matters. A permissive presumption in a criminal case, properly referred to as an inference, permits but does not require the trier of fact to infer the presumed fact from the basic facts. A mandatory presumption as used in *Ulster* is a true presumption requiring that the jury find the presumed fact from the basic facts unless the defendant produces some evidence, i.e., satisfies a burden of production of some evidence. However a mandatory presumption as thus defined may not constitutionally be given the effect intended. As reiterated in *Sandstrom*, which followed *Ulster* by fourteen days, if the defendant fails to produce evidence to rebut the presumption, the jury may still not be directed to find against the defendant for a verdict may never be directed against an accused. Accordingly a mandatory presumption is not mandatory at all, i.e., the burden of production may not as a matter of law be shifted to the defendant.

A full discussion of the confusion rampant in *Ulster* is clearly beyond the scope of this Nutshell. Nevertheless, the following propositions are suggested as consistent with the Supreme Court's overall teachings in the area of criminal presumptions:

(1) A conclusive or irrebuttable presumption operating against a criminal defendant is unconstitutional.

(2) The burden of persuasion with respect to an element of a crime as defined may never be shifted to a criminal defendant by means of a presumption.

(3) Since a verdict may not be directed against an accused, the burden of production with respect to an element of a crime as defined may never be shifted to the defendant.

(4) Accordingly, since a presumption is a rule of law which requires that the existence of the presumed fact be taken as established in the absence of evidence to the contrary, presumptions operating against the accused can never exist in criminal cases.

(5) The trier of fact may, however, be instructed with respect to the inference that arises from the basic fact to the inferred fact provided there is a sufficient rational connection between the basic fact and the fact to be inferred. Whether sufficient rational connection exists between the basic fact and the fact to be inferred to warrant the giving of an instruction, or the particular instruction given, depends not only upon the natural strength of the logical inference but also upon the wording of the particular instruction given. Rational connection also varies depending on whether the fact to be inferred is an element of the offense or negates a defense or whether the fact to be inferred has a lesser effect. However at a minimum for an instructed inference to be given the court must determine that the fact to be inferred more probably than not flows from the basic fact. The more probably true than not true threshold standard is imposed to prevent the jury from overvaluing the weight to be given to the inference having a lesser probative value simply because the inference is instructed by the court.

(a) If the fact to be inferred has a lesser effect, a rational connection exists when the natural inference arising from the basic fact, if proved to be more probably true than not true, to the inferred fact, is sufficient to support a finding by a reasonable juror that the inferred fact is more probably true than not true. Under such circumstances the trier of fact may be instructed that if they find the basic fact, they may, but are not required to, infer from this fact the inferred fact. This may be called an instructed factual inference.

(b) If the fact to be inferred is an element of a crime or negates a defense, if a sufficient rational connection exists the jury may be instructed that if they find the basic fact beyond a reasonable doubt, they may, but are not required to, infer the inferred fact. A sufficient rational connection exists if the court determines that proof of the basic fact establishes the fact to be inferred to be more probably true than not true. Of course, inferences having less probative value going to an element or negating a defense are relevant and may be argued by counsel to the jury. However such inferences may not be instructed. The existence of the inferred fact may be submitted to the jury to determine if, but only if, a reasonable juror on the evidence as a whole, including evidence of the basic fact, could find the inferred fact beyond a reasonable doubt. The jury must also be instructed accordingly. This may occur where when viewed in light of all evidence in the case, the inference from the basic fact together with evidence of the inferred fact other than the basic fact would permit the jury to find the inferred fact beyond a reasonable doubt. In such circumstances the jury may also be instructed that they may not find the presumed fact solely based upon the existence of the basic fact. It may also occur when the inference solely from the basic fact established beyond a reasonable doubt to the inferred fact, when viewed in light of all the evidence, is itself sufficient to support a finding of the inferred fact beyond a reasonable doubt. This may be called an instructed elemental inference.

(c) When the fact to be inferred is an element of a crime or negates a defense, if a sufficient rational connection exists, the jury may be instructed that if they find the basic fact exists beyond a reasonable doubt the law declares that they may, but are not required to regard the basic fact as sufficient evidence of the inferred fact. Arguably equivalent but far less desirable language for such an instruction includes that the basic fact is "prima facie evidence," is "presumptive evidence" or that from the basic fact the inferred fact may be "presumed." A sufficient rational connection exists if the court determines that a reasonable juror could find from the basic fact alone that the inferred fact has been established beyond a reasonable doubt. Moreover the existence of the fact to be inferred may be submitted to the jury to determine if, but only if, a reasonable juror on the evidence as a whole, including evidence of the basic fact, could find the inferred fact beyond a reasonable doubt. This may be called an instructed prima facie inference. The jury must also be instructed accordingly.

## § 303.5    Presumption of Innocence

The presumption of innocence in criminal cases is not a presumption in the usual sense but rather a forceful way of saying that the prosecution must prove guilt beyond a reasonable doubt and that there is to be no inference against the defendant because of his arrest, indictment, or presence as a defendant in court. If requested by the defendant, an instruction with respect to the presumption of innocence is required by the Due Process Clause of the Fourteenth Amendment.

# ARTICLE IV

# RELEVANCY AND ITS LIMITS

*Table of Rules*

## Rule 401.

## DEFINITION OF "RELEVANT EVIDENCE"

**"Relevant evidence" means evidence having any tendency to make the existence of any fact that is of consequence to the determination of the action more probable or less probable than it would be without the evidence.**

### § 401.1   Relevant Evidence: Materiality and "Fact of Consequence"

"Relevant evidence" is defined in Rule 401 as evidence having any tendency to make the existence of any fact that is of consequence to the determination of the action more probable or less probable than it would be without the evidence. The rule employs "fact of consequence to the determination of the action" in place of the term "material," a term which has proved ambiguous. Evidence, direct or circumstantial, is relevant when it possesses any tendency to establish a fact of consequence. Evidence affecting the weight accorded such relevant evidence by the trier of fact falls within the concept of relevancy employed in Rule 401. Use of the phrase "fact of consequence" in place of materiality serves to clarify that the breadth of admissibility of relevant evidence extends to facts not in dispute. Rulings on admissibility of evidence upon a point conceded by an opponent must be made by considering probative value in light of trial concerns such as waste of time and unfair prejudice, Rule 403. Rule 401 also makes clear that evidence which is essentially background in nature offered as an aid to understanding may be admitted. Such items include, for example, biographical information concerning a witness, charts, photographs, views of real estate, and murder weapons connected solely to the crime.

Whether evidence is relevant depends upon it possessing "any" tendency to make a fact of consequence more or less probable than it would be without the evidence in the light of logic, experience, and accepted assumptions concerning human behavior. As Thayer stated, "The law furnishes no test of relevancy." The court in making its determination, Rule 104(a), must exercise broad discretion in drawing on its own experience in the affairs of mankind in evaluating the probabilities upon which relevancy depends. The concept of logical relevancy employed in Rule 401 must be kept separate from issues of sufficiency of evidence for any purpose such as to satisfy a burden of production. "A brick is not a wall" ; relevancy is the brick, sufficiency is the wall. Thus minimal logical relevancy is all that is required. In formulating the Rule 401 definition of relevancy, the Advisory Committee rejected the concerns underlying Wigmore's concept of "plus value" as applied to determining relevancy as being "unworkable and unrealistic." Such concerns, and more, were, however, incorporated in Rule 403, which provides that relevant evidence may be excluded if its probative value is substantially outweighed by the danger of unfair prejudice, confusion of the issues, or misleading the jury, or by considerations of undue delay, waste of time, or needless presentations of cumulative evidence.

Relevant evidence may be either direct or circumstantial. Direct evidence is evidence where the sole inference which must be made to establish a fact of consequence is the truth of the matter asserted. Testimony such as "I saw X shoot B," is direct evidence as to a fact of consequence. Circumstantial evidence involves evidence offered to establish a fact of consequence where an inference in addition to the truth of the matter asserted need be made. Thus testimony that X fled the scene would be both direct evidence of flight and circumstantial evidence of the murderous act.

The terms "material," now "fact of consequence," and "relevant" to a considerable extent prior to the Federal Rules of Evidence were used interchangeably. Evidence which was objected to as immaterial was likely also to be objected to as irrelevant and vice verse. Considerable clarification of analysis is gained by distinguishing between the propriety of the proposition to be established and the propriety of the proof to establish it. "Fact of consequence" describes a proposition which is in the case, and "relevant" describes evidence which has a tendency to prove or disprove the proposition. Whether a fact is of consequence is determined by the substantive law within the framework of the pleadings. Under Rule 401, the objection "irrelevant" raises both concepts, i.e., the evidence does not tend to make more or less probable the fact it is offered to establish or the fact for which offered to establish is not itself of consequence in the litigation. To illustrate, the fact that an eleven year old has had numerous previous consensual sexual encounters is irrelevant as the ultimate fact such evidence tends to prove, i.e., consent, is not a fact of consequence in a prosecution for sexual battery of a minor.

The term "fact of consequence to a determination of the action" includes three general categories of fact. First, it includes facts which comprise direct evidence of an element of a claim or defense. Elements of a claim or defense were referred to at common law as "material propositions." Second, "fact of consequence" includes those facts from whose establishment may be inferred facts amounting to elements of claims or defenses. In other words, intermediate facts which are circumstantial evidence of elements of claims or defenses. Finally, the term "fact of consequence" includes facts bearing circumstantially upon the evaluation of the probative value to be given to other evidence in the case, including demonstrative evidence and the credibility of witnesses. Included in this later category are demeanor, impeachment, rehabilitation, and background information. Questions of logical relevancy arise solely with respect to the latter two categories dealing with circumstantial evidence.

Evidence which is relevant, Rule 401, is admissible except as otherwise provided by law, Rule 402; evidence which is not relevant is not admissible, Rule 402. Relevant evidence may be excluded under Rule 403 if its probative value is substantially outweighed by the danger of unfair prejudice, confusion of the issues, or misleading the jury, or by considerations of undue delay, waste of time, or needless presentation of cumulative evidence. In considering the admissibility of the categories of evidence discussed in the sections which follow, the determination of logical relevancy in practice frequently merges with the concerns comprising grounds for exclusion under Rule 403. Both aspects of admissibility are discussed together in each section as a matter of convenience to the reader.

## § 401.2 Demonstrative and Real Evidence: Definition

The term "demonstrative" evidence is often used to describe all evidence from which the trier of fact may derive a relevant firsthand sense impression in contradistinction to the conventional presentation of oral testimony and the introduction of documentary exhibits. However the foregoing definition is so broad as to be of little assistance; analysis is fostered by treating separately its component parts, real and demonstrative evidence as well as experiments and views.

Real evidence involves the production of an object which usually but not always (e.g., a bullet used as an exemplar for comparison purposes) had a direct or indirect part in the incident, such as a murder weapon, piece of exploding bottle, or article of clothing. It also includes the exhibition of injured parts of the body. Real evidence provides the trier of fact with an opportunity to draw a relevant first hand sense impression. Such evidence may be either direct, such as an exploding bottle, or circumstantial, such as an article of clothing worn at the time of arrest by the defendant in a robbery prosecution exhibited to the jury to show conformity with eyewitness description.

Demonstrative evidence, including such items as a model, map, drawing, chart, photograph, tangible item, or demonstration is distinguished from real evidence in that it has no probative value itself, but serves merely as a visual aid to the jury in comprehending the verbal testimony of a witness or other evidence. Thus demonstrative evidence illustrates and clarifies. It is sometimes referred to as illustrative evidence or as evidence employed solely for illustrative purposes as distinguished from substantive evidence. While it is a common practice for demonstrative evidence to be displayed and referred to without formally being admitted into evidence, the formal offering and introduction of demonstrative evidence into the record as part of the witness' testimony is preferred.

The immediacy and reality of both real and demonstrative evidence accounts for their convincing power and appeal. Employment of real or demonstrative evidence creates a potential that the jury will overvalue such evidence, a risk which is characterized in the terms of Rule 403 as a danger of misleading the jury or creating confusion of the issues. In addition certain real and demonstrative evidence, such as gruesome photographs and the exhibition of hideous injuries, raise the danger of unfair prejudice. However there is no flat rule that the presence of such dangers require exclusion of the evidence. Application of the balancing provisions of Rule 403 to the admissibility of such evidence is required.

## § 401.3  Demonstrative and Real Evidence: Relevancy

The relevancy aspects of demonstrative and real evidence are no different from other evidence: if its appearance or other physical characteristics render a fact of consequence more or less probable, the demonstrative or real evidence is relevant. The requirement is met by demonstrative evidence which promotes understanding of other relevant evidence. The verbal testimony, which the demonstrative evidence aids in understanding, must of course itself be relevant to a fact of consequence in the litigation.

Real evidence may be direct as when the condition of the object itself is in issue, or it may be circumstantial affording inferences as to facts of consequence. The showing required of direct real evidence is that it is genuinely what it purports to be and, if essential to probative value, that its condition is unchanged. Circumstantial real evidence and demonstrative evidence share the problems of circumstantial evidence generally. More detailed treatment is given in connection with particular topics.

### § 401.4  Real Evidence: Tangible Objects; Instrumentalities of Crime

Tangible objects involved in an incident of almost every kind have been admitted into evidence in recognition of the explanative value of the sense impressions derived from the object. The fact of consequence to which the object relates need not be in dispute. Relevant real evidence may be excluded, however, on the grounds of unfair prejudice or needless presentation of cumulative evidence in accordance with Rule 403. Nevertheless, in view of the present general acceptance of evidence of this nature, the exclusion of an object of undoubted relevance and probative value on either ground is unlikely. Moreover as a matter of overall policy, if the fact of consequence for which offered is important in the litigation and if the probative value of the tangible evidence is high, exclusion of the evidence under Rule 403 should occur only in the most unusual circumstances. If "seeing is believing," the jury should be permitted to see.

The tangible object must be proved to be genuinely what it purports to be. If probative value depends upon similarity of condition in a particular respect, that condition must be proved to be unchanged. However, changed conditions do not require exclusion where after the changes are explained, the trier of fact will not be misled.

Instruments allegedly used in the commission of a crime and offered to prove the accused committed the crime must be connected up both with the accused and with the crime, thereby furnishing a link between the accused and the crime. The connection with the crime may be circumstantial, such as establishment of the defendant's possession of masks, burglary tools or quantities of weapons, or direct, such as possession of bait money from the robbed bank or positive eyewitness identification of items employed in committing the crime. Connection with respect to items used in the crime is also satisfied by establishment that the item, such as a gun or knife is similar to the item employed by the accused in the crime. Moreover, if an object is shown to be connected with a defendant, admissibility does not require a showing that such an object was actually used in the offense charged so long as it is shown that the object is at least suitable for the commission of the crime, or otherwise related to the offense. Instrumentalities sufficiently shown to have been employed in the commission of the crime but not connected with the defendant, such as a bloody knife found at the scene of a murder, may be admitted for a purpose other than to show the defendant committed the crime. Instrumentalities, like all tangible evidence, are subject to exclusion under Rule 403.

## § 401.5  Real Evidence: Exhibiting Personal Injuries; Bodily Demonstrations

In light of the fact that the display of a physical injury sustained will almost always be the most probative evidence available as to a fact of consequence, exhibition of physical injuries before the jury is permitted. The absence of controversy as to the existence of the injury or its nature and extent will not preclude display. Even if the injury is particularly shocking, display is considered proper. While of course the introduction of such evidence is subject to Rule 403, the jury should be deprived of such evidence only under the most unusual of circumstances.

While demonstrating the extent of impairment or disability resulting from injury is recognized as proper, caution should be exercised in permitting the injured person to perform certain acts or be manipulated by a physician. Such actions raise significant problems such as feigning, difficulty in conducting cross-examination, and the inducement of an undue emotional response in the trier of fact by manifestations of pain.

## § 401.6   Demonstrative Evidence: Maps, Models, Drawings, Charts and Tangible Items

Use by a witness of visual illustrations to explain testimony is a common courtroom occurrence. Resort to such techniques expands each year; the variety of available techniques is limited only by counsel's ingenuity. Unless the illustration is essential to an understanding of the testimony, it is largely cumulative in effect, and admission or exclusion rests technically within the discretion of the trial judge, Rule 403. In practice, however, the use of maps, models, drawings and charts is now almost universally permitted.

The effectiveness of visual presentation imposes certain limits on its use. The line of demarcation falls between explanation of testimony, which is entirely proper, and the reduction of testimony to graphic form in such manner as to create the possibility of undue emphasis. Thus when the witness illustrates his testimony with a blackboard drawing, or points out on a plat the manner in which a collision occurred, his testimony is clarified but is not likely to be regarded by the trier as being anything more than oral testimony. On the other hand, when an exhibit actually presents in graphic form the testimony of a witness concerning a particular matter, it may be argued that the memorialization is likely to be given undue weight by the trier of fact and thus excludable on the grounds of misleading the jury, Rule 403. If such an exhibit nevertheless fairly and accurately depicts what it purports to represent, the exercise of discretion in favor of exclusion should be employed sparingly.

Mathematical accuracy is not required of a drawing, map, model, or chart for use for illustrative purposes either by a witness or in argument. However if the drawing, map, model, or chart does not aid in understanding by reason of such inaccuracies, i.e., is misleading even after being explained, the exhibit will properly be excluded. Of course, if essential matters depicted in the drawing, map, model, or chart are not supported by the proper foundation, introduction of the exhibit is error.

Demonstrative evidence may also consist of tangible items which are not contended themselves to have played a part in the incident, but which are instead offered for the purpose of rendering other evidence more understandable. A sufficient foundation establishing substantial similarity is, of course, required.

## § 401.7 Demonstrative Evidence: Photographs, Videotapes, Animations

Still photographs, motion pictures, and videotapes, once properly authenticated, are admissible in evidence if helpful to the trier of fact's understanding of a fact of consequence in the litigation. Relevant photographic evidence may however be excluded on the basis of any of the grounds specified in Rule 403, particularly the dangers of misleading the jury and unfair prejudice.

**Still photograph.** A sufficient foundation is laid for a still photograph by testimony of any person or group of persons with personal knowledge *at a time relevant to the issues* of the subject matter depicted in the photograph sufficient to support a finding that the photograph is a fair and accurate representation of the subject matter depicted at that time. The photographer is not required. Lapse of time between the taking the photograph and the time of consequence in the litigation is irrelevant if conditions have not changed. Complete similarity of conditions is not required of photographs used in the same way as maps to illustrate physical relations. Changed conditions alone do not render any photograph inadmissible if after the changes are explained the trier of fact can understand the correct and helpful representation and thus will not be misled by the photograph. However, since the nature of a photograph makes difficult any separation of illustration from assertion, a change of conditions may make the picture so confusing or misleading as to require exclusion, Rule 403.

**Enlarged, color, slow motion, and enhanced.** Enlarged photographs may be used; color photographs are also permitted within the discretion of the court. Slow motion as well as computer enhancement is also permitted within the discretion of the court.

**Motion pictures and videotapes.** Motion pictures and videotapes are admissible on the same basis as still photographs. Although normally not necessary in principle, frequently additional proof that the operator was experienced, the camera or videotape equipment was in good working order, the film or tape was not tampered with, and with respect to motion pictures the film was developed in the usual and customary manner is introduced. In the exercise of its discretion, the court may properly consider that the setting up of projection equipment, darkening the courtroom and showing the film may serve to overemphasize such evidence in the minds of the jury, Rule 403. Videotapes may serve to reduce in part such distraction.

**Posed photographs.** Posed still photographs, motion pictures, and videotapes reconstructing an event while sometimes admitted are also sometimes regarded with disfavor in light of the propensity of the trier of fact to be misled into conferring disproportionate emphasis, Rule 403.

**Animations.** Computer animations are admissible provided a foundation of sufficient similarity is presented, subject to Rule 403. Computer animations that go beyond illustration incorporating experimental elements raise additional concerns relating to similarity as well as the reliability of the explanative theory being employed.

**Illustrative versus substantive.** Still photographs, motion pictures, and videotapes are generally admitted solely to "illustrate" the testimony of the witness and not as substantive evidence. The artificiality and theoretical soundness of such a distinction is certainly subject to criticism. Any supposed practical consequences of such a distinction are minimal at best. Moreover, where the fiction of illustrative purpose is not available, as for example with respect to x-rays and the automatic photograph of a bank robbery, or where the contents of the photograph are clearly sought to be proved, the photograph will be admitted as substantive evidence.

**Personal injuries.** Still photographs, motion pictures and videotapes of an injury may be admitted to the same extent that the injury itself might be exhibited. While admissibility is stated to be within the sound discretion of the court, introduction of photographs is clearly favored. Accordingly, photographic evidence should not be excluded merely because it *might* arouse feelings of horror or indignation in the jury. Moreover, such photographs may be admitted over objection that the evidence is cumulative in light of other evidence of the injury, such as expert testimony or displays, or that the injury is not actually in dispute. The admission of photographs showing treatment, such as traction, is within the discretion of the trial judge, as are motion pictures or videotapes showing a day in the life of the plaintiff.

**Criminal prosecutions.** Despite their gruesomeness and thus arguably prejudicial effect on the jury, relevant photographs generally will be admitted in the court's discretion where they tend to prove such things as the existence of a crime, the cause of death, the number and location of the wounds, the manner in which they were inflicted, the amount of force used, the wilfulness of the act in question, a person's identity, or to corroborate evidence concerning an unusual cause of death. By its very nature, the more gruesome the crime, the more gruesome the photographs which will be admitted. However, although photographs will be admitted where they help the jury better to understand medical testimony, if the gruesome nature of the photographs is caused by autopsy or emergency room procedures, the photographs may be excluded by reason of their relatively slight probative value, Rule 403.

Photographs in criminal prosecutions do not necessarily become cumulative and inadmissible merely because there is also oral testimony or a stipulation on the same general subject. Even where a defendant stipulates to each of the facts as to which the photograph is relevant, the photograph may be admitted on the theory either that the prosecution has the right to prove each and every element of its case or that the photograph may be introduced for the moral weight of the evidence.

**Hearsay.** A photograph, motion picture, videotape, or animation is ordinarily not hearsay. However if the image depicted is a person making an oral or written assertion, or performing non verbal conduct intended as an assertion, such depiction is hearsay when offered to prove the truth of the matter asserted. Thus a videotape of an accident scene showing the position of the cars as they came to rest does not raise a hearsay issue. Conversely, a videotape of the same scene capturing the driver of one car stating that the other driver ran a red light would be hearsay when offered to prove that the other driver ran a red light.

**Rule 403.** Generally speaking, it is relatively unlikely that a properly authenticated and highly probative photograph will be excluded on the grounds of unfair prejudice alone. Naturally, where either the probative value is slight, or the fact of consequence sought to be proved is either itself relatively unimportant in the litigation or undisputed, the likelihood of the photograph being excluded under Rule 403 increases. However the overall importance of photographs to the trier of fact in understanding the matter they are being asked to decide, taken in light of the trier of fact's ability to withstand any inclination to punish the defendant in either a civil or criminal case without regard to culpability simply because of the gruesomeness shown in the photographs, makes admission of photographic evidence the norm.

## § 401.8 Demonstrative Evidence: X-rays

X-rays essentially are no different from ordinary photographs. However the fact that the X-ray shows an image not visible to the unaided eye requires a different type of foundation proof to establish the correctness of the portrayal. Correctness may be shown by comparison with what the witness saw through a fluoroscope or by proving skill in X-ray techniques, proper working condition and accuracy of equipment, manner of taking the picture, and correctness of result based on experience. Of course evidence must be introduced showing that the X-ray offered is actually of the person purported to have been X rayed.

Since an X-ray goes beyond mere illustration of the witness's testimony, it is admitted as substantive evidence. Accordingly, the Original Writing Rule, Rule 1002, applies.

## § 401.9 Demonstrative Evidence: Courtroom and Out of Court Demonstrations

Demonstrations, sometimes but not always employing models or tangible objects, are permissible for explanatory purposes but not for dramatic effect or emotional appeal. Accordingly, the use by medical experts of a model of a human foot, or a model of a human skeleton to explain the nature of injuries is clearly proper. Similarly, during closing argument, within appropriate bounds, counsel may use demonstrative evidence previously employed in the litigation to illustrate and explain. Since the dividing line between proper and improper demonstrations is by no means a sharp one, considerable discretion must be left to the trial judge, Rule 403. Demonstrations may be recorded out of court for presentation in court.

## § 401.10  Experiments

The results of experiments are substantive evidence, admissible to show cause and effect, characteristics, and the like. Common illustrations include ballistics tests, blood tests in paternity matters, and analysis of substances in narcotics cases. Sometimes the purpose of the experiment is to determine how a particular event occurred or did not occur. With respect to such experiments, since the possibility of varying a condition to produce the desired result clearly exists, insistence of substantial similarity of conditions is usually strict. Dissimilarities will be tolerated when shown to be without significance or to create a minor variance in result such that once explained the evidence assists rather than misleads. Experiments not designed to recreate the incident, such as testing to determine the nature of a substance or a presentation offered to illustrate a scientific principle, often require no control or less stringent control over similarity of conditions. The line between experiments designed to recreate the incident and those designed solely to illustrate a scientific principle is often difficult to draw.

Experiments are generally conducted out of court with the results being reported in court, often employing photographic representation. Where a litigant wishes actually to conduct an experiment before the trier of fact, the court must decide whether the confusion, delay and potential misleading of the jury substantially outweighs its probative value, Rule 403. Of course the requirement of similarity of conditions must initially be satisfied.

## § 401.11    View by Trier of Fact

Whether a view of property which is the subject of litigation or the location where a relevant event occurred is taken by the trier of fact has long been within the discretion of the trial judge. The court has inherent discretion, not only to permit a view of property and the scene of the occurrence, but also to allow a view of any object, demonstration, or experiment which is relevant and otherwise admissible in evidence. A view may be appropriate in products liability actions where, for example, the witness can assume his actual position as he operated the piece of machinery, or in criminal proceedings where, for example, a witness may demonstrate the relevant positions and actions of persons or objects. How ever the alternative and frequently preferable procedure of employing testimony, diagrams, photographs, video-tape etc., should not be overlooked. Whether a view is or is not ordered by the trial court is subject to review for abuse of discretion.

Changed conditions do not preclude exercise of discretion in favor of a view particularly if either the change does not effect any relevant feature or where, if after the changes are explained, the jury can understand and be helped by the correct representation.

Neither the evidentiary status nor procedures to be followed at a view are specified in the Federal Rules of Evidence. Since a view cannot be totally incorporated in the record, it involves problems of control by the trial judge over the jury and by the reviewing court over the trial court. Accordingly it has been said that a view is not evidence but is to enable the trier to understand and apply the evidence. This view of views has been subject to sustained and vigorous attack. Although the position adopted by federal decisions was once stated to be unclear, the preferable view treating views as independent substantive evidence appears now to have won out. With respect to procedures to be followed at a view, while the presence of the judge and parties is probably not required in civil as compared to criminal cases, the preferable procedure with respect to attendance and conduct is that followed in California Code of Civil Procedure § 651(b):

> [T]he entire court, including the judge, jury, if any, court reporter, if any, and any necessary officers, shall proceed to the place, property, object, demonstration, or experiment to be viewed. The court shall be in session throughout the view. At the view, the court may permit testimony of witnesses. The proceedings at the view shall be recorded to the same extent as the proceedings in the courtroom.

## Rule 402.

## RELEVANT EVIDENCE GENERALLY ADMISSIBLE; IRRELEVANT EVIDENCE INADMISSIBLE

**All relevant evidence is admissible, except as otherwise provided by the Constitution of the United States, by Act of Congress, by these rules, or by other rules prescribed by the Supreme Court pursuant to statutory authority. Evidence which is not relevant is not admissible.**

## § 402.1  Relevant Evidence Generally Admissible; Irrelevant Evidence Inadmissible

The general rule that all relevant evidence is admissible unless otherwise provided by law states a touchstone of any rational system of justice. Relevant evidence will be inadmissible whenever applicable federal statute, a Federal Rule of Evidence or other court rule, or the United States Constitution so requires. Where federal law provides the rule of decision, admissibility of evidence is governed by Rule 402. Where state law provides the rule of decision, whether the United States Constitution may require that in a particular case a state rule relating to admissibility or inadmissibility of relevant evidence be applied is beyond the scope of this Nutshell.

With respect to other Federal Rules of Evidence, Rules 404, 405 and 407–412 call for exclusion of relevant evidence in various specific situations. Sometimes such relevant evidence is excluded because the risk of misleading, confusion or prejudice is so great that truth would probably be obscured. Sometimes it is thought necessary to provide for the inadmissibility of such relevant evidence to encourage socially desirable conduct which would be discouraged if admissible at trial. The rules governing the competency of witnesses (Article VI), excluding hearsay (Article VIII), requiring authentication or identification (Article IX), and requiring use of the original writing (Article X) are designed to protect the jury from testimony that may not be worthy of belief. The rules on privilege (Article V) reject highly relevant evidence because they protect relationships which are regarded of sufficient social importance to justify some sacrifice of sources of facts that would aid in bringing out the truth. In addition Rule 403 provides in a generalized way that the court may exclude relevant evidence if its probative value is substantially outweighed by the danger of unfair prejudice, confusion of the issues, or misleading the jury, or by considerations of undue delay, waste of time, or needless presentation of cumulative evidence. Such power is necessary to facilitate the ascertainment of truth and to keep the conduct of the trial within bounds.

With respect to other rules, for example, Fed.R.Civ. Proc. 32(a)(3) by requiring a showing of unavailability of the deponent restricts use of relevant depositions. Various statutory provisions similarly restrict the admissibility of relevant evidence.

Of course, irrelevant evidence is not admissible.

## Rule 403.

## EXCLUSION OF RELEVANT EVIDENCE ON GROUNDS OF PREJUDICE, CONFUSION, OR WASTE OF TIME

**Although relevant, evidence may be excluded if its probative value is substantially outweighed by the danger of unfair prejudice, confusion of the issues, or misleading the jury, or by considerations of undue delay, waste of time, or needless presentation of cumulative evidence.**

### § 403.1 Exclusion of Relevant Evidence: Factors to Be Considered; Standard Applied

Evidence which meets the standard of relevancy, Rule 401, may nevertheless possess attendant disadvantages of sufficient importance to call for its exclusion. These disadvantages according to Rule 403 consist of unfair prejudice, confusion of the issues, misleading the jury, and considerations of undue delay, waste of time and the needless presentation of cumulative evidence. A particular item of evidence may involve more than one of them. Collectively these disadvantages may be referred to as trial concerns.

Rule 403 favors the admissibility of relevant evidence. Evidence which is relevant is to be excluded only if its probative value is substantially outweighed by any of the foregoing factors alone or in combination. Exclusion of relevant evidence under Rule 403 is employed sparingly as it is an extraordinary remedy. The burden is on the objecting party. Where relevant evidence is subject to exclusion, the trial court should advise counsel of the specific ground for exclusion so that counsel, if possible, can obviate the objection. The balancing test of Rule 403 applies to evidence being admitted against less than all opposing parties or for a limited purpose such as for its effect upon the credibility of a witness.

In exercising its discretion in applying this standard, the court should consider the importance of the fact of consequence for which the evidence is offered in the context of the litigation, the strength and length of the chain of inferences necessary to establish the fact of consequence, the availability of alternative means of proof, whether the fact of consequence for which the evidence is offered is being disputed, and, where appropriate, the potential effectiveness of a limiting instruction, Rule 105. In evaluating the incremental probative value of the evidence, the trial judge must assume that the evidence will be believed by the trier of fact. Obviously where either the probative value of the offered evidence or the importance of the fact sought to be proved is relatively slight, the likelihood of exclusion under Rule 403 is enhanced.

Rule 403 provides for the exclusion of relevant evidence on the grounds of unfair prejudice. Since all effective evidence is prejudicial in the sense of being damaging to the party against whom it is offered, prejudice which calls for exclusion is given a more specialized meaning: an undue tendency to suggest decision on an improper basis, commonly but not necessarily an emotional one, such as bias, sympathy, hatred, contempt, retribution or horror. An improper basis also includes consideration of the evidence by the jury for a purpose for which it has not been admitted in spite of a limiting instruction not to do so. Where a danger of unfair prejudice is perceived, the degree of likely prejudice must also be considered. The mere fact that evidence possesses a tendency to suggest a decision upon an improper basis does not require exclusion; evidence may be excluded only if the danger of unfair prejudice substantially outweighs the probative value of the proffered evidence. In a similar vein it has been asserted in Rivers v. United States (9th Cir.1959) that "[i]f the mere gruesomeness of the evidence were ground for its exclusion, then it would have to be said that the more gruesome the crime, the greater the difficulty of the prosecution in proving its case."

Where unfair surprise is asserted, enforcement of discovery sanctions or the granting of a continuance are more appropriate remedies than exclusion of the evidence on the basis of balancing harm against incremental probative value. Accordingly, unfair surprise is not included as a factor to be considered in Rule 403.

While Rule 403 speaks in terms of both confusion of the issues and misleading of the jury, the distinction between such terms is unclear in the literature and in the cases. McCormick, Evidence § 185 at 646 (5th ed.1999) refers to the probability that "certain proof and the answering evidence that it provokes might unduly distract the jury from the main issues." 2 Wigmore, Evidence § 442 at 528–29 (Chadbourn rev.1979) describes the concept as follows:

[I]n attempting to dispute or explain away the evidence thus offered, new issues will arise as to the occurrence of the instances and the similarity of conditions, new witnesses will be needed whose cross-examination and impeachment may lead to further issues; and that thus the trial will be unduly prolonged, and the multiplicity of minor issues will be such that the jury will lose sight of the main issue, and the whole evidence will be only a mass of confused data from which it will be difficult to extract the kernel of controversy.

Both commentators are clearly describing the notion of confusion of the issues. While of course a jury confused in the foregoing manner can also be said to have been misled, it is suggested that the concept of misleading the jury refers primarily to the possibility of the jury incorrectly evaluating the probative value of a particular item of evidence, usually by overvaluing, for any reason other than the emotional reaction associated with unfair prejudice. To illustrate, evidence of the results of a lie detector, even where an attempt is made to explain fully the significance of the results, is likely to be overvalued by the trier of fact. Demonstrative evidence in the form of a photograph, map, model, drawing, chart, etc., which varies substantially from the fact of consequence sought to be illustrated similarly may mislead. Finally, a jury may be misled by the sheer amount of time spent upon a question into believing the issue to be of major importance and accordingly into attaching too much significance to it in its determination of the factual issues involved.

Occasionally evidence is excluded not because distracting side issues will be created but rather because an unsuitable amount of time would be consumed in clarifying the situation. Concerns associated with the proper use of trial time also arise where the evidence being offered is relevant to a fact as to which substantial other evidence has already been introduced, including evidence bearing on the question of credibility, where the evidence itself possesses only minimal probative value, such as evidence admitted as background, or where evidence is thought by the court to be collateral. In recognition of the legitimate concern of the court with expenditures of time, Rule 403 provides for exclusion of evidence where its probative value is substantially outweighed by considerations of undue delay, waste of time or needless presentation of cumulative evidence. Thus evidence which in the context of the litigation is merely repetitious or time consuming may be excluded, but only if time considerations substantially outweigh the incremental probative value of the proffered evidence.

In evaluating the incremental probative value of the proffered evidence, the fact that the opponent has offered to stipulate or is not disputing the proposition for which the evidence is being offered should be considered. However, in evaluating such a stance taken by the party opposing admissibility, the powerfulness attached to the concept that the proponent of the evidence need not accept a stipulation but rather is entitled to present otherwise admissible evidence for the fair and legitimate weight introduction of the evidence would have on the trier of facts cannot be overestimated. As the United States Supreme Court stated in Old Chief v. United States (S.Ct.1997), the accepted rule that the prosecution or other litigant is entitled to prove its case free from any defendants option to stipulate the evidence away rests on good sense. If the offer to stipulate or not to dispute does not cover all purposes for which the evidence is relevant, the evidence certainly will not be excluded.

The fertility of the legal mind in attacking practical problems of proof presents situations of infinite variety. Some have recurred with sufficient frequency to evolve fairly definite rules, as is seen in later sections of Article IV. Generally, however, the variables which are present, not only in the disadvantages enumerated above but in the extent to which they outweigh or are outweighed by the proper aspects of the evidence, indeed the variations in the force of relevancy itself, make the entire area one in which the judgment of the trial court ought to be disturbed only if the exercise of discretion was abused.

A finding on the record by the trial court of the result of conducting the balancing mandated by Rule 403 is to be encouraged but is not required.

## Rule 404.

### CHARACTER EVIDENCE NOT ADMISSIBLE TO PROVE CONDUCT; EXCEPTIONS; OTHER CRIMES

**(a) Character Evidence Generally. Evidence of a person's character or a trait of character is not**

admissible for the purpose of proving action in conformity therewith on a particular occasion, except:

(1) **Character of Accused.** Evidence of a pertinent trait of character offered by an accused, or by the prosecution to rebut the same, or if evidence of a trait of character of the alleged victim of the crime is offered by an accused and admitted under Rule 404(a)(2), evidence of the same trait of character of the accused offered by the prosecution;

(2) **Character of Alleged Victim.** Evidence of a pertinent trait of character of the alleged victim of the crime offered by an accused, or by the prosecution to rebut the same, or evidence of a character trait of peacefulness of the alleged victim offered by the prosecution in a homicide case to rebut evidence that the alleged victim was the first aggressor;

(3) **Character of Witness.** Evidence of the character of a witness, as provided in Rules 607, 608, and 609.

**(b) Other Crimes, Wrongs, or Acts.** Evidence of other crimes, wrongs, or acts is not admissible to prove the character of a person in order to show action in conformity therewith. It may, however, be admissible for other purposes, such as proof of motive, opportunity, intent, preparation, plan, knowledge, identity, or absence of mistake or accident, provided that upon request by the accused, the prosecution in a criminal case shall provide reasonable notice in advance of trial, or during trial if the court excuses pretrial notice on good

**cause shown, of the general nature of any such evidence it intends to introduce at trial.**

## § 404.1 Character Evidence: An Overview

Character is the nature of a person, his disposition generally, or his disposition in respect to a particular trait such as peacefulness or truthfulness. Reputation is the community estimate of him. Failure to make the distinction results in confusion which is compounded by the fact that reputation may enter as a method of proving character, Rules 405 and 608. Over the years, owing perhaps to the far greater frequency with which it is encountered in criminal cases, the concept of character has acquired strong moral overtones. Inquiry into the nature of the person has largely been confined to considerations which can be characterized as either goodness or badness.

Rule 404(a) deals with the basic question of when evidence of character or a trait of character is admissible for the purpose of proving that a person acted in conformity with it on a particular occasion, sometimes described as "circumstantial" use of character. Methods of proof are dealt with in Rule 405(a) which provides that in all cases in which evidence of character or a trait of character of a person is admissible for the purpose of proving conformity, proof may be made by testimony as to reputation or by testimony in the form of an opinion; evidence of specific instances of conduct is not admissible. On cross-examination of such a reputation or opinion witness inquiry is allowable into relevant specific instances of conduct, Rule 405(a). Specific instances of conduct are admissible to prove character when character is an essential element of a charge, claim or defense, Rule 405(b).

The general principle enunciated in Rule 404 is that character evidence is not admissible for the purpose of showing that a person acted in conformity therewith on a particular occasion.

"[C]haracter evidence is of slight probative value and may be very prejudicial. It tends to distract the trier of fact from the main question of what actually happened on the particular occasion. It subtly permits the trier of fact to reward the good man and to punish the bad man because of their respective characters despite what evidence in the case shows actually happened." Advisory Committee's Note to Rule 404(a).

Moreover, a person is entitled to have his guilt or innocence of the crime charged determined strictly on the basis of evidence regarding the crime charged.

Rule 404(a)(1) covers the exception which allows an accused to offer evidence of a pertinent trait of his character and allows the prosecution to rebut such evidence once the accused has done so. Rule 404(a)(2) provides a similar exception with respect to evidence of a pertinent character trait of the alleged victim of the crime, with a further exception made for prosecution proof of the character trait for peacefulness in a homicide case. Rule 404(a)(1) further provides that if evidence of a trait of character of the alleged victim of the crimes is offered by an accused and admitted under Rule 404(a)(2), evidence of the same trait of character of the accused may be offered by the prosecution. These exceptions are for criminal cases only, as evidenced by use of the words "accused" and "alleged victim". Finally, Rule 404(a)(3) refers to the exception for evidence of the character of a witness as effecting the witness' credibility provided in Rules 607, 608 and 609.

The foregoing is subject to the exceptions provided in Rules 413–415 relating to the character of the defendant when the defendant is charged with an offense of sexual assault or child molestation or when a civil case is brought against the defendant alleging commission of conduct constituting an offense of sexual assault or child molestation and to the provisions of Rule 412 relating to the character of the victim in sex offense cases.

Rule 404(b) provides for the admissibility of evidence of other crimes, wrongs, or acts for a purpose other than to prove character of a person in order to show that he acted in conformity therewith, such as proof of motive, opportunity, or intent. Evidence of prior crimes, wrongs, or acts to impeach a witness' credibility is dealt with in Rules 608 and 609.

## § 404.2 Rule 404: Character Evidence; Circumstantial Use in Civil Cases

The circumstantial use of character must be distinguished from character in issue discussed in Rule 405(b). Character is used circumstantially when the inference suggested is that a person's character or particular trait of character tends to make it more probable that the person acted or is acting consistently with that character than it would be without such evidence.

Circumstantial use of character evidence is not permitted in civil cases, Rule 404(a), except to impeach or support the character of a witness for truthfulness as provided for in Rules 607, 608 and 609, Rule 404(a)(3). Habit of a person, as distinguished from character, and the routine practice of an organization may be admitted as provided in Rule 406.

The foregoing is subject to the exception provided in Rule 415 relating to the character of the defendant when a civil case is brought against the defendant alleging commission of conduct constituting an offense of sexual assault or child molestation and the exception provided in Rule 412 relating to the character of the victim in civil sex offense cases.

## § 404.3  Rule 404(a)(1): Character Evidence of the Accused

In criminal cases, Rule 404(a)(1) provides that the prosecution may *not* in the first instance introduce evidence of a pertinent character trait of the accused as part of the case in chief against him. By longstanding tradition the unfair prejudice to the defendant in being portrayed as a "bad man" is felt to substantially outweigh any probative value the evidence might possess. On the other hand, the accused in the first instance may offer proof as to a pertinent trait of his character. If he does, the prosecution may then offer evidence as to the same character trait by way of rebuttal, Rule 404(a)(1).

In addition, Rule 404(a)(1) provides that if evidence of a trait of character of the alleged victim of the crime is offered by an accused and admitted under Rule 404(a)(2), evidence of the same trait of character of the accused may be offered by the prosecution. Thus, the accused is not permitted to attack the alleged victim's character and yet remain shielded from the disclosure of equally relevant evidence concerning the same character trait of the accused. For example, in a murder case with a claim of self-defense, the accused, to bolster this defense, might offer evidence of the alleged victim's violent disposition. If the prosecution has evidence that the accused has a violent character, the prosecution is permitted under

Rule 404(a)(1) to offer this evidence as part of its rebuttal. The jury now has information relating to both the accused and the alleged victim necessary for an informed assessment of the probabilities as to who was the initial aggressor.

When offered, evidence of the pertinent character trait must be in the form of either reputation or opinion testimony; proof of specific instances of conduct is not permitted, Rule 405(a).

The procedure provided for in Rule 404(a)(1) is sometimes incorrectly described as "putting his character in issue by the accused." Obviously, however, character does not become an actual issue in the case but is being used circumstantially, the suggested inference being that the accused acted consistently with his character.

The accused may introduce evidence as to a pertinent trait of his character regardless of whether or not the accused testifies at the trial. If the accused does elect to testify, he becomes subject to impeachment, including as provided for in Rule 404(a)(3), attack upon his character for truthfulness in accordance with Rules 607, 608 and 609. This again is not a case of "putting character in issue."

The foregoing is subject to the exceptions provided in Rules 413 and 414 relating to the character of the accused when the accused is charged with an offense of sexual assault or child molestation.

## § 404.4 Rule 404(a)(2): Character Evidence of the Alleged Victim

Evidence of a pertinent character trait of the alleged victim of a crime is circumstantial evidence admissible if offered by the accused, or by the prosecution to rebut the same, Rule 404(a)(2). Evidence of specific acts is not admissible for the purpose of showing character; proof must be by reputation or opinion, Rule 405(a).

The accused in a homicide case is, for example, thus entitled under Rule 404(a)(2) to introduce evidence that the deceased was reputed to be or in the character witness' opinion was a violent and dangerous person. If this pertinent character trait was known to the accused, such knowledge is a factor to be considered in determining whether he reasonably apprehended bodily harm. Regardless however of whether the accused knew of the reputation or had formed his own opinion, such testimony is admissible when offered through another witness for the purpose of showing the character of the deceased, with the suggested inference that the latter was more probably the aggressor. Moreover, if the accused in a homicide prosecution introduces evidence that the alleged victim was the first aggressor, whether or not employing opinion or reputation testimony, the prosecution may offer in rebuttal reputation or opinion testimony as to the character trait of peacefulness of the alleged victim, Rule 404(a)(2).

## § 404.5  Rule  404(b):  Other  Crimes,  Wrongs  or Acts

As an aspect of the rule that the prosecution cannot introduce evidence of a character trait of the accused as part of its case in chief, evidence of the commission of other crimes, wrongs or acts by him is inadmissible for the purpose of showing a disposition or propensity to commit crimes, Rule 404(b). Thus the suggested inference that the accused therefore committed the crime in question or is a bad man deserving of punishment in any event is avoided.

However great inroads upon this rule of exclusion occur because Rule 404(a) does not bar and Rule 404(b) specifically allows evidence of other crimes, wrongs, or acts for purposes other than merely showing a disposition to commit such crimes, wrongs, or acts for the inference that he acted in conformity therewith. Evidence of other crimes, wrongs or acts is admissible when relevant for another purpose such as proof of motive, opportunity, intent, preparation, plan, knowledge, identity, or absence of mistake or accident, Rule 404(b). This list is not intended to be exhaustive for the range of relevancy outside the ban is almost infinite. Nor are the stated categories mutually exclusive. Evidence of other crimes, wrongs, or acts has also been admitted to establish the existence of a conspiracy, a person's participation in a conspiracy, consciousness of guilt, to corroborate crucial testimony, and to rebut a defense of entrapment, for example. The proponent must specifically identify the particular other purpose for which the other crime, wrong, or act evidence is relevant.

Evidence which comprises the crime for which the accused is on trial, whether or not the crime of conspiracy, is offered as direct evidence of the crime and thus not "other" crimes, wrongs, or acts evidence. Similarly falling outside the scope of Rule 404(b) is evidence of other crimes, wrongs, or acts "intricately related," "inextricably intertwined," i.e., so linked together in point of time and circumstances with the crime charged that one cannot be fully shown without proving the other.

In summary, Rule 404(b) permits the introduction of evidence of another crime, wrong, or act *unless* the sole purpose for the offer is to establish the defendant's propensity for crime, i.e., evidence of other crimes is admissible if relevant in the litigation for any purpose other than "to prove the character of a person in order to show he acted in conformity therewith," Rule 404(b).

Relevance for a purpose other than to show the defendant to be a bad man is, however, not always enough for admissibility is subject of Rule 403. As McCormick, Evidence § 190 at 672–73 (5th ed.1999) states:

> [T]he problem is not merely one of pigeonholing, but of classifying and then balancing. In deciding whether the danger of unfair prejudice and the like substantially outweighs the incremental probative value, a variety of matters must be considered, including the strength of the evidence as to the commission of the other crime, the similarities between the crimes, the interval of time that has elapsed between the crimes, the need for the evidence, the efficacy of alternative proof, and the degree to which the evidence probably will rouse the jury to overmastering hostility.

Accordingly, evidence of other crimes, wrongs or acts may be received, if relevant for any purpose other than to show a mere propensity or disposition on the part of the defendant to commit the crime, provided that the court may exclude the evidence if its probative value is substantially outweighed by the risk that its admission will result in unfair prejudice to the accused, Rule 403.

In determining under Rule 403 whether the incremental probative value of the other crime, wrong or act is substantially outweighed by the danger of unfair prejudice, various matters in addition to evaluating the real danger of unfair prejudice must be considered. The strength of evidence as to the commission of the other crime, wrong, or act is a relevant consideration. Evidence sufficient to support a finding of the existence of the other crime, wrong, or act, Rule 104(b), is however all that is required; a showing of clear and convincing evidence is *not* necessary. In addition, the necessity for the evidence should be considered, which is effected by whether the fact of consequence for which offered is being contested, whether a party has agreed to stipulate to the existence of the fact of consequence, or whether a real dispute exists as to the fact of consequence, and if so, whether such fact may otherwise be sufficiently established.

With respect to an offer to stipulate, in Old Chief v. United States (S.Ct.1997), the United States Supreme Court opined that the accepted rule that the prosecution is entitled to prove its case free from any defendant's option to stipulate the evidence away rests on good sense. Thus absent extraordinary circumstances, the proponent of the evidence is entitled to present otherwise admissible evidence for the fair and legitimate weight introduction of the evidence would have on the trier of fact.

The probative value of the evidence itself must of course be considered in light of various factors such as remoteness of time, and where relevancy so depends, upon the degree of resemblance between the other crime and the crime charged. Finally, as with all balancing under Rule 403, the probable effectiveness of a limiting instruction, Rule 105, should also be taken into account. In reaching a balance, the process is complicated by the fact that if the other offense resembles the crime charged, probative value and prejudice will often vary directly.

Upon request by the accused, the prosecution in a criminal case must provide reasonable notice in advance of trial, or during trial if the court excuses pretrial notice on good cause shown, of the general nature of any such evidence it intends to introduce at trial regardless of how the prosecution intends to use such evidence, i.e., during its case-in-chief, for impeachment, or for possible rebuttal.

To ensure that prejudice is avoided if the other crimes evidence is excluded by the court, in questionable cases a proffer should initially be made outside the hearing of the jury. It has been asserted that a final determination on admissibility should normally await the conclusion of the defendant's case, since the court will then be in the best position to balance the probative value of, and the Government's need for, such testimony against the prejudice to the defendant. An obvious exception which in practice seems to have almost swallowed the rule is when the government requires the other crime evidence to present a compelling prima facie case. In fact it is probably more accurate to say that the government can introduce evidence of another crime, wrong, or act during its case in chief unless either the parties have affirmatively taken the issue to which such evidence is relevant out of the case such as by the acceptance of a concession or stipulation, the evidence is relevant solely to the question of specific intent and specific intent is not an element of the offense charged, or the crime is one of general intent and such intent is clearly inferable from the nature of the act.

The process of balancing is largely committed to the sound discretion of the trial court subject to reversal only upon a showing of abuse of discretion. While the practice of entering a written finding as to this balancing is encouraged, if the court in fact gives proper consideration to the question, its absence is of no consequence.

Where evidence of other crimes, wrongs or acts is admitted under Rule 404(b), the jury should be given a limiting instruction, Rule 105, to the effect that they are not to consider the evidence as going to the character of the accused but only as going to the particular purpose for which offered. However, failure of the court to give such an instruction *sua sponte* is unlikely to be considered plain error, Rule 103(d).

As the foregoing discussion indicates, the question of admissibility of a prior crime, wrong or act when offered for one or more of the numerous accepted purposes brings into play a complex array of factors and facts. Since admissibility properly turns upon an evaluation of these factors in light of the particular facts of the case, prior authority will in many cases be of only limited utility.

## Rule 405.

## METHODS OF PROVING CHARACTER

(a) **Reputation or Opinion. In all cases in which evidence of character or a trait of character of a person is admissible, proof may be made by testimony as to reputation or by testimony in the form of an opinion. On cross-examination, inquiry is allowable into relevant specific instances of conduct.**

(b) **Specific Instances of Conduct. In cases in which character or a trait of character of a person is an essential element of a charge, claim, or defense, proof may also be made of specific instances of that person's conduct.**

## § 405.1 Rule 405(a): Method of Proof of Character; Reputation or Opinion; Specific Instances Permitted Only on Cross-Examination

Proof of character or a trait of character as permitted by Rules 404(a)(1), (2) and (3) is confined to evidence of reputation and opinion; specific instances of conduct are not admissible, Rule 405(a). The reputation or opinion of the person testified to cannot be a general one for being law abiding but must be limited to the pertinent trait in accordance with Rule 404(a), unless a more specific character trait is simply not available given the nature of the offense charged. To illustrate, reputation or opinion testimony as to honesty is the pertinent character trait where the charge is larceny or theft; being law abiding is permitted where the charge is narcotics possession. Where reputation testimony is offered, the reputation may be that in the neighborhood in which the person resides or among any group of his associates; the witness must of course establish familiarity with it. Opinion testimony is given similar treatment. Since good reputation for a pertinent character trait is unlikely to excite discussion, the fact that the witness has actually heard no discussion does not bar him from testifying to that reputation. The testimony must relate to reputation or opinion at the time of the act in question rather than at trial.

The trial court has discretion to limit the number of character witnesses.

On cross-examination of a witness who has testified as to the reputation of another with respect to a pertinent character trait, inquiry is of course proper with respect to with whom, where and when the reputation was actually discussed and the nature of the relationship with the person about whom testifying. Similar exploration on cross-examination of the bases of a witness who testifies in the form of an opinion is proper. Under Rule 405(a) specific instances of relevant conduct and rumors and reports thereof may be brought out on cross-examination: the reputation or opinion witness may be asked either "if he knows" or "has he heard" of such matters. Relevant specific instances of conduct include, but are not limited to, those for which there has been a conviction or an arrest; specific instances of conduct which are not criminal may also be relevant. The specific instances of conduct must relate to reputation or opinion at the time of the act in question rather than at trial. Lack of familiarity with such matters is relevant to an assessment of the basis of the character witness' testimony. Familiarity with such matters explores the character witness' standard of "goodness" and "badness." The cross-examiner must possess a good faith basis for inquiry. In the court's discretion counsel may be required to disclose his good faith basis outside the jury's presence prior to cross-examination.

Extrinsic evidence is not permitted with respect to the specific acts; counsel must take the witness' answer. Moreover, inquiry into specific acts on cross-examination of the reputation or opinion witness may be prohibited if the court concludes that the unfair prejudice likely to result substantially outweighs the probative value of such inquiry in assisting the jury in evaluating the witness' testimony, Rule 403. It is improper to ask the character witness whether his or her testimony would be affected if the character witness assumed the existence of the particular act for which the accused is on trial. Where cross-examination is permitted, a limiting instruction, Rule 105, is appropriate advising the jury that they are to consider the inquiry as to the specific act as bearing solely upon its evaluation of the weight to be given to the character witness' testimony.

Where character evidence has been offered in the form of reputation or opinion, it may be rebutted by the testimony of other witnesses only in the form of reputation or opinion.

With respect to opinion testimony, the Advisory Committee's Note clearly states that where a pertinent character trait is involved "the opinion of [a] psychiatrist based upon examination or testimony" is permissible under Rule 405(a).

## § 405.2  Rule 405(b): Character as an Element; Specific Instances of Conduct

Character or a trait of character of a person may itself be an essential element of a charge, claim or defense in a civil or criminal case and thus, in the strict sense, be in issue. When character is in issue, it deserves searching inquiry and the most convincing proof. Hence in addition to reputation and opinion testimony proof by specific instances of conduct is recognized as proper as part of the case in chief despite the attendant disadvantages, Rule 405(b).

In reality, it seldom arises that character or trait of character amounts to an essential element of a charge, claim or defense. The Advisory Committee's Note to Rule 404 provides two illustrations: "The chastity of the victim under a statute specifying her chastity as an element of the crime of seduction, or the competency of the driver in an action for negligently entrusting a motor vehicle to an incompetent driver." To these may be added the character of a person in an action for defamation. Argued additions include the character of a house charged with being used for immoral traffic, the character of the plaintiff or decedent in a personal injury or wrongful death case as bearing upon the question of damages, negligent hiring, the accused's predisposition to commit the crime following the raising of an entrapment defense, truthfulness in a perjury prosecution, and in a Hobbs Act prosecution character evidence to show that the threats of the defendant were not idle. While in each of these later cases admissibility of specific acts is proper, see Rule 404(b), only with the illustrations provided by the Advisory Committee along with negligent hiring and defamation can it be said that character is truly an element of the charge, claim or defense. With each of the other cases previously mentioned, specific instances of conduct are being employed circumstantially for a pur pose other than to prove the character of the person in order to show that he acted in conformity therewith to establish an element of the charge, claim or defense, Rule 404(b). Thus in none of the other cases is the trait of character of a person an actual element of a charge, claim or defense.

## Rule 406.

## HABIT; ROUTINE PRACTICE

**Evidence of the habit of a person or of the routine practice of an organization, whether corroborated or not and regardless of the presence of eyewitnesses, is relevant to prove that the conduct of the person or organization on a particular occasion was in conformity with the habit or routine practice.**

## § 406.1   Habit and Routine Practice: An Overview

While habit may be defined as the regular practice of meeting a particular kind of situation with a specific type of conduct, and character as a generalized description of one's disposition, or of one's disposition with respect to a particular trait, such as honesty, temperance, or peacefulness, the dividing line between habit and character is far from distinct. As recognized in the Advisory Committee's Note to Rule 406, McCormick, Evidence § 162 at 340 (1954) is particularly adept at effectively contrasting habit and character:

> Character and habit are close akin. Character is a generalized description of one's disposition, or of one's disposition in respect to a general trait, such as honesty, temperance, or peacefulness. "Habit," in modern usage, both lay and psychological, is more specific. It describes one's regular response to a repeated specific situation. If we speak of character for care, we think of the person's tendency to act prudently in all the varying situations of life, in business, family life, in handling automobiles and in walking across the street. A habit, on the other hand, is the person's regular practice of meeting a particular kind of situation with a specific type of conduct, such as the habit of going down a particular stairway two stairs at a time, or of giving the hand-signal for a left turn, or of alighting from railway cars while they are moving. The doing of the habitual acts may become semi-automatic.

> Character may be thought of as the sum of one's habits though doubtless it is more than this. But unquestionably the uniformity of one's response to habit is far greater than the consistency with which one's conduct conforms to character or disposition.

Even though character comes in only exceptionally as evidence of an act, surely any sensible man in investigating whether X did a particular act would be greatly helped in his inquiry by evidence as to whether he was in the habit of doing it.

Rule 404 states the general rule that evidence of a person's character or a trait of his character for the purpose of proving that he acted in conformity therewith on a particular occasion is not admissible in civil cases and admissible in criminal proceedings only in limited situations. On the other hand, Rule 406 recognizes the relevancy in both civil and criminal cases of a person's habit or the routine practice of an organization in proving that conduct on a particular occasion was in conformity therewith.

Habit describes one's regular response to a repeated specific situation to the extent that doing the habitual response becomes semi-automatic and extremely regular. The routine practice of an organization is comparable to the habit of an individual. In fact, the business nature of facts usually associated with the routine practice of an organization in comparison with the purely voluntary personal acts comprising habit will frequently provide a greater degree of regularity. It is the notion of extreme regularity that gives both habit and routine practice evidence its probative force. In determining whether the proponent has established "one" regular response to a repeated specific situation, evaluation of the adequacy of the sample and the uniformity of response are key factors. Precise standards for measuring sufficiency however er cannot be formulated.

Rule 406 by its terms admits evidence of habit or routine practice whether corroborated or not and regardless of the presence of eyewitnesses. The requirement of corroboration is inappropriate because it relates to sufficiency of the evidence rather than admissibility.

The admissibility of evidence sufficient to establish a habit or routine practice is of course still subject to exclusion on any of the grounds enunciated in Rule 403.

## § 406.2  Habit of an Individual

Rule 406 provides for the admissibility of habit testimony of an individual to prove that his conduct on a particular occasion was in conformity with that habit. Habit describes one's regular response to a repeated specific situation to the extent that doing the habitual response becomes semi-automatic and extremely regular. Evidence of habit is admissible whether corroborated or not and regardless of the presence of an eyewitness.

While it has been stated that habit is never to be lightly established, the reluctance of some courts at earlier times to accept habit evidence was probably due to a failure to draw a clear line between character and habit. Rule 406 recognizes that where habit, as distinguished from character, is at issue, the reluctance of such courts is misplaced. Of course habit testimony may be admitted only if a sufficient pattern of repeated responses is established so that the conduct of the person may be considered a habit. Evidence that a person had on one or more other occasions acted in a particular manner is alone insufficient to establish an extremely regular practice of meeting a particular kind of situation with a specific kind of conduct.

The Advisory Committee's Note indicates that ordinarily evidence of a "habit" of intemperance to prove drunkenness, evidence of other assaults to prove the instant assault, and evidence of religious "habit" to establish presence at a particular time are not sufficiently semi-automatic and extremely regular to constitute habit. Such instances should be compared with the habit of a person to take a bus home from his place of employment considered in connection with whether the person was a passenger on the bus immediately prior to being run over.

## § 406.3   Routine Practice of an Organization

The operation of organizations depends to a large extent upon the establishing and following of routines, hence evidence of a routine practice (sometimes referred to as custom) of an organization is admissible as tending to prove that it was followed on the occasion in question, Rule 406. Prior to Rule 406, evidence of existence of a routine practice standing alone was often held insufficient to prove the doing of an act; corroboration that the routine was then followed was required. Given the natural lack of recollection as to any one of thousands of routine transactions considered in light of the turnover of personnel, strictly applied corroboration would not only defeat the purpose of Rule 406 but would also result in substantial injustice in certain cases. Corroboration as a condition of admissibility is specifically rejected in Rule 406 on the ground that it relates to sufficiency of the evidence rather than admissibility, thereby greatly facilitating proof of routine practice in many contexts. Of course evidence of the routine practice of an organization may be admitted only if a sufficient pattern of repeated responses is established to warrant a finding that the practice was routine.

## § 406.4  Method of Proof of Habit or Routine Practice

Rule 406 is silent as to the method of proof permitted. Rule 406 as proposed to Congress contained a subdivision (b):

> Method of proof. Habit or routine practice may be proved by testimony in the form of an opinion or by specific instances of conduct sufficient in number to warrant a finding that the habit existed or that the practice was routine.

Proof of specific instances of conduct to establish habit or routine practice is subject to Rule 403. As suggested in the Advisory Committee's Note to Proposed Rule 406(b), the court in exercising its discretion may certainly decide to admit "testimony by W that on numerous occasions he had been with X when X crossed a railroad track and that on each occasion X had first stopped and looked in both directions, but * * * exclude offers of 10 witnesses, each testifying to a different occasion."

Rules 602 and 701 in combination provide that an opinion of a nonexpert witness is admissible if based upon personal knowledge and helpful to the trier of fact in determining a fact of consequence. Opinions of witnesses as to the routine practice of an organization or habit of an individual based upon personal knowledge of the witness should normally be permitted on such grounds. If undisputed, opinion testimony would avoid wasting time. Where in controversy, specific instances of conduct may in the discretion of the court be required to be disclosed as part of development of the witness' basis for his opinion. Specific instances forming the basis of the witness' opinion may of course be developed on cross-examination.

## Rule 407.

## SUBSEQUENT REMEDIAL MEASURES

When, after an injury or harm allegedly caused by an event, measures are taken that, if taken previously, would have made the injury or harm less likely to occur, evidence of the subsequent measures is not admissible to prove negligence, culpable conduct, a defect in a product, a defect in a product's design, or a need for a warning or instruction. This rule does not require the exclusion or evidence of subsequent measures when offered for another purpose, such as proving ownership, control, or feasibility of precautionary measures, if controverted, or impeachment.

### § 407.1   Subsequent Remedial Measures

Subsequent remedial measures, whether a change, repair or precaution, taken by a party after an injury or harm allegedly caused by an event, that if taken previously would have made the injury or harm less likely to occur, may not be introduced to prove negligence, culpable conduct, a defect in a product, a defect in a product's design, or a need for a warning or instruction, Rule 407.

The rationale for exclusion is twofold. First, even though such a measure if taken previously would have made the event less likely to occur, the taking of remedial measures may be motivated by a desire to exercise the highest care and thus in fact not be an admission of negligence or culpable conduct. Second, the taking of corrective steps likely to be overvalued by the jury should not be discouraged by allowing evidence thereof to be introduced against the party.

Evidence of this kind may, however, be received when offered for another purpose such as proving ownership, control, or feasibility of precautionary measures, if controverted, or impeachment, Rule 407. The phrase "if controverted" enables a party to forestall the introduction of evidence of remedial measures to prove such things as ownership, control, or feasibility of precautionary measures by admitting them. Where the other purpose is controverted, introduction of evidence of a subsequent remedial measure is subject to exclusion under Rule 403. In determining whether the probative value of such evidence offered for another purpose is substantially outweighed by the trial concerns provided for in Rule 403, consideration must be given to the potential effectiveness of a limiting instruction, Rule 105.

Rulings on admissibility of subsequent remedial measures are exclusively within the province of the court, Rule 104(a).

## Rule 408.

### COMPROMISE AND OFFERS TO COMPROMISE

**Evidence of (1) furnishing or offering or promising to furnish, or (2) accepting or offering or promising to accept, a valuable consideration in compromising or attempting to compromise a claim which was disputed as to either validity or amount, is not admissible to prove liability for or invalidity of the claim or its amount. Evidence of conduct or statements made in compromise negotiations is likewise not admissible. This rule does not require the exclusion of any evidence other-**

wise discoverable merely because it is presented in the course of compromise negotiations. This rule also does not require exclusion when the evidence is offered for another purpose, such as proving bias or prejudice of a witness, negativing a contention of undue delay, or proving an effort to obstruct a criminal investigation or prosecution.

## § 408.1 Compromise and Offers to Compromise

Pursuant to Rule 408 neither an offer to compromise, acceptance of such offer, nor an actual completed compromise of a disputed claim is admissible to prove liability for or invalidity of the claim or its amount. The reasons recognized for exclusion are (1) irrelevancy, since the offer or compromise may depending upon the circumstances in reality involve a purchase or attempt to purchase peace rather than an admission of liability, and most importantly (2) policy, in that compromises favored by public policy would be discouraged by admitting the evidence. Under Rule 408 such evidence is not admissible provided either liability or amount was disputed.

Prior to enactment of the Federal Rules of Evidence, facts expressed as "assumed" to be true for the purpose of compromise negotiations only were inadmissible. To assure falling within this principle, counsel would preface his statement of fact with a phrase such as "hypothetically speaking," "without prejudice," or "for purposes of discussion only." In addition, facts stated during compromise negotiation were inadmissible if so "inseparably connected with the offer so that it could not be correctly understood without reading the two together." On the other hand an admission neither accompanied by an assuming phrase nor inseparable from the offer itself, sometimes called an independent fact, was admissible even though made in the course of compromise negotiations. This distinction, difficult to apply in practice, is rejected in Rule 408 which makes conduct and statements made in the course of compromise negotiation inadmissible without reference to the presence or absence of assuming phrases or inseparability. Undisclosed internal reports prepared as a basis for compromise negotiations fall within the protection of Rule 408.

Rule 408 was amended by Congress to add the third sentence, "The rule does not require the exclusion of any evidence otherwise discoverable merely because it is presented in the course of compromise negotiations." As stated in the Report of Senate Committee on the Judiciary, the added sentence "insure[s] that evidence, such as documents, is not rendered inadmissible merely because it is presented in the course of compromise negotiations if the evidence is otherwise discoverable. A party should not be able to immunize from admissibility documents otherwise discoverable merely by offering them in a compromise negotiation." In addition the Conference Report makes clear that a party by presenting a fact during compromise negotiations does not thereby prevent an opposing party from offering evidence of that fact at trial if the evidence was obtained from independent sources. Thus the factual matter disclosed in the course of compromise negotiations may be admissible, although the statement disclosing it would not. No "fruit of the poisonous tree" doctrine is intended.

If for purposes of impeachment, proof is offered that the witness received or made a payment by way of compromise, a conflict develops between the principle that bias or prejudice may be shown and the policy of encouraging compromise. Evidence of compromise may be relevant for other purposes as well. In response, the final sentence of Rule 408 provides, "This rule also does not require exclusion when the evidence is offered for another purpose, such as proving bias or prejudice of a witness, negativing a contention of undue delay, or proving an effort to obstruct a criminal investigation or prosecution." As in other instances where evidence is admissible for one purpose but not another, Rule 403 requires an evaluation of the probative value and need for such evidence versus the danger of unfair prejudice and misleading of the jury. In reaching this determination, consideration must be given to the probable effectiveness of a limiting instruction, Rule 105.

A question arises with respect to whether evidence of conduct or statements made in connection with compromise negotiations are admissible as inconsistent statements for purposes of impeachment. The clear import of the Conference Report as well as the general understanding among lawyers is that such conduct or statements may *not* be admitted for impeachment purposes. Rule 408, however, states that evidence of conduct or statements is "likewise not admissible," referring to admissibility of such evidence to prove liability or invalidity of the claim, and furthermore states that the exclusion of evidence is not required when offered for a purpose other than to prove liability for or invalidity of claims. While a majority of decisions permit impeachment, it is nevertheless suggested that conduct or statements made during compromise negotiations should not be admissible as inconsistent statements to impeach.

A determination of whether a statement falls within the protection of Rule 408 is exclusively for the court pursuant to Rule 104(a).

# Rule 409.

# PAYMENT OF MEDICAL AND SIMILAR EXPENSES

**Evidence of furnishing or offering or promising to pay medical, hospital, or similar expenses occasioned by an injury, is not admissible to prove liability for the injury.**

## § 409.1 Payment of Medical and Similar Expenses

Under the broad definition of relevancy in Rule 401, evidence of furnishing, offering or promising to pay medical, hospital, or similar expenses occasioned by an injury is relevant as having some tendency to prove liability. However Rule 409 excludes introduction of such evidence in furtherance of the policy of encouraging assistance to an injured party, it being felt that assistance might be withheld if there were a risk of its use as an admission in a subsequent trial.

No requirement is imposed that there be an actual dispute as to liability or amount at the time of the furnishing or when an offer or promise to pay medical, hospital, or similar expense is made. Statements or conduct not a part of the offer, promise or payment itself are *not* precluded from being introduced into evidence by the provisions of Rule 409. Moreover, evidence of furnishing, promising or offering to pay such expenses is not admissible only when offered to prove liability for the injury; it may be admitted if otherwise relevant to a fact of consequence in the litigation. Where offered for another purpose, the evidence is of course still subject to exclusion under Rule 403.

## Rule 410.

## INADMISSIBILITY OF PLEAS, PLEA DISCUSSIONS AND RELATED STATEMENTS

Except as otherwise provided in this rule, evidence of the following is not, in any civil or criminal proceeding, admissible against the defendant who made the plea or was a participant in the plea discussions:

(1) a plea of guilty which was later withdrawn;

(2) a plea of nolo contendere;

(3) any statement made in the course of any proceedings under Rule 11 of the Federal Rules of Criminal Procedure or comparable state procedure regarding either of the foregoing pleas; or

(4) any statement made in the course of plea discussions with an attorney for the prosecuting authority which do not result in a plea of guilty or which result in a plea of guilty later withdrawn.

However, such a statement is admissible (i) in any proceeding wherein another statement made in the course of the same plea or plea discussions has been introduced and the statement ought in fairness be considered contemporaneously with it, or (ii) in a criminal proceeding for perjury or false statement if the statement was made by the defendant under oath, on the record and in the presence of counsel.

## § 410.1  Rule 410: Inadmissibility of Pleas, Plea Discussions, and Related Statements

In any civil or criminal proceeding evidence of (1) a plea of guilty later withdrawn; (2) a plea of nolo contendere; (3) any statement made in the course of any proceedings under Rule 11 of the Federal Rules of Criminal Procedure or comparable state procedure regarding either of the foregoing pleas; or (4) any statement made in the course of plea discussions with an attorney for the prosecuting authority which do not result in a plea of guilty or which result in a plea of guilty later withdrawn, is not admissible against the defendant who made the plea or was a participant in the plea discussions either as substantive evidence or for impeachment, Rule 410.

The purpose of exclusion is the promotion of the disposition of criminal cases by plea bargaining. The United States Supreme Court emphasized the importance of guilty pleas and plea negotiations in Blackledge v. Allison (S.Ct.1977):

> Whatever might be the situation in an ideal world, the fact is that the guilty plea and the often concomitant plea bargain are important components of this country's criminal justice system. Properly administered, they can benefit all concerned. The defendant avoids extended pretrial incarceration and the anxieties and uncertainties of a trial; he gains a speedy disposition of his case, the chance to acknowledge his guilt, and a prompt start in realizing whatever potential there may be for rehabilitation. Judges and prosecutors conserve vital and scarce resources. The public is protected from the risks posed by those charged with criminal offenses who are at large on bail while awaiting completion of criminal proceedings.

Implementation of the policy of encouraging plea bargaining requires encouraging frank communication between the defendant and his counsel and the government. No defendant or his counsel will pursue such an effort if the remarks uttered during the course of it dare to be admitted in evidence as proof of guilt. Moreover, it is inherently unfair for the government to engage in such an activity, only to use it as a weapon against the defendant when negotiations fail.

Rule 410 makes inadmissible statements made in the course of any of the proceedings mentioned in the rule regarding either a plea later withdrawn or a plea of nolo contendere as well as related statements when made in the course of plea bargaining with an attorney for the government which do not result in a plea of guilty or which result in a plea of guilty later withdrawn. The scope of Rule 410 is not limited to statements by the defendant himself, and thus covers also statements by defense counsel regarding defendant's incriminating admissions to him, as well as statements made by government officials. The prohibition extends only to actions in which the person making the plea or statement barred by Rule 410 is a party. Thus a non-party witness in a civil or criminal case may be impeached by a plea or statement given under any of the circumstances specified in Rule 410; such a plea or statement is not being used "against the defendant" when offered solely to impeach a non-party witness. Similarly a witness may be impeached by a statement given under any of the circumstances specified in Rule 410 if the statement is not "against" the interests of the defendant.

Plea bargaining consists of a discussion wherein a defendant seeks to obtain concessions from the government in return for a plea. Thus plea bargaining entails a bargaining process, a *quid pro quo*. Mere hope, anticipation, or expectation of leniency is insufficient; the accused must be attempting to strike a deal. While usually the concessions sought relate to the defendant, bargaining for concessions as to a third party may properly be considered to fall within the ambit of the rule.

Rule 410 applies to statements made in the course of discussions with an attorney for the prosecuting authority whenever the defendant in fact had exhibited a reasonable subjective expectation that plea negotiations were in progress. Accordingly, the trial court must apply a two-tiered analysis and determine, first, whether the accused exhibited an actual subjective expectation to negotiate a plea at the time of the discussion, and, second, whether the accused's expectation was reasonable given the totality of the objective circumstances. Where the defendant clearly manifested an intent to explore a plea in exchange for a concession, this determination creates little difficulty. On the other hand, where such a preamble is not stated, the totality of the circumstances may nevertheless evidence a reasonable subjective expectation that plea negotiations had been commenced. However, under a totality of the circumstances approach, an accused's subsequent account of his prior subjective mental impressions cannot be considered the sole determinative factor. Otherwise, every confession would be vulnerable to such subsequent challenge. Thus in order for the court to find "actual" and "reasonable" subjective expectation, the accused must have "exhibited" by expressing in some way the hope that a concession in exchange for his plea will come to pass. In short, hope of obtaining leniency is not enough; to have plea bargaining a discussion seeking a concession in exchange for a plea must occur. Unconditional, unbargained for, volunteered admissions or confessions by the accused are thus outside the scope of exclusion provided for in Rule 410.

In determining the reasonableness of the accused's expectation that he was entering into plea negotiations, whether or not the attorney for the prosecuting authority induces the accused to make a statement by promising leniency directly or indirectly such as indicating a willingness to recommend a particular disposition to the court or to permit the entering of a plea to a lesser offense will, of course, be highly relevant. Also to be considered in evaluating the total circumstances surrounding the discussion is whether the attorney with whom the defendant is discussing the matter indicates authority or lack thereof to enter into plea negotiations, without regard to whether such authority was actually possessed. Thus, actual authority is irrelevant—the accused's actual and reasonable exhibition of subjective expectations at the time he was plea negotiating controls.

**Law enforcement personnel.** An area of special significance in Rule 410 concerns the limitation of the rule as amended in 1980 to plea discussions between the attorney for the government and the attorney for the defendant or the defendant whether or not acting pro se. Excluded from the scope of Rule 410 are statements made during plea negotiations to law enforcement officers, unless the law enforcement officer is acting with express authority from a government attorney. The Advisory Committee's Note to Fed.Crim.Proc. 11(e)(6), applicable as well to Rule 410, is careful to state that "This change, it must be emphasized, does not compel the conclusion that statements made to law enforcement agents, especially when the agents purport to have authority to bargain, are inevitably admissible. Rather, the point is that such cases are not covered by the per se rule of 11(e)(6) and thus must be resolved by that body of law dealing with police interrogations." The Advisory Committee's Note later on quotes from the Commentary to the A.B.A. Standards relating to pleas of guilty:

> The above standard is limited to discussions and agreements with the prosecuting attorney. Sometimes defendant will indicate to the police their willingness to bargain, and in such instances these statements are sometimes admitted in court against the defendant. State v. Christian, 245 S.W.2d 895 (Mo.1952). If the police initiate this kind of discussion, this may have some bearing on the admissibility of the defendant's statement. However, the policy considerations relevant to this issue are better dealt with in the context of standards governing in-custody interrogation by the police.

While it is certainly correct that statements made to law enforcement personnel as part of plea negotiations are not "inevitably admissible," it is important to realize that neither are they "inevitably inadmissible." Moreover the clear import of exclusion of such statements from the coverage of the rule with accompanying reference to the law governing police interrogation is an expression of a policy favoring admissibility. As a practical matter assuming *Miranda* is complied with, rarely would exclusion seem to be compelled. If the police commence discussions, claim actual authority to conclude a deal where such authority did not in fact exist, and then continue to lead the accused on into making incriminating statements, maybe, just maybe, the body of law dealing with police interrogation would require exclusion. Anything short of the foregoing will rarely suffice. As indicated in the above quoted Commentary "If the police initiate this kind of discussion, this may have some bearing on the admissibility of the defendant's statement"; the quote is "some bearing", not compelled exclusion. Similarly even if the accused manifests expressly a desire to negotiate with the police officer, the Commentary states that "in such instances these statements are sometimes admitted in court against the defendant"; this is clearly not a rule of compelled exclusion. Prior to the 1980 amendment to Rule 410 statements made under the foregoing circumstances would clearly have been inadmissible. The accused entered into plea negotiations and exhibited a reasonable subjective expectation of negotiating a concession in exchange for a plea.

**Admissibility of statements.** In any civil or criminal case, statements made in the course of plea discussions with an attorney for the prosecuting authority which do not result in a plea of guilty or which result in a plea of guilty later withdrawn and statements made in the course of any proceeding under Rule 11 of the Federal Rules of Criminal Procedure or comparable state procedures regarding either a plea of guilty which was either never entered or was entered but was later withdrawn or a plea of nolo contendere, together with the statements constituting a plea of guilty which was later withdrawn or a plea of nolo contendere are not admissible against the defendant who made the plea or was a participant in the plea discussions either as substantive evidence or for impeachment, Rule 410. Waiver of the protections of Rule 410 is permissible i.e., statements made during plea negotiations may be employed to impeach and as substantive evidence. In addition, evidence of a statement made in connection with, and relevant to, a plea of guilty later withdrawn, a plea of nolo contendere, or in the course of plea bargaining with an attorney for the prosecuting authority concerning an offer to plead guilty or nolo contendere to the crime charged or any other crime, is admissible in a criminal proceeding for perjury or false statement if the statement was made by the defendant under oath, on the record, and in the presence of counsel. Finally, such a statement is admissible in any proceeding wherein another statement made in the course of the same plea or plea discussions has been introduced and the statement ought in fairness be considered contemporaneously with it, Rule 410. A "fruit of the poisonous tree" doctrine is not applied.

A statement is not made in the course of plea discussions if made prior to any plea discussion commencing, if made subsequent to the agreement upon a plea bargain that did not call for the making of the statement, or if made subsequent to the agreement but in breach of the agreement.

Rule 410 applies only to withdrawn pleas, nolo contendere pleas whether or not withdrawn, and statements made to an attorney of the prosecuting authority in the course of plea negotiations not resulting in a plea of guilty or resulting in a plea of guilty later withdrawn. A guilty plea not withdrawn is often admissible in a subsequent civil action arising out of the same facts, as well as sometimes in other situations, since an unwithdrawn plea of guilty admits all matters well pleaded in the indictment or information. Admission of the guilty plea must be distinguished from admission of the judgment of conviction resulting from it. The judgment constitutes an exception to the hearsay rule under Rule 803(22), admissible to prove any fact essential to sustain the judgment. A plea of guilty is not offered to prove the facts recited in the charge but to prove that the offender, not necessarily the defendant in the case at bar, admitted the facts. The plea of guilty may be admissible as an admission of a party-opponent under Rule 801(d)(2) or as a statement against interest of a nonparty under Rule 804(b)(3).

**Nolo contendere.** A plea of nolo contendere whether or not withdrawn, or an offer to plead nolo contendere made in the course of plea discussions with an attorney for the prosecuting authority, together with all statements made in connection therewith, is not admissible in a later civil or criminal action against the defendant. An unwithdrawn plea of nolo contendere, while like a plea of guilty, constitutes an admission only for the purposes of the criminal case at hand. Thus in any subsequent action, whether arising out of the same facts or not, neither the nolo contendere plea nor the conviction based on the plea may be admitted as either an admission of a party-opponent, as a judgment of conviction, or as an inconsistent statement to impeach. Nolo contendere pleas serve to avoid the effect on an impending civil case of a recorded plea of guilty and thereby serve to encourage the disposition of criminal cases. Whether a judgment of conviction following a plea of nolo contendere may be employed under Rule 609 against the defendant when a party for purposes of impeachment is unsettled but very likely. A judgment of conviction following a plea of nolo contendere is admissible for other purposes as well.

## Rule 411.

## LIABILITY INSURANCE

**Evidence that a person was or was not insured against liability is not admissible upon the issue whether the person acted negligently or otherwise wrongfully. This rule does not require the exclusion of evidence of insurance against liability when offered for another purpose, such as proof of agency, ownership, or control, or bias or prejudice of a witness.**

### § 411.1  Liability Insurance

Evidence that a defendant is insured against liability is inadmissible as marginally relevant at best on the issue of fault, for a person by reason of being insured is felt hardly to be no more likely to act negligently or otherwise wrongfully. More importantly, such evidence is excluded as being an invitation to the jury to share the resources of the insurer with the plaintiff, regardless of the merits of the case, Rule 411. Similarly evidence of lack of insurance is also excluded when offered upon the issue of negligence or otherwise wrongful conduct.

An apparently inadvertent disclosure in a jury trial by a witness for plaintiff, with no indication of bad faith on the part of the witness or counsel, whether as the result of an unresponsive answer on direct examination or on cross-examination, does not require a mistrial. Nor is disclosure necessarily fatal in a non-jury trial. Where the fact of insurance has been improperly disclosed, striking of the testimony and instructing the jury to disregard is generally sufficient. It is also appropriate for the court to question the jurors as to whether they can decide the matter without letting the fact of insurance affect their judgment in any way. Reluctance to declare a mistrial is supported in part by the knowledge that in today's society reasonable jurors can be expected to contemplate, if not assume, the presence of insurance in regard to many actions such as automobile accidents and malpractice.

The existence of insurance may be shown in connection with issues other than fault, such as agency, ownership, or control, or bias or prejudice of a witness, Rule 411. Admissibility of evidence of liability insurance for a purpose other than fault is, of course, subject to the requirements of Rule 403, including consideration of the potential effectiveness of a limiting instruction, Rule 105.

## Rule 412.

## SEX OFFENSE CASES; RELEVANCE OF ALLEGED VICTIM'S PAST SEXUAL BEHAVIOR OR ALLEGED SEXUAL PREDISPOSITION

**(a) Evidence Generally Inadmissible. The following evidence is not admissible in any civil or criminal proceeding involving alleged sexual misconduct except as provided in subdivisions (b) and (c):**

**(1) evidence offered to prove that any alleged victim engaged in other sexual behavior; and**

**(2) evidence offered to prove any alleged victim's sexual predisposition.**

**(b) Exceptions.**

**(1) In a criminal case, the following evidence is admissible, if otherwise admissible under these rules:**

(A) evidence of specific instances of sexual behavior by the alleged victim offered to prove that a person other than the accused was the source of semen, injury, or other physical evidence;

(B) evidence of specific instances of sexual behavior by the alleged victim with respect to the person accused of the sexual misconduct offered by the accused to prove consent or by the prosecution; and

(C) evidence the exclusion of which would violate the constitutional rights of the defendant.

(2) In a civil case, evidence offered to prove the sexual behavior or sexual predisposition of any alleged victim is admissible if it is otherwise admissible under these rules and its probative value substantially outweighs the danger of harm to any victim and of unfair prejudice to any party. Evidence of an alleged victim's reputation is admissible only if it has been placed in controversy by the alleged victim.

(c) Procedure to Determine Admissibility.

(1) A party intending to offer evidence under subdivision (b) must:

(A) file a written motion at least 14 days before trial specifically describing the evidence and stating the purpose for which it is offered unless the court, for good cause requires a different time for filing or permits filing during trial; and

(B) serve the motion on all parties and notify the alleged victim or, when appropriate, the alleged victim's guardian or representative.

**(2) Before admitting evidence under this rule the court must conduct a hearing in camera and afford the victim and parties a right to attend and be heard. The motion, related papers, and the record of the hearing must be sealed and remain under seal unless the court orders otherwise.**

## § 412.1    Sex Offense Cases: Relevance of Alleged Victim's Behavior or Alleged Sexual Predisposition

In a criminal proceeding involving alleged sexual misconduct Rule 412, and only Rule 412, governs the admissibility of reputation and opinion evidence relating to any alleged victim's sexual predisposition as well as the admissibility of evidence of specific instances of conduct of any alleged victim offered to prove that the alleged victim engaged in other sexual behavior.

Rule 412 aims to safeguard the alleged victim against the invasion of privacy, potential embarrassment and sexual stereotyping that is associated with public disclosure of intimate sexual details and the infusion of sexual innuendo into the factfinding process. By affording victims protection in most instances, the rule is designed to encourage victims of sexual misconduct to institute and to participate in legal proceedings against alleged offenders. Rule 412 seeks to achieve these objectives by barring evidence relating to the alleged victim's sexual behavior or alleged sexual predisposition, whether offered as substantive evidence or for impeachment, except in designated circumstances in which the probative value of the evidence significantly outweighs possible harm to the victim.

In a criminal proceeding the introduction of reputation and opinion evidence as well as the introduction of evidence of specific instances of conduct of an alleged victim involving other sexual behavior offered to prove the alleged victim's sexual predisposition is never admissible, as substantive evidence or for impeachment, Rule 412(a) and (b). Evidence as to specific instances of conduct offered to prove that any alleged victim engaged in other sexual behavior for a purpose other than to prove the alleged victim's sexual predisposition is similarly not admissible as substantive evidence or for impeachment unless the evidence meets an exception: (1) evidence of specific instances of sexual behavior by the alleged victim offered to prove that a person other than the accused was the source of semen, injury, or other physical evidence, Rule 412(b)(1)(A); (2) evidence of specific instances of sexual behavior by the alleged victim with respect to the person accused of the sexual misconduct offered by the accused to prove consent or by the prosecution, Rule 412(b)(1)(B); or (3) evidence the exclusion of which would violate the constitutional rights of the defendant, Rule 412(b)(1)(C).

Similarly, in a civil proceeding involving alleged sexual misconduct Rule 412, and only Rule 412, governs the admissibility of reputation and opinion evidence relating to any alleged victim's sexual predisposition as well as the admissibility of evidence of specific instances of conduct of any alleged victim offered to prove that the alleged victim engaged in other sexual behavior as substantive evidence or for impeachment. Pursuant to Rule 412(b)(2), in a civil proceeding the introduction of opinion and reputation evidence as well as the introduction of evidence of specific instances of conduct of the alleged victim involving sexual behavior is admissible to prove the alleged victim's reputation "only if [the alleged victim's reputation] has been placed in controversy by the alleged victim." The alleged victim may place reputation in controversy without making a specific allegation in a pleading. Evidence of specific instances of conduct as well as evidence in the form of reputation or opinion evidence offered to prove the sexual behavior or sexual predisposition of any alleged victim is admissible as substantive evidence or for impeachment if it is otherwise admissible under the Federal Rules of Evidence and its probative value substantially outweighs the danger of harm to any victim and of unfair prejudice to any party, Rule 412(b)(2).

A party intending to offer evidence under subdivision (b) must pursuant to Rule 412(c)(1) file a written motion at least 14 days before trial specifically describing the evidence and stating the purpose for which it is offered unless the court, for good cause requires a different time for filing or permits filing during trial, and must serve the motion on all parties and notify the alleged victim or, when appropriate, the alleged victim's guardian or representative. Before admitting evidence under Rule 412 the court must conduct a hearing in camera and afford the victim and parties a right to attend and be heard, Rule 412(c)(2). The motion, related papers, and the record of the hearing must be sealed and remain under seal unless the court orders otherwise, Rule 412(c)(2).

The Advisory Committee's Note asserts that the reason for extending the rule in all criminal cases to protect any person alleged to be a victim of sexual misconduct regardless of the charge actually brought against an accused is obvious; "the strong social policy of protecting a victim's privacy and encouraging victims to come forward to report criminal acts is not confined to cases that involve a charge of sexual assault." The need to protect the victim is equally great, for example, when a defendant is charged with kidnapping, and evidence is offered, either to prove motive or as background, that the defendant sexually assaulted the victim.

The Advisory Committee's Note also asserts that the reason for extending Rule 412 to civil cases is equally obvious; "the need to protect alleged victims against invasions of privacy, potential embarrassment, and unwarranted sexual stereotyping, and the wish to encourage victims to come forward when they have been sexually molested do not disappear because the context has shifted from a criminal prosecution to a claim for damages or injunctive relief." There is a strong social policy in not only punishing those who engage in sexual misconduct, but in also providing relief to the victim. Accordingly, Rule 412 now applies in any civil case in which a person claims to be the victim of sexual misconduct, such as actions for sexual battery or sexual harassment.

Rule 412 applies in all cases involving sexual misconduct without regard to whether the alleged victim or person accused is a party to the litigation. Rule 412 extends to "pattern" witnesses in both criminal and civil cases whose testimony about other instances of sexual misconduct by the person accused is otherwise admissible, § 404.5 supra. When the case does not involve alleged sexual misconduct, evidence relating to a third-party witness' alleged sexual activities is not within the ambit of Rule 412. The witness will, however, be protected by other rules such as Rules 404 and 608, as well as Rule 403.

The terminology "alleged victim" is used because there will frequently be a factual dispute as to whether sexual misconduct occurred. The Advisory Committee's Note indicates that the terminology "alleged victim" does not connote any requirement that the misconduct be alleged in the pleadings. Rule 412 does not, however, apply unless the person against whom the evidence is offered can reasonably be characterized as a "victim of alleged sexual misconduct." When this is not the case, as for instance in a defamation action involving statements concerning sexual misconduct in which the evidence is offered to show that the alleged defamatory statements were true or did not damage the plaintiff's reputation, neither Rule 404 nor Rule 412 operates to bar the evidence; Rules 401 and 403 control. Rule 412 does, however, apply in a Title VII action in which the plaintiff has alleged sexual harassment.

The Advisory Committee's Note also indicates that reference to a person "accused" is also used in a non-technical sense. There is no requirement that there be a criminal charge pending against the person or even that the misconduct would constitute a criminal offense. Evidence offered to prove allegedly false prior claims by the victim is not barred by Rule 412. However, this evidence is subject to the requirements of Rule 404.

**Rule 412(a).** Except as provided in Rule 412(b) discussed infra, evidence offered to prove the victim's "other" sexual behavior or alleged sexual predisposition is barred in both civil and criminal proceedings by Rule 412(a). Past sexual behavior connotes all activities that involve actual physical conduct, i.e. sexual intercourse and sexual contact, or that imply sexual intercourse or sexual contact. Evidence, which might otherwise be admissible under Rules 402, 404(b), 405, 607, 608, 609, or some other evidence rule, must be excluded when Rule 412 so requires. The word "other" is used to suggest some flexibility in admitting evidence "intrinsic" to the alleged sexual misconduct. Rule 412(a) also excludes all other evidence relating to an alleged victim of sexual misconduct that is offered to prove a sexual predisposition, including evidence that does not directly refer to sexual activities or thoughts but that the proponent believes may have a sexual connotation for the factfinder. Admission of such evidence contravenes Rule 412's objectives of shielding the alleged victim from potential embarrassment and safeguarding the victim against stereotypical thinking. Consequently, unless a Rule 412(b) exception is satisfied, evidence such as that relating to the alleged victim's mode of dress, speech, or life-style will not be admissible.

**Rule 412(b)(1).** In a criminal case, evidence is admissible under Rule 412(b)(1) pursuant to three possible exceptions, provided the evidence also satisfies other requirements for admissibility specified elsewhere in the Federal Rules of Evidence, including Rule 403. Subdivisions (b)(1)(A) and (b)(1)(B) require proof in the form of specific instances of sexual behavior "in recognition of the limited probative value and dubious reliability of evidence of reputation or evidence in the form of an opinion," i.e., evidence in the form of reputation or opinion testimony relating to past sexual behavior of the alleged victim is inadmissible.

Under the exception in subdivision (b)(1)(A), evidence of specific instances of sexual behavior with persons other than the person whose sexual misconduct is alleged is admissible when offered to prove that another person was the source of semen, injury or other physical evidence, if otherwise admissible under the Federal Rules of Evidence. Where the prosecution has directly or indirectly asserted that the physical evidence originated with the accused, the defendant must be afforded an opportunity to prove that another person was responsible. Evidence offered for a specific purpose identified in this subdivision may still be excluded if it does not satisfy Rule 401 or 403.

Under the exception in subdivision (b)(1)(B), evidence of specific instances of sexual behavior with respect to the person whose sexual misconduct is alleged is admissible if offered by the accused to prove consent, or offered by the prosecution, if otherwise admissible under the Federal Rules of Evidence. Admissible pursuant to this exception would be evidence of prior instances of sexual activities between the alleged victim and the accused, as might be, subject to Rules 401 and 403, statements in which the alleged victim expressed an intent to engage in sexual intercourse with the accused, or voiced sexual fantasies involving the specific accused. With respect to the prosecution offering such evidence, for example, in a prosecution for child sexual abuse, evidence of uncharged sexual activity between the accused and the alleged victim offered by the prosecution is admissible under Rule 414(a) to show a pattern of behavior. Evidence relating to the victim's alleged sexual predisposition is not admissible pursuant to any of the exceptions provided in Rule 412(b)(2).

Under the exception in subdivision (b)(1)(C), evidence of specific instances of conduct may not be excluded if the result would be to deny a criminal defendant the protections afforded by the Constitution. The scope of this subdivision is of course uncertain. The Advisory Committee's Note provides the example of statements in which the victim has expressed an intent to have sex with the first person encountered on a particular occasion as statements that "might not be excluded without violating the due process right of a rape defendant seeking to prove consent." In addition, evidence that tends to prove that the victim has been convicted of prostitution, that rebuts prosecution evidence relating to the victim's sexual activities, that establishes that the alleged victim has a history of falsely reporting sexual assault, and where either consent or fabrication is the defense in the case, evidence of specific past sexual acts occurring within the prior year tending to establish a common scheme or plan of similar sexual conduct under circumstances similar to the case of issue, have each been specifically included as admissible in at least one state statute on the same subject. To this list may be added others such as where the alleged victim has a motive to falsely accuse the defendant. For example, a young girl who is late returning home may falsely accuse someone of rape in order to provide an explanation of her tardiness.

**Rule 412(b)(2).** Subdivision (b)(2) governs the admissibility of otherwise proscribed evidence in civil cases. It employs a balancing test rather than the specific exceptions stated in subdivision (b)(1) in recognition of the difficulty of foreseeing future developments in the law. Greater flexibility is needed to accommodate evolving causes of action such as claims for sexual harassment. Evidence of an alleged victim's reputation is admissible only if it has been placed in controversy by the alleged victim.

The balancing test of Rule 412(b)(2) requires the proponent of the evidence, whether plaintiff or defendant, to convince the court that the probative value of the proffered evidence "substantially outweighs the danger of harm to any victim and of unfair prejudice to any party." This test for admitting evidence offered to prove sexual behavior or sexual propensity in civil cases differs in three respects from the general rule governing admissibility set forth in Rule 403. First, it reverses the usual procedure spelled out in Rule 403 by shifting the burden to the proponent to demonstrate admissibility rather than making the opponent justify exclusion of the evidence. Second, the standard expressed in subdivision (b)(2) raises the threshold for admission by requiring that the probative value of the evidence *substantially* outweigh the specified dangers. Finally, the Rule 412 test puts "harm to the victim" on the scale in addition to prejudice to the parties.

**Rule 412(c).** The subdivision dealing with the procedure for determining admissibility provides both for a motion at least 14 days before trial as well as for a late motion for good cause shown. In deciding whether to permit late filing, the court may take into account the conditions previously included in the rule: namely whether the evidence is newly discovered and could not have been obtained earlier through the existence of due diligence, and whether the issue to which such evidence relates has newly arisen in the case. The rule recognizes that in some instances the circumstances that justify an application to introduce evidence otherwise barred by Rule 412 will not become apparent until trial.

Rule 412(c) provides that before admitting evidence that falls within the prohibition of Rule 412(a), the court must hold a hearing in camera at which the alleged victim and any party must be afforded the right to be present and an opportunity to be heard. All papers connected with the motion and any record of a hearing on the motion must be kept and remain under seal during the course of trial and appellate proceedings unless otherwise ordered. This is to assure that the privacy of the alleged victim is preserved in all cases in which the court rules that proffered evidence is not admissible, and in which the hearing refers to matters that are not received, or are received in another form.

The procedures set forth in subdivision (c) do not apply to discovery of a victim's past sexual conduct or predisposition in civil cases, which continue to be governed by Fed.R.Civ.P. 26. The Advisory Committee's Note opines that in order not to undermine the rationale of Rule 412, however, courts should enter appropriate orders pursuant to Fed.R.Civ.P. 26(c) to protect the victim against unwarranted inquiries and to ensure confidentiality. Courts should also presumptively issue protective orders barring discovery unless the party seeking discovery makes a showing that the evidence sought to be discovered would be relevant under the facts and theories of the particular case, and cannot be obtained except through discovery. In an action for sexual harassment, for instance, while some evidence of the alleged victim's sexual behavior and/or predisposition in the workplace may perhaps be relevant, non-work place conduct will usually be irrelevant. A confidentiality order should be presumptively granted as well.

**Unfair prejudice.** Rule 412(b)(1) provides that in criminal cases evidence meeting the requirements of an exception to the bar to admissibility contained in subdivisions (A), (B), and (C), is admissible only "if otherwise admissible under these rules." The Advisory Committee's Note specifically mentions as applicable Rule 403. In civil cases the exception to the bar to admissibility contained in subdivision (b)(2) provides for a balancing test, i.e., the probative value of the evidence must substantially outweigh the "danger of harm to the victim" and "of unfair prejudice to any party." Neither phrase is defined in either Rule 412 or the Advisory Committee's Note.

As used in Rule 403, unfair prejudice refers to an undue tendency of an item of evidence to suggest a decision on an improper basis, commonly an emotional one, such as sympathy, hatred, contempt, retribution or horror. With respect to evidence of the alleged victim's other sexual behavior, it is on the basis of an adverse emotional reaction to the other sexual behavior of the alleged victim. The emotional reaction may take various forms such as, "this kind of woman doesn't deserve to be protected" or "why should we send a man to jail for having intercourse with a woman who voluntarily sleeps with every Tom, Dick and Harry." Evidence of other sexual behavior may in addition raise the dangers of confusion of the issue creating a side issue unduly distracting the jury from the main issue, and misleading the jury the possibility of the jury overvaluing the probative value of the past sexual conduct evidence for a reason other than an emotional one. The danger of misleading the jury is substantial. In fact legislative reassessment of the actual probative value in today's sexually liberated society of other sexual behavior in light of the jury's likelihood to overvalue is one of the critical underpinnings of the recent movement in favor of rape shield statutes such as Rule 412. The term "harm to the victim" is undoubtedly intended to protect the witness from harassment and undue embarrassment, Rule 611(a)(3), as well as foster the interests of society in encouraging victims to actively redress claims. How this interest in protecting alleged victims and thereby encouraging the prosecution of meritorious civil claims is to be integrated into any equation evaluating probative value versus unfair prejudice is extremely unclear.

## Rule 413.

## EVIDENCE OF SIMILAR CRIMES IN SEXUAL ASSAULT CASES

**(a) In a criminal case in which the defendant is accused of an offense of sexual assault, evidence of the defendant's commission of another offense or offenses of sexual assault is admissible, and may be considered for its bearing on any matter to which it is relevant.**

**(b) In a case in which the Government intends to offer evidence under this rule, the attorney for the Government shall disclose the evidence to the defendant, including statements of witnesses or a summary of the substance of any testimony that is expected to be offered, at least fifteen days before the scheduled date of trial or at such later time as the court may allow for good cause.**

**(c) This rule shall not be construed to limit the admission or consideration of evidence under any other rule.**

**(d) For purposes of this rule and Rule 415, "offense of sexual assault" means a crime under Fed-**

eral law or the law of a State (as defined in section 513 of title 18, United States Code) that involved—

(1) any conduct proscribed by chapter 109A of title 18, United States Code;

(2) contact, without consent, between any part of the defendant's body or an object and the genitals or anus of another person;

(3) contact, without consent, between the genitals or anus of the defendant and any part of another person's body;

(4) deriving sexual pleasure or gratification from the infliction of death, bodily injury, or physical pain on another person; or

(5) an attempt or conspiracy to engage in conduct described in paragraphs (1)-(4).

## § 413.1 Evidence of Similar Crimes in Sexual Assault Cases

In a criminal case in which the defendant is accused of an offense of sexual assault, evidence of the defendant's commission of another offense or offenses of sexual assault is admissible, and may be considered for its bearing on any matter to which it is relevant, Rule 413(a). In a case in which the Government intends to offer evidence under this rule, the attorney for the Government must disclose the evidence to the defendant, including statements of witnesses or a summary of the substance of any testimony that is expected to be offered, at least fifteen days before the scheduled date of trial or at such later time as the court may allow for good cause, Rule 413(b). Rule 413(c) provides specifically that Rule 413 "shall not be construed to limit the admission or consideration of evidence under any other rule."

For purposes of Rules 413 and 415, Rule 413(d) provides that "offense of sexual assault" means a crime under Federal law or the law of a State (as defined in section 513 of title 18, United States Code) that involved (1) any conduct proscribed by chapter 109A of title 18, United States Code; (2) contact, without consent, between any part of the defendant's body or an object and the genitals or anus of another person; (3) contact, without consent, between the genitals or anus of the defendant and any part of another person's body; (4) deriving sexual pleasure or gratification from the infliction of death, bodily injury, or physical pain on another person; or (5) an attempt or conspiracy to engage in conduct described in paragraphs (1)–(4).

Rule 413 raises many questions, the most important of which is the mandatory language of Rule 413(a) providing that "[i]n a criminal case in which the defendant is accused of an offense of sexual assault, evidence of the defendant's commission of another offense or offenses of sexual assault is admissible, and may be considered for its bearing on any matter to which it is relevant." Thus in a prosecution for an offense of sexual assault, Rule 413(a) clearly states that evidence of a specific instance of sexual assault by the accused is admissible for any "matter to which it is relevant," including "the defendant's propensity to commit sexual assault or child molestation offenses, and assessment of the probability or improbability that the defendant has been falsely or mistakenly accused of such an offense." The Report of the Judicial Conference of the United States on the Admission of Character Evidence in Certain Sexual Misconduct Cases, opined that arguably the mandatory language, i.e., "is admissible," of Rule 413(a) makes other Federal Rules of Evidence such as the hearsay rule or Rule 403 inapplicable. Such an interpretation has been rejected; Rule 403 is applicable. Even Representative Susan Molinari, co-sponsor of the enacting legislation, recognized that "the general standards of the rules of evidence will continue to apply, including the restrictions on hearsay evidence and the court's authority under Evidence Rule 403 to exclude evidence whose probative value is substantially outweighed by its prejudicial effect."

## Rule 414.

## EVIDENCE OF SIMILAR CRIMES IN CHILD MOLESTATION CASES

(a) In a criminal case in which the defendant is accused of an offense of child molestation, evidence of the defendant's commission of another offense or offenses of child molestation is admissible, and may be considered for its bearing on any matter to which it is relevant.

(b) In a case in which the Government intends to offer evidence under this rule, the attorney for the Government shall disclose the evidence to the defendant, including statements of witnesses or a summary of the substance of any testimony that is expected to be offered, at least fifteen days before the scheduled date of trial or at such later time as the court may allow for good cause.

(c) This rule shall not be construed to limit the admission or consideration of evidence under any other rule.

**(d)** For purposes of this rule and Rule 415, "child" means a person below the age of fourteen, and "offense of child molestation" means a crime under Federal law or the law of a State (as defined in section 513 of title 18, United States Code) that involved—

**(1)** any conduct proscribed by chapter 109A of title 18, United States Code, that was committed in relation to a child;

**(2)** any conduct proscribed by chapter 110 of title 18, United States Code;

**(3)** contact between any part of the defendant's body or an object and the genitals or anus of a child;

**(4)** contact between the genitals or anus of the defendant and any part of the body of a child;

**(5)** deriving sexual pleasure or gratification from the infliction of death, bodily injury, or physical pain on a child; or

**(6)** an attempt or conspiracy to engage in conduct described in paragraphs (1)–(5).

## § 414.1 Evidence of Similar Crimes in Child Molestation Cases

In a criminal case in which the defendant is accused of an offense of child molestation, evidence of the defendant's commission of another offense or offenses of child molestation is admissible, and may be considered for its bearing on any matter to which it is relevant, Rule 414(a). In a case in which the Government intends to offer evidence under Rule 414, the attorney for the Government must disclose the evidence to the defendant, including statements of witnesses or a summary of the substance of any testimony that is expected to be offered, at least fifteen days before the scheduled date of trial or at such later time as the court may allow for good cause, Rule 414(b). Rule 414(c) provides specifically that Rule 414 "shall not be construed to limit the admission or consideration of evidence under any other rule."

For purposes of Rules 414 and 415, Rule 414(d) provides that "child" means a person below the age of fourteen, and "offense of child molestation" means a crime under Federal law or the law of a State (as defined in section 513 of title 18, United States Code) that involved (1) any conduct proscribed by chapter 109A of title 18, United States Code, that was committed in relation to a child; (2) any conduct proscribed by chapter 110 of title 18, United States Code; (3) contact between any part of the defendant's body or an object and the genitals or anus of a child; (4) contact between the genitals or anus of the defendant and any part of the body of a child; (5) deriving sexual pleasure or gratification from the infliction of death, bodily injury, or physical pain on a child; or (6) an attempt or conspiracy to engage in conduct (1)–(5).

With respect to interpretation of Rule 414, particularly in light of its mandatory language in Rule 414(a), i.e., "is admissible," see § 413.1 supra.

## Rule 415.

### EVIDENCE OF SIMILAR ACTS IN CIVIL CASES CONCERNING SEXUAL ASSAULT OR CHILD MOLESTATION

**(a) In a civil case in which a claim for damages or other relief is predicated on a party's alleged**

commission of conduct constituting an offense of sexual assault or child molestation, evidence of that party's commission of another offense or offenses of sexual assault or child molestation is admissible and may be considered as provided in Rule 413 and Rule 414 of these rules.

(b) A party who intends to offer evidence under this Rule shall disclose the evidence to the party against whom it will be offered, including statements of witnesses or a summary of the substance of any testimony that is expected to be offered, at least fifteen days before the scheduled date of trial or at such later time as the court may allow for good cause.

(c) This rule shall not be construed to limit the admission or consideration of evidence under any other rule.

## § 415.1  Evidence of Similar Acts in Civil Cases Concerning Sexual Assault of Child Molestation

In a civil case in which a claim for damages or other relief is predicated on a party's alleged commission of conduct constituting an offense of sexual assault or child molestation, evidence of that party's commission of another offense or offenses of sexual assault or child molestation is admissible and may be considered as provided in Rules 413 and 414, Rule 415(a). A party who intends to offer evidence under Rule 415 must disclose the evidence to the party against whom it will be offered, including statements of witnesses or a summary of the substance of any testimony that is expected to be offered, at least fifteen days before the scheduled date of trial or at such later time as the court may allow for good cause. Rule 415(c) provides specifically that Rule 415 "shall not be construed to limit the admission or consideration of evidence under any other rule."

With respect to interpretation of Rule 415, particularly in light of its mandatory language in Rule 415(a), i.e., "is admissible," see § 413.1 supra.

# ARTICLE V

# PRIVILEGES

*Table of Rules*

## Rule 501.

## GENERAL RULE

**Except as otherwise required by the Constitution of the United States or provided by Act of Congress or in rules prescribed by the Supreme Court pursuant to statutory authority, the privilege of a witness, person, government, State, or political subdivision thereof shall be governed by the principles of the common law as they may be interpreted by the courts of the United States in light of reason and experience. However, in civil actions and proceedings, with respect to an element of a claim or defense as to which State law supplies the rule of decision, the privilege of a witness, person, government, State, or political subdivision thereof shall be determined in accordance with State law.**

## § 501.1  Rule 501: General Rule of Privilege; An Overview

The purpose of the ordinary rules of evidence is to promote the ascertainment of the truth. Another group

170

of rules, however, is designed to permit the exclusion of evidence for reasons wholly unconnected with the quality of the evidence or the credibility of the witness. These reasons are found in the desire to protect an interest or relationship. The term "privilege" as employed in Rule 501 is used broadly to describe these latter rules of exclusion. Since the effect of a privilege is to suppress the truth, a privilege should be recognized only if the interest or relationship is of outstanding importance and would undoubtedly be harmed by denying the protection of privilege.

As proposed by the Advisory Committee and prescribed by the Supreme Court, Rule 501 would have provided that, except as required by the Constitution of the United States, by Act of Congress, or by other rules adopted by the Supreme Court including the nine specific privileges recognized in proposed rules 502-510, no person had a privilege to (1) refuse to testify, (2) refuse to disclose any matter, (3) refuse to produce any object in writing or (4) prevent another from seeing a witness or disclosing any matter or producing any object in writing. Congress, however, amended Article V to eliminate all of the Court's proposed rules on privilege. Instead, Congress in a single Rule 501 left the law of privileges in its prior state.

Rule 501 provides that in federal criminal cases and in civil cases where federal law provides the rule of decision, privileges should continue to be developed by the courts of the United States under a uniform standard applicable both in civil and criminal cases. That standard, derived from then existing Rule 26 of the Federal Rules of Criminal Procedure, mandates the application of the principles of the common law as interpreted by the courts of the United States under a uniform standard applicable both in civil and criminal cases. That standard, derived from then existing Rule 26 of the Federal Rules of Criminal Procedure, mandates the application of the principles of the common law as interpreted by the courts of the United States in the light of reason and experience. The intent of Congress was thus not to freeze the law of privilege but rather to provide courts with the flexibility to develop rules of privilege in the light of reason and experience on a case by case basis. In so developing rules of privilege, the Supreme Court in Trammel v. United States (S.Ct.1980) advised that since "privileges contravene the fundamental principle that 'the public ... has a right to every man's evidence,'" privileges must be strictly construed and accepted "only to the very limited extent that permitting a refusal to testify or excluding relevant evidence has a public good transcending the normally predominant principle of utilizing all rational means for ascertaining truth."

Federal courts have recognized as a matter of federal common law the most basic and traditional privileges, but have not been very receptive to more modern, sometimes novel, privileges which typically have come into existence in various states by statutory enactment. A communication made in confidence has been recognized as privileged only if fostering of the relationship is considered important to society and the injury to such relationship that would result from disclosure exceeds the benefit gained from a fully informed determination of litigation. Thus federal courts recognize a lawyer-client privilege, a spousal testimonial privilege, a spousal confidential communications privilege, a psychotherapist-patient privilege, a political vote privilege, a clergyman-penitent privilege, and qualified privileges for trade secretes, secrets of state, and informer's identity. Federal courts have not recognized a physician-patient privilege or an accountant-client privilege.

Federal courts also accept that journalists possess a qualified privilege to refuse to testify about their news sources or to produce their unpublished work product. The basis of this privilege is society's interest in a free and accurate flow of information, an interest courts believe could be subverted by the chilling effect the absence of such a privilege might have on both journalists and their sources. In balancing the policies underlying the privilege against the rights of the courts, the prosecution, criminal defendants and private litigants to every person's evidence, the courts have weighed several factors: (1) the materiality or necessity to the case of the information allegedly privileged, (2) the attempts of the side seeking the information to obtain it from sources other than the journalists, and (3) whether the information sought is in fact available from such sources. Whether a qualified academic freedom privilege exists with respect to appointments matters is disputed.

Rule 501 as redrafted by Congress provides that in civil actions and proceedings, with respect to an element of a claim or defense as to which state law supplies the rule of decision, the privilege of a witness, person, government, State or political subdivision thereof shall be determined in accordance with state law. The rationale for such application of state law with respect to privilege was stated in the Report of the House Committee on the Judiciary:

[F]ederal law should not supersede that of the States in substantive areas such as privilege absent a compelling reason. The Committee believes that in civil cases in the federal courts where an element of a claim or defense is not grounded upon a federal question, there is no federal interest strong enough to justify departure from State policy. In addition, the Committee considered that the Court's proposed Article V would have promoted forum shopping in some civil actions, depending upon differences in the privilege law applied as among the State and federal courts. The Committee's proviso, on the other hand, under which the federal courts are bound to apply the State's privilege law in actions founded upon a State-created right or defense, removes the incentive to "shop".

Rule 501 governing privilege applies to all stages of actions, cases, and proceedings, Rule 1101(c).

Rule 501 excepts from its coverage privileges required by the Constitution of the Untied States, privileges provided by Act of Congress, and privileges created by other rules prescribed by the Supreme Court pursuant to statutory authority. Detailed discussion of constitutional, statutory privileges, and common law privileges recognized under Rule 501 is beyond the scope of this Nutshell. The lawyer-client privilege and the husband-wife privileges are, however, discussed below.

The ordinary rules of evidence are invoked or waived by the parties in their capacity of litigants as an essential aspect of the adversary system. Privileges, to the contrary, are invoked or waived by their owners, who may or may not be parties to the litigation. The person asserting a privilege has the burden of showing facts which give rise to the privilege; a mere assertion of the privilege does not suffice. The existence of a privilege is a matter for the court, Rule 104(a).

## § 501.2  Lawyer–Client Privilege

Federal decisions have long given full recognition to the common law privilege against disclosure of confidential communications between lawyer and client. The obvious purpose of the lawyer-client privilege is to encourage clients to make full disclosure to their attorneys. "As a practical matter, if the client knows that damaging information could more readily be obtained from the attorney following disclosure than from himself in the absence of disclosure, the client would be reluctant to confide in his lawyer and it would be difficult to obtain fully informed legal advice." Fisher v. United States (S.Ct.1976).

A client has a privilege to refuse to disclose and to prevent any other person from disclosing "confidential" communications made for the purpose of facilitating the rendition of professional legal services to the client. Thus a communication made as a mere friend to a lawyer or a communication relating to business without contemplation of legal advice or representation does not create the relationship. A communication is "confidential" if not intended to be disclosed to third persons other than representatives of the lawyer to whom disclosure is in furtherance of the rendition of professional legal services to the client or to those reasonably necessary for the transmission of the communication. A representative of a lawyer includes associates, secretaries, file clerks, etc., as well as the lawyer's investigator. Also included is an expert employed to assist the lawyer in the rendering of legal services including the planning and conduct of litigation. However an expert hired to testify at trial is outside the scope of the lawyer-client privilege. Whether the expert's compensation is derived immediately from the lawyer or the client is not material. The concept of confidential communications' extends to documents exchanged between lawyer and client. Thus a document created for the purpose of facilitating the rendition of professional legal services, such as a letter, is privileged in the hands of the lawyer. However, where the document is pre-existing, the document by virtue of being forwarded to the lawyer does not acquire a privileged status.

The lawyer-client privilege also includes communications by the lawyer or the lawyer's representative to the client if the communication constitutes legal advise, or tends directly or indirectly to reveal the substance of a client confidence.

For purposes of the lawyer-client privilege, a client is defined as a person, public officer, or corporation, association, or other organization or entity, either public or private who is rendered professional legal services by a lawyer, or who consults a lawyer with a view to obtaining professional legal services from him. An issue arises as to who is a representative of a corporation, association, or other organization or entity, either public or private, whose communication is protected by the lawyer-client privilege. Two alternatives have been put forth. Under the control group test, representatives of the client is limited to persons having authority to obtain professional legal services, or to act on advice rendered pursuant thereto, on behalf of the client. Under the subject matter test, representatives of the client also includes employees not in the control group, if (1) the communication was made for the purpose of securing legal advice; (2) the employee making the communication did so at the direction of his corporate superior; (3) the superior made the request so that the corporation could secure legal advice; (4) the subject matter of the communication is within the scope of the employee's corporate duties; and (5) the communication is not disseminated beyond those persons who, because of the corporate structure, need to know its contents. In Upjohn Co. v. United States (S.Ct. 1981) the Supreme Court, as a practical matter, declared the subject matter test to be consistent with the principles of the common law as interpreted in light of reason and experience, Rule 501.

The lawyer-client privilege belongs to the client, not to the attorney. The privilege may be claimed by the client, his guardian or conservator, the personal representative of a deceased client, or the successor, trustee, or similar representative of a corporation, association, or other organization, whether or not in existence. The privilege once attaching thus persists unless waived without regard to whether the lawyer-client relationship has been terminated. The person who was the lawyer at the time of the communication can and should claim the privilege but only on behalf of the client. His authority to do so is presumed in the absence of evidence to the contrary. Like other privileges, the lawyer-client may be claimed by its owner, whether or not a party to the litigation.

The lawyer-client privilege does not apply: (1) if the services of the lawyer were sought or obtained to enable or aid anyone to commit or plan to commit what the client knew or reasonably should have known to be a crime or fraud; (2) as to a communication relevant to an issue of breach of duty by the lawyer to his client or by the client to his lawyer; (3) as to a communication relevant to an issue concerning an attested document to which the lawyer is an attesting witness; (4) as to a communication relevant to a matter of common interest between two or more clients if the communication was made by any of them to a lawyer retained or consulted in common, when offered in an action between any of the clients. In addition while upon the death of the client the privilege survives in favor of his estate in regard to claims by outsiders against the estate, it does not apply to a communication relevant to an issue between parties who claim through the same deceased client, regardless of whether the claims were by testate or intestate succession or by *inter vivos* transaction.

## § 501.3   Husband–Wife Privileges

Federal courts recognize that in the interests of marital harmony the testifying spouse has a privilege, in criminal but not civil cases, to refuse to testify against the other. The holder of the privilege, referred to as the anti-marital facts privilege, is solely the testifying spouse; the non-testifying spouse may not assert the privilege on his or her behalf. The scope of the anti-marital facts testimonial privilege extends only to the right to refuse to answer questions which tend to incriminate the non-testifying spouse. Questions which do not tend to incriminate the non-testifying spouse do not jeopardize the marriage. The testimonial husband-wife privilege ceases to exist if the parties do not remain married. Moreover, no privilege exists if the marriage is a sham or invalid. Since the anti-marital facts testimonial privilege is not based primarily upon the notion of fostering confidential communications, it is not waived by prior voluntary disclosure by the spouse called at trial to testify.

In criminal cases and civil cases where federal law provides the rule of decision, a privilege exists with respect to confidential marital communications. This privilege bars testimony concerning intra-spousal confidential expressions made during the marital relationship. Like the testimonial husband-wife privilege, existence of the confidential communication husband-wife privilege depends on there being a valid marriage. The privilege, however, does not apply where the communications occur between permanently separated spouses. Unlike the testimonial privilege, the confidential communication privilege survives termination of the marriage by annulment, divorce or death. The husband-wife confidential communication privilege barring disclosure by either spouse belongs to both spouses and may be asserted by either in his or her own right.

## § 501.4 Waiver of Privilege; Disclosure Without Opportunity to Claim

The holder of a privilege against disclosure of the confidential communication waives the privilege if he or his predecessor while holder of the privilege voluntarily discloses or consents to disclosure of any significant part of the matter or communication. To illustrate, the giving of written consent to a psychiatrist to release records, the calling and eliciting of testimony of a lawyer at trial by the holder, as well as the repeating to a third person the content of privileged communication by the holder of the privilege, each constitutes a waiver. Failure to assert the privilege at trial also constitutes a waiver. Once confidentiality is destroyed through voluntary disclosure, it cannot be restored by a subsequent claim of privilege. Knowledge or lack thereof of the existence of the privilege by the holder at the moment of disclosure is irrelevant. Voluntary disclosure of privileged information waives the privilege with respect to all other communications on the same subject matter. Waiver does not occur, however, if voluntary disclosure is itself a privileged communication.

The holder will not be held to have waived the privilege where disclosure of the privileged confidential communication was either compelled erroneously or made without opportunity to claim the privilege. Where disclosure was wrongfully judicially compelled the argument that the holder of the privilege should, in order to preserve the privilege, be required to stand firm and take the consequences, including a judgment for contempt, is rejected as exacting of the holder greater fortitude in the face of authority than ordinary individuals are likely to possess, and assuming unrealistically that a judicial remedy is always available. Similarly no waiver results when disclosure is made without the holder having an opportunity to claim the privilege. Thus a third person may not testify against an accused in a criminal case to a confidential communication disclosed to him by a spouse to whom the confidential marital communication was made. Neither could the spouse so testify. The same rule would apply in the unlikely event a lawyer, psychiatrist, or clergyman made an unauthorized disclosure of a confidential communication. The problem arises most frequently in connection with eavesdroppers. Where for example electronic surveillance is employed, the holder should not be held to have waived the privilege. However where the parties know that another person was in a position to easily hear a communication with the naked car, no privilege would attach for an intent to have the communication be confidential is lacking.

# ARTICLE VI

# **WITNESSES**

### *Table of Rules*

## Rule 601.

## GENERAL RULE OF COMPETENCY

**Every person is competent to be a witness except as otherwise provided in these rules. However, in civil actions and proceedings, with respect to an element of a claim or defense as to which State law supplies the rule of decision, the competency of a witness shall be determined in accordance with State law.**

## § 601.1 General Rule of Competency: An Overview

Rule 601 eliminates all grounds of witness incompetency with respect to a claim or defense as to which federal law provides the rule of decision except those specifically recognized in the Federal Rules of Evidence. Included in the grounds for incompetency *not* recognized are age, religious·belief, mental incapacity, color of skin, moral incapacity, conviction of a crime, marital relationship, and connection with the litigation as a party, attorney, or interested person. Such matters, long ago regarded as grounds of incompetency, survive in most instances as avenues of impeachment of the witness. In the great majority of respects, Rule 601 merely reflects the common law as it has developed with respect to the competency of witnesses.

The only general competency requirements specified in these rules are contained in Rule 603 which requires that every witness declare that he will testify truthfully by oath or affirmation and Rule 602 which requires that the witness possess personal knowledge. Together these rules require that (1) the witness had the capacity to accurately perceive, record and recollect impressions of facts (physical and mental capacity) at the time of the event, (2) the witness in fact did perceive, record and can recollect impressions having any tendency to establish a fact of consequence in the litigation (personal knowledge), (3) the witness declares that he will tell the truth, understands the duty to tell the truth (oath or affirmation) as well as understands the difference between the truth and a lie or fantasy, and (4) the witness possesses the capacity to comprehend questions and express himself understandably, where necessary with aid of an interpreter, Rule 604 (narration). Before a witness will be permitted to testify, evidence must be introduced sufficient to support a finding of personal knowledge, Rule 602, i.e., that the witness has the capacity to and actually did observe, receive, record and can now recollect and narrate impressions obtained through any of his senses having any tendency to establish a fact of consequence, and the witness must declare by oath or affirmation that he will testify truthfully, Rule 603. No other personal qualifications of a witness are required. No mental qualification is specified. The Advisory Committee's Note reasons that standards of mental capacity have proved elusive, few witnesses were actually disqualified, and moreover that a witness wholly without mental capacity is difficult to imagine. However, while mental incapacity is not a specified ground of incompetency, testimony of a witness whose mental capacity has been seriously questioned may still be excluded on the grounds that no reasonable juror could possibly believe that the witness in fact possesses personal knowledge, Rule 602, or understands the difference between the truth and a lie or fantasy and the duty to tell the truth, Rule 603.

Competency of a witness to testify thus requires a minimum ability to observe, record, recollect and recount as well as an understanding of the duty to tell the truth. Where the capacity of a witness has been brought into question, the ultimate question is whether a reasonable juror must believe that the witness is so bereft of his powers of observation, recordation, recollection and narration as to be so untrustworthy as a witness as to make his testimony lack relevancy. Such a test of competency has been characterized as requiring minimum credibility. The tendency is increasingly to resolve doubts as to minimum credibility of the witness in favor of permitting the jury to hear the testimony and judge the credibility of the witness for itself. Thus, for example, mental capacity generally functions as an effect on the weight to be given to testimony rather than precluding admissibility.

Rule 601 specifying that where federal law provides the rules of decision all witnesses are competent is clearly designed to further effectuate this trend. Testimony of all witnesses to be relevant must still meet a minimum credibility level with respect to observation, recordation, recollection, narration and duty to testify truthfully. However, paraphrasing the Advisory Committee's Note referred to above, a witness wholly without capacity with respect to acquiring personal knowledge and understanding the duty to testify truthfully is difficult to imagine. Testimony of a witness passing the test of minimum credibility may nevertheless be excluded under Rule 403; the more deficient the witness' capacities the more likely the probative value of the witness' testimony will be outweighed by the trial concerns enumerated in Rule 403.

The Federal Rules of Evidence do provide in Rules 605 and 606 respectively that neither the presiding judge nor a member of the jury is competent to testify at a trial in which participating.

In civil actions and proceedings with respect to an element of a claim or defense as to which State law supplies the rule of decision, the competency of a witness shall be determined in accordance with State law, Rule 601. Given the general current state of the common law with respect to elimination of grounds of incompetency of witnesses, the major impact of application of state law in such instances concerns the so-called Dead Man's Statutes.

In all actions without regard to whether state or federal law provides the rule of decision, otherwise competent witnesses may be barred from testifying as to a particular matter by a claim of privilege. Determining a claim of privilege and determining whether a witness is competent to testify sometimes intertwine. For example, issues relating to a husband or wife testifying for or against each other are treated under federal law as matters of privilege and not competency. However, under state law, such questions are occasionally discussed in terms of competency and not privilege. Since both Rule 601, competency, and Rule 501, privilege, require application of state law where state law provides the rule of decision, whichever treatment is provided by applicable state law will be followed in such cases in federal court.

Other than to the extent intimately connected with questions relating to the possession of personal knowledge, Rule 602, the competency of a witness is to be determined solely by the court, Rule 104(a).

## § 601.2  Mental Capacity: Preliminary Hearings; Ordering of Psychiatric Examinations; Children

Rule 601 does not specify a measure of mental capacity as a condition precedent to the giving of testimony. Mental deficiency ordinarily affects only the weight accorded testimony, not its admissibility. The Advisory Committee's Note states:

> No mental or moral qualifications for testifying as a witness are specified. Standards of mental capacity have proved elusive in actual application. A leading commentator observes that few witnesses are disqualified on that ground. Weihofen, Testimonial Competency and Credibility, 34 Geo.Wash.L.Rev. 53 (1965). Discretion is regularly exercised in favor of allowing the testimony. A witness wholly without capacity is difficult to imagine. The question is one particularly suited to the jury as one of weight and credibility, subject to judicial authority to review the sufficiency of the evidence.

Accordingly an adjudication of feeblemindedness does not render a witness incompetent, nor does having spent time in a mental institution. Similarly the mere fact that a witness has been found incompetent to stand trial does not preclude the witness from testifying. Moreover neither age nor sanity is a test of competency.

A witness must nevertheless possess personal knowledge of a particular fact, Rule 602, understand the duty to tell the truth and be willing to declare by oath or affirmation to tell the truth, Rule 603, in order to testify.

Evidence sufficient to support a finding of such personal knowledge must be introduced. The ultimate question to be asked is whether the witness is so bereft of his powers of observation, recordation, recollection or narration as to be so thoroughly untrustworthy as a witness as to make his testimony lack relevancy. Thus upon viewing all the evidence of personal knowledge in a light most favorably to the proponent of the witness alleged to be mentally deficient, if a reasonable juror in viewing his manifest deficiencies could not believe that the witness in fact observed, recorded, recollects, can narrate, and understands the duty to tell the truth, Rule 603, the witness' testimony may not be introduced. Testimony of a witness meeting such a minimal credibility requirement may nevertheless be excluded under Rule 403.

Difficulties surrounding the fact that while mental capacity is not required under Rule 601, it nevertheless remains a consideration in evaluating personal knowledge, Rule 602, and duty to testify truthfully, Rule 603, surface with respect to whether a preliminary hearing as to competency should be conducted. The competency of a witness is a matter to be decided by the court, Rule 104(a). Prior to the enactment of Rule 601, the trial court would frequently conduct "preliminary hearings" outside the presence of the jury to determine the competency of a child witness, an alleged drug addict, or a witness alleged to be mentally deficient. In spite of the import of the Advisory Committee's Note presented above, courts routinely continue to conduct such hearings to determine competency; expert witness testimony may be received. Discretion exists for the court to require psychiatric examinations of witnesses in aid of its determination of witness competency.

In summary, when Rule 601 is viewed in light of Rules 602, 603 and 403, it becomes manifest that, in spite of any contrary implication in the Advisory Committee's Note to Rule 601, a witness must possess sufficient mental capacity to observe, record, recollect, and narrate as well as an ability to understand the duty to tell the truth, and that the court in its discretion may both conduct a preliminary hearing and order a psychiatric examination in aid of its determination. If the witness by reason of age, retardation, injury, medication, or illness is so severely mentally deficient that a reasonable juror could not put any credence in the witness's testimony, i.e., the witness lacks minimum credibility, the court must find that the witness is incompetent to testify. Minimum credibility should be evaluated in light of the need for the witness' testimony as well as the factors listed in Rule 403. As McCormick, Evidence § 62 at 267–69 (5th ed.1999) states:

> [T]he * * * test is whether the witness has intelligence enough to make it worthwhile to hear him at all and whether he recognizes a duty to tell the truth. Is his capacity to perceive, record, recollect, and narrate, such that he can probably add knowledge of the facts to the record? * * * Conceding the jury's deficiencies, the remedy of excluding such a witness [of minimum credibility], who may be the only person available who knows the facts, seems inept and primitive. Though the tribunal is unskilled, and the testimony difficult to weigh, on balance it is still better to let the evidence come in for what it is worth with cautionary instructions.

A witness who has been found minimally credible is subject to cross-examination with respect to his ability to observe, record, recollect, and narrate as well as his ability to understand the duty to testify truthfully. Such inquiry affecting the credibility of the witness is not collateral; extrinsic evidence may be introduced. Whether psychiatric testimony offered by a party relating to the credibility of the witness is admissible rests in the discretion of the court. Similarly whether under unusual circumstances either a psychiatrist will be appointed by the court to examine a witness, or the witness ordered to submit to an examination by a psychiatrist retained by a party for the purpose of assisting a litigant in attacking the credibility of a witness rests in the discretion of the court.

18 U.S.C.A. § 3509(c) provides as follows with respect to determining the competency of a child witness:

(1) Effect of Federal Rules of Evidence. Nothing in this subdivision shall be construed to abrogate rule 601 of the Federal Rules of Evidence.

(2) Presumption. A child is presumed to be competent.

(3) Requirement of a Written Motion. A competency examination regarding a child witness may be conducted by the court only upon written motion and offer of proof of incompetency by a party.

(4) Requirement of Compelling Reasons. A competency examination regarding a child may be conducted by the court only if the court determines, on the record, that compelling reasons exist. A child's age alone is not a compelling reason.

(5) Persons Permitted to be Present. The only persons who may be permitted to be present at a competency examination are—

(A) the judge;

(B) the attorney for the government;

(C) the attorney for the defendant;

(D) a court reporter; and

(E) persons whose presence, in the opinion of the court, is necessary to the welfare and well-being of the child, including the child's attorney, guardian ad litem or adult attendant.

(6) Not Before Jury. A competency examination regarding a child witness shall be conducted out of the sight and hearing of a jury.

(7) Direct Examination of Child. Examination of a child related to competency shall normally be conducted by the court on the basis of questions submitted by the attorney for the Government and the attorney for the defendant including a party acting as an attorney pro se. The court may permit an attorney but not a party acting as an attorney pro se to examine a child directly on competency if the court is satisfied that the child will not suffer emotional trauma as a result of the examination.

(8) Appropriate Questions. The questions asked at the competency examination of a child shall be appropriate to the age and developmental level of the child, shall not be related to issue at trial, and shall focus on determining the child's ability to understand and answer simple questions.

(9) Psychological and Psychiatric Examinations. Psychological and psychiatric examinations to assess the competency of a child witness shall not be ordered without a showing of compelling need.

Common questions asked to children to determine the ability of the child to distinguish truth from a lie or fantasy are inquiries such as "If I told you my robe was white, would that be a lie or the truth?" and "Is Superman real or just make believe?"

## § 601.3   Alcohol or Drug Use as Affecting Competency

Habitual use of intoxicants or drug addiction does not by itself make a witness incompetent to testify. Even the fact that a witness was under the influence at the time of observing the event in question or testifies while under the influence is not disqualifying; competency is determined by an assessment of minimum credibility.

## § 601.4   Dead Man's Statutes

A highly significant change provided by proposed Rule 601 but not accepted by Congress was the abolition of incompetency of witnesses by virtue of state Dead Man's Statutes in all actions tried in the federal court. While state Dead Man's Statutes vary in content, they generally provide for the exclusion of an interested witness' testimony concerning a conversation or event which took place in the decedent's or incompetent's presence when offered against the latter's representative. The rationale is the notion that where death or incompetency has closed the mouth of one party, the law seeks to effect equality by closing the mouth of the other. Dead Man's Statutes manifest the cynical view that a party will lie when he cannot be directly contradicted and the unrealistic assumption that jurors, knowing the situation, will believe anything they hear in these circumstances. While motivated by the laudable desire to protect decedent's and incompetent's assets from attack based on perjured testimony, such statutes have been a failure in practice while generating a considerable amount of litigation. There is no federal Dead Man's Statute.

The Advisory Committee's Proposed Rule 601 abolishing such witness incompetency in all actions tried in federal courts reflected the belief that this surviving relic of the common law disqualification of parties as witnesses leads to more miscarriages of justice than it prevents. However Congress, while acknowledging the substantial disagreement existing as to the merits of Dead Man's Statutes, felt that since they represent state policy, they should not be overturned in the absence of a compelling federal interest. Accordingly Rule 601 was amended to provide that where state law supplies the rule of decision, state law with respect to the competency of witnesses, which includes a state's Dead Man's Statute will be applied. Where federal law provides the rule of decision, the competency of a witness is to be determined solely with reference to federal law.

## Rule 602.

## LACK OF PERSONAL KNOWLEDGE

**A witness may not testify to a matter unless evidence is introduced sufficient to support a finding that the witness has personal knowledge of the matter. Evidence to prove personal knowledge may, but need not, consist of the testimony of the witness' own testimony. This rule is subject to the provisions of rule 703, relating to opinion testimony by expert witnesses.**

## § 602.1   The Requirement of Personal Knowledge

Admissible testimony is limited to matters of which the witness has acquired personal knowledge through any of his own senses, Rule 602. The requirement of personal knowledge is closely related to the inadmissibility of hearsay, Rule 802. If a witness testifying to an event acknowledges being in a distant location at the exact time, the proper objection is lack of personal knowledge. If the witness on the other hand states that he was told of the event by another person, the proper objection is hearsay. In many situations where it is clear that the witness is relying upon the statements of others although not specifically so stating, the objection "hearsay" generally suffices.

A witness testifying to an extrajudicial statement which is defined as not hearsay, Rule 801(d), or is admissible under an exception to the hearsay rule, Rules 803, 804, or 807, is not, however, required to have personal knowledge of the matter related in the statement. A witness testifying to such a statement admitted as not hearsay, Rule 801(d), or as an exception pursuant to Rules 803, 804, or 807 must, however, possess personal knowledge as to the fact of the statement itself. Moreover, to be admitted pursuant to an exception contained in Rule 803, 804, or 807 the declarant of the extrajudicial statement also must be shown to have personal knowledge as to the matter related. Personal knowledge of the declared is also required of statements defined as not hearsay by Rule 801(d)(1). Personal knowledge may appear from the statement itself, Rule 602, or be inferable from the circumstances. Statements admissible as an admission of a party opponent, Rule 801(d)(2), do not require a showing of personal knowledge on the part of the declarant.

The requirement of personal knowledge is one of conditional relevancy governed by Rule 104(b). The proponent of the evidence must thus introduce evidence sufficient, if believed, to support a finding by a reasonable juror of personal knowledge of the matter related. Evidence to prove personal knowledge may but need not consist of the testimony of the witness himself, Rule 602. The foundation must be sufficient when viewed most favorably to the proponent to support a finding by a reasonable jury that it is more probably true than not true that the witness had the capacity and opportunity to observe through his senses and record a relevant sense impression, did in fact observe, record and can now recollect the relevant sense impression, and finally can comprehend questions and narrate the relevant sense impression. Where such a foundation is laid, the witness must be permitted to testify unless a reasonable juror on all the evidence could not believe that the witness observed, recorded, recollects and can narrate what he claims to have perceived. Testimony previously received may be stricken if it later appears that personal knowledge was lacking.

The last sentence of Rule 602 makes the requirement of personal knowledge expressly subject to the provisions of Rule 703 which allows an expert witness to express opinions based on facts of which he does not have personal knowledge. A lay witness offering an opinion under Rule 701 is however required to have personal knowledge of the facts upon which the opinion is based.

# Rule 603.

# OATH OR AFFIRMATION

**Before testifying, every witness shall be required to declare that the witness will testify truthfully, by oath or affirmation administered in a form calculated to awaken the witness' conscience and impress the witness' mind with the duty to do so.**

## § 603.1 Oath or Affirmation

Before testifying, every witness must declare that he will testify truthfully by oath or affirmation, Rule 603. An oath contains a formal calling upon God; an affirmation is merely a statement that one will tell the truth. A typical oath is "Do you swear to tell truth, the whole truth, and nothing but the truth, so help you God?" A typical affirmation is "Do you affirm to tell the truth under penalty of perjury?"

The object of requiring the witness to declare that he will testify truthfully is twofold. The first and principal design is to affect the conscience of the witness to impress his mind with the duty to speak the truth. The second is that if the witness willfully falsifies his testimony, he may then be punished for perjury. The declaration may be either by oath or affirmation which may be administered by either the judge or court clerk. The oath or affirmation should be of a form and administered in a manner calculated to awaken the witness' conscience and impress his mind with his duty to testify truthfully.

Neither Rule 603 nor Rule 601 imposes any requirement of moral capacity in the sense of requiring that the witness actually possess a sense of responsibility to speak the truth. Similarly no requirement of a belief in God is imposed. Rule 603 adopts the position that the true purpose of the oath is not to exclude any competent witness, but merely to add a stimulus to truthfulness wherever such a stimulus is feasible.

Whether a witness has sufficiently declared by oath or affirmation that he will testify truthfully is a determination to be made by the court, Rule 104(a).

## Rule 604.

## INTERPRETERS

**An interpreter is subject to the provisions of these rules relating to qualification as an expert and the administration of an oath or affirmation to make a true translation.**

### § 604.1  Interpreters

Rules of procedure applicable in both civil and criminal actions provide that the court may appoint an interpreter of its own selection and may fix reasonable compensation. Neither rule specifies those situations where an interpreter must be appointed leaving the matter for case law determination. Interpreters have generally been required where a witness does not speak English at all or well enough to testify fully, where the witness speaks in sign language, and where the criminal defendant does not speak English at all or well enough to communicate with counsel and understand the proceedings.

In civil proceedings the interpreter's compensation is either paid out of funds provided by law or paid by one or more of the parties at the direction of the court. Fees paid to an interpreter may in the court's discretion be taxed ultimately as costs. In criminal proceedings compensation to the interpreter is paid either out of funds provided by law or by the government, as the court may direct.

When an interpreter is appointed, the interpreter is to be administered an oath or affirmation, Rule 604. The oath or affirmation of the interpreter is to make a "true translation" which requires that the interpreter communicate exactly what the witness is expressing in his testimony. An interpreter for a criminal defendant is also required to interpret everything said in the courtroom, whether by a witness, attorney, or the court.

Rule 604 specifically provides that the interpreter must meet the qualifications for an expert witness contained in Rule 702 which requires in the case of an interpreter that by reason of knowledge, skill, experience, training, or education, the interpreter is capable of providing a true translation.

## Rule 605.

## COMPETENCY OF JUDGE AS WITNESS

**The judge presiding at the trial may not testify in that trial as a witness. No objection need be made in order to preserve the point.**

### § 605.1   Competency of Judge as Witness

According to the older view of the common law, a judge was competent to testify in a trial over which he was presiding, but in his discretion might decline to do so. A second view developed under which the judge was disqualified from testifying to material disputed facts but free to testify with respect to matters merely formal and undisputed. Finally, a third view emerged, one adopted in Rule 605, providing for a blanket prohibition against testimony at trial by the presiding judge.

The reasons for automatically rendering the judge incompetent are obvious. The role of witness is plainly destructive of the court's image of impartiality, however impartial the trial judge may in fact be. Moreover testimony by the trial judge must of necessity create problems concerning jury overvaluing of his testimony, ruling on objections to his testimony, the conduct of cross-examination, the virtual impossibility of impeachment, and the continuation of the trial before the same judge.

As specified in Rule 605, no objection need be made in order to preserve the objection to the presiding judge testifying as a witness.

## Rule 606.

## COMPETENCY OF JUROR AS WITNESS

**(a) At the Trial. A member of the jury may not testify as a witness before that jury in the trial of the case in which the juror is sitting. If the juror is called so to testify, the opposing party shall be afforded an opportunity to object out of the presence of the jury.**

**(b) Inquiry Into Validity of Verdict or Indictment. Upon an inquiry into the validity of a verdict or indictment, a juror may not testify as to any matter or statement occurring during the course of the jury's deliberations or to the effect of anything upon that or any other juror's mind or emotions as influencing the juror to assent to or dissent from the verdict or indictment or concern-**

ing the juror's mental processes in connection therewith, except that a juror may testify on the question whether extraneous prejudicial information was improperly brought to the jury's attention or whether any outside influence was improperly brought to bear upon any juror. Nor may a juror's affidavit or evidence of any statement by the juror concerning a matter about which the juror would be precluded from testifying be received for these purposes.

### § 606.1    Rule 606(a): Competency of Juror as Witness at Trial

A member of the jury is barred from testifying as a witness before that jury in the case in which he is sitting, Rule 606(a). The rule is thus a counterpart of Rule 605 which renders the trial judge incompetent. The words "before that jury" make clear that the rule does not prevent the questioning of jurors by the judge or counsel as part of the jury selection process. The likelihood of a juror ever being called to testify in a case in which he is sitting is extremely small since any prospective juror disclosing personal knowledge would undoubtedly be excused during the jury selection process. In the unlikely event a juror is called to testify, the opposing party must be afforded an opportunity to object out of the presence of the jury, Rule 606(a).

### § 606.2    Rule 606(b): Competency of Juror to Attack Validity of Verdict or Indictment

Jurors are prohibited from attacking their verdict or indictment by testifying directly or indirectly by means of affidavits or statements as to any matter or statement occurring during the course of the jury's deliberations or to the effect of anything upon his or any other juror's mind or emotions as influencing him to assent to or dissent from the verdict or indictment or concerning his mental processes in connection therewith, Rule 606(b). Thus improper intrinsic influences on a jury's verdict are not competent to impeach the verdict. By insulating the jury decision making process and juror mental processes, Rule 606(b) adopts the philosophy expressed in McDonald v. Pless (S.Ct.1915), that "[j]urors would be harassed and beset by the defeated party in an effort to secure from them evidence of facts which might establish misconduct sufficient to set aside a verdict. If evidence thus secured could be thus used the result would be to make what was intended to be a private deliberation, the constant subject of public investigation to the destruction of all frankness and freedom of discussion and conference." A juror thus may not attack his verdict for example on the grounds of a quotient verdict, that a fellow juror was intoxicated, that jury instructions were misinterpreted, that the jury drew adverse inferences from the defendant's failure to testify, or on the basis of jury speculation as to insurance. Similarly excluded as grounds of attack are internal discussions, arguments, mental and emotional reactions, votes, or statements, even a statement purporting to relate specific factual information which was incorrect.

Jurors may however attack their verdict on the grounds that prejudicial extraneous influence or information was injected into or brought to bear upon the deliberation process, Rule 606(b). Thus a juror may testify on the question whether extraneous prejudicial information was brought to the jury's attention (e.g., a radio newscast or a newspaper account), whether any outside influence was improperly brought to bear upon a juror (e.g., a threat to the safety of a member of his family), as well as whether an unauthorized view, experiment, or jury investigation had transpired. In addition a verdict may be attacked on the grounds of dishonest answers by a juror on voir dire.

A party seeking an inquiry must first make a sufficient preliminary showing of misconduct that would warrant reversal for a hearing to be held. At the hearing the jury verdict will be set aside if there is a reasonable possibility that such influence or information affected the verdict. Improper extraneous influence or information will not however result in a new trial if it is apparent that no prejudice resulted. A preliminary showing of reversible misconduct gives rise to a presumption of prejudice placing the burden of proof on the victorious party to show harmlessness, at least in some cases. The court should not decide this question ex parte but rather should determine the circumstances, the impact thereof upon the juror, and whether or not it was prejudicial, in a hearing with all interested parties permitted to participate. While the juror may testify describing the extraneous influence or information, the juror may not testify about its impact.

Testimony of a juror may also be admitted in support of the verdict to rebut a charge of extraneous influence or information.

Rule 606(b) does not prohibit inquiry by the trial judge to ascertain that the verdict delivered was the verdict actually agreed upon, or inquiry otherwise designed to confirm or clarify the verdict.

## § 606.3   Competency and Propriety of Lawyer for a Party as Witness at Trial

Rule 601 confirms that a lawyer for a party is not as such incompetent to testify. Nevertheless, the court has wide discretion to refuse to permit a lawyer to testify in favor of his client. Discretion will often be exercised to prevent such testimony where other sources of evidence as to the fact of consequence are available or where the necessity for testimony by the lawyer could have been avoided. Even where no other witness is available and the lawyer is willing to withdraw, discretion will sometimes be exercised in favor of preventing the lawyer from testifying.

The ABA Model Rules of Professional Conduct, Rule 3.7, Lawyer as Witness, enacted in 1983 provides as follows:

(a) A lawyer shall not act as advocate at a trial in which the lawyer is likely to be a necessary witness except where:

(1) the testimony relates to an uncontested issue;

(2) the testimony relates to the nature and value of legal services rendered in the case; or

(3) disqualification of the lawyer would work substantial hardship on the client.

(b) A lawyer may act as advocate in a trial in which another lawyer in the lawyer's firm is likely to be called as a witness unless precluded from doing so by Rule 1.7 or Rule 1.9.

## Rule 607.

## WHO MAY IMPEACH

**The credibility of a witness may be attacked by any party, including the party calling the witness.**

## § 607.1　Impeachment: Components of Credibility

Since circumstantial evidence bearing on the credibility of a witness tends to make the existence of a fact of consequence in the determination of the action more or less probable than without such evidence, circumstantial evidence bearing on the credibility of a witness is relevant, Rule 401. The credibility of any witness may be attacked by any party, including the party calling the witness, Rule 607. The common law voucher rule which traditionally served to prohibit a party from impeaching his own witness is abandoned as based upon false premises. The credibility of a witness may not be bolstered in the absence of an attack.

Credibility is dependent upon the willingness of the witness to tell the truth and upon his ability to do so. His ability to tell the truth as to an event of which he purports to possess personal knowledge is the product in turn of his physical and mental capacity, actuality of employment of such capacity to perceive, record, and recollect in the matter at hand, and his ability to narrate. Impeachment of a witness may be directed to one or more components of credibility. Thus the objective or objectives being sought in any given situation may be to draw into question the accuracy of the witness' perception, recordation, recollection, narration or sincerity. With respect to capacity and actuality of perception, recordation, recollection and narration, discrediting may often be accomplished by the simple means of a leading question. For example, a witness may be asked if it wasn't nighttime when the event occurred or whether he was over 400 feet away at the time. Where the attack is upon sincerity, since a simple leading question will tend to be argumentative, resort to a specific mode of impeachment is generally required, such as a prior conviction or prior inconsistent statement. Of course with respect to certain modes of impeachment, particularly contradiction and prior inconsistent statements, the attack also extends to personal knowledge. To illustrate, if the witness denies being 400 feet away asserting instead that he was only 20 feet from the event, a prior inconsistent statement that he was 400 feet away constitutes an attack not only upon sincerity but also upon perception, recordation and recollection.

In assessing the credibility of a witness, the trier of fact looks not only to the content of the witness' testimony on direct and his answers to questions asked on cross-examination, the trier of fact also assesses the demeanor of the witness throughout.

The modes of impeachment potentially permissible depending upon the circumstances are (1) reputation for truth and veracity, Rule 608(a), (2) prior acts of misconduct probative of untruthfulness, Rule 608(b), (3) prior convictions, Rule 609, (4) partiality, i.e., interest, bias, corruption or coercion, (5) contradiction by other evidence including conduct of the witness himself, and (6) self-contradiction with one's own prior inconsistent statement, Rules 801(d)(1)(A) and 613. Impeachment by reference to matters of religion is never allowed, Rule 610.

The accused in a criminal case by taking the stand in his own behalf becomes a witness and subject to impeachment as to his credibility, although his character otherwise is not placed in issue.

Matters brought out on cross-examination attacking credibility of a witness are generally a proper subject for rehabilitation upon redirect examination. However in the

interest of avoiding excessive collateral issues certain
limitations upon rebutting attacks upon witnesses are
recognized.

## § 607.2   Contradiction: Collateral and Non–Collateral Matters; Good Faith Basis

On cross-examination of a witness, every permissible
type of impeachment may be employed for cross-examination has as one of its purposes the testing of the
credibility of the witness. The use of extrinsic evidence to
contradict is more restricted due to considerations of
confusion of the issues, misleading the jury, undue consumption of time, and unfair prejudice raised by the
introduction of so-called collateral matters. If a matter is
considered collateral, the testimony of the witness on
direct or cross-examination stands the cross-examiner
must take the witness' answer; extrinsic evidence, i.e.,
evidence offered other than through the witness himself,
in contradiction is not permitted. If the matter is not
collateral, extrinsic evidence may be introduced disputing
the witness' testimony on direct examination or denial of
truth of the facts asserted in a question propounded on
cross-examination.

Evidence offered for the purpose of contradiction or
self contradiction such as a prior inconsistent statement
is non-collateral if the subject matter of the evidence is
relevant in the litigation to establish a fact of consequence, i.e., relevant for a purpose other than mere
contradiction of the in-court testimony of the witness—
the subject matter itself tends to directly or circumstantially establish a fact of consequence. In addition, matters bearing directly upon the credibility of the witness
in a manner other than merely through contradiction or
self-contradiction, such as (1) bias, interest, corruption,

or coercion, (2) alcohol or drug use, (3) deficient mental capacity and (4) want of capacity, opportunity, or absence of actual acquisition and retention of personal knowledge are non-collateral and may be contradicted by other evidence. Impeachment of a witness' character for truthfulness by means of a prior conviction is also non-collateral, Rule 609. However, impeachment of a witness' character for truthfulness by means of specific instances of conduct not resulting in a conviction is collateral, Rule 608(b)(1). Similarly, employment of a specific instance of conduct on cross-examination to impeach reputation or opinion testimony as to a pertinent character trait of the principal witness is treated as a collateral matter, Rules 405(a) and 608(b)(2). Treatment of specific instances of conduct offered to impeach by Rules 405(a) and 608(b) as collateral is based upon an assessment of the lack of probative value of extrinsic proof contradicting the denial given by the witness upon the credibility of the witness in comparison to the trial concerns enumerated in Rule 403. Finally, a third category of non-collateral creating a test of necessity exists. A witness may be contradicted as to a part of his testimony where as a matter of human experience he would not be mistaken if the thrust of his testimony was true. These categories were developed at common law to permit introduction of extrinsic evidence relating to the credibility of a witness as now mandated by Rule 403—where the probative value of the evidence is not substantially outweighed by trial concerns including the danger of unfair prejudice. However extrinsic evidence meeting the foregoing test of non-collateral may nevertheless be excluded if in the particular instance at hand the dangers specified in Rule 403 predominate. Thus extrinsic evidence being non-collateral is a necessary but not sufficient condition for admissibility.

Consider the following illustration. Bob is called to testify that the color of the traffic light facing Apple Street was red at the time of an automobile accident he witnessed at the corner of Apple and Main. On direct examination, Bob testifies that he was proceeding east on Apple Street heading toward the Piagano's Pizza Restaurant which was located on the corner of Apple and Peach. On cross-examination counsel asks, "Isn't it true that Piagano's Pizza Restaurant is located on Apple three blocks east of Peach at Maple?" Although this question is permissible as potentially affecting the jury's assessment of Bob's power of recollection and concern for detail, if Bob continues to maintain that the restaurant is on Peach Street, extrinsic evidence may not be offered during the cross-examiner's case in chief as to the location of the restaurant. The matter is collateral, because the location of the restaurant is not relevant in the litigation other than to contradict the testimony of the witness. Even if Bob denied on cross-examination making a prior statement in which he allegedly said that the restaurant was on Apple and Maple, extrinsic evidence establishing the prior statement would be inadmissible because the matter remains collateral. On the other hand, the color of the traffic light is non-collateral, i.e., the color of the traffic light is otherwise relevant in the case. Thus contradictory evidence that the light facing Apple Street was green is admissible. Similarly, if Bob denies on cross-examination having previously stated that the traffic light was green, extrinsic evidence establishing Bob's prior inconsistent statement not only may but must be introduced.

Assuming Bob is then asked on cross-examination if he was wearing his glasses while driving, a yes answer may be contradicted by extrinsic evidence that his only pair of glasses was being repaired at the time of the accident. Evidence disputing the acquisition of personal knowledge by the witness of facts relevant in the case is non-collateral. Similarly, if Bob denied on cross-examination that his wife was related to the plaintiff, extrinsic evidence of such a fact would be admissible. Evidence of partiality of the witness is non-collateral. Extrinsic evidence offered to establish bias, interest, corruption, or coercion of the witness may be admitted following denial by the witness of a fact giving rise to such an inference when put to the witness on cross-examination. A prior inconsistent statement with respect to a subject matter bearing upon acquisition of personal knowledge, for example, a statement by Bob that he was not wearing his glasses, or bearing upon bias, interest, corruption, or coercion, for example, a statement by Bob that his wife is related to the plaintiff, relates to a non-collateral matter; extrinsic evidence is permitted but not required. Finally, restructuring the initial illustration, if Piagano's Pizza Restaurant is ·in fact located on Birch Street, and its location on Birch in relation to Bob's location prior to leaving for the restaurant would naturally place Bob on Main, and not Apple, as he approached the intersection, extrinsic evidence of the location of the restaurant would be admissible on the ground that error as to the location of the restaurant brings into question the trustworthiness of Bob's entire testimony. Bob may have seen the light facing Main, and not the light facing Apple.

Extrinsic evidence concerning a collateral matter may be admitted under the doctrine of "door opening." Admissibility of evidence under the notion of "door opening" tends to arise where the government seeks to introduce evidence on rebuttal to contradict specific factual assertions raised during the direct examination of the criminal defendant.

A good faith basis on the part of examining counsel as to the truth of the matter contained in questions propounded to a witness on cross-examination is required. Innuendoes and insinuations of inadmissible or nonexistent matters are improper. Thus counsel on cross-examination may not ask Bob, "Isn't it true that Piagano's is located on Birch?" without having a reasonable basis in fact for believing that Piagano's is in fact on Birch and not Apple. Nor may counsel on cross-examination inquire of Bob whether his wife was related to the plaintiff absent a good faith basis. Note that the requirement of a good faith basis applies only when the cross-examiner is effectively asserting in the form of a question the truth of a factual statement included within the question. If the cross-examiner is merely inquiring whether something is or is not true, a good faith basis is not required. Thus the question, "Your glasses were being repaired at the time of the accident, weren't they?" requires a good faith basis, while the question, "Were you wearing your glasses at the time of the accident?" does not. The principle of a good faith basis applies in the laying of a foundation for impeachment by prior inconsistent statement. Moreover the examining party must have the intent and ability to introduce extrinsic evidence establishing the making of the statement as to a non-collateral matter in the event the making of the statement is not admitted by the witness.

## § 607.3 Impeachment of a Party's Own Witness

Pursuant to the common law's voucher rule, a party could not impeach a witness whom he had called. After prolonged and vigorous attack by commentators it became generally recognized that the traditional rationale supporting the voucher rule did not withstand analysis and that a party should generally be able to attack the credibility of his own witness. However, it was also recognized that a party should not be able to place a prior statement of his witness before the jury under the mere guise of impeachment, and that a jury, in spite of a limiting instruction, Rule 105, would likely give substantive effect to prior inconsistent statements employed by a party to impeach his own witness.

Prior to the adoption of the Federal Rules of Evidence, federal courts permitted impeachment of a party's own witness by prior inconsistent statements only where the witness' testimony both surprised and affirmatively damaged the calling party. The requirement of surprise and affirmative damage permitted a party to impeach his own witness when truly necessary. At the same time, the requirement prevented a party from calling a witness solely to place a substantively inadmissible prior inconsistent statement before the jury in the hope that the jury would disregard a limiting instruction and consider the statement as substantive evidence.

The Federal Rules of Evidence, as originally proposed, would have eliminated any problem of a party's impeachment of his own witness by prior inconsistent statements. Proposed Rule 801(d)(1)(A) provided that all prior statements inconsistent with testimony given by a witness during trial were defined as not hearsay. Accordingly, Proposed Rule 607 provided only that "[t]he credibility of a witness may be attacked by any party, including the party calling him." Since courts were to admit all prior inconsistent statements as substantive evidence, there was no need for a requirement of surprise and affirmative damage to prevent a calling party from using impeachment as a technique to place before the jury statements that were not substantively admissible. However Rule 801(d)(1)(A) as enacted by Congress limits prior inconsistent statements denominated as not hearsay to those "given under oath subject to the penalty of perjury at a trial, hearing, or other proceeding, or in a deposition." This restriction as to prior inconsistent statements that are admissible as substantive evidence without any corresponding restriction of the right of a calling party under Rule 607 to impeach his own witness again raises the problem of the calling party's potential misuse of impeachment by prior inconsistent statement.

Two basic resolutions of this dilemma were offered, neither of which was subsequently adopted by the courts. It was asserted that federal courts should meet the problem by continuing to require surprise and affirmative damage as a prerequisite for a party to impeach his own witness with a nonsubstantively admissible prior inconsistent statement. The requirement of surprise and damage does not depend on the voucher rule, which the Advisory Committee rejected in drafting Rule 607, but has the independent justification that it prevents improper use of prior inconsistent statements under the guise of impeachment. Furthermore Congress' unwillingness to permit the admission of all prior inconsistent statements as substantive evidence was motivated in part by a concern that juries might convict criminal defendants on the basis of unreliable prior inconsistent statements. Thus reading Rule 607 in the light of Rule 801(d)(1)(A) and reimposing the requirement of surprise and affirmative damage especially in criminal cases when the Government seeks to impeach its own witness—would fur-

ther Congressional purpose in amending Rule
801(d)(1)(A).

With respect to impeachment of a party's own witness
with a prior inconsistent statement not substantively
admissible, in the absence of both surprise and affirmative damage, determined separately with respect to each
portion of the witness' testimony, impeachment of one's
own witness is inappropriate. If the witness does not give
affirmatively damaging testimony, i.e., testimony of positive aid to the adversary, the party simply does not need
to attack his credibility. If the witness' testimony does
not surprise the party, the litigant should not be permitted to impeach his testimony by placing before the jury
the witness' prior statement because he could have re-
frained from eliciting the statement he seeks to impeach.
The requirement of surprise would prevent the party
from consciously introducing affirmatively damaging testimony under the only circumstances in which he would
do so when the potential effect on the jury of the prior
inconsistent statement outweighs the affirmatively damaging effect of the elicited testimony.

Weinstein's Evidence ¶ 607–18 (1995) recognized the
problem created by the amendment of Rule 801(d)(1)(A)
without a corresponding change in Rule 607, but suggested a different approach to its resolution:

   Instead of placing so much emphasis on the motive of
   the profferer, an approach more consistent with the
   underlying policy of the federal rules of evidence would
   be to analyse the problem in terms of Rule 403 is the
   probative value of the impeachment evidence outweighed by its prejudicial impact?

It is suggested that in practice the balancing test of Rule 403 is inferior to the simple surprise and affirmative damage requirement for several reasons. Initially it is questionable in light of the clear language of Rule 607 whether a court would even consider balancing pursuant to Rule 403. Moreover ad hoc balancing requires that the court under the pressures of a trial situation sort out and weigh the probative value of evidence upon witness credibility against the possibility that it will confuse the issues or mislead the jury. Accordingly balancing is unlikely to produce uniform or predictable results. In addition two of the key factors suggested by Weinstein's Evidence, probative value and prejudicial impact, appear to vary directly: the more probative a prior statement is of credibility, the greater the unfair prejudice caused by the jury considering the inconsistent statement as substantive evidence; the less probative of credibility, the less danger of unfair prejudice likely to arise from substantive consideration. Finally balancing pursuant to Rule 403 is likely to be time-consuming and of limited effectiveness in screening the jury from potentially prejudicial prior statements. As Weinstein's Evidence envisions the process, the court would make its Rule 403 ruling only after the witness had been confronted with his alleged prior statement in the presence of the jury. It is not clear that such procedures would adequately prevent prejudice, since the jury would become aware of the prior inconsistent statement before the court initiated its inquiry. Moreover the court would most likely find, given the availability of a limiting instruction, that the probative value of the impeaching evidence upon credibility outweighed any potential prejudice. In addition, impeachment of a witness who testifies to a matter which merely disappoints the calling party will frequently be permitted by a trial judge impressed by the apparent reliability of the prior inconsistent statement and sympathetic to the plight of the embarrassed examiner. Such impeachment will frequently be permitted in spite of the fact that no legitimate purpose is served by an attack upon the credibility of a witness called by the party in the absence of affirmative damage. Thus, while Weinstein's Evidence asserts, "In most cases, of course, the Rule 403 analysis and the surprise-damage requirements will lead to the same result," this assertion is certainly questionable.

Although no conclusive pattern has developed in the cases, not surprisingly, on balance, a literal interpretation of Rule 607, with one important caveat, predominates over either surprise and affirmative damage or Rule 403 balancing. The caveat is that impeachment of a party's own witness by means of a prior statement may not be employed as a "mere subterfuge" or for the "*primary* purpose of placing before the jury substantive evidence which is not otherwise admissible" when the party is aware prior to calling the witness that the witness will not testify consistent with the witness' prior statement. Application of the "mere subterfuge" or "*primary* purpose" caveat focuses upon the content of the witness' testimony as a whole. Thus if the witness' testimony is important in establishing any fact of consequence significant in the context of the litigation, the witness may be impeached as to any other matter testified to by means of a prior inconsistent statement, including any matter the witness now simply claims not to recall. Contrast the requirements of surprise and affirmative damage which focus upon each segment of the witness' testimony rather than the witness' testimony taken as a whole.

A party taking a deposition is not by virtue of the taking precluded from impeaching the deponent. Since prior inconsistent statements made at a deposition are substantively admissible pursuant to Rule 801(d)(1)(A), the foregoing problem does not arise with respect to depositions.

Under Rule 607, a party's own witness may be impeached by means other than prior inconsistent statements to the same extent as a witness called by an adversary. Protection against abuse is afforded by both Rules 403 and 611(a). A witness whose testimony is known in advance to be adverse may not be called for the sole purpose of attacking the witness' credibility.

## § 607.4 Personal Knowledge: Mental Capacity; Expert Testimony

The capacity and actuality of a witness' perception, his ability to record and remember sense impressions, and his ability to comprehend questions and narrate are relevant to an assessment of the weight to be given a witness' testimony. Each of these areas is a proper subject of cross-examination. None of these areas are considered collateral, extrinsic evidence is permissible.

The mental capacity of a witness is thus a proper subject of cross-examination. With respect to a witness possessing minimum credibility and thus competence to testify, an adversary is entitled to explore on cross-examination the effect that age, retardation, injury, or mental illness has had on the witness' ability to observe, record, recollect, and recount, as well as his ability to understand the duty to tell the truth. Such inquiry is non-collateral; extrinsic evidence may be introduced. Whether psychiatric testimony offered by a party relating to the credibility of a witness is admissible rests in the discretion of the court. Similarly whether the court will order a psychiatric examination of the witness for the purpose of permitting full exploration of the credibility of the witness also rests in the court's discretion.

## § 607.5  Alcohol or Drug Use as Affecting Credibility

Use of drugs at the time of the event related by a witness or at the time of the giving of his testimony is a proper subject of cross-examination. Drunkenness at the time of the event related or at the time of testimony may also be explored on cross-examination. Both drugs and alcohol may affect a witness' ability to perceive, record, recollect and narrate, i.e., personal knowledge. Neither drug use nor drunkenness is collateral; the cross-examiner is not foreclosed by a denial of the witness and may prove the condition in question by other witnesses.

With respect to the question of establishment of narcotic addiction as relevant in assessing personal knowledge, the cases are in disagreement. While earlier cases prohibit such evidence, there is now some support for permitting the introduction of evidence of narcotic addiction as bearing on the acquisition of personal knowledge. Pursuant to Rule 401, evidence of drug addiction possesses at least the minimum probative value necessary to establish relevancy with or without the aid of an expert witness to interpret the effect of narcotic addiction on the particular witness. However, introduction of such evidence is of course subject to exclusion under Rule 403 whenever unfair prejudice or misleading of the jury is likely to result; a majority of cases seem to prohibit introduction. Whether evidence has been offered, including but not limited to expert witness testimony, as to the effect narcotic addiction has had on the particular witness' ability to perceive, record, recollect, narrate and understand the obligation to testify truthfully will be an important factor in assessing the probative value of such evidence in light of the trial concerns recognized in Rule 403.

Proof of chronic alcoholism as affecting personal knowledge has been generally excluded. Several commentators have however argued in favor of admissibility.

Neither drug or alcohol use at a relevant time nor chronic alcoholism or drug addiction is admissible for the inference that the witness is therefore more likely to lie.

## § 607.6 Name, Occupation and Residence of the Witness

The occupation and related background of the witness are regarded as having value in determining the credit to be given his testimony and may be inquired into as a matter of right on both direct and cross-examination. It is also proper to elicit on direct or cross-examination a witness' place of residence. In fact in both Alford v. United States (S.Ct.1931) and Smith v. Illinois (S.Ct. 1968), the Supreme Court indicated that defense counsel has the right to obtain on cross-examination the place of residence of all prosecution witnesses. Nevertheless, where a serious question has been raised as to the safety of the witness if his address is disclosed, several courts have required submission by the government of the relevant information to the district judge *in camera* for him to decide whether disclosure would present a real problem. Where the witness has recently changed residence for his protection, one possible solution is to require disclosure solely of the witness' former residence and

other facts relating to the witness' background. Similarly
while the actual name used by a witness testifying for
the prosecution at the relevant time must be disclosed,
the court in its discretion may withhold the name currently used by the witness in the interest of the witness'
safety.

## § 607.7 Untrustworthy Partiality: Interest, Bias, Corruption, or Coercion; Foundation

Matters which may reasonably be expected to color the
testimony of a witness or cause him to testify falsely are
proper subjects of inquiry of any witness by any party.
Emotions likely to be created under the influence of such
matters, referred to collectively by 3A Wigmore, Evidence
§ 945 at 782 (Chadbourn rev.1970) as untrustworthy
partiality, consist of:

> Bias, in common acceptance, covers all varieties of
> hostility or prejudice against the opponent personally
> or of favor to the proponent personally.

> Interest signifies the specific inclination which is apt
> to be produced by the relation between the witness and
> the cause at issue in the litigation.

> Corruption is here to be understood as the conscious
> false intent which is inferrible from giving or taking a
> bribe or from expressions of a general unscrupulous-
> ness for the case in hand.

In order to complete the definition of partiality, the
inclusion of a fourth category is suggested: coercion,
intended to include any form of mental, emotional, or
physical duress or compulsion that overcomes a witness'
duty to tell the truth.

Partiality may be established by evidence first relating to the circumstances of the witness' situation, making it "a priori" probable that he has some partiality of emotion for one party's cause; or second relating to the conduct or statements of the witness himself, indicating the presence of such partiality, the inference here being from the expression of the feeling to the feeling itself.

The variety of matters potentially giving rise to untrustworthy partiality is almost infinite. Such matters include love, hate, fear, family relationship, sexual preference, financial interest in outcome, business relationship, employment, membership in an organization, shared beliefs, payment by a party such as that made to an expert witness, and in criminal matters the fact that the witness has not been charged with a crime, been granted immunity or is currently awaiting sentence. The commission of prior acts of misconduct may also give rise to an inference of untrustworthy partiality. A good faith basis as to the truth of the matter contained in the question seeking to establish partiality is required. The cross-examiner is not limited to questioning the witness concerning the circumstances of the witness' situation, his conduct and his feelings about a party, but may also inquire into statements by the witness concerning matters relating to possible untrustworthy partiality.

In criminal proceedings the defendant has a constitutional right to cross-examine a witness concerning any matter which goes to explain, modify, or discredit what he said on direct examination. Moreover, though the scope of such cross-examination is generally within the trial court's discretion, wide latitude must be afforded the defendant in cross-examination for the purpose of establishing partiality or otherwise challenging the credibility of a government witness. Where charges are dropped in exchange for testimony, where the witness is a coindictee or has unrelated charges pending, is a paid informer, has been granted immunity, has been promised or expects leniency, is awaiting sentence, is being held in protective custody, has been given special treatment at government expense, or has entered into a plea agreement, amongst others, foreclosure of the right to inquire may constitute reversible error. On the other hand, the right to cross-examination is not without its limitations.

Matters in this area are not considered collateral within the rule precluding contradiction on collateral matters. Hence the answers are not conclusive on the cross-examiner; they may but need not be contradicted by other testimony. Of course both the scope of cross-examination and the introduction of extrinsic evidence are subject to judicial discretion with respect to the trial concerns expressed in Rule 403 and the protection of the witness from harassment or undue embarrassment, Rule 611(a)(3). Extrinsic evidence is also admissible under appropriate circumstances to rebut an inference of partiality. Similarly, considerations underlying Rule 403 may demand that the party attacking the witness introduce the extrinsic proof in the face of the witness' denials.

Reasoning by analogy from Rule 613(b), extrinsic evidence of a statement of a witness evidencing partiality may be introduced provided the witness is afforded at some time an opportunity to deny or explain. The same arguments suggesting that under normal circumstances the witness be asked concerning the alleged prior inconsistent statement initially on cross-examination are equally applicable to alleged prior statements evidencing partiality. Thus while extrinsic evidence of the conduct or status of a witness evidencing partiality is not subject to the formal requirement of an opportunity on cross-examination to deny or explain, the practice of confronting the witness on cross-examination with such conduct or status should nevertheless be encouraged.

## § 607.8    Contradiction by Other Evidence

The principle is recognized that a witness may be contradicted by evidence introduced by any party, Rule 607. McCormick, Evidence § 45 at 168–69 (5th ed.1999) describes contradiction by other evidence including evidence of conduct of the witness as follows:

Statements are elicited from Witness One, who has testified to a material story of an accident, crime, or other matters, to the effect that at the time he witnessed these matters the day was windy and cold and he, the witness, was wearing his green sweater. Let us suppose these latter statements about the day and the sweater to be "disproved." This may happen in several ways. Witness One on direct or cross-examination may acknowledge that he was in error. Or judicial notice may be taken that at the time and place it could not have been cold and windy, e.g., in Tucson in July. But commonly disproof or "contradiction" is attempted by calling Witness Two to testify to the contrary, i.e., that the day was warm and Witness One was in his shirt-sleeves.

The effect upon the credibility of the witness is that if it is assumed that Witness Two's testimony is correct, then it may be inferred that Witness One has made either an honest mistake or has falsified with respect to a particular fact. It also tends to follow that if Witness One fabricated or is mistaken as to a particular fact, he may have done likewise with respect to other points or all of his testimony. However given the fact that a witness possibly mistaken or fabricating as to the weather or what he was wearing may still be testifying correctly as to the more important aspects of his testimony, considerations expressed in Rule 403 result in the exclusion of extrinsic evidence of contradiction where the fact to be contradicted is "collateral."

The introduction of evidence offered to contradict upon a collateral matter is sometimes admitted under the doctrine of "door opening." Admissibility of evidence under the concept of "door opening" tends most frequently to arise where the government seeks to introduce evidence on rebuttal to contradict specific factual assertions raised during the direct examination of the criminal defendant.

## Rule 608.

## EVIDENCE OF CHARACTER AND CONDUCT OF WITNESS

**(a) Opinion and Reputation Evidence of Character. The credibility of a witness may be attacked or supported by evidence in the form of opinion or reputation, but subject to these limitations: (1) the evidence may refer only to character for truthfulness or untruthfulness, and (2) evidence of truthful character is admissible only after the character of the witness for truthfulness has been attacked by opinion or reputation evidence or otherwise.**

**(b) Specific Instances of Conduct. Specific instances of the conduct of a witness, for the pur-**

pose of attacking or supporting the witness' character for truthfulness, other than conviction of crime as provided in rule 609, may not be proved by extrinsic evidence. They may, however, in the discretion of the court, if probative of truthfulness or untruthfulness, be inquired into on cross-examination of the witness (1) concerning the witness' character for truthfulness or untruthfulness or (2) concerning the character for truthfulness or untruthfulness of another witness as to which character the witness being cross-examined has testified.

The giving of testimony, whether by an accused or by any other witness, does not operate as a waiver of the accused's or the witness' privilege against self-incrimination when examined with respect to matters that relate only to character for truthfulness.

## § 608.1  Character of Witness for Truthfulness or Untruthfulness: An Overview

Testimony can scarcely be considered apart from the individual who gives it. Consequently the character of the witness is relevant under the definition of relevancy, Rule 401, and a proper area for exploration. However the likelihood of misleading, confusion, unfair prejudice, and undue consumption of time expressed in Rule 403, plus the policy consideration that excessive scrutiny may increase the reluctance of people to come forward and testify, all have resulted in rather stringent limitations upon inquiry into the character of the witness. Rule 404(a) states the general proposition that character evidence is not admissible for the purpose of proving that a person acted in conformity therewith. Rule 404(a) is subject to several exceptions, one of which, Rule

404(a)(3), is character evidence bearing upon the credibility of a witness for truthfulness or untruthfulness as specified in Rules 607, 608 and 609.

The underlying rationale of Rule 608 is that the character of an individual for truthfulness or untruthfulness makes it more or less likely that the individual will testify truthfully. Under Rule 608(a)(1), the character of a witness for truthfulness or untruthfulness may be attacked or supported by evidence in the form of reputation or opinion. Evidence in the form of reputation or opinion in support of the character of a witness for truthfulness is permitted only if the character of the witness for truthfulness has been attacked by opinion or reputation evidence or otherwise, Rule 608(a)(2).

Specific instances of conduct, other than conviction for a crime, may in the discretion of the court, if probative of truthfulness or untruthfulness, be inquired into on cross-examination of the witness (1) concerning his character for truthfulness or untruthfulness, or (2) concerning the character for truthfulness or untruthfulness of another witness as to which character the witness being cross-examined has testified, Rule 608(b). The cross-examiner must possess a good faith basis for his inquiry. Other than conviction for a crime as provided in Rule 609, specific instances of conduct when offered for the purpose of attacking or supporting the character of a witness for truthfulness may not, however, be established by extrinsic evidence, Rule 608(b). The matter is collateral; the cross-examiner must take the answer provided by the witness. Prior convictions of any witness may be employed for purposes of impeachment in accordance with Rule 609.

The distinction between a criminal defendant who takes the stand and thus becomes subject as a witness to an attack upon his credibility, and an accused who introduces evidence of a pertinent trait of his character, Rule 404(a)(1), with or without himself testifying must be borne in mind.

When the criminal defendant or any other person testifies, thereby making an assessment of credibility relevant, it does not operate as a waiver of his privilege against self-incrimination when examined with respect to matters that relate only to character for truthfulness, Rule 608.

Rule 608 relates solely to the introduction of opinion or reputation testimony and specific instances of conduct offered as probative of the witness' character for truthfulness or untruthfulness. Admissibility of specific acts of misconduct or opinion or reputation testimony offered for any other purpose lies outside the scope of Rule 608.

## § 608.2 Rule 608(a): Opinion or Reputation Testimony Relating to Truthfulness; When Permitted

The credibility of any witness, including the accused once he takes the stand, may be attacked by evidence in the form of opinion or reputation testimony as to the character of the witness for truthfulness, Rule 608(a)(1). If the witness' character for truthfulness has been attacked by means of opinion or reputation testimony, his character for truthfulness may then be supported but only in the form of opinion or reputation testimony, Rule 608(a)(2); specific instances of conduct in support of the witness' character for truthfulness remain inadmissible. Moreover as also provided in Rule 608(a)(2), if the character of the witness for truthfulness has been attacked "otherwise" than by opinion or reputation testimony, opinion or reputation testimony in support becomes admissible. Impeachment of the witness by means of a prior conviction, Rule 609, prior acts of misconduct, Rule 608(b)(1), or a showing of coercion or corruption are attacks on character and thus make opinion or reputation testimony admissible in rebuttal. However a showing of interest or bias does not constitute a sufficient attack upon character to permit introduction of evidence in support of the character of the witness for truthfulness.

Supporting evidence in the form of opinion or reputation testimony for truthful character may also be admissible in situations where the witness has had his character for truthfulness assaulted upon cross-examination or by means of self-contradiction. With respect to cross-examination, the trial court must initially determine whether the net effect of the cross-examination constitutes a sustained direct attack on the witness' character for truthfulness. This is often a difficult decision. Even if the court finds that a sustained direct attack has occurred, whether opinion and reputation testimony for truthfulness becomes admissible is disputed. Where the witness is impeached by a prior inconsistent statement, a court in its discretion may allow subsequent proof of opinion or reputation for truthfulness where the impeachment raises an inference impinging truthfulness of the witness but not where such impeachment merely charges lack of memory or mistake. While the Advisory Committee's Note points out that whether contradiction constitutes a sufficient attack upon the character of the witness depends upon the circumstances, it has generally been held that mere contradiction by other evidence does not suffice.

Opinion and reputation testimony of truthfulness is not admissible in the first instance; it is admissible only after the character of the witness for truthfulness has been attacked by opinion or reputation testimony or otherwise.

### § 608.3   Rule 608(b): Opinion or Reputation Testimony Relating to Truthfulness; Basis and Content

With respect to reputation testimony, the proper procedure is to ask the character witness whether he knows the general reputation of the principal witness for truth and veracity in the neighborhood in which the latter lives, or among those with whom the person works, attends school or socializes. The testimony must relate to reputation of the witness at or near the time of trial. Testimony as to reputation must be based upon the witness having discussed the reputation with others, having heard it discussed by others, or of never having heard it discussed although he would have heard contrary comments had they existed. Upon testifying as to knowledge of the witness' reputation for truthfulness or untruthfulness, the witness may further be asked, "In view of that reputation, would you believe him under oath?"

Opinion testimony of the character witness as to the character for truthfulness or untruthfulness of the principal witness must be rationally based upon the personal knowledge of the character witness. Sufficient personal knowledge to render such an opinion may be acquired as a result of contact with the principal witness in any aspect of the principal witness' life. Only the opinion of the character witness held at or near the time of trial is relevant. A character witness testifying in the form of an opinion may also be asked whether or not he would believe the witness under oath.

## § 608.4 Rule 608(b)(1): Cross–Examination as to Specific Acts of Conduct of the Witness; Extrinsic Evidence

The credibility of any witness, including a reputation or opinion witness, may be attacked upon cross-examination by questioning the witness concerning specific instances of his conduct not leading to a conviction if the court in the exercise of discretion finds that the specific instance is probative of the witness' character for untruthfulness, Rule 608(b)(1). Thus provided the cross-examiner possesses a good faith basis, inquiry on cross-examination may be permitted by the court with respect to the commission of offenses not leading to a conviction as well as acts of misconduct not constituting a crime.

The court must determine whether in its discretion the particular instance is probative of character for untruthfulness and whether under Rule 403 the probative value of the question and answer upon the credibility of the witness is substantially outweighed by the danger of unfair prejudice. Particular instances of conduct satisfying this standard will normally involve dishonesty or false statement as employed in Rule 609(a)(2). In this determination the probable effectiveness of a limiting instruction, Rule 105, is appropriately considered. While the question of "remoteness in time" of specific acts was deleted by Congress as an express requirement, remoteness remains a relevant consideration in assessing the probative value of the evidence in the application of the

Rule 403 balancing test. The court also possesses discretion to preclude such cross-examination under Rule 611(a)(3) to protect witnesses from harassment or undue embarrassment.

A ruling made in response to a motion in limine to permit or prohibit impeachment under Rule 608(b) is advisory only; the trial court is free in the exercise of sound discretion, even if nothing unexpected happens at trial, to alter a previous in limine ruling. A definitive ruling to an objection permitting or prohibiting the impeachment under Rule 608(b)(1), made either at or before trial, preserves a claim of error for appeal, Rule 103(a). A court ruling which is not definitive, however, does not do so. In addition in order to preserve for review a claim of improper impeachment under Rule 608(b), the witness must testify.

Specific instances of conduct probative of character for truthfulness or untruthfulness of the witness on the stand may not be developed under Rule 608(b) upon direct or redirect examination; inquiry on cross-examination only is specified.

Cross-examination as to a specific instance relating to the character for untruthfulness of the particular witness being examined, including the witness who testifies as to the character of the principal witness, should be phrased in terms of the underlying act itself. Thus where the specific act is probative of untruthfulness of the witness being cross-examined, the question should not inquire about rumors, reports, arrests or indictments but rather about the underlying specific act of misconduct itself. The act of misconduct alone is relevant when cross-examining the alleged actor, not whether someone else might think that the witness committed the act. Extrinsic evidence with respect to the specific act of conduct of the witness is not admissible, Rule 608(b). The cross-examiner thus must take the answer given by the witness. Of course, evidence of a specific instance of conduct of the witness may be received when relevant for another purpose such as showing bias, motive, intent, identity, etc., even though such evidence will have an impact on the character of the witness for truthfulness as well.

The giving of testimony, whether by an accused or by any other witness, does not operate as a waiver of his privilege against self-incrimination when examined with respect to matters that relate only to character for truthfulness, Rule 608.

In spite of the text of Rule 608(b)(1), it is suggested that cross-examination of a witness, especially the criminal defendant, with respect to his prior acts of misconduct not leading to a conviction is too inherently prejudicial in light of probative value and thus should rarely if ever be permitted. This aspect of Rule 608(b)(1) is simply a mistake.

## § 608.5  Rule  608(b)(2):  Cross-examination  of Character Witness as to Specific Acts of Conduct of Principal Witness; Extrinsic Evidence

A witness who has testified as to his favorable opinion or the good reputation of the principal witness for truth and veracity can be cross-examined with respect to prior convictions as well as prior acts of misconduct not leading to a conviction of the principal witness if probative of untruthfulness. While it seems to rarely happen, with respect to a witness who testifies as to his unfavorable opinion or the bad reputation of the principal witness for truth and veracity, cross-examination is permitted as to specific instances of conduct of the principal witness probative of truthfulness, Rule 608(b)(2).

When a character witness testifies as to the reputation of the principal witness for truthfulness or untruthfulness, the proper question on cross-examination with respect to specific acts of conduct of the principal witness at common law is "Have you heard?". Where the testimony of the character witness is in the form of an opinion, the proper form of the question at common law in addition to "Have you heard?" is either "Do you know?" or "Are you aware?". The foregoing distinction, while correct in theory, is of such slight practical importance that it could easily be eliminated if elimination has not already been accomplished. The character witness may be asked not only concerning the specific acts of the principal witness probative of truthfulness or untruthfulness, but may be cross-examined concerning familiarity with convictions as well as arrests, rumors, reports, indictments, etc., concerning such acts of the principal witness. Such facts have a natural bearing upon the reputation of the principal witness and the character witness' opinion of the principal witness. Lack of familiarity with such facts is relevant to an assessment of the basis for the character witness' testimony. Familiarity with such matters explores the character witness' standard of "truthfulness" or "untruthfulness." Whatever the form of the question, the cross-examiner must, of course, have a good faith basis supporting his inquiry.

A character witness whether testifying as to the reputation of the principal witness as to truthfulness or untruthfulness, may testify on direct examination and be cross-examined concerning with whom, where and when he actually discussed the reputation of the principal witness. Opinion testimony must be based upon personal knowledge of the principal witness by the character witness; the extent of the relationship with the principal witness is a proper subject of inquiry on cross-examination.

Specific instances of conduct probative of the truthfulness or untruthfulness of the principal witness may not be brought out upon direct or redirect examination; inquiry on cross-examination only is permitted under Rule 608(b)(2). Extrinsic evidence with respect to specific acts of conduct of the principal witness, other than conviction of crime as provided in Rule 609, is not admissible; the cross-examiner must take the witness' answer.

Inquiry on cross-examination of the character witness as to acts of the principal witness probative of truthfulness or untruthfulness not resulting in a conviction is subject to Rule 403. cross-examination will be precluded if the court determines that the probative value of such cross-examination is substantially outweighed by the danger of unfair prejudice. The rather tenuous nature of character testimony as to truth and veracity in the first place, coupled with the inherent risk of unfair prejudice associated with such cross-examination when the principal witness is also a party, militate in favor of the court exercising its discretion in favor of prohibiting inquiry into specific acts. In fact, a blanket prohibition upon cross-examination as to specific acts of the principal witness would be preferable to current Rule 608(b)(2).

## Rule 609.

## IMPEACHMENT BY EVIDENCE OF CONVICTION OF CRIME

(a) General Rule. For the purpose of attacking the credibility of a witness,

(1) evidence that a witness other than an accused has been convicted of a crime shall be admitted, subject to Rule 403, if the crime was punishable by death or imprisonment in excess of one year under the law under which the witness was convicted, and evidence that an accused has been convicted of such a crime shall be admitted if the court determines that the probative value of admitting this evidence outweighs its prejudicial effect to the accused; and

(2) evidence that any witness has been convicted of a crime shall be admitted if it involved dishonesty or false statement, regardless of the punishment.

(b) Time Limit. Evidence of a conviction under this rule is not admissible if a period of more than ten years has elapsed since the date of the conviction or of the release of the witness from the confinement imposed for that conviction, whichever is the later date, unless the court determines, in the interests of justice, that the probative value of the conviction supported by specific facts and circumstances substantially outweighs its prejudicial effect. However, evidence of a conviction more than 10 years old as calculated herein, is not admissible unless the proponent gives to the adverse party sufficient advance written notice of intent to use such evidence to provide the adverse party with a fair opportunity to contest the use of such evidence.

(c) **Effect of Pardon, Annulment, or Certificate of Rehabilitation.** Evidence of a conviction is not admissible under this rule if (1) the conviction has been the subject of a pardon, annulment, certificate of rehabilitation, or other equivalent procedure based on a finding of the rehabilitation of the person convicted, and that person has not been convicted of a subsequent crime which was punishable by death or imprisonment in excess of one year, or (2) the conviction has been the subject of a pardon, annulment, or other equivalent procedure based on a finding of innocence.

(d) **Juvenile Adjudications.** Evidence of juvenile adjudications is generally not admissible under this rule. The court may, however, in a criminal case allow evidence of a juvenile adjudication of a witness other than the accused if conviction of the offense would be admissible to attack the credibility of an adult and the court is satisfied that admission in evidence is necessary for a fair determination of the issue of guilt or innocence.

(e) **Pendency of Appeal.** The pendency of an appeal therefrom does not render evidence of a conviction inadmissible. Evidence of the pendency of an appeal is admissible.

## § 609.1 Impeachment by Evidence of Conviction of a Crime: The Dilemma

The extent to which a witness and in particular the criminal defendant may be impeached by evidence that he has been convicted of a crime has long been extremely controversial. Rule 609 engendered more debate in Congress than any other single rule of evidence, and the final result was a conference compromise settling the differences between the House and Senate versions. The focus of the dispute was whether to confine admissibility to convictions for a crime believed to be directly relevant to veracity, the so-called crimen falsi, whether to admit proof of conviction for serious crimes of whatever nature, the latter being the orthodox rule, or whether to introduce a discretionary balancing test with respect to either or both of the foregoing approaches.

Employment of a prior conviction to impeach is premised upon the assumption that a person with a criminal record has a bad general character, evidenced by his willingness to disobey the law, and that his bad general character would lead him to disregard his oath to testify truthfully. According to Justice Holmes speaking for the Supreme Judicial Court of Massachusetts in Gertz v. Fitchburg R.R. Co. (1884):

> [W]hen it is proved that a witness has been convicted of a crime the only ground for disbelieving him which such proof affords is the general readiness to do evil which the conviction may be supposed to show. It is from that general disposition alone that the jury is asked to infer a readiness to lie in a particular case, and thence that he has lied in fact. The evidence has no tendency to prove that he was mistaken, but only that he has perjured himself, and it reaches that conclusion solely through the general proposition that he is a bad character and unworthy of credit.

This rationale has been asserted to be tenuous, particularly where the conviction was for a crime of violence.

Evidence of the prior conviction is admissible under Rule 609 only to impeach the witness' character for truthfulness and not as evidence bearing on the witness' character for being law abiding. Exclusion of evidence of prior crimes of the defendant in relation to the character trait of being law abiding is a specific instance of the broader prohibition against a party offering evidence of a person's character for the purpose of proving that he acted in conformity therewith on a particular occasion, Rule 404. The rationale for exclusion of evidence of prior convictions to prove character has been stated succinctly by the Supreme Court in Michelson v. United States (S.Ct.1948):

> [T]he inquiry is not rejected because character is irrelevant; on the contrary, it is said to weigh too much with the jury and to so overpersuade them as to prejudge one with a bad general record and deny him a fair opportunity to defend against a particular charge.

The trier of fact is thus required to determine a defendant's guilt or innocence of the crime charged solely on the basis of evidence relevant to that particular crime. A conviction may not, at least in theory, be based upon the trier of fact's belief that the defendant is a person of bad character.

An accused nevertheless faces a serious dilemma whenever a prior conviction may be employed for the purpose of impeachment. If he testifies and is impeached with the prior conviction, he risks conviction upon the current charge simply because the jury thinks he is a bad man. This bad man inference takes two forms. First, the trier of fact may infer that since he previously committed a crime, he must have also committed the crime for which on trial. The more similar the nature of the prior offense disclosed to the jury is to the crime charged, the stronger the natural but impermissible inference likely to be drawn by the jury that if the defendant did it before he probably did it this time. Second, the trier of fact may reason that since the defendant has been convicted of an offense, he probably has committed other offenses for which he has never been apprehended. Based on this reasoning, the trier of fact will be more ready to convict for the offense at hand, being less concerned with convicting a "truly innocent man." Although the jury is instructed that they are to consider the evidence of a prior conviction solely in determining the credibility of the defendant as a witness and not as evidence of guilt of the crime for which the defendant is on trial, Rule 105, it is rarely seriously asserted that the trier of fact is fully capable much less interested in making such a distinction. On the other hand, if the defendant chooses to remain silent, the jury may conclude that he is guilty despite instructions that no inference is to be drawn against him by reason of his failure to testify.

On direct examination or gratuitously in the course of cross-examination, the witness may make representations regarding the existence or nature of prior convictions. In either event, prior convictions of the witness may become admissible as rebuttal evidence.

Rule 609 deals solely with the admissibility of prior convictions of a witness to impeach credibility by an attack upon character for truthfulness through the establishment of a willingness to disobey the laws of society. Use of a prior conviction for other purposes, such as showing bias or interest, falls outside the scope of Rule 609.

The approach adopted in Rule 609 is treated in the sections which follow.

## § 609.2    Rule 609(a): Impeachment by Evidence of Conviction; The General Rule; An Overview

In both civil and criminal cases, Rule 609(a) provides that evidence of conviction of a crime not remote in time may be employed to attack the credibility of a witness under certain specified circumstances if elicited from the witness on direct or cross-examination, or established by public record or otherwise provided initially that the crime (1) was punishable by death or imprisonment in excess of one year under the law under which the witness was convicted, or (2) involved dishonesty or false statement regardless of the punishment. "Punishable" means the punishment that might have been imposed, not that which was actually imposed; it is the law of the place of conviction rather than that governing a comparable federal crime which is relevant in determining the length of potential imprisonment. Impeachment with any conviction as to which ten years has elapsed since the date of the conviction or the release of the witness from confinement impound for that conviction, whichever is later, is governed by Rule 609(b).

Crimes of dishonesty or false statement, whether felony or misdemeanor, may be employed to impeach regardless of punishment and without satisfaction of a balancing test, Rule 609(a)(2). However with respect to crimes not involving dishonesty or false statement punishable by death or imprisonment in excess of one year, a balancing test is imposed. Rule 609(a)(1) provides that for the purpose of attacking the credibility of a witness, "evidence that a witness other than an accused has been convicted of a crime shall be admitted, subject to Rule 403, if the crime was punishable by death or imprisonment in excess of one year under the law under which the witness was convicted, and evidence that an accused has been convicted of such a crime shall be admitted if the court determines that the probative value of admitting this evidence outweighs its prejudicial effect to the accused."

When the criminal defendant testifies, evidence that the criminal defendant has been convicted of a crime punishable by death or imprisonment in excess of one year is admissible if the court determines that the probative value of admitting the evidence outweighs its prejudicial effect to the criminal defendant, Rule 609(a)(1). Since the probative value must outweigh the prejudicial effect, the burden of establishing admissibility is placed upon the government, the party proposing to employ the conviction, contrary to the practice with regard to unfair prejudice generally under Rule 403. The conviction is admissible to impeach the criminal defendant under Rule 609(a)(1) provided its probative value "outweighs" its prejudicial effect; the general balancing test contained in Rule 403 provides for admissibility unless the unfair prejudicial effect "substantially outweighs" the probative value. Whether the foregoing shift of burden in comparison to Rule 403, when considered in light of the variation in standard, actually results in fewer convictions being employed to impeach the criminal defendant is extremely doubtful.

With respect to every witness in a civil or criminal court case other than the criminal defendant, evidence that the witness has been convicted of a crime is admissible, subject to Rule 403, if the crime was punishable by death or imprisonment in excess of one year under the law under which the witness was convicted, Rule 609 (a)(1).

## § 609.3 Rule 609(a)(1): Crimes Punishable by Death or Imprisonment in Excess of One Year; Discretionary Balancing Test

Rule 609(a)(1) provides that before any conviction for a crime punishable by death or imprisonment in excess of one year under the law under which convicted may be employed to impeach the criminal defendant, the court must first determine that the probative value of admitting the evidence outweighs its prejudicial effect to the criminal defendant. The burden of proof is upon the government. With respect to the factors to be considered, the Advisory Committee's Note to the 1971 draft of Rule 609 states:

The provision finds its genesis in Luck v. United States, 121 U.S.App.D.C. 151, 348 F.2d 763 (1965). Prior to that decision, slight latitude was recognized for balancing probative value against prejudice, though some authority allowed or required the trial judge to exclude convictions remote in point of time. Referring to 14 D.C.Code § 305, the court said:

"It says, in effect, that the conviction 'may,' as opposed to 'shall,' be admitted; and we think the choice of words in this instance is significant. The trial court is not *required* to allow impeachment by prior conviction every time a defendant takes the stand in his own defense. The statute, in our view, leaves room for the operation of a sound judicial discretion to play upon the circumstances as they unfold in a particular case. There may well be cases where the trial judge might think that the cause of truth would be helped more by letting the jury hear the defendant's story than by the defendant's foregoing that opportunity because of the fear of prejudice founded upon a prior conviction. [Footnote omitted.] There may well be other cases where the trial judge believes the prejudicial effect of impeachment far outweighs the probative relevance of the prior conviction to the issue of credibility. This last is, of course, a standard which trial judges apply every day in other contexts; and we think it has both utility and applicability in this field. [Footnote omitted.]

In exercising discretion in this respect, a number of factors might be relevant, such as the nature of the prior crimes, [footnote omitted] the length of the criminal record, the age and circumstances of the defendant, and, above all, the extent to which it is more important to the search for truth in a particular case for the jury to hear the defendant's story than to know of a prior conviction. The goal of a criminal trial is the disposition of the charge in accordance with the truth. The possibility of a rehearsal of the defendant's criminal record in a given case, especially if it means that the jury will be left without one version of the truth, may or may not contribute to that objective. The experienced trial judge has a sensitivity in this regard which normally can be relied upon to strike a reasonable balance between the interests of the defendant and of the public. We think Congress has left room for that discretion to operate." 348 F.2d at 768.

The application of *Luck* has been refined and clarified in numerous subsequent decisions of the court which rendered it, notably in Gordon v. United States, 127 U.S.App.D.C. 343, 383 F.2d 936 (1967). Pointing out that *Luck* placed on the accused the burden of demonstrating that the prejudice from his prior convictions " 'far outweigh' the probative relevance to credibility" (p. 939), Judge, now Chief Justice, Burger suggested in *Gordon* various factors to be considered in making the determination: the nature of the crime, nearness or remoteness, the subsequent career of the person, and whether the crime was similar to the one charged. It will be noted that subdivision (b) of the rule imposes a specific time limit and that subdivision (c) deals with aspects of rehabilitation; these provisions should be construed only as imposing outer limits upon the judge's determination and not as restricting his decision within them.

Also important to an assessment of probative value versus prejudice is the centrality of the credibility issue.

In summary, the following factors should be considered in determining whether the probative value of admitting the evidence upon the credibility of the criminal defendant outweighs its prejudicial effect: (1) the nature of the prior crime; (2) the length of the defendant's criminal record; (3) defendant's age and circumstances; (4) the likelihood that the defendant would not testify; (5) the nearness or remoteness of the prior crime; (6) defendant's subsequent career; (7) whether the prior crime was similar to the one charged; (8) the centrality of the issue of credibility; and (9) the need for defendant's testimony. To this one might add a tenth facts surrounding the conviction including whether or not the defendant pled guilty or was convicted after trial, and whether the defendant testified at the trial.

Exactly how each factor is to be assessed and balanced pursuant to the prescribed standard cannot be stated with precision; it must be left to the sensitivity of the trial judge to strike a reasonable balance. Similarity between the prior offense and the crime for which on trial is always an important consideration in evaluating unfair prejudice.

The process of balancing the various factors in a rational manner is extremely difficult at best if not in fact an impossibility. Difficulties associated with identifying, evaluating and balancing up to ten factors in determining whether the probative value of a prior conviction as it bears on the credibility of the criminal defendant outweighs its prejudicial effect to the defendant is further complicated by the fact that several of the factors relevant to assessing probative value themselves cut in different directions, such as centrality of the issue of credibility versus similarity of the offense and need for the defendant's testimony. It is not surprising that a ruling permitting use of a prior conviction to impeach will be reversed on appeal only upon a showing of clear abuse of discretion.

While it is probably not necessary that the record contain an affirmative statement by the court concerning the particular factors considered and weight each was accorded, trial judges have been strongly urged and occasionally required to make a specific finding on the record with respect to the outcome of balancing probative value versus unfair prejudice concerning use of the prior conviction in the context of the given litigation.

Rule 609(a)(1) also provides that for the purpose of attacking the credibility of *every* witness other than the criminal defendant whether testifying in a civil or criminal case, evidence that the witness has been convicted of a crime punishable by death or imprisonment in excess of one year and the law under which the witness was convicted is admissible subject to the balancing test of Rule 403. Thus, the prior conviction may be employed to impeach unless its probative value is substantially outweighed by the danger of unfair prejudice.

## § 609.4 Rule 609(a)(2): Crimes of Dishonesty or False Statement

Since it is generally accepted that a conviction for a crime involving "dishonesty or false statement" is probative upon the issue of a witness' truthfulness, such convictions, regardless of punishment, may be employed to impeach any witness, including a criminal defendant, without first satisfying a balancing test, Rule 609(a)(2).

The nature of specific offenses properly included within the phrase "dishonesty and false statement" has been subject to debate. The Report of the Conference Committee stated:

> By the phrase "dishonesty and false statement" the Conference means crimes such as perjury or subornation of perjury, false statement, criminal fraud, embezzlement, or false pretense, or any other offense in the nature of a crimen falsi, the commission of which involves some element of deceit, untruthfulness, or falsification bearing on the accused's propensity to testify truthfully.

McCormick, Evidence § 42 at 160 (5th ed.1999) has maintained that under the view of the Report of the Conference Committee limiting the phrase "dishonesty or false statement" to crimes involving crimen falsi little meaning attaches to the term "dishonesty," with the possible exception of embezzlement. The controversy spilled over into reported decisions trying to give meaning to the term "dishonesty or false statement" with respect to convictions involving petty larceny, robbery, shoplifting and narcotics. It quickly became settled however that crimes involving solely the use of force such as assault and battery, and crimes such as drunkenness and prostitution do not involve dishonesty or false statement, while the crime of fraud does.

The pattern that has emerged over time from the cases evidences a willingness to follow the Conference Committee's Report and define dishonesty or false statement as a crime "which involves some element of deceit, untruthfulness, of falsification bearing on the accused's propensity to testify truthfully," i.e., involve some element of active misrepresentation. Several additional crimes have now been held on their face to meet this definition such as failure to file tax returns, passing counterfeit money, and filing a false police report. On the other hand courts seem generally unwilling to conclude that offenses such as petty larceny, shoplifting, robbery, possession of a weapon, and narcotic violations are per se crimes of dishonesty or false statement. A physical attempt to remain undetected does not alone make the crime one involving dishonesty or false statement. If the party wishing to employ a conviction not considered per se a crime of dishonesty or false statement is able to show by going behind the judgment that the particular conviction rested upon facts establishing deceit, untruthfulness or falsification, i.e., involved some element of active misrepresentation, the prior conviction may be employed to impeach credibility under Rule 609(a)(2).

## § 609.5 Rule 609(b): Conviction as to Which More Than Ten Years Has Elapsed

Evidence of a conviction under Rule 609 is not admissible if a period of more than ten years has elapsed since the date of the conviction or of the release of the witness from the confinement imposed for that conviction, whichever is the later date, unless the court determines, in the interests of justice, that the probative value of the conviction supported by specific facts and circumstances substantially outweighs its prejudicial effect, Rule 609(b).

Rule 609(b) alters the pattern established in Rule 609(a) in five principal respects. First, Rule 609(b) requires that admissibility be supported by a finding on the record as to the specific facts and circumstances considered in reaching a determination in favor of admissibility. Second the probative value of the conviction must substantially outweigh rather than merely outweigh its prejudicial effect. Third, the foregoing balancing test is applied to all witnesses including the criminal defendant. Fourth, Rule 609(b) applies its balancing test to all prior convictions even those involving dishonesty or false statement. Fifth, evidence of a conviction more than ten years old is not admissible unless the proponent gives the adverse party sufficient advance written notice of intent to use such evidence to provide the adverse party with a fair opportunity to contest the use of such evidence, Rule 609(b).

The Report of the Senate Committee on the Judiciary states that "it is intended that convictions over ten years old will be admitted very rarely and only in exceptional circumstances." Reported decisions, however, indicate that while prior convictions over ten years old are not usually admitted, instances of admissibility appear to occur with more frequency than "very rarely."

## § 609.6 Rule 609(a) and (b): Method of Establishing Convictions; Preserving Error for Appeal; Timing of Ruling; Limiting Instructions

**Method of establishing.** Once the court determines that a particular conviction is provable, Rule 609(a) and (b), the conviction may be elicited from the witness on direct or cross-examination or established by public record, usually in the form of a certified copy, Rule 902(4), or otherwise. Whether elicited on direct or cross-examination, the witness may be questioned as to matters appearing on the public record including the court, date and nature of offense. If the witness admits that he was so convicted, the anticipatory disclosure or impeachment has been completed. If, however, the witness fails to admit the conviction in any respect, for example by specifically denying or by claiming a lack of recollection, the impeaching party must introduce evidence of the conviction preferably the public record of conviction, as well as evidence proving that the witness was the individual so convicted. Alternatively, the public record of conviction along with proof of identity may be offered in the first instance.

While inquiry into related matters on cross-examination such as the details of the offense, length of time served, fact paroled, and guilt or innocence is improper, there is conflicting authority with respect to whether the witness may himself be permitted to offer general statements in explanation, mitigation or denial. If permitted at all, the scope of the statement lies in the trial judge's discretion subject to the general policy of Rule 403 dictating exclusion of prejudicial, confusing and time-consuming evidence unredeemed by sufficient probative value. On the other hand, it is clear that the pendency of an appeal of the conviction may be established as a qualifying circumstance.

It is common practice for the party who calls a witness with a provable criminal record to bring out the prior conviction on direct examination. This process was never treated as impeachment of a party's own witness but rather as anticipatory disclosure designed to reduce the prejudicial effect of the evidence if revealed for the first time on cross-examination. Anticipatory disclosure is particularly common when the criminal defendant testifies on his own behalf. If the introduction on direct examination may create a danger of unfair prejudice to a party, for example, where there is evidence of a past association between the prosecution witness and the criminal defendant, the conviction may not be disclosed on direct examination by the prosecution if the probative value of admitting the conviction is substantially outweighed by its prejudicial effect to the defendant, Rule 403. Given the characterization of such disclosure as "anticipatory," a representation by the criminal defendant claiming unfair prejudice that the prior conviction will not be employed upon cross-examination of the witness should be a factor of considerable significance in determining the propriety of employing the prior conviction under such circumstances to impeach.

**Preserving error for appeal.** If a defendant introduces the fact of a prior conviction without the trial court having an opportunity at trial sometime following the defendant's direct testimony to rule on admissibility, the defendant will have waived his right to raise error on appeal. Thus, if a ruling had not been obtained either before or earlier at trial, anticipatory disclosure constitutes a waiver. If on an earlier occasion the trial court had reserved ruling or issued only a tentative or provisional ruling as to admissibility, anticipatory disclosure without renewal of the objection at trial also constitutes a waiver. Finally, anticipatory disclosure on direct examination or otherwise of a prior conviction definitively ruled admissible in advance of or earlier at trial on a motion in limine similarly waives the right to assert error on appeal; the opposing party must be given the choice as to whether or not to offer the prior conviction to impeach at trial.

**Timing of ruling.** The admissibility of prior convictions for purposes of impeachment is an appropriate matter for a motion in limine, i.e., a motion in advance of trial. It would certainly assist counsel to know what the ruling will be on this important matter so that he can make appropriate tactical decisions. For example, questioning of potential jurors, the opening of defense counsel and the decision of the defendant to take the stand may be affected. While appropriate for decision prior to trial, the court is not obliged to so rule. Factors associated with application of the discretionary balancing test of Rule 609(a)(1) or Rule 609(b) and consideration of waste of time often result in the decision being made either at the conclusion of the government's case, immediately prior to the time the defendant takes the stand, or even at the conclusion of the defendant's direct testimony. A ruling made in advance of trial is subject to change; the trial court is free in the exercise of sound discretion even if nothing unexpected happens at trial to alter a previous in limine ruling. Moreover in order to preserve for review a claim of improper impeachment under Rule 609(a)(1) or Rule 609(b), the defendant must testify.

**Limiting instruction.** Where a witness is impeached by means of prior conviction, the immediate giving of a cautionary instruction is appropriate as is the giving of a limiting instruction concerning the proper use of the prior conviction when the jury is instructed on the law at the conclusion of the case. Failure to give a limiting instruction will more likely result in plain error where the prior conviction is similar.

## § 609.7 Rule 609(c): Effect of a Pardon, Annulment, or Certificate of Rehabilitation

Evidence of a conviction is not admissible if (1) the conviction has been the subject of a pardon, annulment, certificate of rehabilitation, or other equivalent procedure based on a finding of the rehabilitation of the person convicted, and that person has not been convicted of a subsequent crime which was punishable by death or imprisonment in excess of one year, or (2) the conviction has been the subject of a pardon, annulment, or other equivalent procedure based on a finding of innocence, Rule 609(c).

For a conviction to be inadmissible under Rule 609(c)(1), the procedure whatever called, must have made a finding of rehabilitation of the person convicted. A pardon or its equivalent granted solely for the purpose of restoring civil rights lost by virtue of the conviction is not equivalent to a finding of rehabilitation, nor is an expungement or the dismissal of the conviction following fulfillment of certain conditions, where the state law under which granted provides that the prior conviction may be proved in any subsequent prosecution of the defendant. Accordingly, neither a certification showing a sentence has been satisfactorily served, nor pardon not based upon a finding of innocence, nor parole successfully completed, nor release from a halfway house, is sufficient alone to bar use of the conviction for purposes of impeachment, Rule 609(c)(1).

A pardon, annulment, or equivalent procedure based upon a finding of innocence makes the conviction inadmissible, Rule 609(c)(2).

## § 609.8   Rule 609(d): Juvenile Adjudications

Juvenile adjudications are not admissible to attack the credibility of a witness under Rule 609 with the sole exception that evidence of a juvenile adjudication of a witness other than the defendant may be employed in a criminal case for purposes of impeachment if (1) the conviction would be admissible to attack credibility if of an adult and (2) its admission in evidence is necessary to a fair determination of guilt or innocence, Rule 609(d).

The Supreme Court in Davis v. Alaska (S.Ct.1974), held that the denial of the right to cross-examine a key prosecution witness about possible bias and prejudice deriving from his probationary status as a juvenile delinquent was a violation of the defendant's right of confrontation guaranteed by the Sixth Amendment. However, *Davis* neither holds nor suggests that the Constitution confers a right in every case to impeach the general credibility of a witness through cross-examination about his past juvenile adjudications.

Whether a fair determination of guilt or innocence requires the employment of a juvenile conviction to attack the credibility of a witness other than the criminal defendant on the basis of either bias or willingness to disobey the law must be determined by the court on the facts of the particular case. Whether the rehabilitative process has been demonstrated a failure and the strategic importance of the witness' testimony are relevant considerations.

## § 609.9   Rule 609(e): Pendency of Appeal

The pendency of an appeal from a conviction does not render the conviction inadmissible; evidence of the pendency of the appeal is itself admissible, Rule 609(e).

Obviously a conviction that has been reversed on appeal may not be employed to impeach in a subsequent trial. Employment of a conviction to impeach which is later reversed on appeal will not normally be considered reversible error. However where the conviction is reversed for constitutional error involving lack of counsel, the standard for determining whether the error is reversible in a criminal case is whether use of the conviction is harmless beyond a reasonable doubt.

## Rule 610.

## RELIGIOUS BELIEFS OR OPINIONS

**Evidence of the beliefs or opinions of a witness on matters of religion is not admissible for the purpose of showing that by reason of their nature the witness' credibility is impaired or enhanced.**

### § 610.1 Religious Beliefs or Opinions

Evidence with respect to the religious beliefs or opinions of a witness is not admissible for the purpose of enhancing or impairing credibility by virtue of the nature of the beliefs, Rule 610. Inquiry into religious beliefs or opinions is not sufficiently probative as to the credibility of a witness to be admitted when considered in light of the potential for unfair prejudice. Rule 610 prohibits inquiry as to religious beliefs or opinions rather than providing the witness with a privilege not to be examined as to his religious beliefs or opinions. Evidence of religious belief or opinion may be admitted for other purposes, however, such as to show bias where the witness' church is a party to the litigation.

## Rule 611.

## MODE AND ORDER OF INTERROGATION AND PRESENTATION

(a) **Control by Court.** The court shall exercise reasonable control over the mode and order of interrogating witnesses and presenting evidence so as to (1) make the interrogation and presentation effective for the ascertainment of the truth, (2) avoid needless consumption of time, and (3) protect witnesses from harassment or undue embarrassment.

(b) **Scope of Cross–Examination.** Cross-examination should be limited to the subject matter of the direct examination and matters affecting the credibility of the witness. The court may, in the exercise of discretion, permit inquiry into additional matters as if on direct examination.

(c) **Leading Questions.** Leading questions should not be used on the direct examination of a witness except as may be necessary to develop the witness' testimony. Ordinarily leading questions should be permitted on cross-examination. When a party calls a hostile witness, an adverse party, or a witness identified with an adverse party, interrogation may be by leading questions.

## § 611.1  Mode and Order of Interrogation and Presentation: An Overview

Rule 611 is an extremely encompassing rule speaking to a variety of aspects of the mode and order of interrogation of witnesses and presentation of evidence at trial.

Rule 611(a) provides generally for the exercise of reasonable control by the court over the mode, order, and presentation of evidence. Rule 611(b) limits the scope of cross-examination to the subject matter of direct and matters of credibility, subject to the discretion of the court to permit additional inquiry as if on direct examination. Rule 611(c) delineates when leading questions should be permitted. Thus while Rule 611 in its title refers to the order of interrogation and presentation of evidence at trial, none of the three subdivisions speaks directly to the sequence of presentation at trial.

The commentary that follows takes a relatively broad look at the order of presentation of evidence and argument at trial. It then examines in detail the presentation of testimony through direct, cross, redirect and recross and finally rebuttal. Also included are references to specific objections to both the form of the question and to offered evidence available at various stages throughout the trial. Such objections are collectively referred to as trial objections. Trial courts are vested with considerable discretion in ruling upon trial objections. Objections of this nature, as well as objections generally, are governed by Rule 103.

## § 611.2 Order of Presentation: Voir Dire, Opening Statements and Closing Arguments

Rule 611(a) directs the court to exercise "reasonable" control over the mode and order of interrogating witnesses and presentation of evidence. With respect to those aspects of the trial not involving the presentation of evidence or the interrogation of witnesses such as voir dire, opening statement and closing argument, the court similarly exercises "reasonable" control over the mode and order of the proceedings. Not surprisingly customary patterns have developed over time in each of these areas, in some instances leading to the formulation of a statute or rule. The plaintiff/government, the party possessing the burden of production and burden of persuasion, is given the right to open the various aspects of the litigation such as voir dire (when counsel is permitted to question), opening statement and presentation of evidence. With respect to closing argument, a civil plaintiff most frequently has the right to both open and close while the government is always placed in that position.

Voir dire examination of prospective jurors is conducted in civil cases pursuant to Fed.R.Civ.P. 47(a), and in criminal cases pursuant to Fed.R.Crim.Proc. 24(a). For all practical purposes the two rules are identical. Fed. R.Civ.Proc. 47(a) provides·

> The court may permit the parties or their attorneys to conduct the examination of prospective jurors or may itself conduct the examination. In the latter event, the court shall permit the parties or their attorneys to supplement the examination by such further inquiry as it deems proper or shall itself submit to the prospective jurors such additional questions of the parties or their attorneys as it deems proper.

The predominant method employed in the federal courts in both civil and criminal cases is for the court alone to conduct the voir dire examination. If counsel wishes additional questions asked, he may tender them to the court for its consideration. Peremptory challenges are governed by statute in civil matters and by court rule in criminal cases. The procedure for selecting alternative jurors is pursuant to court rule in both civil and criminal proceedings.

The opening statement by the plaintiff in civil cases and the government in criminal cases, the party with the burden of persuasion, is invariably made as soon as the jury is empanelled. This is ordinarily followed immediately by the defendant's opening statement. If requested, the court usually possesses discretion to permit the defendant to withhold the presentation of an opening statement until immediately prior to presentation of his or her case in chief.

The procedure for closing argument, mandated in criminal proceedings and generally followed in civil cases, consists of the opening final argument of the plaintiff/prosecution, the defendant's closing argument, and by a rebuttal argument of the plaintiff/prosecution. The rebuttal argument is limited to responding to arguments made by the defendant. If defendant waives closing argument, the plaintiff/prosecution has no right to offer further argument. The court may, however, in its discretion permit further argument or argument not in the nature of rebuttal if, for example, counsel by inadvertence has omitted something he intended to state.

## § 611.3   Order of Presentation: Evidence Introduced at Trial

**Plaintiff's case in chief.** The plaintiff in a civil case or prosecution in a criminal matter, possessing the burden of production, must initially present his case in chief, i.e., introduce facts sufficient to establish each controverted element of the claim asserted or the offense charged. This is known as a prima facie case. Thus at the first stage the plaintiff/prosecution will bring forward successively all the witnesses on whom he will rely to establish these facts together with the documents and other tangible evidence pertinent for this purpose, which will be offered when they have been authenticated by the testimony of the witnesses, Rule 901. During this stage each witness of the plaintiff/prosecution will first be questioned by plaintiff/prosecution counsel upon direct examination, then cross-examined by opposing counsel. These examinations may be followed by redirect and recross examination. When all of the plaintiff/prosecution witnesses to his main case have been subjected each in turn to this process of questioning and cross-questioning, the plaintiff/prosecution signifies the completion of his case in chief by announcing that he rests.

**Defendant's denials and affirmative defenses.** The defendant then presents his witnesses and offers into evidence documents and other tangible evidence in support of his case including those items authenticated during cross-examination of plaintiff's witnesses. At this stage the defendant produces evidence that denies, repels, counteracts, explains or disproves the plaintiff/prosecution's claims. In addition, the civil defendant will introduce evidence in support of any affirmative defense raised in the answer; the criminal defendant will introduce evidence of any so-called or true affirmative defense including those as to which the giving of notice of intent to assert is required. Here again each witness' story on direct examination is subject to be tested by cross-examination and supplemented on redirect, etc., before he leaves the stand. When the defendant has thus completed the presentation of his proof of so-called and true affirmative defenses, if any, and his evidence in denial of the plaintiff's claims, the defendant announces that he rests.

**Plaintiff's rebuttal and defendant's surrebuttal.** The plaintiff/prosecution now is entitled to present its case in rebuttal. The plaintiff/prosecution may not at this stage present witnesses who merely lend support to the evidence originally presented as to the elements of the offense or claim for relief, but is confined to testimony directed to refuting the defendant's evidence. The proper scope and function of rebuttal is thus refutation, which involves evidence which denies, explains, qualifies, disproves, repels or otherwise sheds light on evidence offered by the defense including evidence rehabilitating the credibility of witnesses. To answer points first raised by the defendant's witnesses, the plaintiff/prosecution in rebuttal may present new witnesses or it may recall witnesses who have testified on the case in chief. The admissibility of evidence on rebuttal is committed to the discretion of the trial court. In the court's discretion, evidence tending to refute is admissible in rebuttal even if it would also have been admissible as part of the plaintiff/prosecution's case in chief, and even if repetitive of matters actually introduced during the case in chief. In this, as in the other stages, the witness may not only be examined on direct, but cross-examined and reexamined. When the plaintiff/prosecution's case in rebuttal is finished, he closes his case. If new points are brought out during rebuttal, the defendant may meet them by evidence in surrebuttal, sometimes called rejoinder. In addition, defendant may offer evidence to rehabilitate witnesses whose credibility has been attacked in plaintiff/prosecution's rebuttal. The defendant then closes his case.

**Defendant's counterclaim.** Where the defendant has interposed a counterclaim, the defendant's case in chief with respect to the counterclaim is normally presented together with defendant's evidence in opposition to plaintiff's main case and in support of defendant's affirmative defenses. Plaintiff presents his evidence in opposition and affirmative defenses to the counterclaim when he presents rebuttal evidence. Such evidence is responded to by defendant on surrebuttal.

**Both sides close.** When both parties have announced that they have closed, the hearing on the facts comes to an end and the trial proceeds with the closing arguments of counsel and the court's instructions to the jury.

## § 611.4   Rule 611(a): Control by Court of Order of Presentation of Evidence

It is the responsibility of the court to control the mode and order of interrogating witnesses and the presentation of evidence so as to foster the ascertainment of truth, avoid needless consumption of time, and at the same time protect witnesses from harassment or undue embarrassment, Rule 611(a). The normal pattern at trial with respect to voir dire, opening statements, presentation of evidence and closing argument assists counsel and the court in conducting the trial in an orderly manner.

As long as each party is afforded the opportunity to present his own evidence and to meet that of his opponent, he is scarcely in a position to complain of deviation or lack thereof from the normal pattern. Thus occasionally a witness, such as an expert, may be examined by a party during his opponent's case in chief, or a party may request the opportunity to recall a witness for additional examination. At other times it is simply difficult to ascertain where a particular item fits within the normal pattern. Certain distortions of the normal pattern, such as the offering of evidence in rebuttal which is merely cumulative of plaintiff's case in chief or attempting to establish a new ground of liability in rebuttal, do not make for the ascertainment of truth and will not be countenanced. When the admissibility of evidence depends upon other evidence, the court has discretion to admit it subject to being "connected up".

While ordinarily cross-examination is deferred until completion of the direct examination, cross-examination of a witness as to his qualifications, personal knowledge or competency prior to giving his principal testimony, sometimes described as "voir dire", avoids exposing the jury to inadmissible evidence if the witness proves to be unqualified, lack personal knowledge or be incompetent. Hence, for example cross-examination as to an expert's qualifications, the personal knowledge of a lay witness, or competency of a witness to testify under a state's Dead Man's Statute, should be permitted prior to the witness' principal testimony if requested. Similar considerations surround the conducting of voir dire examination as to the foundation laid with respect to authenticity or identification as a condition precedent to admissibility of an exhibit or other item of evidence, Rule 901.

In summary, the entire matter of the mode of witness examination and the order of presentation of evidence rest largely in the discretion of the trial judge, Rule 611(a). Abuse of discretion is likely to arise only if opportunity is completely denied to present evidence, impeach witnesses, support the credibility of impeached witnesses, or refute new points raised by the opponent.

## § 611.5 Introduction of Evidence After Parties Rest

The court's discretion discussed in the preceding section extends to reopening a case for the taking of further evidence after a party or even both parties have closed. Discretion may be exercised in favor of reopening the case even after argument and instruction, and the opposite party seems not to be in a position to complain unless he is denied the opportunity to meet the additional evidence. While liberality in favor of reopening is to be encouraged to afford the fullest possible hearing (particularly in nonjury cases), the additional evidence should not be allowed absent a showing of diligence and most certainly should not be allowed if deliberately withheld in an attempt to deprive the opponent of an opportunity to meet it.

Where reopening is denied, the nature of the additional evidence sought to be introduced should be disclosed in the form of an offer of proof to preserve possible error for review.

## § 611.6  Direct Examination

During the presentation of evidence throughout the trial, each party seeks to elicit from witnesses testimony establishing certain facts and to introduce documentary and other tangible evidence. To facilitate the presentation of testimony, witnesses may be subpoenaed to appear at trial and exhibits may be required to be produced.

The process of eliciting facts from a witness called by a party is termed direct examination. Rule 611(c) provides that leading questions, those suggesting the answer, are not permitted upon direct examination unless necessary to develop the witness' testimony. When a party calls a hostile witness, an adverse party or a witness identified with an adverse party, however, interrogation may be by leading questions.

The credibility of a witness may not be bolstered during direct examination by evidence of specific instances of conduct or otherwise; background information is admissible within the discretion of the court. Impeachment of a witness on direct examination is permitted by Rule 607.

## § 611.7  Attendance of Witnesses and Production of Documents at Trial: Witness Fees

Persons may be compelled to appear at trial by service of a subpoena, a writ commanding the witness to appear and testify in a designated cause or matter at a specified time and place. A subpoena may also command the person to bring books, papers, documents and other tangible items properly designated therein. They are issued by the clerk at the request of either party in both civil and criminal cases. Subpoenas should not be confused with a notice to produce served on an opposing party in connection with the Original Writing Rule.

Witness fees are set by statute.

## § 611.8  Rule 611(c): Form of Testimony on Direct; Leading Questions

A party calling a witness to testify at trial must ordinarily elicit testimony from the witness in response to nonleading questions. Use of specific nonleading questions such as "Please describe the weather conditions at the time of the accident," tend to keep the witness within the bounds of relevancy and the exclusionary rules of evidence. They also serve to afford the opponent an opportunity to object to inadmissible evidence before it is given. A narrative answer on the other hand in response to a general nonleading question such as "Please tell us everything that happened on the day of the accident," possesses the advantages of naturalness and freedom from interruption. The extent to which testimony tends to fall in one pattern or the other depends largely on the extent to which the nonleading question is specific or general, a matter much within the discretion of trial counsel and the trial judge. This discretion sensibly permits the adoption of a course best suited to the characteristics of the particular witness, considered in light of testimony to be given in the context of the litigation.

Rule 611(c) provides that leading questions should not be employed on direct examination of a witness, except as may be necessary to develop his testimony, or where a hostile witness, an adverse party or a witness identified with an adverse party is called to testify. The rule is phrased in suggestive ("should not") rather than mandatory terms. The test of a leading question is whether it suggests the answer desired by the examiner; the vice lies in substituting the suggestions of counsel for the actual testimony of the witness. A question may be leading because of its form, for example, "Didn't he * * *?", its detail, or be made suggestive by reason of the examiner's emphasis on certain words, the tone used by the examiner in asking the question as a whole, or by the examiner's nonverbal conduct. While not always the case, questions which may be answered either "Yes" or "No" are considered leading. Merely using the term "whether or not" or other form of alternative does not of itself keep a question from being leading. On the other hand, a witness can scarcely be examined without calling attention to the subject matter on which his testimony is sought, and a question so doing is not considered leading.

Sustaining an objection to a leading question may be more or less an empty gesture. Effective enforcement requires foreclosing all further inquiry into the subject, or permitting counsel to return to it only after an exploration of other matters have reduced the effect of the communication of the answer to the witness. These measures are available to the trial judge. The fact that they are seldom invoked may well lead to the conclusion that the rule against leading questions is lacking in true substance and operates merely to create a false sense of spontaneity which the examiner might otherwise destroy by use of leading questions.

Rule 611(c) provides for the use of leading questions on direct examination (1) when necessary to develop the witness' testimony and (2) when directed to a witness regarded as hostile as a matter of law.

**Necessary to develop.** Leading questions are proper as necessary to develop the witness' direct testimony in the following situations:

(a) Undisputed preliminary or inconsequential matters. Leading questions focus the witness' attention upon a topic; leading upon a point about which no controversy exists is harmless and saves time.

(b) A witness who is hostile or unwilling. A witness who demonstrates recalcitrance by giving damaging testimony, or by answering reluctantly, obstinately or belligerently, i.e., a witness hostile in fact, may be led. Notice that the mere giving of damaging answers in the absence of recalcitrance does not permit counsel to lead. A witness who is unwilling, i.e., a witness who shows himself by demeanor or testimony to be reticent, deceptive, hesitant, evasive or uncooperative, may also be led.

(c) A child witness or an adult with communication problems either physical or mental.

(d) A witness whose recollection is exhausted.

(e) A witness who is being impeached by the party calling the witness as provided in Rule 607.

(f) A witness who is frightened, nervous, or upset while testifying, frequently a child victim of a sexual assault.

(g) A witness who is unresponsive or shows a lack of understanding.

**Hostile in law.** Some witnesses, such as an adverse party, are automatically considered hostile so that leading questions are permitted on direct examination without a prior in court showing that leading questions are in fact necessary for the orderly development of the witness' testimony. Rule 611(c) defines hostile in law witnesses to include "a hostile witness, an adverse party or a witness identified with an adverse party." Since such a witness will not be responsive to the suggestions of counsel, leading questions are permitted. Whether a witness is to be considered automatically hostile is determined as of the time of his examination. Ordinarily an officer, director, managing agent, or even an employee of a party, and a relative of the party should be considered a witness identified with an adverse party and thus subject to leading questions.

The party calling the witness may impeach to the extent provided by Rules 607 and 403. A coparty whose interests are adverse to the witness is also entitled to lead and impeach. Following the examination, the side to which the witness presumably is friendly is entitled to examine as if on redirect, i.e., to deny, explain, qualify, modify, counteract, repel, disprove, or otherwise shed light on the testimony given but not to bring out new matters. Leading questions may be employed in the process to the same extent permitted on redirect examination.

Whether leading is harmful depends on the circumstances, including the nature of the witness and the context within which the question is asked. As previously discussed, leading may be necessary if any testimony at all is to be elicited for example from an unwilling witness or from a witness whose recollection is exhausted. Hence the propriety of questions which are admittedly leading is peculiarly within the competency of the trial judge. Deciding whether a question is unnecessarily leading under the circumstances is poorly suited for determination on appeal; reversals for abuse of discretion are rare.

## § 611.9 Lack of Foundation: "Voir Dire" as to Admissibility of Evidence

The objection "lack of foundation" is employed at trial in reference to many different situations. Whenever a preliminary factual finding is required to be made by either the court alone, Rule 104(a), or in connection with a matter of conditional relevancy, Rule 104(b), opposing counsel may object that the evidence presented fails to support introduction of the evidence being offered, i.e., the evidence lacks a sufficient foundation to be admitted. To illustrate, the objection "lack of foundation" may be employed with respect to at least each of the following:

(1) Competency of a lay witness, Rule 601.

(2) Qualifications of an expert witness, Rule 702.

(3) Introduction of opinion testimony including a determination the reliability of scientific, technical, or other specialized knowledge, Rules 701–705.

(4) Personal knowledge, Rule 602.

(5) Unavailability in connection with a hearsay exception, Rule 804(a).

(6) Satisfaction of the requirements of a hearsay exemption or exception, Rules 801(d), 803 and 804(b).

(7) Authentication or identification, Art. IX.

(8) Admissibility of evidence other than the Original Writing, Art. X.

(9) The existence or waiver of a privilege, Art. V.

(10) Relevancy, Rule 401.

Counsel objecting to introduction of evidence on the grounds of lack of introduction of a sufficient foundation will, if requested, frequently be given an opportunity to cross-examine the witness at the time of offer limited solely to the question of the sufficiency of the foundation. This process is referred to as "voir dire". If opposing counsel is successful in his objection to the adequacy of the foundation for the testimony of the witness or introduction of an item of evidence, inadmissible evidence will never come to the attention of the trier of fact. If opposing counsel, on the other hand, were to wait until general cross-examination to explore more fully the foundation laid, if ultimately successful in showing inadequacy of foundation, the only remedy available is the striking of the evidence accompanied by an instruction to the jury to disregard since the evidence is already before the jury.

The objection "lack of foundation" may also arise where a party attempts to introduce extrinsic evidence to impeach without having satisfied the preliminary requirements of laying a proper foundation upon cross-examination of the witness or otherwise.

## § 611.10 Cross–Examination: An Overview; Rule 611(c), Leading Questions

Cross-examination is a matter of right. cross-examination constitutes an important aspect of due process and in criminal cases of the right of confrontation. The scope of cross-examination is restricted in Rule 611(b) to the subject matter of direct examination and matters affecting the credibility of the witness; Rule 611(a) imposes restraints upon cross-examination to protect witnesses from harassment or undue embarrassment. In addition various other rules of evidence such as Rules 403, 608, and 609, to name a few, place restrictions on the scope of the cross-examination which may properly be undertaken of any given witness. The extent of cross-examination within any area properly the subject of cross-examination rests within the discretion of the court. In criminal proceedings, however, the defendant must be afforded wide latitude on cross-examination for the purpose of establishing partiality or otherwise challenging the credibility of a government witness, as well as for the purpose of presenting a defense.

While cross-examination is commonly thought of as being destructive in nature with examining counsel attempting in one way or another to affect the trier of fact's assessment of the weight to be accorded the testimony of the witness given during direct examination employing leading questions in the process, cross-examination entails much more. Counsel on cross-examination may (1) attempt to elicit disputed facts from the witness favorable to his case, (2) have the witness repeat those facts testified to on direct favorable to the cross-examiner, (3) have the witness testify to nondisputed facts essential to presentation of his theory of the case, (4) attempt to have the witness qualify, modify or otherwise shed light upon his testimony with respect to unfavorable versions of disputed facts given on direct examination, (5) establish that the witness' testimony is not harmful to the advocate's case on the critical points under dispute and/or (6) ask questions of the witness designed primarily to keep the cross-examiner's theory of the case before the trier of fact. Whether the cross-examiner chooses to attempt to elicit favorable facts from a witness called by an opponent, have the witness testify to nondisputed facts, etc., and/or ask questions designed to discredit the witness or his testimony, naturally depends upon various factors including the importance of the testimony of the witness in the context of the litigation considered in light of the realistic possibilities for a successful cross-examination given the ammunition available. cross-examination is also sometimes much less. It is less in that on cross-examination leading questions are sometimes prohibited and certain kinds of impeachment will not always be allowed.

Rule 611(c) provides that leading questions should ordinarily be permitted on cross-examination. The reason for prohibiting leading questions, i.e., the witness will be responsive to the suggestions of counsel, generally does not apply to the witness being cross-examined. However if the particular witness is partial to the party cross-examining, there is the same danger in leading questions as on direct, and the court has discretion to prohibit their use. One circumstance in which a prohibition upon the use of leading questions on cross-examination is appropriate is when the witness was called by an opponent and automatically regarded and treated as hostile pursuant to Rule 611(c) and is then cross-examined by his own or other friendly counsel.

The criminal defendant who chooses to testify of course becomes subject to cross-examination as a witness in the case. The extent to which the criminal defendant waives his privilege against self-incrimination is not addressed by Rule 611(c).

When employed loosely, cross-examination refers to both the right to lead a witness and to employ a technique of impeachment such as use of a prior inconsistent statement or otherwise attempt to "destroy" the testimony of the witness. cross-examination is both more and less. It is more in that objectives other than destroying the credibility of the witness are very often pursued. It is less in that on cross-examination leading questions are sometimes prohibited and certain kinds of impeachment will not always be allowed. Proper rulings on cross-examination are greatly facilitated by analysis rather than a knee jerk response by the court to the knee jerk response by counsel in reply to an objection made to a question asked on cross-examination "Your Honor, this is cross-examination."

## § 611.11 Rule 611(b): Scope of Cross–Examination

The scope of cross-examination is limited to the subject matter of direct examination and matters affecting the credibility of the witness, Rule 611(b). The purpose of the limited scope of cross-examination rule is to foster the orderly presentation of the case by having each side introduce the evidence upon which it relies in support of those matters as to which it has the burden of production during its turn to present its case in chief. Courts in applying the limited scope rule, however, tend to construe liberally what falls within the subject matter of direct examination. Inquiry affecting the credibility of the witness is generally perceived to extend to include whatever tends to explain, modify, qualify, discredit or otherwise shed light upon the testimony given on direct without regard to whether such matters are also supportive of the adversary's case in chief. The criminal defendant is given wide latitude with respect to cross-examination for the purpose of establishing partiality and to present a theory of defense. Evidence previously suppressed may be employed to impeach testimony elicited on cross-examination within the scope of the accused's direct examination.

The fact that the scope of cross-examination as thus defined is not susceptible to being determined with exactness, together with the practical necessity of curbing interminable and pointless inquiries combine to make reviewing courts reluctant to disturb decisions of trial judges absent a clear showing of abuse of discretion resulting in manifest prejudice to a party. To this end, Rule 611(b) is phrased in suggestive ("should be limited") rather than mandatory terminology. The extent of cross-examination with respect to an appropriate subject of inquiry is also within the sound discretion of the trial court; trial judges retain wide latitude to impose reasonable limits on such cross-examination based on concerns about, among other things, harassment, prejudice, confusion of the issues, the witness' safety, or interrogation that is repetitive or only marginally relevant. Where the court's restriction on cross-examination relates to the scope of permitted examination rather than the extent of exploration with respect to a permitted line of inquiry, the chances for reversal on appeal on the grounds of clear abuse of discretion and, where applicable, denial of the right of confrontation are increased.

A party in the court's discretion may be permitted to exceed the scope of direct examination, in which case inquiry shall be conducted as if on direct examination, Rule 611(b). Thus leading questions would not be permitted and impeachment, including by inconsistent statement, would be governed by Rule 607. Under such circumstances, the party originally calling the witness may then proceed to examine the witness with leading questions and impeach the witness with respect to those matters raised beyond the scope of direct.

## § 611.12  Redirect and Recross Examination

The function of redirect examination is to meet new facts or rehabilitate a witness with respect to impeaching matter brought out on cross-examination through the introduction of evidence tending to refute, i.e., deny, explain, qualify, disprove, repel or otherwise shed light upon evidence developed during cross-examination. The witness may be asked questions designed to explain apparent inconsistencies between statements made on direct and cross-examination; to deny or explain the making of an alleged prior inconsistent statement, Rule 613; to correct inadvertent mistakes made on cross-examination; to bring out circumstances repelling unfavorable inferences raised on cross-examination; to bring out prior consistent statements admissible pursuant to Rule 801(d)(1)(B); and to bring out other aspects of an event, transaction, conversation or document shedding light on those aspects previously developed during cross-examination.

In order to accomplish these objectives, it is frequently necessary to direct the witness' attention to the exact subject matter of the testimony sought. Hence some questions which might be objectionable as leading if asked during direct examination will often be permitted on redirect examination as necessary to the development of the witness' testimony. It is also generally proper to employ a leading question incorporating particular factual matters where refutation takes the form of a denial or affirmation. However where refutation takes another form such as explanation, is it improper to incorporate the explanation or other testimony desired into the question itself.

A witness may not be asked on redirect whether his testimony on direct examination was the truth since the answer is not rehabilitating, nor will a witness normally be permitted merely to repeat on redirect statements made upon direct examination.

Questions such as whether redirect exceeds the scope of cross-examination, whether the testimony offered is in the nature of refutation, as well as the propriety of the form of the question, all ultimately rest in the discretion of the court. The court also has discretion to permit the development of new matters, usually matters not brought out on direct examination through oversight, or even allow repetition of matters testified to on direct, subject of course to allowance of appropriate recross-examination thereon.

The function of recross is to meet new factual matters or rehabilitate a witness with respect to matters of credibility brought out for the first time during redirect examination. Inquiry merely repeating testimony developed during cross-examination is normally improper. The scope and extent of recross-examination rests in the discretion of the court.

## § 611.13 Rebuttal and Surrebuttal: Corroboration of Witness; Rebutting Attacks

The function and scope of rebuttal and surrebuttal is the presentation of evidence in refutation of evidence presented by an opponent during his last opportunity to offer evidence. Refutation evidence is that which denies, explains, qualifies, disproves, repels or otherwise sheds light on evidence offered by an opponent as to a fact of consequence in the litigation including the credibility of witnesses. The scope of rebuttal is restricted to non-collateral matters. Refutation evidence may be offered by the defendant when he presents his case in chief. Refutation evidence offered by the plaintiff/prosecution after the close of defendant's case in chief is called rebuttal. The refutation evidence of the plaintiff/prosecution must rebut new evidence or new theories proffered during the defendant's case in chief. If new points are brought out during rebuttal, refutation by the defendant is called either surrebuttal or rejoinder. Whether to allow or disallow rebuttal or surrebuttal, the scope and extent of rebuttal and surrebuttal, as well as whether new matters may be introduced, rests in the sound discretion of the court.

Rebuttal is also the time for the plaintiff/prosecution to introduce extrinsic evidence with respect to impeachment of the defendant's witness such as evidence as to the making of a prior inconsistent statement, Rule 613. Where the defendant impeaches a plaintiff/prosecution witness in like manner, extrinsic evidence is offered along with defendant's case in chief.

In order to accomplish either refutation or the introduction of extrinsic evidence, pinpoint questions directed
to the specific topic on which testimony is desired will
frequently be needed. Leading questions will be permitted to thus focus the witness' attention. Where refutation
takes the form of denial or affirmation, a leading question incorporating the matter to be denied or affirmed is
generally permitted. However where refutation is in another form such as explanation, or where extrinsic evidence is being offered, the examination should proceed
on rebuttal with leading questions focusing the witness'
attention while not suggesting the ultimate response, i.e.,
it is improper to incorporate into the question the desired refutation evidence or extrinsic evidence itself and
then inquire whether or not the foregoing is true.

In the interest of avoiding excessive collateral issues,
certain limitations on corroboration of testimony on direct and redirect examination and on refutation of attacks upon a witness on rebuttal are recognized. Such
limitations on corroboration are expressed for example in
Rule 608, reputation testimony for truthfulness, and
Rule 801(d)(1)(B), prior consistent statements.

## § 611.14  Trial Objections: An Overview; Form of the Question

In the process of examining witnesses there arise occasions where the party opposing the examination, whether
it be direct, cross, redirect, or recross, feels that the
question itself being propounded by counsel is improper
for one reason or another. If the witness is on direct or
redirect examination, the question may, for example, be
leading, call for a narrative answer, be compound, be
repetitive, call for speculation on the part of the witness,
characterize testimony or simply be unintelligible. Ques-

tions propounded on cross-examination or recross may suffer from the deficiency of being compound, repetitive, calling for speculation or unintelligibility. In addition questions on cross-examination or recross may be argumentative, assume facts either not in evidence or in dispute, or misquote the prior testimony of the witness. Occasionally the difficulty is not with the question but with the fact that the witness' answer is not responsive. Together the foregoing deficiencies may be referred to as trial objections. Trial objections thus focus primarily on the form of the question or responsiveness of the answer rather than the content of the answer itself.

Occasionally counsel opposing an examination of a witness believes something is improper in the questioning process but can't put a label on it. On other occasions counsel may realize he is getting hurt badly by the testimony of the witness and wishes to interrupt the flow of the testimony. Counsel in such situations have been known to rise and state, "Your Honor, I object, he can't do that." A more acceptable method of objecting where one thinks something is wrong but can't think immediately of the exact reason is merely to make the general objection, "I object." If there is something amiss the court may simply sustain the objection. If the court does not perceive any irregularity or itself can't put a label on it, counsel when asked to state the ground of the objection frequently responds as follows: If the witness is on direct examination, opposing counsel asserts either "form of the question" or "lack of foundation," whichever is believed to more nearly approximate what he has in mind. If the witness is on cross-examination, counsel generally asserts "form of the question". Given the imprecise nature of trial objections and thus the broad discretion placed in the court in this area, courts will frequently reply, "Counsel lay additional foundation," "Counsel, rephrase the question," or simply "Counsel, move along."

While the objection "form of the question" may suffice to raise most of the trial objections which follow, specificity will clearly enhance the likelihood of the court exercising its discretion to sustain the objection.

### § 611.15    Question Is Too Broad or Calls for a Narrative Answer

A question which is too broad or general permits the witness to give a narrative answer which may include irrelevant or otherwise objectionable testimony such as hearsay or inadmissible opinion. Since opposing counsel cannot discern from the broad general question what testimony is being sought, he cannot frame a proper objection on such grounds prior to hearing the witness' answer, at which point the jury has also heard the inadmissible matter. While a motion to strike would be granted under such circumstances, its effectiveness in having the jury disregard what it heard is suspect. Illustrative of general questions calling for a narrative response are "Tell us everything that was said that night," and "How did the accident happen?"

On the other hand, narrative responses are frequently more persuasive to the trier of fact as well as being less influenced by the suggestions of counsel than are answers to specific nonleading questions. There is also some scientific indication that spontaneous narrative is more accurate, while interrogation by specific questions is said to present a more complete picture of the facts.

In practice of course questions that tend to call for a narrative response as well as specific though nonleading questions are employed. Frequently witnesses are examined in the narrative form, being interrupted at appropriate junctures with specific inquiries to establish additional material or to more fully develop facts included in the witness' answer. Specific inquiries may be desirable for other purposes, such as to ensure the presentation of facts in a desirable order, to give the witness more confidence in the courtroom, to supplement the testimony with demonstrative evidence, to lay a foundation for the introduction of evidence whether it be documentary or real, and to establish the competency of lay or expert witnesses including establishment, when applicable, of personal knowledge.

The use of narrative versus specific questions rests very much in the discretion of the court. Where hearsay or other inadmissible evidence is unlikely to be included in a response, narrative questions will generally be permitted. Where hearsay or other inadmissible evidence is likely to be forthcoming, while the alternative of instructing the witness not to include specified matter in response to a narrative question is available, specific questions providing the opponent an opportunity to object before an answer is given tend to be required in practice.

## § 611.16 Compound Questions

A question is objectionable as compound if it contains two or more questions. A compound question increases the risk of inaccuracy since the witness may be confused by the question. Moreover the answer of the witness will be ambiguous as it is hard to determine which question is being answered. To illustrate, the question "Did you go to the store or did you go to the park?" is a compound question to which an intelligible yes or no answer could not be made.

## § 611.17   Question Is Repetitive: Asked and Answered

A question is objectionable if the witness has previously asked and answered a substantially identical question. Such a question, being repetitive, has the tendency to unduly emphasize the testimony. The objection asked and answered frequently arises on redirect or recross-examination when counsel attempts to have the witness repeat a favorable answer to obtain emphasis. Repetition is more frequently allowed on cross-examination. However, even on cross-examination once the exact question has been asked and fully answered, discretion will normally be exercised in favor of sustaining the objection.

The objection asked and answered does not apply where counsel wishes to repeat a question propounded by opposing counsel to a witness during a prior segment of the witness' examination. The objection asked and answered does apply to questions asked by counsel for a co-party similarly situated.

## § 611.18   Question Calls for Conjecture, Speculation or Judgment of Veracity

A question addressed to a witness lacking personal knowledge of the event, Rule 602, is objectionable if it asks the witness to guess or surmise what occurred. Thus a question asking the witness what "probably" occurred or for his "impression" is objectionable as calling for speculation or conjecture. Questions inquiring of the witness on cross-examination as to whether something "is possible" or "could have been" if asked to a witness lacking sufficient personal knowledge are objectionable as calling for speculation or conjecture. Similarly, questions inquiring "what if" are generally impermissible.

With respect to a question calling for opinion testimony of a lay witness, Rule 701, if the witness' opinion is not based upon personal knowledge, Rule 602, or is based upon ambiguous matters, the question is objectionable as calling for speculation or conjecture. The objection is sometimes confusingly couched in terms of calling for a conclusion of the witness. Similarly if the basis of an expert's opinion, Rule 703, includes so many varying or uncertain factors that he is required to guess or surmise in order to reach an opinion, the expert's opinion is objectionable as speculation or conjecture.

A question which requires a lay witness to comment directly on the veracity of another witness, a matter exclusively within the province of the trier of fact, is considered improper. Thus the question on cross-examination, "Are you saying, Mr. Jones is a liar?", will be prohibited. However some trial courts have been known to permit the question, "Do you disagree with Mr. X who testified that * * *?" Questions designed to elicit an opinion on veracity of another witness are equally improper on direct or redirect examination.

## § 611.19 Question Is Ambiguous, Imprecise, Unintelligible or Calls for a Vague Answer

In the interrogation of a witness, questions should be intelligibly phrased, concise, and clear in meaning. Neither the witness, the court, nor counsel should have to guess what a question is supposed to mean. If the question cannot be understood, it is objectionable as being ambiguous, imprecise, unintelligible, or calling for a vague answer.

## § 611.20   Question Is Argumentative or Contains an Improper Characterization

A question on cross-examination is argumentative if asked for the purpose of persuading the trier of fact, rather than to elicit information. Questions are also argumentative if they call for an argument in answer to an argument contained in a question. Thus, for example, the question "Are you lying now or were you lying then?" is argumentative, as is the question to an informer who says she had not been paid, "In other words, you did it for the good of the country, is that correct?" Finally, a question is argumentative if it merely invokes the witness' assent to the questioner's inferences from or interpretation of facts proved or assumed.

Whether a particular question will be found to be argumentative rests in the discretion of the trial court. The definition of an argumentative question is extremely inexact. Moreover, the relationship between counsel and the witness, the volume, tone of voice, inflection, emphasis and gestures all affect the thrust of the question. It is thus not surprising that what appears argumentative to some courts is perfectly proper cross-examination in others.

The direct examination analogue of the argumentative question is the question containing within it counsel's characterization of the previous testimony of the witness couched in favorable terminology. Questions such as "After Jones lost total control of his senses, what * * * ?" and "After you gave this crook your hard earned money, what * * * ?" are illustrative.

## § 611.21 Questions Assuming Facts Either Not in Evidence or in Dispute

A question that assumes a fact not in evidence is improper in that it presents before the jury a fact that has not been proved. The jury hearing such a fact stated in a question may erroneously assume its truth. Similarly a question which assumes a fact in dispute is calculated to suggest the adoption of the assumption by the witness. Moreover the answer may leave it unclear whether the witness actually did adopt the assumption, leaving the true purport of the answer unclear. The classic illustration is, "When did you stop beating your wife?" So does the question "At any time during this assault, did anyone attempt to leave?" which assumes the existence of the assault, a fact that is being contested. Questions of this sort are objectionable. If the witness has previously testified to the fact, the reasons for the objection do not exist. Nor is it objectionable to assume the existence of a fact not in dispute provided sufficient support for such fact exists in the record.

The use of questions assuming a fact not in evidence or in dispute generally but not exclusively arise upon cross-examination. Questions assuming a fact not in evidence on cross-examination often begin with such phrases as "Did you know," "Have you heard," or "Would it surprise you if I told you." Many of these questions will also be objectionable on the ground of relevancy. Questions merely insinuating the existence of facts not proved are also objectionable. This prohibition does not, however, extend to assuming that the witness' answer is untrue for the purpose of putting various questions to show that fact since such questions do not thereby assume that the witness has testified to a fact which he has not testified to.

The court in its discretion may accept a representation of counsel that a fact assumed or insinuated on direct or cross-examination to be true will be connected up later in the trial through the introduction of admissible evidence. Failure to introduce evidence establishing the facts previously assumed or insinuated will result in the evidence adduced being stricken. Such actions may also constitute reversible error.

## § 611.22  Misquoting a Witness in a Question

A question that misstates the testimony of the witness as part of a subsequent question to that or another witness is improper. Misquoting the prior testimony of the witness misleads and creates confusion similar to the assuming of facts not in evidence or in dispute.

## § 611.23  Unresponsive Answer: No Question Pending

An answer which is not responsive to the question should be stricken on motion of the questioner, whether on direct or cross-examination. Counsel may also where appropriate request the court to advise the trier of fact to disregard the witness' stricken answer. Counsel may also advise or preferably ask the court to advise the witness to respond directly to questions asked. The objection does not extend to statements of the witness either in answer to a question or concerning a matter involved in the litigation made as part of an improper argument between counsel and the witness.

The motion is available only to the questioner, unresponsiveness not being a matter of concern to the opposite party if the answer is otherwise admissible. If the answer is otherwise admissible, sustaining an objection by opposing counsel would be both fruitless and time wasting for examining counsel could simply ask a question designed to elicit the exact same information. However in order to prevent a witness from continuing to give an unresponsive answer, opposing counsel may object on the ground that there is no question pending before the witness, or that the answer is being volunteered. The objection is predicated upon the notion that in the absence of a pending question, it is impossible to predict and therefore to object in advance to inadmissible evidence.

## Rule 612.

## WRITING USED TO REFRESH MEMORY

**Except as otherwise provided in criminal proceedings by section 3500 of title 18, United States Code, if a witness uses a writing to refresh memory for the purpose of testifying, either—**

**(1) while testifying, or**

**(2) before testifying, if the court in its discretion determines it is necessary in the interests of justice,**

**an adverse party is entitled to have the writing produced at the hearing, to inspect it, to cross-examine the witness thereon, and to introduce in evidence those portions which relate to the testimony of the witness. If it is claimed that the writing contains matters not related to the subject matter of the testimony the court shall examine**

**the writing in camera, excise any portions not so related, and order delivery of the remainder to the party entitled thereto. Any portion withheld over objections shall be preserved and made available to the appellate court in the event of an appeal. If a writing is not produced or delivered pursuant to order under this rule, the court shall make any order justice requires, except that in criminal cases when the prosecution elects not to comply, the order shall be one striking the testimony or, if the court in its discretion determines that the interests of justice so require, declaring a mistrial.**

## § 612.1   Refreshing Recollection: General Considerations; Use of Leading Questions

The recollection of a witness under appropriate circumstances may be refreshed on direct examination by means of either a leading question or the showing of a writing. Rule 612 addresses solely employment of a writing to refresh recollection. Use of leading questions to refresh recollection falls within Rule 611(c) which provides for the use of leading questions on direct examination of a witness when necessary to develop his testimony. For the sake of convenience, however, general considerations applicable to the use of leading questions as well as writings to refresh recollection are discussed in this section; those aspects unique to the use of writings are discussed in the section which follows.

With respect to refreshment of recollection generally, it is sometimes stated that a party may seek to refresh the recollection of a witness only if the witness testifies that his recollection is exhausted and that he can't recall the matter forming the subject of the inquiry. Thus under such authority, if a witness replies in an absolute fashion, for example, that nothing else was said or nothing else happened, refreshment of recollection would not be permitted. However other decisions reach the sensible position that refreshing recollection is proper even if the witness gives a positive albeit unanticipated answer. As McCormick, Evidence § 9 at 37 (5th ed.1999) states, "The witness may believe that she remembers completely but on looking at the memorandum, she would recall additional facts." Counsel can sometimes avoid having to face the issue by incorporating lack of recollection in the question asked, such as "Do you recall whether anything else was said?" Where such a question would be inconvenient as a matter of form or where counsel does not wish to suggest to the jury that the witness has memory problems, counsel must fall back on a general instruction to the witness to respond to questions such as "Was anyone else present?" with the answer, "I don't recall."

The process of refreshing recollection must be conducted as provided in Rule 103(c) so as "to prevent inadmissible evidence from being suggested to the jury by any means, such as . . . asking questions in the hearing of the jury." Where refreshment of recollection is by means of a writing, this mandate is easily accomplished by the handing of the writing to the witness accompanied by a request to the witness to read the writing to himself. The witness may then be asked whether his recollection has been refreshed. If the answer is yes the initial question is repeated. If the witness however states that his recollection has not been refreshed, it is improper for counsel or the witness to read the writing aloud before the trier of fact.

Where the matter under consideration is of significance in the litigation, such as, for example, where the government seeks to refresh the recollection of a witness it has called as to a statement bearing directly on the guilt of the defendant, it is similarly improper to employ a leading question incorporating the content of the alleged statement before the trier of fact. The proper procedure is either to reduce the oral statement to writing and proceed as set out above or on rare occasion excuse the jury and attempt to refresh the witness' recollection. Only if the witness states that his recollection has in fact been refreshed, may the question be repeated before the jury. As stated in Goings v. United States (8th Cir. 1967):

> [I]f a party can offer a previously given statement to substitute for a witness's testimony under the guise of 'refreshing recollection,' the whole adversary system of trial must be revised. *The evil of this practice hardly merits discussion. The evil is no less when an attorney can read the statement in the presence of the jury and thereby substitute his spoken word for the written document.*

On the other hand where the witness cannot recall a preliminary or otherwise relatively unimportant matter such as which direction Main Street runs, a leading question in open court incorporating the answer may be employed. Similarly leading questions which suggest that something else may have occurred without directly stating what that event was are also proper to refresh recollection. Thus following the answer "Not that I can recall" to the question "Was anything else said?", the question "Was anything said concerning the proposed Acme merger?" is proper.

## § 612.2 Rule 612: Writings Used to Refresh Memory

A witness may refresh his memory by referring to a writing while testifying. The writing itself need not be admissible in evidence; all that is required is for the witness to state the facts from his own present recollection after inspecting it. The writing need not have been prepared by the witness or at his direction, nor need the writing have been made at or near the time of the event recorded. Moreover, the Original Writing Rule, Rule 1002, does not apply. In short, anything may be used for this purpose, the only question being whether it genuinely is calculated to revive the witness' recollection.

There is, of course, a real possibility that the witness will testify from what purports to be a revived present memory when his testimony is actually a reflection, conscious or unconscious, of what he has read rather than what he remembers. The court has considerable discretion to reject such testimony by finding that the writing did not in fact revive the witness' recollection. In reaching this determination the court may initially require the witness to read the writing to himself and surrender possession of it before responding to any questions. A finding that his memory is not revived may, however, pave the way for admission of the writing under the hearsay exception for past recollection recorded, Rule 803(5).

Where the matter is so lengthy that even a witness with a refreshed memory unaided by the writing would have trouble reciting all the facts without frequent looking at the writing, the court frequently will exercise its discretion to permit the witness to consult the writing as he speaks. This practice is so common with respect to .

experts such as doctors that counsel without objection will often simply advise the expert witness early in the examination to feel free to consult his medical records at any time during his testimony.

Rule 612 confers upon opposing counsel the absolute right to inspect the writing referred to by the witness while testifying, to cross-examine regarding it, and introduce into evidence for the purpose of impeachment those portions which relate to the testimony of the witness. These provisions of Rule 612 serve to afford protection against abuse. As McCormick, Evidence § 9 at 35–6 (5th ed.1999) states, "With the memorandum before her, the cross-examiner has a good opportunity to test the credibility of the witness's claim that her memory has been revived, and to search out any discrepancies between the writing and the testimony."

A witness may also refer to a writing to refresh his recollection prior to testifying at a trial, hearing, or other proceeding. While the version of Rule 612 proposed by the Supreme Court provided that an opponent should have the same rights with regard to writings so consulted as with those consulted on the stand, Rule 612 as amended by Congress provides for opposing counsel to have access to the writings only if the court in its discretion determines it is necessary in the interests of justice. This requirement was imposed to prevent time consuming fishing expeditions at trial among the multitude of papers which a witness may have used in preparing for his testimony as well as to avoid disclosure of information protected by a privilege.

Under Rule 612 neither inspection by the writing nor its employment upon cross-examination by itself makes the document admissible on behalf of the proponent of the witness.

The Report of the House Committee on the Judiciary states an intention that nothing in Rule 612 bar an assertion of privilege, usually lawyer-client, Standard 503, with respect to the document referred to whether before or at trial. Nevertheless support exists for the proposition that use of a writing protected by the lawyer-client privilege to refresh recollection waives the privilege. If a claim of privilege is successfully asserted as reason for not allowing access to opposing counsel, the court may make any order justice requires. If the claim of privilege is made known in advance, one obvious solution is to simply forbid the witness to refresh his recollection at any time from the writing.

When a writing is reviewed on the witness stand, and when in the court's discretion disclosure of writings reviewed prior to testifying is necessary in the interests of justice, if it is claimed that the writing reviewed contains matters not related to the subject matter of the testimony, the court shall examine the writing in camera, excise any portions not so related, and order delivery of the remainder to the party entitled thereto. If a writing is not produced or delivered pursuant to order under this rule, the court shall make any order justice requires including striking the testimony, contempt, dismissal or finding issues against the offender; except that in criminal cases when the prosecution elects not to comply, the order shall be one striking the testimony or, if the court in its discretion determines that the interests of justice so require, declaring a mistrial, Rule 612.

## Rule 613.

# PRIOR STATEMENTS OF WITNESSES

(a) Examining Witness Concerning Prior Statement. In examining a witness concerning a prior statement made by the witness, whether written or not, the statement need not be shown nor its contents disclosed to the witness at that time, but on request the same shall be shown or disclosed to opposing counsel.

(b) Extrinsic Evidence of Prior Inconsistent Statement of Witness. Extrinsic evidence of a prior inconsistent statement by a witness is not admissible unless the witness is afforded an opportunity to explain or deny the same and the opposite party is afforded an opportunity to interrogate the witness thereon, or the interests of justice otherwise require. This provision does not apply to admissions of a party-opponent as defined in Rule 801(d)(2).

### § 613.1 Rule 613(a) and (b): Prior Statements of Witnesses; An Overview

A witness testifying in court may be impeached by proof that the witness made a statement outside of court contradicting his or her in-court testimony, or failed to speak under circumstances where it would have been natural to relate the matters testified to in court if true. The rationale is a witness who testifies one way at trial while speaking inconsistently prior to trial is blowing hot and cold thereby raising doubts as to the truthfulness of both statements.

A prior statement of a witness may be employed for purposes of impeachment only if inconsistent with the witness' in-court testimony. An inconsistent statement by a witness meeting the definition of hearsay, Rule 801(a)-(c), is admissible as substantive evidence only if the statement is exempted from the category of hearsay, Rules 801(d)(1) and (2) and particularly Rule 801(d)(1)(A), or if the statement meets the requirements of a hearsay exception, Rules 803 and 804. Otherwise its effect is limited to impairing the credibility of the witness. Rule 613 applies only with respect to prior inconsistent statements admissible solely to impeach credibility of the witness or as substantive evidence solely by virtue of Rule 801(d)(1)(A). Prior inconsistent statement impeachment is subject to Rule 403.

Rule 613(a) abolishes the requirement emanating from Queen Caroline's Case (Eng.1820) that cross-examining counsel show or disclose to the witness an inconsistent writing prior to examination concerning its contents. This requirement was abolished in England long ago by statute. The requirement, which for the most part had not been followed by trial courts in actual practice, is now discarded officially in favor of surprise; the truth seeking process is better served by cross-examination without first providing the witness a warning, Rule 613(a). The provision for disclosure upon request to opposing counsel is designed to curtail unwarranted insinuations as to the existence of a prior statement.

The traditional foundation requirement that the attention of the witness be directed to the statement on cross-examination is relaxed in Rule 613(b) in favor of simply requiring that the witness be provided an opportunity to explain or deny and the opposite party an opportunity to examine the witness with respect to the statement, with no specification of any particular time or sequence.

A prior inconsistent statement should not be confused with an admission of a party opponent, Rule 801(d)(2), which like statements admitted as a hearsay exception are not subject to the provisions of Rule 613(b).

## § 613.2 Prior Statements of Witnesses: Requirement of Inconsistency

Prior inconsistent statements are not limited to those which are directly contradictory; it is sufficient if the inconsistency has a reasonable tendency to discredit the testimony of the witness. McCormick, Evidence § 34 at 127 (5th ed.1999) suggests the following: "[C]ould the jury reasonably find that a witness who believed the truth of the facts testified to would have been unlikely to make a prior statement of this tenor?" 3A Wigmore, Evidence § 1040 at 1048 (Chadbourn rev.1970) proposes a similarly liberal test: "Do the two expressions appear to have been produced by inconsistent beliefs?" The liberal view of inconsistency has generally been applied in the federal courts

The prior inconsistent statement may consist of a previously expressed opinion whether or not the subject matter would be a proper one for opinion evidence offered at trial. The inconsistency may also consist of the omission from a prior statement of a matter which would reasonably be expected to have been mentioned if true, or the failure to speak at all of a matter asserted at trial under circumstances in which it would have been natural to do so. In a similar vein, under circumstances which would normally call for a denial if untrue, the failure to respond to the statement of another may be treated as an adoption by silent acquiescence. Furthermore, the inconsistency may consist of a statement made by a third party adopted by the declarant as true. Finally, an inconsistency may consist of a photograph, sketch, or identikit picture previously adopted by the witness as an accurate portrayal of an individual differently described or identified by that witness in court.

A witness who testifies to a fact at trial may be impeached with a prior statement of the witness claiming a lack of recollection as to the fact; current recollection and prior lack of recollection are inconsistent. When, however, a witness claims lack of recollection on the stand as to the existence of an earlier event, a prior statement describing that event is arguably not on its face inconsistent with the witness' current lack of recollection. The establishment of a prior statement describing the event which the witness claims on the witness stand not to recall does, however, bring into question the weight to be afforded the witness' overall ability to recall, along with whether the witness' claimed lack of recollection is real of feigned. Since adversely affecting the credibility of a witness called by an opponent is one of the purposes of cross-examination, inquiry with respect to the prior statement on cross-examination may be permitted in the discretion of the court. When a witness on direct examination asserts a lack of recollection as to the underlying event, provided the court initially determines that current lack of recollection and a prior statement as to the underlying event are in fact inconsistent, the calling party's right to impeach the witness with an inconsistent statement is governed by Rule 607. Substantive admissibility of some but by no means all such prior inconsistent statements is provided for in Rule 801(d)(1)(A).

## § 613.3   Prior Statements of Witnesses: Foundation Requirement; Good Faith Basis; Extrinsic Proof; Limiting Instruction

At common law a proper foundation had to be laid during cross-examination of the witness prior to the introduction of extrinsic proof as to the existence of a prior inconsistent statement. This traditional foundation consisted of directing the attention of the witness to the time, place, and circumstances of the statement, often called "persons present," along with the content of the statement. The foundation requirement served several purposes including avoiding unfair surprise to the adversary by alerting him to the possible existence of a prior inconsistent statement and thus enabling him to prepare to meet the issue and preventing unfairness to the witness by permitting him to explain or deny an apparent inconsistency at the time it was first suggested. Most importantly with respect to prior inconsistent statements admissible only for purposes of impeachment, the foundation requirement fostered the use of such statements to affect credibility while discouraging the trier of fact from giving them substantive consideration. The foundation requirement placed the prior statement in juxtaposition with the testimony at trial of the witness sought to be impeached. In addition, by enabling the witness to admit that a prior statement is his own, the foundation requirement reduced the likelihood that extrinsic evidence of the prior inconsistent statement would be introduced, evidence which is much harder for the jury not to accept substantively.

Accomplishment of these objectives did not require strict enforcement of the "time, place, and persons present" aspect of the traditional rule in comparison to the content of the statement; courts generally required only that the witness' attention be sufficiently directed to the content of the prior inconsistent statement and the circumstances surrounding its making so that he could admit, deny, or explain. On the other hand, the content of the alleged prior inconsistent statement must be presented to the witness with particularity. The impeaching cross-examiner himself did not actually have to provide the opportunity for explanation. The cross-examiner could instead require the witness to answer the question whether he made the particular statement yes or no. As long as counsel on redirect was permitted to elicit an explanation, the foundation requirement was deemed satisfied. However, courts applying the commonlaw foundation requirement strictly enforced the requirement that the opportunity for such explanation must occur before the introduction of extrinsic evidence.

While the traditional foundation is still generally laid in practice, the formal insistence that the attention of the witness be directed to the statement on cross-examination is relaxed in Rule 613(b) in favor of simply providing the witness an opportunity to explain or deny and the opposite party an opportunity to examine on the statement, with no specification of any particular time or sequence. Rule 613(b) thus permits extrinsic proof to be introduced before the witness is allowed to admit, deny, or explain the prior statement. Moreover what is important under Rule 613(b) is the opportunity to deny or explain, not whether any denial or explanation actually occurs; the foundation requirement is satisfied if the witness remains available for recall by the calling party later in the course of the trial, even if that party chooses not to recall the witness. Rule 613(b) in addition provides that the opportunity to explain or deny may be refused altogether to a witness where the interests of justice so require. Thus for example, if counsel does not learn of an inconsistent statement until after a witness ceased being amenable to the court's jurisdiction, in the court's discretion impeachment absent the foundation may be permitted.

A good faith basis for inquiring regarding a prior inconsistent statement is required: innuendoes or insinuations of a nonexistent statement are improper. Protection against unwarranted insinuation is provided in part by the requirement of Rule 613(a) for prior disclosure of the contents of the statement on request to opposing counsel. In addition, the court in its discretion may demand prior to any cross-examination an on the record assurance of counsel that if required to do so that he can support the foundation question as to whether the witness had made a prior statement with evidence of the alleged statement.

If the witness denies making the prior inconsistent statement, states that he cannot remember making the prior inconsistent statement, or otherwise equivocates, the prior inconsistent statement if collateral may not be proved; extrinsic evidence is inadmissible. However if the prior inconsistent statement relates to a subject matter that is relevant for a purpose other than mere contradiction, i.e., the subject matter itself tends directly or circumstantially to establish a fact of consequence, the matter is noncollateral; extrinsic evidence must, not may, be introduced. If the witness admits making the statement, the party calling him is entitled on redirect to have him make such explanation as he can, show the circumstances under which made, or to introduce portions of the other conversation, document or testimony tending to explain, qualify or otherwise shed light on the inconsistency. Whether the statement may be proved by extrinsic evidence even though the witness unequivocally admits having made it is the subject of dispute. Questions to the impeaching witness presenting extrinsic proof should state the time, place, circumstances of the statement and the subject matter of the statement but not its content. Leading questions are permitted as necessary to develop the witness' testimony, Rule 611(c). Such questions serve to focus the witness' attention on the testimony sought and thus avoid the bringing out of incompetent matters which might result if the conversation were asked for generally. Extrinsic evidence as to a collateral matter is not admissible. The cross-examiner thus must take the denial or explanation given by the witness.

Where a prior inconsistent statement is admitted solely to impeach the witness, the jury upon request will be cautioned at the time the statement is introduced and/or a limiting instruction given when the court charges the jury as to the law that they are to consider the statement only as affecting the credibility of the witness, Rule 105. Where neither a cautionary nor limiting instruction is requested by counsel, if the prior inconsistent statement is extremely damaging if considered by the jury as substantive evidence and the proponent of such evidence is the prosecution in a criminal case otherwise having a weak case, the court to avoid plain error must *sua sponte* give such an instruction, but not otherwise. In the absence of plain error, if no request is made to have the jury advised that the prior inconsistent statement was admitted solely to impeach, the statement may be considered as substantive evidence by the jury.

## § 613.4  Requiring a Foundation on Cross–Examination

As the Advisory Committee's Note to Rule 613(b) indicates, "[t]he traditional insistence that the attention of the witness be directed to the statement on cross-examination is relaxed in favor of simply providing the witness an opportunity to explain and the opposite party an opportunity to examine on the statement, with no specification of any particular time or sequence." The Advisory Committee's Note suggests that Rule 613(b) facilitates the questioning of collusive witnesses by permitting several such witnesses to be examined before disclosure of a joint prior inconsistent statement. That rather infrequent benefit hardly explains Rule 613(b) dispensing with the requirement that a foundation be laid on cross-examination. The rationale for Rule 613(b) in fact derives from a combination of two factors: (1) that Rule 801(d)(1)(A) as proposed by the Advisory Committee and the Supreme Court gave substantive effect to all prior inconsistent statements, and (2) perceived lawyer incompetence.

To understand why the Advisory Committee proposed Rule 613(b) one must keep in mind that if prior inconsistent statements are admissible only for purposes of impeachment, the foundation requirement fosters the use of such statements to affect credibility while discouraging the trier of fact from giving them substantive consideration. In practice, the foundation requirement served to place a prior statement in juxtaposition to the testimony at trial of the witness sought to be impeached. In addition, by enabling the witness to admit a prior statement as his own, the foundation requirement reduced the likelihood that extrinsic evidence of the prior inconsistent statement would be introduced, evidence that is much harder for the jury not to accept substantively. Under the scheme of the proposed evidence rules, however, all prior inconsistent statements were to be admissible as substantive evidence pursuant to Rule 801(d)(1)(A). With the substantive admissibility of all such prior statements this objective fostered by the foundation requirement was no longer relevant and a practical consideration became paramount. Trial lawyers for some unknown reason often forget to lay or in some cases never learned how to lay a proper foundation for extrinsic evidence. The Advisory Committee politely referred to such forgetfulness or incompetence as the "dangers of oversight." With substantive admissibility, these "oversight[s]" could be legitimized by permitting introduction of prior inconsistent statements at any time so long as the witness was eventually given an opportunity to deny or explain.

As enacted by Congress, however, Rule 801(d)(1)(A) does not permit the substantive admission of all prior inconsistent statements. Thus the traditional foundation requirements' utility in encouraging the jury to consider a prior inconsistent statement solely as an indication of credibility and not as substantive evidence remains relevant. Since all prior inconsistent statements are not substantively admissible, counsel should not have the unfettered right to introduce extrinsic evidence of such a statement before the witness has an opportunity to admit, deny, or explain the declaration. Initial introduction of extrinsic evidence permits a prior statement to be placed before the trier of fact on multiple occasions and under circumstances encouraging the statement's acceptance as substantive evidence. Accordingly, the court should require under Rule 403 and Rule 611(a)(1) that the traditional foundation be laid on cross-examination prior to the introduction of extrinsic evidence with respect to prior inconsistent statements admissible solely to impeach unless the interests of justice otherwise require.

## § 613.5 Prior Conduct of a Witness

A witness may be impeached by proof that he acted in a manner contradictory of his testimony. As with contradiction generally, extrinsic evidence may not be introduced relating solely to collateral matters. Inconsistent conduct relied upon for impeachment does not require the providing of an opportunity to explain or deny.

## § 613.6 Use of Suppressed Statements and Illegally Seized Evidence to Impeach

Statements taken from a defendant in violation of *Miranda* and thus inadmissible when offered by the prosecution as part of its case in chief are admissible to impeach statements made by defendant on direct examination. Illegally seized evidence is also admissible to impeach the testimony of the defendant. Moreover, answers by the defendant to questions propounded on cross-examination that are plainly within the scope of defendant's direct examination, Rule 611(b), are subject to impeachment by the government albeit by evidence that has been illegally obtained. Finally, reliance by a party upon Rule 703 may open the door to the admissibility of otherwise inadmissible evidence to rebut.

# Rule 614.

## CALLING AND INTERROGATION OF WITNESSES BY COURT

(a) **Calling by Court.** The court may, on its own motion or at the suggestion of a party, call witnesses, and all parties are entitled to cross-examine witnesses thus called.

(b) **Interrogation by Court.** The court may interrogate witnesses, whether called by itself or by a party.

(c) **Objections.** Objections to the calling of witnesses by the court or to interrogation by it may be made at the time or at the next available opportunity when the jury is not present.

## § 614.1 Rule 614(a): Calling of Witnesses by the Court

While it is clear that the court may on its own motion or at the suggestion of a party call a witness not called by a party, Rule 614(a), rarely should the court's discretion be so exercised with respect to a lay witness. The calling of nonexpert witnesses by the court is generally an unwarranted intrusion into the adversary system and thus should be undertaken only when clearly required in the interests of justice. Instances where the action may be warranted arise in situations such as custody matters where a special obligation is placed upon the court to protect the interests of a nonparty.

The power of the court to itself call a witness was historically most often exercised where the government expected that a witness would be perceived as untrustworthy and desired to escape the necessity of calling him, thereby avoiding any apparent association with the witness before the jury. Making the witness a "court's witness" also served to circumvent the common law rule against impeachment of a party's own witness. If the witness was called at the request of the government as a "court's witness," as is true under Rule 614(a), either party could then cross-examine, i.e., lead and impeach, the witness.

Under the Federal Rules of Evidence, a witness possessing crucial testimony for whose veracity a party does not wish to vouch will almost invariably be declared a hostile witness under Rule 611(c). Accordingly, the party calling such a witness will be permitted to propound leading questions. Impeachment of such a witness should be conducted in accordance with Rule 607, which provides generally that the party calling the witness may impeach. Whether the party calling the particular witness would in fact be entitled to impeach with a prior inconsistent statement is a matter which should be addressed squarely and not circumvented by the inadequate expedient of having the witness declared a "court's witness". Difficulties accompanying witness association with a party can be ameliorated, if not totally removed, by the court advising the jury when the witness is called by a party that the witness has been declared hostile to the calling party.

## § 614.2   Rule 614(b): Interrogation by the Court

The court may ask questions of a witness. He must, however, avoid conveying to the jury his views regarding the merits of the case, the veracity of the witness, or the weight of the evidence. Throughout the trial the court must maintain an appearance of impartiality and neither become an advocate for a particular party nor display hostility to anyone. If the questions asked by the court are improper, the embarrassing position of counsel is obvious. Avoidance of these hazards confines the court largely to questions designed to clarify confused factual issues, to correct inadequacies of direct or cross-examination, to aid an embarrassed witness, or otherwise to insure that the trial proceeds efficiently and fairly.

## § 614.3   Rule 614(c): Objection to Calling or Interrogation of Witness

A specific objection is required to preserve for appeal any alleged error with respect to the court calling or interrogating a witness, Rule 103. However, under Rule 614(c) the objection need not be made contemporaneously with the calling or interrogation if the jury is present. Thus counsel is relieved of the embarrassment attendant upon objecting to the court's action in the presence of the jury. The objection can be made at the next available opportunity when the jury is absent, or preferably at the first reasonable opportunity for a side bar conference. Objections so made will be considered timely under Rule 103(a)(1).

## Rule 615.

## EXCLUSION OF WITNESSES

**At the request of a party the court shall order witnesses excluded so that they cannot hear the testimony of other witnesses, and it may make the order of its own motion. This rule does not authorize exclusion of (1) a party who is a natural person, or (2) an officer or employee of a party which is not a natural person designated as its**

representative by its attorney, or (3) a person whose presence is shown by a party to be essential to the presentation of the party's cause, or (4) a person authorized by statute to be present.

## § 615.1 Exclusion and Separation of Witnesses

If a witness hears the testimony of others before he himself takes the stand, he will find it much easier to deliberately tailor his own story to that of other witnesses. Witnesses may also be influenced subconsciously. In either event, the cross-examiner will find it more difficult to expose fabrication, collusion, inconsistencies, or inaccuracies with respect to witnesses who have heard others testify. Separation prevents improper influence during the trial by prohibiting witness to witness communication both inside and outside the courtroom

At common law the court in its discretion could exclude witnesses in the interests of the ascertainment of truth. Rather than adopting a discretionary approach, Rule 615 treats the exclusion of witnesses as a matter of right "At the request of a party, the court *shall* order witnesses excluded." The court is also empowered to order exclusion on its own motion. A request to exclude witnesses is often referred to as "invoking the rule on witnesses." No time period is specified in which to make the request. Several standards have been applied in determining whether a failure of the court to order exclusion of a witness requires a reversal of the judgment.

Under Rule 615 not all witnesses may be excluded and separated. The rule does not authorize exclusion of (1) a party who is a natural person, or (2) an officer or employee of a party which is not a natural person designated as its representative by its attorney which includes an investigative agent of the government, or (3) a person whose presence is shown by the party to be essential to the presentation of the cause, or (4) a person authorized by statute to be present.

An example of a witness whose presence may be essential is an expert witness. It is certainly essential to give counsel the benefit of his expert's assistance while an expert for the other party is testifying. Similarly assistance may be needed in connection with other technical matters as to which counsel lacks sufficient familiarity to try the case effectively on his own. A strong argument can be made for also permitting the presence of an expert witness who intends to give his opinion at trial based in part on evidence presented at trial, Rule 703.

Exclusion and separation does not extend to rebuttal witnesses or witnesses called to impeach credibility.

While Rule 615 provides solely for the exclusion of witnesses from the courtroom, the court may take further measures of separation designed to prevent communication between witnesses, such as ordering them to remain physically apart, ordering them not to discuss the case with one another, and ordering witnesses not to read a transcript of the trial testimony of another witness.

If a witness violates an order of exclusion or separation, the appropriate remedy is committed to the sound discretion of the court. The court may declare a mistrial, refuse to permit a witness to testify, permit cross-examination concerning the violation, or instruct the jury to weigh the credibility of the witness in light of the witness' presence in court or discussions with another witness. The court may also hold the witness in contempt.

However the thrust of judicial opinion absent compelling circumstances is against the simple remedy of either declaring a mistrial or disqualifying the witness. Unfortunately once it is decided to permit the witness to testify, the remaining alternatives are not without their drawbacks. A contempt citation punishes the witness and may perhaps deter future misconduct but does nothing to extinguish any false testimony which the witness may have fabricated by listening to other witnesses. The comment, while useful, may have unwarranted repercussions where the witness remained in the courtroom but his testimony was unaffected. A derogatory comment on his credibility may actually distort the truth. The best remedy is to avoid the problem as much as possible by the court impressing upon both the witness and counsel in the first place the importance of obeying the court's ruling excluding and separating the witness.

# ARTICLE VII

# OPINIONS AND EXPERT TESTIMONY

*Table of Rules*

## Rules 701–706.

## OPINIONS OF LAY AND EXPERT WITNESSES

### Prelude

## § 701.0 Opinions of Lay and Expert Witnesses: Historical Perspective and Introduction

Implicit in the modern cases dealing with opinions of both lay and expert witnesses is the recognition that the making of an intelligent decision on a contested issue of fact requires the trier of fact to be supplied with data which is useful in resolving the issue. This sensible policy applies regardless of whether the data consist of matters observed by an ordinary witness or specialized technical information supplied by an expert. Conversely, testimony which merely tells the jury to decide an issue in a particular way is both useless and confusing. Illustrative are the exclusion of an expert's opinion that the defendant had no legal excuses for non-performance, and of an opinion that an oil distributor was under a contractual duty to make a shipment. Obviously these were both situations in which more detailed facts, readily understood by the trier of fact, were available and should have been supplied. Unfortunately the soundness of excluding opinion evidence in cases of this kind led at common law to the generalization that witnesses should state "facts" rather than "opinions" and that opinions on ultimate issues should not be allowed. The result was to deprive triers of fact of useful and needed assistance, especially when specialized technical information was necessary for proper evaluation. Nevertheless even when the rule against opinions was in full flower, courts recognized that a witness, whether lay or expert, could testify in the form of an opinion under limited circumstances.

The admissibility of lay opinions is now governed by Rule 701 and expert opinions by Rules 702, 703 and 705; opinions on the ultimate issue are controlled as to both by Rule 704. The standard to be applied with regard to lay opinions is whether the opinion, rationally based on the perception of the witness, Rule 701(a), will assist the trier of fact in understanding the witness' testimony or the determination of a fact in issue, Rule 701(b). With respect to an expert witness, Rule 702 provides for the admissibility of opinions which will assist the trier of fact to understand the evidence or determine a fact in issue. In both instances, opinions are admissible if they will be of assistance, "of help," to the trier of fact. Opinion testimony of both lay and expert witnesses is subject to exclusion under Rule 403.

The overall liberality of the "of help" standard as to both lay and expert witness opinions coupled with the position taken in Rule 704 permitting opinions on the ultimate issue provides a clear indication that opinions previously admissible under the common law are also admissible under Rules 701 and 702. Moreover many opinions that once would have been excluded are now admissible as well.

The frequency with which expert witnesses have testified in modern times coupled with their importance in the litigation has focused considerable attention on the rules of evidence governing the admissibility of expert witness testimony.

Upon enactment in 1975, Rules 703 and 705 of the Federal Rules of Evidence altered the common law rules with respect to the basis of an expert's opinion as well as the manner such basis is disclosed to the jury. More recently, the United States Supreme Court imposed a gatekeeping requirement with respect to every explanative theory employed by an expert witness, a requirement now reflected in Rule 702 itself.

## Rule 701.

### OPINION TESTIMONY BY LAY WITNESSES

**If the witness is not testifying as an expert, the witness' testimony in the form of opinions or inferences is limited to those opinions or inferences which are (a) rationally based on the perception of the witness, (b) helpful to a clear understanding of**

**the witness' testimony or the determination of a fact in issue, and (c) not based on scientific, technical or other specialized knowledge within the scope of Rule 702.**

## § 701.1 Opinion Testimony of Lay Witnesses

Rule 701 provides for the admissibility of opinions or inferences of a witness not testifying as an expert. Prior to testifying to his opinion or inference, the witness must first lay a foundation establishing personal knowledge of the facts which form the basis of the opinion or inference, Rule 602. In addition, where relevancy requires, a foundation must be laid as to the witness' personal knowledge of facts to which the observed facts are being compared. Thus a witness may not testify that something smelled like dynamite unless it is sufficiently established that the witness from prior experience knows what dynamite smells like. The opinion or inference of the witness must be rationally based on the witness' perception, meaning only that it must be one which a person could normally form from observed facts. Moreover the testimony in the form of an opinion or inference must not be based on scientific, technical or other specialized knowledge within the scope of Rule 702, but rather must be the result of the type of experiences common to many human beings. Finally, the testimony of a lay witness in the form of an opinion or inference must be helpful to a clear understanding of his testimony or to the determination of a fact in issue. Whether a particular opinion or inference is in fact both rationally based and helpful naturally depends upon the facts of the case. This determination is made by the court, Rule 104(a).

A clear line between fact and opinion is impossible to draw. In a sense all testimony to matters of fact is the conclusion of the witness formed from observed phenomena and mental impressions. Witnesses who are accustomed in speaking to include opinions and inferences in describing events often find any line difficult to draw. It is more helpful to the jury to hear such a witness speak naturally than to have him harried by objections that he is improperly giving his opinion. Absolute certainty on the part of the lay witness is not required; opinions expressed with qualifications such as "I believe" or "I can't be positive, but" may be admitted , as may opinions expressed in terms such as "could", "most probably", or "is similar to". Helpful opinions rationally based upon the perception of the witness couched in terms of an estimate are also admissible. Generally speaking a lay witness may testify in the form of an opinion, (1) when an expression of the witness' personal knowledge could be conveyed in no other form, (2) when a witness formed an accurate total impression, although unable to account for all the details upon which it was based, or (3) most importantly, when an accounting of the details alone would not accurately convey the total impression received by the witness. These circumstances frequently overlap. To illustrate, in a prosecution for receiving stolen property, a witness was permitted to testify to his opinion based on personal knowledge that the accused knew how the merchandise was obtained.

Rule 701 is stated in the nature of a general principle of helpfulness, leaving specific application much to the discretion of the trial court. In applying the standard of helpfulness, the more detailed description is preferred to the more abstract. The closer the subject of the opinion approaches critical issues, the greater the likelihood the court will require more concrete expression from the witness either alone or prior to the offering of an opinion conveying the witness' overall impression. The court may insist that loaded words like "murdered," "stolen" or "assaulted" be avoided in a shorthand rendering. Obviously an opinion amounting to no more than a belief that the plaintiff or the defendant ought to win is inadmissible; such opinions are not helpful to a clear understanding of his testimony or the determination of a fact in issue.

The topics upon which lay witnesses have been permitted to express an opinion are extremely varied. They include the appearance of persons or things, identity, the manner of conduct, competency of a person, feeling, degrees of light or darkness, sound, size, weight, distance and an endless number of things that cannot be described factually in words apart from inferences. Also included are speed of a vehicle, the value of personal property, the financial condition of an entity, the nature of a substance, the meaning of a statement, the witness' own physical, mental or emotional status, the identity and physical condition of another person including such things as age, condition of health, ability to work, sanity, suffering, possession of mental faculties, hearing, eyesight, unconsciousness after an accident, and intoxication to name just a few. Opinions as to the state of mind or emotion of another create special difficulties.

## Rule 702.

## TESTIMONY BY EXPERTS

**If scientific, technical, or other specialized knowledge will assist the trier of fact to understand the evidence or to determine a fact in issue, a witness qualified as an expert by knowledge,**

**skill, experience, training, or education, may testify thereto in the form of an opinion or otherwise, if (1) the testimony is based upon sufficient facts or data, (2) the testimony is the product of reliable principles and methods, and (3) the witness has applied the principles and methods reliably to the facts of the case.**

## § 702.1　Testimony by Experts: An Overview

Testimony providing scientific, technical, or other specialized knowledge, in the form of an opinion or otherwise, is admissible only if (1) the knowledge is based upon sufficient facts, data, or opinions, (2) there are sufficient assurances of trustworthiness present that the explanative theory being employed to create the knowledge produces a correct result to warrant jury acceptance, (3) the explanative theory has been applied in accordance with proper procedures, (4) the witness is qualified as an expert by knowledge, skill, experience, training or education to provide such knowledge, and (5) the knowledge will assist the trier of fact to understand the evidence or to determine a fact in issue, Rule 702.

The admissibility of expert testimony, Rule 702, requires that the trial court make several preliminary determinations, Rule 104(a). The trial court must decide whether the witness called is properly qualified to give the testimony sought. A witness may be qualified as a expert on the basis of either knowledge, skill, experience, training, or education or a combination thereof. The trial court must further determine that the testimony of the expert witness, in the form of an opinion or otherwise, will assist the trier of fact, i.e., be helpful, to understand the evidence or to determine a fact in issue. Finally the trial court must determine that as actually applied in the matter at hand, Rule 702(3), to facts, data, or opinions sufficiently established to exist, Rule 702(1), including facts, data, or opinions reasonably relied upon under Rule 703, sufficient assurances are present that the expert witness' explanative theory produces a correct result to warrant jury acceptance, i.e., testimony that is the product of reliable principles and methods, Rule 702(2). An explanative theory must be supplied by the expert; an opinion without analysis is meaningless. The proponent of the expert witness testimony has the burden of establishing the foregoing admissibility requirements to be more probably true than not true. The weight to be given to expert testimony permitted by the court is for the trior of fact to determine. Expert witness testimony is subject to exclusion under Rule 403.

Expert testimony is not limited to scientific or technical areas, but rather includes all areas of specialized knowledge. Thus within the scope of Rule 702's concept of experts fall individuals, sometimes called "skilled" witnesses, such as bankers and landowners testifying as to land value, and others whose expertise is based largely upon experience.

When scientific, technical, or other specialized knowledge will be helpful to the trier in evaluating facts intelligently, the traditional method of supplying data of this nature is the introduction of an opinion of an expert witness. Rule 702 provides that expert testimony may be "in the form of an opinion or otherwise." Thus the expert may, but need not, testify in the form of an opinion. He may instead give an exposition of relevant scientific or other principles permitting the trier of fact to draw its own inference or conclusion from the evidence presented, or he may combine the two.

The expert whose function is to supply scientific, technical or other specialized knowledge, should be distinguished from the lay witness who is required to have some specific background of experience common to many human beings in order to render his observations significant, i.e., rationally based on the perception of the witness as specified in Rule 701. What is required of the expert witness is the establishment of a sufficiently reliable explanative theory underlying scientific, technical, or other specialized knowledge that will assist the trier of fact to understand the evidence or determine a fact in issue.

Expert witnesses frequently express an opinion in response to a question such as "Do you have an opinion to a reasonable degree of [scientific, medical or other technical] certainty as to * * * ?" While the expert usually replies to follow up questions indicating his opinion in absolute terms such as "did" or "was caused", less than absolute certainty is permissible. Thus opinions expressed in terms such as "could", "most probably", or "is similar to" are properly received. While questions to an expert designed to elicit an opinion as to a fact of consequence including an expression of his estimate of probabilities of the facts expressed in the opinion are frequently couched in terms of reasonable certainty, such phraseology is not mandated.

## § 702.2   Qualifications of Experts

An expert must be shown by the party calling him to possess scientific, technical or other specialized knowledge. Whether the witness is sufficiently qualified as an expert is a matter to be decided by the court, Rule 104(a). The court may permit a voir dire examination into the expert's qualifications to express a particular opinion. If the court finds the witness unqualified, the witness will be excused prior to presenting the opinion to the jury. It is preferable that the court not advise the jury of its determination if it decides that the witness is in fact qualified as an expert as to a particular subject matter.

A witness may be qualified as an expert by reason of knowledge, skill, experience, training or education. Under Rule 702, a witness may be qualified as an expert by virtue of any one such factor, or upon a combination of any of the five factors. Specific degrees, certificates of training or membership in a professional organization are not required. Included within the category of experts are what the Advisory Committee's Note refers to as "skilled" experts, such as bankers or landowners testifying as to land value. The local carpenter, plumber, tilelayer, etc., may be added to this list of experts. The degree and manner of knowledge and experience required of the proffered expert is directly related to the complexity of the subject matter and the corresponding likelihood of error by one insufficiently familiar therewith. Of course a person may be an expert with respect to a related subject matter and still not be qualified as an expert in the subject matter at hand. Overall the court must determine whether testimony by the witness as an expert will assist the trier of fact to understand the evidence or to determine a fact in issue.

Liberality and flexibility in evaluating qualifications should be the rule; the proposed expert should not be required to satisfy an overly narrow test of his own qualifications. The trial court has wide discretion in determining the competency of a witness as an expert with respect to a particular subject. The court's decision is reviewed applying the abuse of discretion standard.

## § 702.3  Compensation of Experts; Compelling Testimony at Trial, Contingent Fees

Expert witnesses hired by a party to testify are paid by that party for their time spent in preparation and while testifying at trial. It is improper for an expert to be compensated on a contingent fee basis. In responding to arguments based upon right to access to courts, the prohibition has been upheld on the ground that the inducement placed upon the expert by a contingent fee to tailor his testimony is too great.

The expert may be compelled to testify at trial by a party, whether as to observed facts or in the form of an expert opinion if previously formed, without payment or compensation other than ordinary witness fees. An agreement to pay special compensation for the giving of such testimony would thus seem to lack consideration. However time spent in preparation or in forming new opinions would no doubt support a contract to pay therefor since preparation is not compellable in the absence of compensation.

## § 702.4  Assist the Trier of Fact; Common Knowledge

Expert testimony is admissible whenever scientific, technical or other specialized knowledge will assist the trier of fact to understand the evidence or to determine a fact in issue, Rule 702. At common law it was sometimes stated that expert testimony is admissible only when the factual issue is one which jurors could not determine without technical assistance. This restriction was frequently stated conversely: expert testimony would be excluded if upon a matter reasonably regarded as within the common knowledge and experience of jurors and hence involving no need of expert assistance. Under Rule 702 the admissibility of expert testimony is to be determined solely on the basis of assisting the trier of fact. Thus even as to matters within the general common knowledge and experience of jurors, where helpful to comprehension or explanation, expert testimony is permitted. Rule 702 thus adopts the position long advocated by 7 Wigmore, Evidence § 1923 at 31–32 (Chadbourn rev.1978):

> The true test of the admissibility of such testimony is not whether the subject matter is common or uncommon, or whether many persons or few have some knowledge of the matter; but it is whether the witnesses offered as experts have any peculiar knowledge or experience, not common to the world, which renders their opinions founded on such knowledge or experience any aid to the court or the jury in determining the questions at issue.

## § 702.5 "Gatekeeping" Under *Daubert/Kumho*/Rule 702: Determining "Reliable"

The United States Supreme Court has declared that the trial court has a gatekeeping obligation to determine whether the explanative theory underlying every expert witness' testimony, regardless of whether based on scientific, technical or other specialized knowledge, is "reliable." A flexible approach is to be employed. Federal Rule of Evidence 702 was amended effective December 1, 2000 to reflect the foregoing by requiring that the trial judge before permitting an expert to testify determine that "(1) the testimony is based upon sufficient facts or data, (2) the testimony is the product of reliable principles and methods, and (3) the witness has applied the principles and methods reliably to the facts of the case." This section explores the concept of reliability gatekeeping in the context of the specific requirements of Amended Rule 702.

**Historical development;** *Frye* **and** *Daubert.* When "scientific" evidence is offered as substantive "evidence" or as forming the basis of an expert's opinion, the "reliability" of the scientific fact derived from a scientific principle generally depends on the following factors: (1) the reliability of the underlying scientific principle; (2) the reliability of the technique or process that applies the principle; (3) the condition of any instrumentation used in the process; (4) adherence to proper procedures; (5) the qualifications of the person who performs the test; and (6) the qualifications of the person who interprets the results. With respect to the first two criteria, the predominant common-law test in the United States for determining that such evidence is sufficiently reliable to be admitted, first enunciated in 1923 in Frye v. United States (D.C.Cir.1923), is based on the general acceptance of the scientific principle:

Just when a scientific principle or discovery crosses the line between the experimental and demonstrable stages is difficult to define. Somewhere in this twilight zone the evidential force of the principle must be recognized, and while the courts will go a long way in admitting expert testimony deduced from a well-recognized scientific principle or discovery, the thing from which the deduction is made must be sufficiently established to have gained general acceptance in the particular field in which it belongs.

In Daubert v. Merrell Dow Pharmaceuticals, Inc. (S.Ct. 1993), the United States Supreme Court declared that the *Frye* "general acceptance" test did not survive adoption of the Federal Rules of Evidence. At the same time, the Supreme Court imposed a requirement that with respect to "scientific" evidence, the trial judge under Rules 702 and 104(a) must act as a gatekeeper, screening "scientific" evidence to ensure reliability. Once again interpreting the legislatively enacted Federal Rules of Evidence as a statute, the Supreme Court not only observed that nothing in the text of Rule 702 incorporates the general acceptance test of *Frye,* it also opined that the test is at odds with the "liberal thrust" of the Federal Rules of Evidence and their "general approach of relaxing the traditional barriers to 'opinion' testimony." The Supreme Court concluded that *Frye* is "incompatible with the Federal Rules of Evidence [and] should not be applied in federal trials."

Although *Frye* was displaced by the Federal Rules of Evidence, the Supreme Court held that the trial judge nevertheless must screen scientific evidence to ensure reliability. The requirement in Rule 702 that the expert's testimony pertain to "scientific knowledge" was found to establish a standard of evidentiary reliability or scientific validity. In addition, the Supreme Court noted that Rule 702 requires that the evidence offered "assist the trier of fact to understand the evidence or to determine a fact in issue," a condition that goes primarily to relevance. Accordingly, the Court said:

> Faced with a proffer of expert scientific testimony, then, the trial judge must determine at the outset, pursuant to Rule 104(a), whether the expert is proposing to testify to (1) scientific knowledge that (2) will

assist the trier of fact to understand or determine a fact in issue. This entails a preliminary assessment of whether that reasoning or methodology properly can be applied to the facts in issue.

The Supreme Court, while declining to set out a definitive checklist or test, provided a series of factors that are appropriately considered when determining whether a theory, technique, reasoning, methodology, etc., referred to sometimes hereafter collectively as an "explanative theory", is scientific knowledge that will assist the trier of fact. The Supreme Court initially suggested that a key question is whether the theory or technique can be (and has been) tested. The importance of testability speaks to the very nature of scientific methodology:

"Scientific methodology today is based on generating hypotheses and testing them to see if they can be falsified; indeed, this methodology is what distinguishes science from other fields of human inquiry." Green, at 645. See also C. Hempel, Philosophy of Natural Science 49 (1966) ("[T]he statements constituting a scientific explanation must be capable of empirical test"); K. Popper, Conjectures and Refutations: The Growth of Scientific Knowledge 37 (5th ed. 1989) ("[T]he criterion of the scientific status of a theory is its falsifiability, or refutability, or testability").

The Supreme Court then suggested that another important consideration is peer review (although it expressly notes that publication is not a sine qua non of admissibility). In fact, the Supreme Court explains:

Publication ... does not necessarily correlate with reliability, see S. Jasanoff, The Fifth Branch: Science Advisors as Policymakers 61–76 (1990), and in some instances well-grounded but innovative theories will

not have been published, see Horrobin, The Philosoph-
ical Basis of Peer Review and the Suppression of
Innovation, 263 J.Am.Med.Assn. 1438 (1990). Some
propositions, moreover, are too particular, too new, or
of too limited interest to be published. But submission
to the scrutiny of the scientific community is a component of "good science," in part because it increases the
likelihood that substantive flaws in methodology will
be detected. See J. Ziman, Reliable Knowledge: An
Exploration of the Grounds for Belief in Science 130–
33 (1978); Relman and Angell, How Good is Peer
Review, 321 New Eng.J. Med. 827 (1989). The fact of
publication (or lack thereof) in a peer-reviewed journal
thus will be a relevant, though not dispositive, consideration in assessing the scientific validity of a particular technique or methodology on which an opinion is
premised.

The third factor appropriately considered, opined the
Supreme Court, is the known or potential rate of error
while the fourth factor mentioned is the existence and
maintenance of standards controlling the technique's operation. The Supreme Court subtly developed the fifth
and final factor:

Finally, "general acceptance" can yet have a bearing
on the inquiry. A "reliability assessment does not
require, although it does permit, explicit identification
of a relevant scientific community and an express
determination of a particular degree of acceptance
within that community." United States v. Downing,
753 F.2d, at 1238. See also 3 Weinstein & Berger
¶ 702[03], pp. 702–41 to 702–42. Widespread acceptance can be an important factor in ruling particular
evidence admissible, and "a known technique that has

been able to attract only minimal support within the community," *Downing*, supra, at 1238, may properly be viewed with skepticism.

The Supreme Court concluded:

The inquiry envisioned by Rule 702 is, we emphasize, a flexible one. Its overarching subject is the scientific validity and thus the evidentiary relevance and reliability of the principles that underlie a proposed submission. The focus, of course, must be solely on principles and methodology, not on the conclusions that they generate.

Throughout, a judge assessing a proffer of expert scientific testimony under Rule 702 should also be mindful of other applicable rules. Rule 703 provides that expert opinions based on otherwise inadmissible hearsay are to be admitted only if the facts or data are "of a type reasonably relied upon by experts in the particular field in forming opinions or inferences upon the subject." Rule 706 allows the court at its discretion to procure the assistance of an expert of its own choosing. Finally, Rule 403 permits the exclusion of relevant evidence "if its probative value is substantially outweighed by the danger of unfair prejudice, confusion of the issues, or misleading the jury...." Judge Weinstein has explained: "Expert evidence can be both powerful and quite misleading because of the difficulty in evaluating it. Because of this risk, the judge in weighing possible prejudice against probative force under Rule 403 of the present rules exercises more control over experts than over lay witnesses." Weinstein, 138 F.R.D., at 6327.

Attempting to understand application of *Daubert* by trial and appellate courts in the years that immediately followed can easily cause frustration. *Daubert* is a very incomplete case if not a very bad decision. It did not, in any way, accomplish what it was meant to, i.e., encourage more liberal admissibility of expert witness evidence. In fact, *Daubert* overall in practice actually created a more stringent test for expert evidence admissibility especially in civil cases. What resulted was a series of confusing and conflicting opinions.

The difficulties with *Daubert* are many. Most significant is that in eradicating the *Frye* test for all cases, *Daubert* only explicitly provided a standard for admissibility of "scientific" evidence under Federal Rule of Evidence 702. Thus *Daubert* complicated matters by speaking of the gatekeeper role solely in the context of "scientific" evidence, making it unclear whether a gatekeeper role applied to "technical or other specialized knowledge." In addition, in rejecting *Frye*, once again speaking about "scientific" evidence, the Court stated that the requirements of Rule 702 applied to all "scientific" evidence and not "specially or exclusively to unconventional evidence," i.e., " 'novel' scientific techniques." In short, *Daubert* on its face did not apply "gatekeeping" to "technical or other specialized knowledge" while stating that Rule 702 itself requires that all "scientific" evidence be subjected to gatekeeping.

The fact *Daubert* resulted in substantial confusion is not surprising. For example, what happens when expert witnesses are testifying based on experience acquired "technical or other specialized knowledge", referred to as "skilled experts", or other expert witnesses are testifying based upon "technical or other specialized knowledge" in product liability cases? Is an expert engineer or person with 30 years of practical experience testifying as to "scientific" knowledge when opining as to how a product could be made safer or is it "technical or other specialized knowledge"? If the former and the five *Daubert* factors are rigorously applied, the chances of such experts being able to opine that this product could have been made safer by doing X and Y is problematic. Satisfaction of the five *Daubert* factors would very often, at a minimum, require the construction and testing of the alternative design beyond the financial capacity of the party or the litigation.

Moreover, if something is not "scientific", under *Daubert* is judicial gatekeeping nevertheless mandated? Is it in fact already incorporated in Rule 702? If so, how should the court go about deciding whether an opinion of an expert skilled witness based on experience or another type of expert, such as a university professor testifying as to "technical or other specialized knowledge", is based upon a sufficiently trustworthy explanative theory? In short, are *Daubert's* five factors to be applied to "technical or other specialized knowledge" as well, is a different probably more inclusive list of factors to be considered, or is a more generalized search for assurance of evidentiary reliability to be conducted?

Historically, as a practical matter, *Frye* was applied solely in criminal cases to "new and novel" explanative theories, and in almost all cases the evidence was forensic evidence offered by the government. *Frye* wasn't applied in product liability cases at all. If a qualified expert was called to opine, assuming a recognized field of expertise clearly existed and an adequate factual basis was established, the expert was permitted to testify. The only objection available relating to an explanative theory asserted by the opponent to be so untrustworthy as to flunk the laugh test was "speculative and conjectural." For example, an expert testifying that a piece of falling glass caused the cancer later observed in the area struck, i.e., post hoc ergo propter hoc, was considered "speculative and conjectural." Now *Daubert* was clearly to be applied to a variety of situations to which *Frye* was never applicable.

When it actually came for the lower courts to determining with particularity where *Daubert* gatekeeping was mandated, the language in *Daubert* produced several interpretations, each of which gave rise to a different result. Some courts, relying on the broad gatekeeper language of *Daubert* or Rule 702 itself, held that all explanative theories must be shown to be reliable. Some of these courts applied the *Daubert* five factors in assessing "technical or other specialized knowledge." Others declared that the task is to develop a more inclusive list of appropriate factors to be considered and a method to evaluate such factors in the context of the litigation when "scientific" evidence is not involved. Still other courts concluded that gatekeeping in the sense of a threshold reliability screening is required while specifically declining to mandate the five *Daubert* factors or an expanded version thereof. Finally other courts concluded that gatekeeping in any sense is mandated only as to "scientific" evidence leaving the explanative theory underlying "technical and other specialized knowledge" subject only to the requirements applicable to expert testimony generally.

*Daubert* boxed the courts into working within a structure that did not function as anticipated by the Supreme Court and can fairly be said not to have functioned well at all. The Supreme Court sought to encourage liberal admissibility. It believed that it was abolishing a strict *Frye* test in favor of a more liberal factor balancing analyses. In fact, liberality of admissibility did not occur, but rather the direct opposite. First, with respect to "scientific" evidence, *all* "scientific" evidence was now subjected to *Daubert's* five factor analyses, including scientific evidence in civil cases never before subjected to significant gatekeeping. When a gatekeeping test is applied where one wasn't before, less rather than more expert witness testimony is admissible hardly a liberalization. Even where *Frye* was applied previously, while *Daubert* probably has not resulted in many, if any, expert opinions being excluded where previously admitted, *Daubert* hardly significantly liberalized admissibility. Very little, if anything, is now admitted in the federal court that is excluded by *Frye* in state courts still following *Frye*. Second, with respect to "technical or other specialized knowledge", once again *Frye* was not applied at all with the exception of social science explanative theories such as eyewitness identification, hypnotic recollection, post traumatic stress disorder, battered wife syndrome, child sexual abuse syndrome, etc. In such social science areas, when *Daubert* gatekeeping is applied, sustaining admissibility is more difficult than under the *Frye* general acceptance test especially if the five *Daubert* factors are employed rigorously. Clearly controlled study falsifiability does not comport well with social science we correctly refuse to abuse a child for the sake of research. No liberalization here. With respect to other "technical or other specialized knowledge" experts, such as skilled experts and university professors in product liability and other cases, application of *Daubert* is obviously more restrictive since *Frye* was never previously applied in these matters.

Federal courts, generally speaking, were unable to legitimately fight their way out of the *Daubert* five factor analyses gatekeeping box. *Daubert* says "new or novel" is not a distinction. More importantly, no other limitation was suggested by *Daubert* at all.

Federal courts confronted with the frustrating *Daubert* gatekeeping box on occasion attempted avoidance to the point of distorting the clear understanding of how the rules of evidence operate relating to expert witnesses. Two illegitimate avoidance approaches were undertaken. First, it was asserted, albeit incorrectly, that as long as the witness has personal knowledge of the factual basis for his or her opinion not acquired for purposes of litigation, no matter the composition of the factual basis, such as reliance on business records and industry experience, the witness may testify as a lay witness. According to such cases a witness must be classified as an expert only if either the expert reasonably relies upon information furnished by others, Rule 703, or acquires information forming the factual basis of an opinion for purposes of litigation. Second, it was asserted, albeit also incorrectly, that an expert testifying as to whether a product is defectively designed is not subject to *Daubert* gatekeeping if the expert's testimony is based upon general scientific principles and years of practical experience because such an expert's testimony is "not based on any particular methodology or technique." To conclude that "no methodology or technique", i.e., explanative theory, is involved with respect to opinion testimony presenting "scientific, technical or other specialized knowledge" is simply untenable. Both of these illegitimate avoidance approaches are now prohibited.

In state courts applying *Frye*, state supreme courts have sought to limit the role of the trial court in acting as a gatekeeper. First, courts have limited *Frye* to "new or novel" explanative theories. Such a limitation assumes that traditional explanative theories have been sufficiently generally accepted under *Frye* to be considered reliable without the introduction of foundational proof. Second, even if the explanative technique is "new or novel", some state courts have attempted to further limit application of the *Frye* test. This limitation focuses on the perceived capacity of the trier of fact to properly evaluate the testimony of the expert. For example, courts may inquire as to whether a "new or novel" explanative theory is pure opinion, not relying upon a machine, sometimes called a little black box. If it is pure opinion, the argument goes that the jury can evaluate the testimony adequately and will not be overwhelmed by an aura of scientific certainty. They are presumed to be sufficiently inherently skeptical of pure opinion testimony. On the other hand, if the expert testimony employs a "new or novel" explanative theory that has a technique or procedure that appears to create an accurate result especially if a black box is involved, it is asserted that the aura of scientific certainty may overwhelm the trier of fact. Before such courts will permit the jury to be possibly overwhelmed, the trial court under *Frye* must assess trustworthiness through application of the general acceptance test. In short, if the jury is likely to simply and uncritically buy into the experts evidence, the courts must exercise a gatekeeping role to assure what is uncritically accepted actually works.

Of course, the lines drawn in the foregoing set of limitations are fuzzy at best. What is pure opinion? When is something a technique or procedure and when is it pure opinion? Are all "new and novel" little black boxes to be treated the same? Moreover, what is the justification for the court concluding that these criteria, assuming they are capable of being applied in practice, distinguish between expert testimony incorporating a "new and novel" explanative theory that can and will be reasonably assessed by the jury from those explanative theories likely to be uncritically accepted by the jury as trustworthy? In any event, *Daubert* on its face permitted none of the forms of limitation employed under *Frye*. Not surprisingly, federal courts by and large did not seek to introduce such limitations.

In summary, after *Daubert* important questions remained unanswered: *Daubert* either does or does not impose a gatekeeping requirement to "technical or other specialized knowledge" and if it does, how is such gatekeeping to be performed.

**The *Kumho* clarification.** The United States Supreme Court answered both questions in Kumho Tire Company, Ltd. v. Carmichael (S.Ct.1999). The *Daubert* "gatekeeping" obligation applies not only to testimony based on "scientific" knowledge, but also to testimony based on "technical" and "other specialized" knowledge. In making the "gatekeeping" determining, the trial court "may" consider one or more of the five specific factors that *Daubert* mentioned when doing so will help determine that the testimony is "reliable." Overall, *Kumho* instructs that the test of "reliable" is "flexible" and that "*Daubert's* list of specific factors neither necessarily nor exclusively applies to all experts in every case." "Rather the law grants a district court the same broad latitude when it decides how to determine reliability as it enjoys in respect of its ultimate reliability determination."

**Defining "reliable"; the Supreme Court.** As employed in *Daubert, Kumho* and elsewhere, "reliable" appears to be given two meanings at the same time. On the one hand, "reliable" is taken to mean that the explanative theory actually works, i.e., produces a correct, accurate, truthful, valid etc. conclusion. The second usage of "reliable" refers to meriting confidence, worthy of dependence or reliance, i.e., possesses sufficient assurance of trustworthiness to warrant acceptance by the trier of fact. The later is the dictionary definition of "reliable." It as also the underlying approach of the now rejected *Frye* test discussed supra. In short, applying the first usage of "reliable" requires the trial court to determine that the explanative theory "works" while the second usage of "reliable" requires that the trial court determine only that there exist sufficient assurances that the explanative theory "works" to warrant acceptance by the trier of fact.

*Daubert* itself speaks with both faces of "reliable." The thrust and tone of the opinion listing appropriate factors to be considered supports a conclusion that "gatekeeping" is a determination of whether the explanative theory works. The opinion even states its confidence that the federal judges possess the capacity to make a "preliminary assessment of whether the reasoning and methodology underlying the testimony is scientifically valid", i.e., "the principal support[s] what it purports to show", and that "*evidentiary reliability* will be based upon *scientific validity*." At the same time, however, *Daubert* states that Rule 702 requires that an "expert's opinion will have a reliable basis in the knowledge and experience of his discipline", a reference to sufficient assurances that the explanative theory works. At one point in the opinion, *Daubert* appears to speak to both meanings at once:

The inquiry envisioned by Rule 702 is, we emphasize, a flexible one. Its overarching subject is the scientific validity and thus the evidentiary relevance and reliability of the principles that underlie a proposed submission. The focus, of course, must be solely on principles and methodology, not on the conclusions that they generate.

The last sentence is certainly subject to interpretation. The Supreme Court itself in General Electric Co. v. Joiner (S.Ct.1997) was forced to acknowledge that "conclusions and methodology are not entirely distinct from one another."

*Kumho* for its part is no better. The discussion of the "flexibility" of factors to be considered in determining "the reliability of expert testimony" implies a search for correctness, accuracy, etc., the explanative theory "works." Moreover, in part III of the opinion, Justice Breyer provides an illustration of what he believes to be a proper application of the flexible *Daubert–Kumho* factor approach concluding that the "relevant issue was whether the expert could reliably determine the cause of this tire's separation", i.e., does the explanative theory as actually applied to the particular facts present produce a correct, accurate, etc. result. Conversely, *Kumho* quotes *Daubert* for the proposition that "the trial judge must determine whether the testimony has 'a reliable basis in the knowledge and experience of [the relevant] discipline.'" More significantly, *Kumho* further states that the trial court's responsibility "is to make certain that an expert, whether basing testimony upon professional studies or personal experience, employs in the courtroom the same level of intellectual rigor that characterizes the 'practice' of an expert in the relevant field."

**Defining reliable; trial and appellate courts.** Numerous questions of interpretation arise when one seeks to determine whether an explanative theory "works". Applying even the five *Daubert* factors in a consistent and rational manner is no easy task. The flexible approach of *Kumho*, according to the Advisory Committee's Note to Rule 702, puts many additional factors on the table further complicating the process. One can certainly argue that the more factors listed, the harder it becomes for the nonexpert trial judge to determine whether an explanative theory "works". It is respectfully suggested that it is the reluctance of trial and appellate judges to determine that an explanative theory actually "works", thereby becoming amateur experts themselves, that led several trial and appellate courts to initiate and sanction the two avoidance techniques discussed above as well as in some opinions to limit application of *Daubert* solely to "scientific" knowledge.

On the other hand, as developed infra, trial and appellate judges favor the sufficient assurances of trustworthiness approach. Pursuant to this approach, which as explored above finds support in both *Daubert* and in particular the flexible approach of *Kumho*, an explanative theory employed by an expert to support his or her testimony is sufficiently "reliable" when it has been shown that sufficient assurances of trustworthiness are present to warrant jury acceptance that the expert's explanative theory, as actually applied in the matter at hand to facts, data, or opinions sufficiently established to exist, produced a correct result.

An explanative theory can be shown to possess sufficient assurances of trustworthiness by proof that the explanative theory, as actually applied, possesses particularized earmarks of trustworthiness. Generally speaking, particularized earmarks of trustworthiness should be found to be established if the expert's explanative theory is shown to have been derived and employed in a manner consistent with processes customarily employed by experts in the particular field, which has been stated in the alternative as (1) adheres to the same standards for intellectual rigor demanded in the experts professional work, (2) conforms to applicable professional standards employed outside the courtroom, (3) possesses the aura of proper expert methodology, or (4) is soundly grounded in the principles and methodology of the particular field. *Clearly, many courts have adopted the foregoing reasoning.*

**Applying Rule 702.** Rule 702, as amended pursuant to the Rules Enabling Act, effective December 1, 2000, states:

## Rule 702.

## TESTIMONY BY EXPERTS

If scientific, technical, or other specialized knowledge will assist the trier of fact to understand the evidence or to determine a fact in issue, a witness qualified as an expert by knowledge, skill, experience, training, or education, may testify thereto in the form of an opinion or otherwise, *if (1) the testimony is based upon sufficient facts or data, (2) the testimony is the product of reliable principles and methods, and (3) the witness has applied the principles and methods reliably to the facts of the case.*

The Advisory Committee's Note maintains that Rule 702 is consistent with *Kumho's* interpretation of *Daubert.*

The structure of the amended rule as evidenced by its three-prong proviso would ordinarily imply that each of the three requirements is separate and distinct. In short, the structure of amended Rule 702 appears to envisage that a court in determining admissibility of expert witness testimony declare that each of the three numbered requirements set forth above are satisfied or declare that one or more of the three have not been sufficiently established. In practice, however, the dividing line between the three requirements is often at best incredibly unclear. Moreover, and more importantly, all three are in fact part and parcel of a single determination.

In *Kumho*, the expert witness for the plaintiff was proffered to opine that the tire blow out causing plaintiff's injury came about because of separation in the tire resulting from a defect in the tire and that conversely the tire separation was not caused by overdeflection, i.e., either overloading or underinflation. The expert testified that in the absence at least two of four signs of abuse, observed through visual and tactile inspection, i.e., proportionately great tread wear on the shoulder, signs of grooves caused by the beads, discolored sidewalks, marks on the rim flange, the separation was caused by a defect.

At the reliable explanative theory level, i.e., (2) above, the Supreme Court concluded that there was no indication in the record that other experts in the industry use the foregoing two factors test or that the particular expert himself if still working for a tire manufacturer "would have concluded in a report to his employer that a similar tire was similarly defective on grounds identical to those upon which he rested his conclusion." In addition, there was no indication in the record that other experts "normally made the very fine distinctions, say, the symmetry of comparatively greater shoulder tread wear that were necessary" according to the expert to support his own theory. In the same vein it was noted that the trial court "could reasonably have wondered about the reliability of a method of visual and tactile inspection sufficiently precise to ascertain with some certainty the abuse-related significance of minute shoulder/center relative tread wear differences, but insufficiently precise to tell 'with any certainty' from the tread wear whether a tire had traveled less than 10,000 or more than 50,000 miles."

As to whether the facts, data, or opinions relied upon as the basis of the experts opinion were sufficiently established, i.e., (1) above, the record indicated that while the expert asserted that the tire tread remaining had a depth of 3/32 inch, "the opposing expert's (apparently undisputed) measurements indicate that the tread depth taken at various positions around the tire actually ranged from .5/32 of an inch to 4/32 of an inch, with the tire apparently showing greater wear along both shoulders than along the center."

As to proper application, i.e (3) above, the expert testified that with respect to the sign of abuse, bead grooving, "that most tires have some bead groove pattern, that where there is reason to suspect an abnormal bead groove he would ideally 'look at a lot of [similar] tires' to know the grooving's significance, and that he had not looked at many tires similar to the one at issue."

Thus in *Kumho* itself the Supreme Court explored all three requirements in applying its "flexible" approach to determining whether plaintiff's expert witness' testimony was "reliable". All three requirements were discussed more or less together, with the court moving between

and among the three specified requirements of Amended
Rule 702 freely without even identifying them in any
manner whatsoever. In short, the Supreme Court in
*Kumho* did what should be done, i.e., look at all three
requirements as in fact one requirement:

> For one thing, and contrary to respondents' sugges-
> tion, the specific issue before the court was not the
> reasonableness in general of a tire expert's use of a
> visual and tactile inspection to determine whether
> over-deflection had caused the tire's tread to separate
> from its steel-belted carcass. *Rather, it was the reason-*
> *ableness of using such an approach, along with Carl-*
> *son's particular method of analyzing the data thereby*
> *obtained, to draw a conclusion regarding the particular*
> *matter to which the expert testimony was directly rele-*
> *vant.*

The following articulation combining the three numbered
separate requirements of Amended Rule 702 is suggested:

> As actually applied in the matter at hand to facts, data,
> or opinions sufficiently established to exist, are there
> sufficient assurances present that the expert witness'
> explanative theory produces a correct result to warrant
> jury acceptance?

This overall approach set forth above and employed in
*Kumho* has the advantage of avoiding problems in analysis which may arise if each of the three requirements is
truly treated as separate. For example, in *Kumho* visual
and tactile observation was assumed to be a reliable
method of determining why tire tread separated from its
steel-belted carcass. Let us assume that visual and tactile
inspection employing a four sign approach, putting aside
problems associated with the subjectivity of ascertaining
the significance of minute difference supposedly observa-

ble through visual and tactile inspection, is shown to possess sufficient assurances of trustworthiness, i.e., "reliable", to warrant jury acceptance. Let us also assume that such explanative theory requires the presence of all four signs for a conclusion of defect to be reached.

What if the evidence supports a finding that three signs are present to the required extent but not the fourth sign?

If the three requirements specified of amended Rule 702 are treated separately, it can be argued that while there is an explanative theory that is the product of reliable principles and methods, i.e., (2) above, there is an inadequate basis of facts, data or opinions to support such an explanative theory, i.e., (1) above, as the fourth sign has not been established. In short, the testimony should be excluded because it is not "based upon sufficient facts, [ ] data [, or opinions]." Alternatively it can be argued that the expert's testimony is not the product of reliable principles and methods, i.e. (2) above, because an explanative theory employing only three signs has not been established to possess sufficient assurances of trustworthiness to warrant acceptance. Finally, if an explanative theory requiring the presence of four signs is applied when only three signs are present, or if the determination of the presence of one or more of the four signs was not itself done by applying that aspect of the explanative theory in accordance with proper procedure, it can be argued that the explanative theory is not being applied in accordance with proper procedures, i.e. (3) above.

The foregoing demonstrates that *Kumho* is correct to view the determination as a single issue involving an assessment of the presence of sufficient assurance of trustworthiness of the explanative theory as actually applied to facts, data, or opinions sufficiently established to exist. Treating each requirement as independent would lead to an unnecessary determination as to whether "an" explanative theory possessing sufficient assurances of trustworthiness exists generally as to the matter at hand. Focusing on such a determination causes two additional questions to be asked. "Has a sufficient basis been established?" and "Was the explanative theory applied properly to such basis?" Once again, the more helpful way to state the entire issue as done in *Kumho* is "Has the explanative theory as actually applied to facts, data or opinions sufficiently established to exist been shown to possess sufficient assurances of trustworthiness to warrant jury acceptance that a correct result was produced?"

**Current status.** With *Kumho's* interpretation of *Daubert* clarifying that the gatekeeping obligation of explanative theory "reliability" screening is applicable to all expert witness testimony regardless of whether scientific, technical or other specialized knowledge, deciding what is meant by "reliable" takes on even more importance. Determining whether an explanative theory actually works is neither appropriate nor wise. Obviously, the role of the trial judge as "gatekeeper" is to prevent the trier of fact from relying upon expert testimony that does not warrant acceptance, not to decide which explanative theories produce "the" correct result. Trial courts are poorly equipped by training, education, experience, etc. to make such a determination. Moreover, judges generally appear uncomfortable in deciding whether an explanative theory actually works. As evidenced by reported decisions, judges believe that their proper role, one they undertake frequently, is to determine if sufficient assurances of trustworthiness have been established to warrant jury acceptance that the expert's explanative theory, as actually applied in the matter at hand to facts, data, or opinions sufficiently established to exist, produced a correct result. The ultimate determination of whether the explanative theory as applied actually produced a correct result or whether a competing explanative theory did so, etc., rests with the jury. While amended Rule 702 of the Federal Rules of Evidence is less clear than one would like as to what is meant by "reliable," the sufficient assurance of trustworthiness interpretation is certainly consistent with the text of the rule as well as relevant segments of the Advisory Committee's Note, consistent with the flexible approach of *Kumho*, as well as being the interpretation of "reliable" favored by judicial opinions speaking to the issue.

## § 702.6 Subjects of Expert Testimony

As described in § 702.5 supra, judicial reliability gatekeeping prior to 1993 under *Frye* was confined as a practical matter to forensic evidence offered by the prosecution in criminal cases coupled with application of the laugh test, i.e., speculative or conjectural, initiated across the spectrum of expert witness testimony. With *Daubert* in 1993 came the application of reliability gatekeeping to "scientific" evidence and sometimes but not always to areas of technical and specialized knowledge as well. Where application of *Daubert* to technical or other specialized knowledge comprised rigid application of the five *Daubert* factors, the results were uneven at best. In 1999 with *Kumho*, as reinforced by Rule 702 as amended effective December 1, 2000, a flexible approach to reliability gatekeeping to all areas of scientific, technical or other specialized knowledge was inaugurated. While much has been learned to date, it is still too soon to know how the flexible approach of *Kumho*/Rule 702 as applied by trial and appellate courts to various subjects in real cases will eventually evolve in practice. Thus the reliability "gatekeeping" saga instituted in *Daubert*, as modified by *Kumho*/Rule 702, continues.

Over the years judicial opinions have addressed the admissibility of numerous expert witness opinions applying an explanative theory employing scientific, technical, or other specialized knowledge. These numerous opinions have applied solely the conjectural or speculative test, applied *Frye,* applied *Daubert*, with or without its five factors, applied *Daubert* with a different set of factors, didn't apply *Daubert*, etc. and now must apply the flexible test of reliability "gatekeeping" expounded by *Kumho*/Rule 702. Thus in looking at reported opinions addressing the admissibility of expert witness testimony employing a given explanative theory upon a particular subject, the opinions must be examined carefully in light of the shifting tests for admissibility being applied over time.

In the criminal arena, many subjects have been examined over the years to determine whether the explanative theory meets one or another gatekeeping "reliability" threshold. These include lie detectors, truth serum, hypnosis, voice prints, ballistics, DNA, handwriting, fingerprints, inductively coupled plasma, compulsive gambling, penile arousal as well as psychological testimony in child sexual abuse cases and elsewhere amongst others. Some but by no means all of the explanative theories examined have been found to possess sufficient assurances of trustworthiness to be presented to the trier of fact first under *Frye* and then under *Daubert*. The most notable exception is, of course, the lie detector. Examination of these explanative theories under *Kumho*/Rule 702 does not alter the situation.

In the civil arena, the imposition of a reliability gate-keeping determination by *Daubert*, where other than speculative or conjectural gatekeeping was not previously undertaken, has had no measurable effect with respect to most subject matter areas obviously involving scientific, technical, or other specialized knowledge. Even in those courts that believed *Daubert* required gatekeeping not just to "scientific" knowledge but with respect to technical or other specialized knowledge as well and regardless of whether the five *Daubert* factors were or were not applied rigorously, most experts in civil cases, including most testifying as medical experts, continued to testify as they had prior to 1993. Motions in limine or motions for summary judgment raising reliability concerns as to most experts explanative theories simply weren't made. With respect to these areas, litigants realized that the explana-tive theory in fact possessed sufficient assurances to be presented to the trier of fact for its consideration and that a challenge would be solely a waste of time and money. As a matter of practice, counsel did not and do not challenge the explanative theory underlying a blood test for cholesterol or the accidentologist on stopping distances. In such cases widespread acceptance alone as a matter of practice sufficiently establishes that the expla-native theory was derived in a manner consistent with the process customarily employed by experts in the field. Of course, admissibility will continue to turn upon the trial court's determination that as actually applied in the matter at hand to facts, data, or opinions sufficiently established to exist, including those reasonably relied upon, sufficient assurances of trustworthiness are present that the expert witness' explanative theory produces a correct result to warrant jury acceptance.

However, in civil litigation with respect to certain subject matters, *Daubert* brought on not only change but substantial chaos and confusion as well. *Kumho* and amended Rule 702 have brought a flexible approach to the gatekeeping determination of reliability, i.e., whether sufficient assurances of trustworthiness are present as discussed in § 702.5 supra. Particularly affected, for example, was expert testimony as to unreasonably dangerous in product liability litigation, expert testimony as to causation in toxic tort as well as other litigation, and to a much lesser extent medical expert testimony employing the explanative theory known as differential diagnosis.

Sometimes the critical question in determining whether an expert will be permitted to testify upon a particular subject in both civil and criminal cases does not in practice involve a gatekeeping reliability assessment of the underlying explanative theory. Instead, admissibility turns upon an assessment of the expert's knowledge, skill, experience, training, and education or upon considerations of helpfulness, common knowledge and trial concerns underlying Rule 403. The testimony of the "skilled" expert witness, e.g., the banker or landowner testifying as to land value and the expert qualifying heavily upon experience such as the local carpenter, plumber or tilelayer are illustrative. Law enforcement officials testifying as to typical crime patterns and language, particularly as to drug transactions, may be included in this category with the adequacy of basis and helpfulness criteria in Rule 702 here taking center stage. Drug courier profile evidence highlights the trial concerns expressed in Rule 403.

Particularly but not exclusively in criminal cases, application of consideration of helpfulness, common knowledge and trial concerns underlying Rule 403 sometimes play an important role in the determination of the admissibility of expert witnesses whose testimony relies more heavily upon education than the "skilled" experts discussed above. Illustrative are eyewitness identification testimony, damage assessment testimony in personal injury actions, and linguistic evidence. The underlying explanative theories employed by such expert witness more obviously raise reliability concerns than those employed by the "skilled" expert witness, and thus *Daubert/Kumho* Rule 702 gatekeeping considerations. Nevertheless, the approach of the court's in determining admissibility focuses upon helpfulness, common knowledge and trial concerns underlying Rule 403, with the expert's testimony, frequently when offered by the criminal, being declared inadmissible. In short, what characterizes and separates these subject matter areas from those mentioned above is in fact the absence of any serious underlying explanative theory gatekeeping reliability screening being undertaken by the courts; such explanative theories, having already received widespread acceptance, are simply accepted as "reliable" by the litigants. A *Daubert/Kumho*/Rule 702 reliability gatekeeping determination is rarely undertaken in practice; admissibility or non admissibility turns upon other considerations.

Finally expert witness testimony may be tendered with respect to the mental state or condition of a defendant in a criminal case. With respect to such testimony, Rule 704(b) prohibits an expert witness from stating an opinion or inference as to whether the defendant did or did not have the mental state or condition constituting an element of the crime charged or defense thereto. Illustrative are premeditation in homicide, lack of predisposition in entrapment, or when the true affirmative defense of insanity is raised. Also included is the mental state or condition of the criminal defendant in tax evasion and more importantly drug cases. These subjects of expert testimony are addressed in § 704.2 infra.

On appeal, the trial court's gatekeeping reliability determination will be reviewed applying the abuse of discretion standard.

## Rule 703.

## BASES OF OPINION TESTIMONY BY EXPERTS

**The facts or data in the particular case upon which an expert bases an opinion or inference may be those perceived by or made known to the expert at or before the hearing. If of a type reasonably relied upon by experts in the particular field in forming opinions or inferences upon the subject, the facts or data need not be admissible in evidence in order for the opinion or inference to be admitted. Facts or data that are otherwise inadmissible shall not be disclosed to the jury by the proponent of the opinion or inference unless the court determines that their probative value in assisting the jury to evaluate the expert's opinion substantially outweighs their prejudicial effect.**

## § 703.1 Bases of Opinion Testimony by Experts

Under Rule 703 in addition to the scientific, technical or other specialized knowledge forming the bases of the witness' expertise, Rule 702, an expert may base his opinion or inference (1) on firsthand observation of facts, data, or opinions perceived by him before trial, (2) on facts, data or opinions presented at trial as by the familiar hypothetical question or by having the expert attend the trial and hear the testimony establishing the facts, data, and opinions relied on, and (3) on facts, data or opinions presented to the expert outside of court other than by his own direct perception. Such facts, data or opinions presented to the expert out of court need not be admitted or even admissible in evidence in order for the opinion or inference to be admitted if of a type reasonably relied upon by experts in the field, Rule 703. The rule thus brings judicial practice into line with the practice of experts themselves when not in court. For example, a physician in his own practice bases his diagnosis on information from a variety of sources, such as hospital records, Xray reports, statements by patients, and reports and opinions from nurses, technicians and other doctors. Most of these could be presented in the form of admissible evidence, but only through a time consuming process of authentication. As the Advisory Committee's Note states: "The physician makes life-and-death decisions in reliance upon them. His validation, expertly performed and subject to cross-examination, ought to suffice for judicial purposes." Rule 703 also offers a more satisfactory basis for ruling upon the admissibility of public opinion poll evidence.

Whether the facts, data or opinions not admitted in evidence are of a type reasonably relied upon is a preliminary question for the court, Rule 104(a). The requirement that the facts, data or opinions be of a type reasonably relied upon by experts in the field provides a check on the trustworthiness of the opinion and its foundation. In determining whether reliance by the expert is reasonable, the proponent of the evidence must satisfy the court, both that such items are of the type customarily relied upon by experts in the field and that such items are sufficiently trustworthy to make such reliance reasonable. A statement by the witness that he and other experts customarily find facts, data, or opinions of a given type reliable in forming an opinion should be considered highly influential but not binding upon the court. To allay the fear that enlargement of the permissible basis might break down the rules of exclusion unduly, the Advisory Committee's Note stresses the reasonable reliance requirement and gives the opinion of an "accidentologist" as to the point of impact based on statements of bystanders as an example of a situation where it is not satisfied.

While a standard as to trustworthiness of facts, data, or opinions relied upon by the expert is not specified in Rule 703, the foregoing example contained in the Advisory Committee's Note indicates that reliance is reasonable only if the facts, data, or opinions possess trustworthiness in excess of that possessed by the ordinary hearsay statement. Circumstantial guarantees of trustworthiness identical or equivalent to that possessed by hearsay statements admissible pursuant to any hearsay exception are apparently contemplated. This better view is known as the restrictive approach in comparison to the liberal approach which finds customary reliance by experts in the field alone sufficient.

The concept of circumstantial guarantees trustworthiness identical or equivalent to that possessed by statements admissible pursuant to a hearsay exception required under the restrictive approach is best explored by means of an illustration. Assume the issue being disputed is the cause of a fire in a warehouse leading to significant property damage and the death of a fireman. In a wrongful death action against Bob Jones, the plaintiff calls to the stand a member of the arson squad of the local fire department who testifies that he arrived on the scene about twenty minutes after the first fireman arrived. The arson expert is prepared to testify that the fire was deliberately set. In support of his opinion, the arson expert relies upon certain oral statements made to him by a fireman on the scene describing his observations during the first few minutes fighting the fire. These oral statements of another fireman relating matters of personal knowledge are of a type reasonably relied upon by experts in the field, i.e., they are customarily relied upon and the statements by virtue of being statements made pursuant to a business duty to report are sufficiently trustworthy to make such reliance reasonable. In addition the arson expert relied upon the results of certain laboratory tests conducted upon material removed by firemen from the wreckage. Once again since these laboratory tests were conducted in the regular course of a regularly conducted business activity, the results of the tests are reasonably relied upon by the arson experts. Finally the arson expert also relies upon two statements. The first made to him by a fireman on the scene relates that ten minutes after he arrived a bystander calmly reported seeing a man run out of the building shortly before it caught fire. The second is a statement by another fireman that the fireman had seen Bob Jones standing at the corner watching the fire and that Bob Jones is rumored among the fireman to be a professional arsonist. While both of the foregoing statements may be of a type customarily relied upon by experts in the field, neither statement is sufficiently trustworthy to make such reliance reasonable. The statement by a bystander, a person under no business duty to report, possessing no indicia of trustworthiness beyond that possessed by hearsay statements at large, may not "reasonably" be relied upon by an expert. A statement by a member of the expert's organization reporting a rumor, a statement not based upon personal knowledge of the underlying facts, is similarly a hearsay statement not sufficiently trustworthy to be "reasonably" relied upon even if of a type customarily relied upon by experts in the field.

While only the terms "facts or data" appear in Rule 703, opinions not in evidence, even those not admissible, may also form the bases of an expert's opinion if reasonably relied upon by experts in the particular field.

Facts, data, or opinions reasonable relied upon by an expert witness are *not* by virtue thereof substantive evidence; reasonably relied on facts, data, or opinions constitute substantive evidence only if otherwise admitted in evidence. When facts, data, or opinions are reasonably relied upon by an expert and yet are admissible only for the purpose of forming part of the bases of the expert's opinion or inference, a question arises as to whether such facts, data, or opinions may be disclosed to the trier of fact. Under Rule 703 the trial court must balance the probative value of the facts, data, or opinions in assisting the jury to evaluate the expert's opinion or inference on the one hand, against the risk of prejudice resulting from the jury's potential misuse of the facts, data, or opinions for substantive purposes on the other. The facts, data, or opinions may be disclosed to the jury by the proponent of the opinion or inference, only if the trial court finds that the probative value of the facts, data, or opinions in assisting the jury to evaluate the expert's opinion substantially outweighs its prejudicial effect. In some circumstances the proponent might wish to disclose facts, data, or opinions reasonably relied upon by the expert in order to "remove the string" from the adverse party's anticipated attack, and thereby prevent the jury from drawing an unfair negative inference. The trial court should take this consideration into account in applying the balancing test. In determining the appropriate course, the trial court should also consider the probably effectiveness or lack of effectiveness of a limiting instruction under the particular circumstances.

If the otherwise inadmissible facts, data, or opinions are disclosed under the balancing test, the trial judge must give a limiting instruction upon request informing the jury that the underlying facts, data, or opinions must not be used for substantive purposes.

As provided in Rule 705, the expert may be required by an adverse party to disclose underlying facts, data, or opinions on cross-examination. As stated in the Advisory Committee's Note, such an adverse party's "attack on an expert's basis will often open the door to a proponent's rebuttal with information that was reasonably relied upon by the expert, even if that information would not have been discloseable initially under the balancing test provided by this amendment."

Where the otherwise inadmissible facts, data, or opinions reasonably relied upon are disclosed to the jury upon application of the balancing test, by the adverse party on cross-examination, or through "door opening," for some but not for all practical although not theoretical purposes, Rule 703 operates as the equivalent of an additional exception to the rule against hearsay. Where facts, data, or opinions are disclosed, Rule 703 creates an exception to the Original Writing Rule, Rule 1002, and serves as an alternative method of satisfying the requirement of authentication with respect to facts, data, and opinions reasonably relied upon by the testifying expert.

Although the rule's purpose is to permit experts to base opinions on reliable hearsay and other facts that are not admissible because of the absence of the declarant or for some other reason, a prosecution witness may, nevertheless, not base an opinion on evidence that has been seized from a defendant in violation of the Fourth Amendment or *Miranda*. Application of the "fruit of the poisonous tree doctrine" mandates such a result. Similarly, where policy considerations such as those surrounding privileges, and subsequent remedial measures, compromises and offers to compromise, etc., require that certain matters not be admitted at trial, the policy may not be thwarted by allowing the same evidence to enter the trial through the "back door" in the form of the basis of an expert's opinion.

Facts, data, or opinions reasonably relied upon by the expert witness in forming his opinion on the subject matter which have not been admitted into evidence are also subject to exclusion on the basis of attendant trial concerns. Thus facts, data, or opinions which would be inadmissible under, for example, Rules 404, 405, 608, 609 and facts, data, or opinions otherwise admissible in evidence which would be excluded under Rule 403, cannot form part of the bases of an expert's opinion under Rule 703. The adverse party may not be placed on the horns of the dilemma of being unable to require disclosure of facts, data, or opinions underlying the expert's opinion or inference on cross-examination without presenting facts, data, or opinions to the jury banned from jury consideration by virtue of other rules of evidence.

If certain facts, data, or opinions are excluded from consideration by the expert, the expert may still render his opinion if an adequate basis nevertheless remains.

## Rule 704.

## OPINION ON ULTIMATE ISSUE

**(a) Except as provided in subdivision (b), testimony in the form of an opinion or inference otherwise admissible is not objectionable because it embraces an ultimate issue to be decided by the trier of fact.**

**(b) No expert witness testifying with respect to the mental state or condition of a defendant in a criminal case may state an opinion or inference as to whether the defendant did or did not have the mental state or condition constituting an element of the crime charged or of a defense thereto. Such ultimate issues are matters for the trier of fact alone.**

### § 704.1 Opinion on Ultimate Issue: An Overview

An expert or a lay witness will not be precluded from testifying in the form of an opinion or inference upon the ultimate issue on the ground that the testimony invades the province of the jury, Rule 704(a). Many common law decisions prohibited an opinion to be expressed upon an ultimate issue. Long ago, however, federal courts came to the realization that since the trier of fact is not required to accept the opinion of the witness, opinion evidence on the ultimate issue does not invade the jury's province.

The modern trend is clearly in accord; 7 Wigmore, Evidence § 1920 at 18 (Chadbourn rev.1978) dismissed the common law ultimate issue rule as "a mere bit of empty rhetoric."

The fact that an opinion or inference is not objectionable because it embraces an ultimate issue does not mean, however, that all opinions embracing the ultimate issue must be admitted for both Rules 701 and 702 embody the criterion of helpfulness for lay and expert witnesses alike. Thus an opinion that plaintiff should win is rejected as not helpful.

Opinions phrased in terms of inadequately explored legal criteria should similarly be excluded as not helpful and possibly misleading. Employing the illustration referred to in the Advisory Committee's Note, a question asked of an expert witness whether he believed the testator had the testamentary capacity to make a will presupposes that both the expert and the trier of fact are familiar with the elements comprising the legal standard. Thus it is preferable, both in terms of effectiveness and the avoidance of an objection, to ask instead whether the testator had the mental capacity to appreciate the nature and extent of his property and the natural objects of his bounty and to formulate a rational scheme of distribution. Of course, with respect to all opinion testimony unfair prejudice, confusion, and misleading the jury are to be avoided under Rule 403.

Care should be taken in interpreting the concept of "inadequately explored legal criteria" and applying Rule 403 not to lose sight of the fact that "the so-called 'ultimate issue' rule is specifically abolished" by Rule 704(a) and that the standard by which to judge opinions, lay and expert, "is to admit them when helpful to the trier of fact." An opinion on an ultimate issue by a lay or expert witness is helpful (1) when an expression of the witness' knowledge can be conveyed in no other form, (2) where an accurate, total impression was formed by a witness who is unable to account for all the details upon which it was based, or (3) most importantly where an accounting of the details by itself alone cannot accurately convey the total impression held by the witness. Thus for one or more of the foregoing reasons testimony as to such matters as intoxication, speed, handwriting, value, causation and proper method will normally be admitted.

Moreover returning to the illustration of testamentary capacity, if an adequate foundation exploring legal criteria is first presented, a lay or expert witness opinion as to testamentary capacity should then be permitted; such an opinion is itself helpful to a determination of a fact of consequence. With respect to negligence actions, an opinion phrased in terms of negligence itself, involving not only the formulation of a legal standard by the witness but also one substantially immune to exploration, seems calculated to confuse or mislead rather than assist the trier. Hence phrasing solely in more factual terms is desirable. Expressions such as "safe," "dangerous," "reasonable," and "good practice" appear appropriate, in that where an adequate factual foundation has been presented, such terms do tend to assist the trier of fact in understanding the testimony of the witness. Similarly after exploration of the facts upon which based, an opinion by an expert in a strict liability action that a product is unreasonably dangerous and in a patent infringement action that a patent was infringed should be permitted as helpful to the trier of fact. In criminal prosecutions it is often helpful for an expert to testify that certain conduct of the accused falls within a complex statutory prohibition.

Rule 704(a) of course permits neither a lay nor expert witness to render an opinion as to questions which are matters of law for the court, to advise the jury to decide the question in a particular way, to offer a speculative opinion upon an unsubstantiated basis, or to testify as to whether another witness is telling the truth.

Determining whether an opinion on the ultimate issue involves a pure question of law, or unexplored legal criteria with respect to a mixed fact and law question on the one hand (and is therefore inadmissible) or conversely is of help to the trier of fact in understanding the evidence or in determining a fact in issue is sometimes extremely difficult. As to the question of unexplored legal criteria with respect to a mixed fact and law question, roughly speaking if the phrase used by the expert witness has a legal meaning which is obviously different than its common meaning, i.e., a separate, distinct, and specialized meaning in law, and the common meaning is clearly being employed, the testimony is admissible. When the two meanings are not clearly different in the minds of the trier of fact, since the legal meaning will involve unexplored legal criteria such as occurs with the terms fraud, discriminate and manipulate, the testimony is inadmissible. If the factual criteria underlying the legal meaning are in fact initially explored through the expert's testimony or otherwise thus helping to make the legal meaning clear to the trier of fact, such as may occur with testamentary capacity, unreasonably dangerous, and deviation from accepted medical practice, then the opinion testimony of the expert once again is admissible. Finally, if the common meaning and the legal meaning are the same, the testimony is admissible. Obviously if the term being explored has no legal meaning, i.e., legal characterization is not involved, the foregoing concerns with respect to testimony involving a legal conclusion are not raised.

## § 704.2  Opinion on Ultimate Issue: Mental State or Condition

Rule 704(b) provides that when the mental state or condition of a defendant in a criminal case is in issue such as premeditation in homicide, lack of predisposition in entrapment, or when the true affirmative defense of insanity has been raised, an expert witness may not testify that the defendant did or did not have the mental state or condition constituting an element of the crime charged or of a defense thereto. Mental state is also frequently at issue in tax evasion and drug cases.

Where lack of mental capacity is asserted, presumably the expert may answer the questions "Was the accused suffering from a mental disease or defect?", "Explain the characteristics of the mental disease and defect.", "Was his act the product of that disease or defect?" and "What is the effect of the disease or defect on the person's mental state?" However the expert may not answer the question "Was the accused able to appreciate the nature and quality of his act?" or "Was the accused able to appreciate the wrongfulness of his acts?"

Whether Rule 704(b) is having its intended effect of substantially moderating the battle of experts when mental state or condition is in issue remains to be determined.

## Rule 705.

# DISCLOSURE OF FACTS OR DATA UNDERLYING EXPERT OPINION

**The expert may testify in terms of opinion or inference and give reasons therefor without first testifying to the underlying facts or data, unless the court requires otherwise. The expert may in any event be required to disclose the underlying facts or data on cross-examination.**

## § 705.1  Disclosure of Facts or Data Underlying Expert Opinion

Rule 705 eliminates the common law requirement that a hypothetical question be employed in eliciting testimony of an expert witness not possessing personal knowledge of all basic facts. The hypothetical question in theory presents the trier of fact with facts, data and opinions forming the bases of the expert's opinion thereby assisting the trier of fact in evaluating the weight to be given to the expert's opinion. In practice, however, the hypothetical question fails to perform as expected. As 2 Wigmore, Evidence § 686 at 962 (Chadbourn rev.1979) notes, "the hypothetical question misused by the clumsy and abused by the clever, has in practice led to intolerable obstruction of truth."

Rule 705 permits the opinion or inference of an expert to be given without first testifying in court to the underlying facts, data or opinions unless the court requires otherwise. Of course, disclosure of facts, data or opinions admitted into evidence is permitted upon direct examination, and most often for tactical reasons such disclosure will occur. Facts, data, or opinions that are reasonably relied upon under Rule 703 that are otherwise inadmissible may not be disclosed to the jury by the proponent of the opinion or inference unless the court determines that their probative value in assisting the jury to evaluate the expert's opinion substantially outweighs their prejudicial effect. If disclosure is permitted, the court must instruct the jury that facts, data, or opinions reasonably relied upon by the expert under Rule 703 may be considered "solely as a basis for the expert opinion and not as substantive evidence." Facts, data, and opinions forming the bases of an expert's opinion, not disclosed on direct examination, may be developed on cross-examination. If the testimony of the witness or other evidence reveals that the expert's bases for his opinion is inadequate, the expert's opinion should be stricken as based upon conjecture or speculation.

If the cross-examiner believes that the witness lacks either sufficient qualifications or sufficient foundation for his opinion, the court in its discretion may require an offer of proof or permit a voir dire examination into such matters either before or outside the presence of the jury. In this manner, if the witness is not qualified or a sufficient basis is lacking, the witness' testimony can be ruled inadmissible without the trier of fact ever being exposed to the inadmissible opinion of the witness. If the witness is ultimately permitted by the court to testify as an expert, it is preferable not to so inform the jury so as not to inadvertently put the trial court's stamp of authority on the witness's testimony.

Rule 705 places a heavy burden on the cross-examiner who must be sufficiently informed about the subject matter to be able to bring out the underlying facts in a manner exposing any weakness inherent in the expert's opinion. The discovery rules in civil cases and to a lesser degree in criminal cases serve to provide the cross-examiner with advance knowledge of the nature of the expert's opinion and its bases. In addition, the cross-examiner may also have the assistance of his own expert in the courtroom, Rule 615. Where the cross-examiner has for one reason or another not been provided with the necessary information to conduct an effective cross-examination, a situation most likely to occur in criminal cases, the court may exercise its discretion under Rule 705 and require that a full foundation be established on direct examination.

## § 705.2  Discretionary Use of Hypothetical Question

While no longer required under Rule 705, if a hypothetical question is put by counsel upon direct examination and permitted by the court, the hypothetical question should include basic facts, data and opinions not in dispute and the version of those disputed facts favorable to the proponent of the question which reasonably appear to have a direct bearing upon the opinion, including those relied upon as provided in Rule 703, for which full disclosure has been sanctioned. With respect to those facts, data and opinions not coming within the reasonable reliance provision of Rule 703 or for which disclosure has not been approved by the trial court, there must be an evidentiary basis for each such item included in the hypothetical question. While there is no requirement that all pertinent facts, data, or opinions in the case be included in the hypothetical, the court possesses discretion to require that additional facts, data, or opinions be added to the original question if it deems such facts, data, or opinions essential to providing an adequate basis for a helpful answer. Similarly, the court possesses discretion to accept the hypothetical question as propounded, thereby leaving it to opposing counsel to explore on cross-examination whether the assumption of such additional facts, data, or opinions would alter the expert's opinion.

Both an objection based on failure to include necessary facts, data, or opinions and an objection that facts, data, or opinion, were included in the hypothetical question not supported by the evidence, should be deemed sufficient only if the particular facts, data, or opinions referred to are specifically identified thereby facilitating the reformulation of the hypothetical question.

## § 705.3   Cross–Examining Experts

On cross-examination, in the process of probing the witness' qualifications, experience, weakness in bases, and the sufficiency of assumptions, opposing counsel may require the expert to disclose the facts, data, and opinions underlying the expert's opinion, Rule 705, including facts, data, or opinions reasonably relied upon pursuant to Rule 703. With respect to facts, data, or opinions forming the basis of the expert's opinion, disclosed on direct examination or during cross-examination, the cross-examiner may explore whether, and if so how, the nonexistence of any fact, data, or opinion or the existence of a contrary version of the fact, data, or opinion supported by the evidence, would affect the expert's opinion. Similarly the expert may be cross-examined with respect to material reviewed by the expert but upon which the expert does not rely. Counsel is also permitted to test the knowledge, experience and fairness of the expert by inquiring as to what changes of conditions would affect his opinion, and in conducting such an inquiry, subject to the requirements of Rule 403, the cross-examiner is not limited to facts finding support in the record. It is, however, improper to inquire of the expert whether his opinion differs from another expert's opinion, not expressed in a learned treatise, if the other expert's opinion has not itself been admitted in evidence. An expert witness may in addition be impeached with a learned treatise admissible as substantive evidence under Rule 803(18). A hypothetical question may be employed upon cross-examination in the court's discretion.

An expert witness may, of course, be impeached in the same manner as any other witness, including by the means of a prior inconsistent. Accordingly, cross-examination of an expert directed at establishing bias through financial interest is proper. In this context the cross-examiner may seek to establish (1) financial interest in the case at hand by reason of remuneration for services, including services performed which enabled him to testify, (2) continued employment by a party, or (3) the fact of prior testimony for the same party or the same attorney. When it comes to questions directed toward establishing (1) the amount of previous compensation from the same party, (2) the relationship between the expert's income from testifying on behalf of a party or a category of party and total income of the expert, or (3) the mere fact of prior testimony most frequently on behalf of other persons or entities similarly situated, the common law authority indicates some lack of agreement. Such inquiries should be permitted.

While the precise scope of cross-examination rests within the discretion of the trial court, this discretion should not be applied in a narrow or restricted manner, especially with respect to experts who deal in opinions as to matters truly not in the common knowledge and experience of laymen.

## Rule 706.

## COURT APPOINTED EXPERTS

(a) Appointment. The court may on its own motion or on the motion of any party enter an order to show cause why expert witnesses should not be appointed, and may request the parties to submit nominations. The court may appoint any expert witnesses agreed upon by the parties, and may appoint expert witnesses of its own selection. An expert witness shall not be appointed by the court unless the witness consents to act. A witness so appointed shall be informed of the witness' duties by the court in writing, a copy of which shall be filed with the clerk, or at a conference in which the parties shall have opportunity to participate. A witness so appointed shall advise the parties of the witness' findings, if any; the witness' deposition may be taken by any party; and the witness may be called to testify by the court or any party. The witness shall be subject to cross-examination by each party, including a party calling the witness.

(b) Compensation. Expert witnesses so appointed are entitled to reasonable compensation in whatever sum the court may allow. The compensation thus fixed is payable from funds which may be provided by law in criminal cases and civil actions and proceedings involving just compensation under the fifth amendment. In other civil actions and proceedings the compensation shall be paid by the parties in such proportion and at such time as the court directs, and thereafter charged in like manner as other costs.

(c) **Disclosure of Appointment.** In the exercise of its discretion, the court may authorize disclosure to the jury of the fact that the court appointed the expert witness.

(d) **Parties' Experts of Own Selection.** Nothing in this rule limits the parties in calling expert witnesses of their own selection.

## § 706.1    Court Appointed Experts: Policy Considerations

The approach taken in Rule 706 with respect to procedures governing the court appointment of experts is intimately tied up with the reasons and circumstances supporting the notion of court appointed experts in the first place. In adopting Rule 706, at least five concerns were being addressed. First, a litigant may be unable to procure the assistance of an expert, either because he cannot afford one or cannot locate an expert willing to testify. The latter circumstance may occur for example to the plaintiff in a medical malpractice litigation. Second, a party will on his own produce the best witness and not the best expert in the sense of being the most qualified. Third, the jury may be helpless to decide which of two scientific theories presented by competing experts is correct. Since the jury depends upon the experts themselves to explain the propositions with which they deal, there is no independent way of measuring the reliability of expert testimony on the basis of experience, intuition, or common sense. Fourth, the use of an impartial expert promotes the settlement of claims. Fifth and finally, as the Advisory Committee's Note states:

"The practice of shopping for experts, the venality of some experts, * * * have been matters of deep concern."

While each of the foregoing concerns is of some importance, probably the critical factor supporting court appointment of expert witnesses is the mistrust generated by experts employed by the litigants. Unfortunately, neither the image possessed by experts nor the concern generated by expert venality is a recent phenomenon. As early as 1858 the United States Supreme Court in Winans v. New York & Erie Railroad (S.Ct.1858) felt compelled to speak to the question: "Experience has shown that opposite opinions of persons professing to be experts may be obtained to any amount." Professor Himes, 135 J Franklin Inst. 409, added the following observation:

It is often surprising to see with what facility and to what an extent [experts'] views can be made to correspond with the wishes or interests of the parties who call them. * * * [T]heir judgment becomes so warped by regarding the subject in one point of view that even when conscientiously disposed, they are incapable of expressing a candid opinion. * * * They are selected on account of their ability to express a favorable opinion, which, there is great reason to believe is in many instances the result alone of employment and the bias growing out of it.

The intensity of such criticism seems to have grown as changes in the litigation process including the expansion of litigation in products liability and medical malpractice have rendered the partisan nature of experts an even more serious problem. The structure of the Federal Rules of Evidence themselves lends additional fuel to the fires of discontent with party selected expert witnesses. In short, there exists the fear that a glib and unscrupulous expert witness with no qualification in his professed field other than a willingness to sell any opinion to anyone who wants it will frequently out sell the conscientious, well-trained and careful expert who gives no opinion that he cannot back up, and that the concept that the jury can detect a fraud is absurd.

In response to the overall problems perceived with expert witness testimony, the suggestion that the court may appoint impartial experts was incorporated into Rule 706. Testimony of experts reluctant to appear on behalf of a particular party may be secured by this procedure. In addition some indication exists that "better" experts may occasionally be obtained by process of court appointment in that certain experts not willing to be retained by any party are agreeable to being appointed by the court.

Whether court appointment of experts is, however, an appropriate solution to the battle of the biased and venal experts is much less clear. It may be argued in opposition to the court appointment of an expert witness that there is no such thing as a truly impartial expert and, even assuming such an expert does exist, why should it be assumed that the court has the ability to discern him. In addition, the procedure associated with the employment of the expert at trial can be said with much justification to foster excessive emphasis by the trier of fact on this witness' opinion at the expense of the adversary system. As the Advisory Committee Note itself acknowledges, "court appointed experts [may] acquire an aura of infallibility to which they are not entitled."

## § 706.2   Court Appointed Experts: Procedure

The court may on its own motion or on motion of any party enter an order to show cause why an expert witness should not be appointed, and may request the parties to submit nominations. The court may appoint any expert witness agreed upon by the parties or may appoint an expert witness of its own selection. However an expert witness may not be appointed by the court unless he consents to act. The court must advise the expert of his duties. The expert so appointed must in turn advise the parties of his findings, if any. The expert's deposition may be taken by any party and he may be called to testify by any party or by the court. If called at trial the expert witness may be cross-examined by any party, including the party calling him as a witness, Rule 706(a).

The trial court thus possesses discretion as to whether to appoint an expert witness at all, and if so which expert to appoint. Where the parties agree to the expert witness to be appointed the court will usually accede to the parties' wishes.

An expert appointed by the court is entitled to reasonable compensation in whatever sum the court may allow. Such compensation is payable from funds provided by law in criminal cases and in civil actions and proceedings involving just compensation under the fifth amendment. As the Advisory Committee's Note indicates the special provision for fifth amendment compensation cases is designed to guard against reducing constitutionally guaranteed just compensation by requiring the recipient to pay costs. In other civil actions and proceedings the compensation is to be paid by the parties in such proportion and at such time as the court directs, and thereafter charged in like manner as other costs, Rule 706(b).

Rule 706(c) provides that the court, in its discretion, may authorize disclosure to the jury of the fact that the expert witness was appointed by the court. The Advisory Committee's Note succinctly and correctly observes that disclosure "seems to be essential if the use of court appointed experts is to be fully effective." Nevertheless, Weinstein's Evidence indicates that the question of disclosure was most strenuously debated in discussions among the Advisory Committee with some members of the bar expressing fear that "the court's imprimatur would overwhelm the jury and cause it to lose sight of the fact that the expert may have a professional bias towards one of the opposing views before it." On the other hand, supporters of disclosure may counter by pointing out that jurors should be encouraged to place special emphasis on the testimony of the court appointed experts for such reliance accords with the reasons for his appointment in the first place. Disclosure was apparently left discretionary to cover those situations where there exists two responsible schools of thought, or where disclosure of the fact of court appointment would otherwise tend to cause undue emphasis being placed on the expert's testimony.

In summary, Rule 706(c) merely provides for discretionary disclosure of the fact that the court appointed the expert witness. Rule 706(c) thus fails to come to grips with the problem of disclosure of court appointment. Sometimes it is possible to permit the expert appointed by the court to testify as a neutral expert without the imprimatur of the court being bestowed. When this is not possible, the adverse effect either express or implied association of the expert with the court has upon the adversary process suggests that it is generally preferable for the court to refrain from appointing an expert under Rule 706(c). In any event, it appears that the arguments of those opposing the court appointment of experts as a solution to the problem of the battle of the venal experts are prevailing, in that, as is also true generally at common law, the appointment of expert witnesses by the court under Rule 706 is a relatively infrequent occurrence.

# ARTICLE VIII

# HEARSAY

*Table of Rules*

## Rules 801–806.

# THE HEARSAY RULE AND HEARSAY EXCEPTIONS

## Prelude

## § 801.0   The Hearsay Rule and Hearsay Exceptions

Article VIII generally approaches hearsay in the traditional manner of a definition, Rules 801(a), (b) and (c) and a rule excluding hearsay, Rule 802, subject to certain exceptions under which evidence is not required to be excluded. In some instances hearsay is admissible pursuant to an exception without regard to the availability of the declarant as a witness, Rule 803, while in other instances the hearsay exception requires that the declarant be unavailable, Rule 804. Rule 807 provides a residual exception for hearsay statements not otherwise admissible under either Rule 803 or Rule 804 but having equivalent circumstantial guarantees of trustworthiness. Provision is also made for hearsay within hearsay, Rule 805 and for attacking and supporting the credibility of the hearsay declarant, Rule 806. Article VIII departs from the common law in Rule 801(d)(1) by treating certain prior statements by a witness as defined as not hearsay, and in Rule 801(d)(2) by treating admissions of a party-opponent as defined as not hearsay rather than as a hearsay exception. Out-of-court statements that are exempt from the bar of the rule against hearsay, Rule 802, through definition as not hearsay or fall within a hearsay exception to be admitted into evidence must, of course, still meet other requirements for admissibility, such as relevance, authenticity, and when the contents of a document are sought to be proved, the Original Writing Rule, Rule 1002.

The Introductory Note: The Hearsay Problem of the Advisory Committee describes the approach taken as follows:

The factors to be considered in evaluating the testimony of a witness are perception, memory, and narration. Morgan, Hearsay Dangers and the Application of the Hearsay Concept, 62 Harv.L.Rev. 177 (1948), Selected Writings on Evidence and Trial 764, 765 (Fryer ed. 1957); Shientag, Cross-Examination: A Judge's Viewpoint, 3 Record 12 (1948); Strahorn, A Reconsideration of the Hearsay Rule and Admissions, 85 U.Pa. L.Rev. 484, 485 (1937), Selected Writings, supra, 756, 757; Weinstein, Probative Force of Hearsay, 46 Iowa L.Rev. 331 (1961). Sometimes a fourth is added, sincerity, but in fact it seems merely to be an aspect of the three already mentioned.

In order to encourage the witness to do his best with respect to each of these factors, and to expose any inaccuracies which may enter in, the Anglo–American tradition has evolved three conditions under which witnesses will ideally be required to testify: (1) under oath, (2) in the personal presence of the trier of fact, (3) subject to cross-examination.

(1) Standard procedure calls for the swearing of witnesses. While the practice is perhaps less effective than in an earlier time, no disposition to relax the requirement is apparent, other than to allow affirmation by persons with scruples against taking oaths.

(2) The demeanor of the witness traditionally has been believed to furnish trier and opponent with valuable clues. Universal Camera Corp v. N.L.R.B., 340 U.S. 474, 495–496, 71 S.Ct. 456, 95 L.Ed. 456 (1951); Sahm, Demeanor Evidence: Elusive and Intangible Imponderables, 47 A.B.A.J. 580 (1961), quoting numerous authorities. The witness himself will probably be impressed with the solemnity of the occasion and the possibility of public disgrace. Willingness to falsify may reasonably become more difficult in the presence of the person against whom directed. Rules 26 and 43(a) of the Federal Rules of Criminal and Civil Procedure, respectively, include the general requirement that testimony be taken orally in open court. The Sixth Amendment right of confrontation is a manifestation of these beliefs and attitudes.

(3) Emphasis on the basis of the hearsay rule today tends to center upon the condition of cross-examination. All may not agree with Wigmore that cross-

examination is "beyond doubt the greatest legal engine ever invented for the discovery of truth," but all will agree with his statement that it has become a "vital feature" of the Anglo–American system. 5 Wigmore § 1367, p. 29. The belief, or perhaps hope, that cross-examination is effective in exposing imperfections of perception, memory, and narration is fundamental. Morgan, Foreword to Model Code of Evidence 37 (1942).

The logic of the preceding discussion might suggest that no testimony be received unless in full compliance with the three ideal conditions. No one advocates this position. Common sense tells that much evidence which is not given under the three conditions may be inherently superior to much that is. Moreover, when the choice is between evidence which is less than best and no evidence at all, only clear folly would dictate an across-the-board policy of doing without. The problem thus resolves itself into effecting a sensible accommodation between these considerations and the desirability of giving testimony under the ideal conditions.

The solution evolved by the common law has been a general rule excluding hearsay but subject to numerous exceptions under circumstances supposed to furnish guarantees of trustworthiness. Criticisms of this scheme are that it is bulky and complex, fails to screen good from bad hearsay realistically, and inhibits the growth of the law of evidence.

Since no one advocates excluding all hearsay, three possible solutions may be considered: (1) abolish the rule against hearsay and admit all hearsay; (2) admit hearsay possessing sufficient probative force, but with procedural safeguards; (3) revise the present system of class exceptions.

(1) Abolition of the hearsay rule would be the simplest solution. The effect would not be automatically to abolish the giving of testimony under ideal conditions. If the declarant were available, compliance with the ideal conditions would be optional with either party. Thus the proponent could call the declarant as a witness as a form of presentation more impressive than his hearsay statement. Or the opponent could call the declarant to be cross-examined upon his statement. This is the tenor of Uniform Rule 63(1), admitting the hearsay declaration of a person "who is present at the hearing and available for cross examination." Compare the treatment of declarations of available declarants in Rule 801(d)(1) of the instant rules. If the declarant were unavailable, a rule of free admissibility would make no distinctions in terms of degrees of noncompliance with the ideal conditions and would exact no quid pro quo in the form of assurances of trustworthiness. Rule 503 of the Model Code did exactly that, providing for the admissibility of any hearsay declaration by an unavailable declarant, finding support in the Massachusetts act of 1898, enacted at the instance of Thayer, Mass.Gen.L.1932, c. 233 § 65, and in the English act of 1938, St.1938, c. 28, Evidence. Both are limited to civil cases. The draftsmen of the Uniform Rules chose a less advanced and more conventional position. Comment, Uniform Rule 63. The present Advisory Committee has been unconvinced of the wisdom of abandoning the traditional requirement of some particular assurance of credibility as a condition precedent to admitting the hearsay declaration of an unavailable declarant.

In criminal cases, the Sixth Amendment requirement of confrontation would no doubt move into a large part of the area presently occupied by the hearsay rule in the event of the abolition of the latter. The resultant split between civil and criminal evidence is regarded as an undesirable development.

(2) Abandonment of the system of class exceptions in favor of individual treatment in the setting of the particular case, accompanied by procedural safeguards, has been impressively advocated. Weinstein, The Probative Force of Hearsay, 46 Iowa L.Rev. 331 (1961). Admissibility would be determined by weighing the probative force of the evidence against the possibility of prejudice, waste of time, and the availability of more satisfactory evidence. The bases of the traditional hearsay exceptions would be helpful in assessing probative force. Ladd, The Relationship of the Principles of Exclusionary Rules of Evidence to the Problem of Proof, 18 Minn.L.Rev. 506 (1934). Procedural safeguards would consist of notice of intention to use hearsay, free comment by the judge on the weight of the evidence, and a greater measure of authority in both trial and appellate judges to deal with evidence on the basis of weight. The Advisory Committee has rejected this approach to hearsay as involving too great a measure of judicial discretion, minimizing the predictability of rulings, enhancing the difficulties of preparation for trial, adding a further element to the already over-complicated congeries of pretrial procedures, and requiring substantially different rules for civil and criminal cases. The only way in which the probative force of hearsay differs from the probative force of other testimony is in the absence of oath, demeanor, and cross-examination as aids in determining credibility. For a judge to ex-

clude evidence because he does not believe it has been described as "altogether atypical, extraordinary. * * * " Chadbourn, Bentham and the Hearsay Rule: A Benthamic View of Rule 63(4)(c) of the Uniform Rules of Evidence, 75 Harv.L.Rev. 932, 947 (1962).

(3) The approach to hearsay in these rules is that of the common law, i.e., a general rule excluding hearsay, with exceptions under which evidence is not required to be excluded even though hearsay. The traditional hearsay exceptions are drawn upon for the exceptions, collected under two rules, one dealing with situations where availability of the declarant is regarded as immaterial and the other with those where unavailability is made a condition to the admission of the hearsay statement. Each of the two rules concludes with a provision for hearsay statements not within one of the specified exceptions "but having comparable [equivalent] circumstantial guarantees of trustworthiness." Rules 803(24) and 804(b)[(5)] [Now Rule 807]. This plan is submitted as calculated to encourage growth and development in this area of the law, while conserving the values and experience of the past as a guide to the future.

For the convenience of the reader, the definition of hearsay, Rules 801(a), (b), and (c), and the two categories of statements exempt from the bar of the rule against hearsay, Rule 802, through definition as not hearsay, i.e. prior statement of witness, Rule 801(d)(1), and admission by party opponent, Rule 801(d)(2), are each treated separately in the sections which follow. With respect to each of the three segments comprising Rule 801, presentation of the text of the rule is followed by commentary addressed to the various subsections comprising the particular segment of Rule 801 under consideration. A similar pattern is followed with respect to the various exceptions delineated in Rules 803 and 804.

## Rules 801(a), (b) and (c).

## DEFINITION OF HEARSAY

**The following definitions apply under this article:**

**(a) Statement.** A "statement" is (1) an oral or written assertion or (2) nonverbal conduct of a person, if it is intended by the person as an assertion.

**(b) Declarant.** A "declarant" is a person who makes a statement.

**(c) Hearsay.** "Hearsay" is a statement, other than one made by the declarant while testifying at the trial or hearing, offered in evidence to prove the truth of the matter asserted.

## § 801.1 Rules 801(a)(1) and (2), (b) and (c): Definition of Hearsay

Hearsay is defined in Rule 801(c) as a statement, other than one made by a declarant while testifying at the trial or hearing, offered in evidence to prove the truth of the matter asserted, i.e., the content of the statement. A statement, Rule 801(a), is (1) an oral or written assertion or (2) nonverbal conduct of a person, if it is intended by him as an assertion. The term "assertion" includes both matters directly expressed and matters necessarily implicitly being asserted. A declarant is simply a person who makes a statement, Rule 801(b). Thus documentary evidence as well as the oral assertions of a witness, whether or not recorded, may fall within the definition of hearsay. The definition of hearsay contained in Rule 801 conforms with that of the common law. Specific applications of the definition of hearsay are presented in the sections that follow.

The four risks to be considered in evaluating the testimony of a witness are (1) perception in the sense of capacity and actuality of observation by means of any of the senses, (2) recordation and recollection (sometimes called memory), (3) narration (sometimes called ambiguity), and (4) sincerity (sometimes called fabrication). In order to encourage the witness to testify to the best of his ability with respect to each of the four risks, and to expose inaccuracies in the witness' testimony, a witness is required to testify at trial (1) under oath or affirmation, (2) personally so that the trier of fact may observe the witness' demeanor, and (3) subject to contemporaneous cross-examination. Hearsay evidence is excluded, Rule 802, because an out of court statement is not subject to each of these three tests for ascertaining truth. Of the three, inability to conduct cross-examination is the essential factor underlying the rule excluding hearsay.

The definition of hearsay contained in Rules 801(a)-(c) together with the four risks relating to trustworthiness of a statement with which the hearsay rule is concerned is depicted in the following "Stickperson Hearsay" diagrams. Figure A portrays the hearsay risks associated with an oral statement of an out of court declarant. Figure B portrays the hearsay risks associated with the introduction of a written or recorded statement of an out of court declarant.

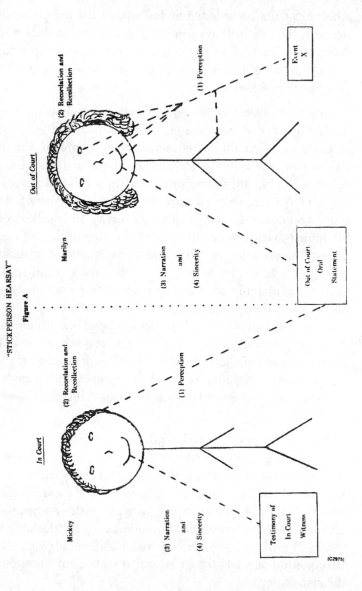

"STICKPERSON HEARSAY"

Figure A

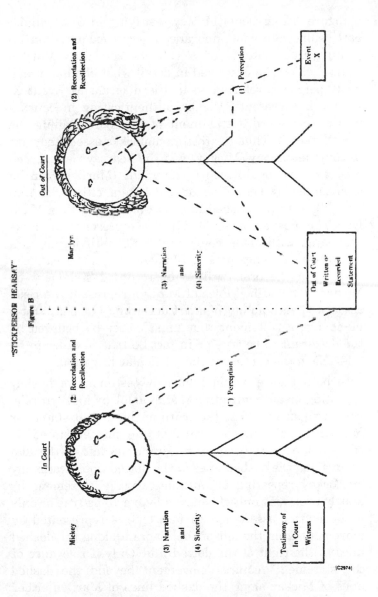

"STICKPERSON HEARSAY"

Figure B

In Court — Mickey

Out of Court — Marlyn

(1) Perception

(2) Recordation and Recollection

(3) Narration and (4) Sincerity

Event X

Out of Court Written or Recorded Statement

Testimony of In Court Witness

[C2974]

Figure A represents Mickey testifying in court, under oath, subject to contemporaneous cross-examination repeating the contents of a conversation with Marilyn during which she described in detail what she had previously perceived-referred to in the diagram as Event X. Figure B represents Mickey authenticating in court a written or recorded statement of Marilyn detailing the same Event X. Thus the testimonial risks associated with in court testimony (Mickey) and the hearsay risks associated with an out of court statement (Marilyn) can be appreciated by beginning at the left of either diagram and following the dashed lines of Mickey and then Marilyn. The dashed lines of Mickey represent the risks associated with an in court declarant testifying as to a fact of which he has personal knowledge, in this case the *making* of the oral, written or recorded statement by Marilyn. The dashed lines of Marilyn represent the risks associated with an out of court declarant's hearsay statement, i.e., a statement that must either be believed by the declarant to be true or in fact be true in order to be relevant in the context of the particular litigation.

In both Figure A and Figure B, testimony of Mickey repeating or authenticating a statement by Marilyn relevant without regard to the truth of the matter stated, or Marilyn's belief in the truth of the matter stated, is represented by the movement from the left of the diagram along the dashed lines *to* the dotted line. Testimony of Mickey repeating or authenticating a statement by Marilyn relevant only if believed by her to be true or only if the matter asserted is in fact true is represented by movement from the left of the diagram along the dashed lines to the right of the dotted line. Only if relevance of the statement requires movement beyond the dashed lines of Mickey along the dashed lines of Marilyn either into her head alone (belief—two hearsay risks) or further down the other side (Event X—four hearsay risks) is the statement hearsay. Such statement is offered to prove the truth of the matter asserted, Rule 801(c). Thus anytime a statement's relevance depends upon movement along the dashed lines of the diagram from the in court testimony of Mickey to the right of the dotted line, the statement is hearsay. Conversely, to the extent that the statement is relevant simply by virtue of Mickey repeating his personal knowledge of the making of the oral statement (Figure A) or authenticating the written or recorded assertion of Marilyn (Figure B), since movement proceeds from the in court testimony of Mickey along the dashed lines only *to* the dotted line, the statement of Marilyn is not hearsay. Such statement is not being offered to prove the truth of the matter asserted but solely for the fact it was said.

Determining whether a statement offered at trial for a particular purpose is hearsay thus involves solely a search for the presence of hearsay risks (belief—two hearsay risks or Event X—four hearsay risks). If such hearsay risks are present the statement is hearsay. *No assessment of the magnitude of hearsay risks present is undertaken.* Magnitude of hearsay risks bears solely upon whether the hearsay statement is felt sufficiently trustworthy to be admitted pursuant to an exception to the rule against hearsay.

The term "matter asserted" as employed in Rule 801(c) and at common law includes both matters directly expressed and matters the declarant necessarily implicitly intended to assert. When the declarant necessarily intended to assert the inference for which the statement is offered, the statement is tantamount to a direct assertion and therefore is hearsay. The declarant necessarily intends to assert, i.e., implicitly asserts, matters forming the foundation for matters directly expressed in the sense that such additional matters must be assumed to be true to give meaning to the matters directly expressed in the context in which the statement was made. To illustrate, the question "Do you think it will stop raining in one hour?" contains the implicit assertion that it is currently raining. The fact that it is currently raining is a necessary foundation fact which must be assumed true for the question asked to make sense.

Under the definition of hearsay contained in Rule 801(c) when a statement offered to prove the truth of the matter asserted is made "other than * * * by the declarant while testifying at the trial or hearing," the statement is hearsay without regard to whether or not the out of court declarant is available to testify or actually testifies at the trial or hearing at which the out of court statement is offered. Therefore the definition of hearsay in Rules 801(a)–(c) applies to all statements not made at the trial or hearing and thus not made subject to contemporaneous cross-examination before the trier of fact. When the out of court declarant does in fact also testify at trial, cross-examination, or direct and redirect examination, at that time provides an opportunity for the party opposing the truth of the out of court statement to explore the truth of the out of court statement before the trier of fact. Nevertheless, general admissibility of prior statements of in court witnesses is not provided for in the Federal Rules of Evidence. Rule 801(d)(1) does exempt from the operation of the rule against hearsay, by definition as not hearsay, certain prior inconsistent statements, Rule 801(d)(1)(A), and certain prior consistent statements, Rule 801(d)(1)(B). In addition statements of prior identification of a person after perceiving him are also exempted as not hearsay, Rule 801(d)(1)(C). The reasons for limiting the definition of not hearsay to only certain situations involving prior statements of an in court witness subject to later cross-examination are discussed elsewhere.

Notice that in deciding whether a statement falls within the definition of hearsay, it is irrelevant whether the statement was self-serving or disserving at the time of being either made or offered. It is similarly irrelevant in deciding whether a statement falls within the definition of hearsay as to whether the statement is being offered as direct or circumstantial evidence.

Occasionally, whether the party against whom a statement is offered was present when the statement was made has a bearing upon whether the statement is hearsay or is exempt under Rule 801(d)(2) as "not hearsay". Thus, an oral statement offered to show notice cannot have been effective as such unless it was made in the presence of the person sought to be charged with notice. Similarly, the presence of the party is essential if it is claimed that she admitted the truth of an oral statement by failing to deny it. In general, however, the presence or absence of the party against whom an extrajudicial statement is offered has no bearing upon either its status as hearsay or its admissibility, and an objection based on such absence betrays a basic lack of understanding of the nature of hearsay. Accordingly, in the great majority of situations, the objection "not in the presence of the defendant," and the converse in support of admissibility, "in the presence of the defendant," both frequently heard in criminal prosecutions, fail to address questions relevant to determining admissibility under the hearsay rule.

## § 801.2 Rule 801(a)(2): Nonverbal Conduct Intended as an Assertion

Nonverbal conduct may on occasion clearly be the equivalent of an assertive statement, that is, done for the purpose of deliberate communication, and thus classified as hearsay, Rule 801(a)(2). Nodding, pointing, and the sign language of the hearing impaired are as plainly assertions as are spoken words. So too is a videotape of the injured plaintiff recreating the accident which caused his injuries.

## § 801.3 Rule 801(a)(2): Nonverbal Conduct Not Intended as an Assertion

Nonverbal conduct not intended as an assertion is not hearsay, Rule 801(a)(2). The provision of Rule 801 declaring nonverbal conduct not intended as an assertion not hearsay resolves a long-time controversy among commentators. The controversy, however, has only been rarely the subject of judicial decision, frequently because the hearsay question has not been perceived. When the issue is whether an event happened, evidence of conduct from which the actor's belief may be inferred from which in turn the happening of the event may be inferred, bears at least a superficial resemblance to an out of court statement by the actor that he believed the event occurred. An analysis in terms of the principal danger which the hearsay rule is designed to guard against, i.e., lack of opportunity to test by cross-examination the capacity and actuality of his perception as well as his recordation, recollection, narration, and sincerity, however, leads to a rejection of the analogy between such an inference, sometimes called an "implied assertion," and an express allegation. When a person acts without intending to communicate a belief, his veracity is not involved. Furthermore there is frequently a guarantee of the trustworthiness of the inference to be drawn because the actor has based his actions on the correctness of his belief. Consider for example a person who is observed opening an umbrella, offered for the inference that it is raining. While the inference to be drawn from such nonverbal conduct is the same as in the case of a direct assertion that it is raining, the fact remains that the intent to assert is absent and thus the all important danger believed to be inherent in hearsay with respect to sincerity is absent as well. While the risk of sincerity is removed, the objection still remains that the accuracy of the actor's perception and recollection are untested by cross-examination as to the possibility of honest mistake. However risks of error in these respects are more sensibly factors to be used in evaluating weight and credibility rather than grounds for exclusion. Practical necessity also supports treating nonverbal nonassertive conduct as falling outside the definition of hearsay. Consider the illustration of a car stopped at a traffic light offered for the inference that the light was red. Treatment of such conduct as hearsay would too often exclude highly trustworthy and probative evidence. Resort to the residual exception of Rule 807 is an inappropriate response to a frequently recurring situation.

The court must be satisfied of the probative value of the proffered proof in light of trial concerns. Thus the inference of belief drawn from the nonassertive conduct and/or the inference drawn from such belief when offered to prove the truth of the fact impliedly being asserted may be too ambiguous to warrant submitting the evidence to the jury; its probative value may be so slight in comparison with the possibility of confusing and misleading the trier of fact that exclusion pursuant to Rule 403 is proper. Thus if the person opening an umbrella was known to be both exiting a store that sells umbrellas and superstitious concerning the opening of umbrellas indoors, ambiguity associated with the offering of such evidence to establish that it was raining at the time would certainly be enhanced. Whether exclusion is warranted under Rule 403 of course would depend upon examination of all relevant circumstances.

When nonverbal conduct is at issue, it is not always perfectly clear whether an assertion was intended by the person whose conduct is in question. If evidence of conduct is offered on the theory that it is not intended as an assertion and hence not hearsay, the burden of showing that an assertion was intended is on the party objecting to the evidence. The question of intention to assert is a preliminary one for the court, Rule 104(a). Even if the person intended to make an assertion, the person's conduct may itself be relevant to establish a fact of consequence in the litigation and if so is not hearsay for such purpose.

Nonverbal conduct not intended as an assertion and thus not hearsay under Rule 801(a)(2) is frequently, but incorrectly, treated as an admission of a party opponent. Illustrations include flight, silence, threats, and the fabrication, destruction, or suppression of evidence. Such evidence may be excluded upon application of Rule 403.

## § 801.4   Rule 801(a)(1): Oral or Written Conduct Not Intended as an Assertion

Considerations present with respect to nonverbal no-nassertive conduct support the position taken in Rule

801(a)(1) that oral or written conduct not intended as an assertion is not hearsay. Examples of such conduct are screams of pain, outbursts of laughter, singing a song or uttering or writing an expletive. Of course any of the foregoing may be intended as an assertion.

## § 801.5   Rule 801(c): Statements Offered Other Than to Prove the Truth of the Matter Asserted; Verbal Act; Characterizing Act; Affect on Listener; Impeachment

Hearsay does not encompass all extrajudicial statements but only those offered for the purpose of proving the truth of matters asserted in the statement, Rule 801(c). Therefore when the mere making of the statement is the relevant fact, i.e., tends to establish a fact of consequence, Rule 401, hearsay is not involved. Such statements are frequently said to be offered solely for the fact said and not for the truth of the matter asserted, i.e., the truth of their contents.

**Verbal act.** As to one group of extrajudicial statements falling outside the category of hearsay, the statement itself, the verbal act, has independent legal significance or gives rise to legal consequences. Thus testimony by an agent as to a statement by the principal granting him authority to act as agent is not hearsay. Other illustrations include statements constituting contracts, constituting the crime, statements offered as evidence of defamation, evidence offered that a statement has been made so as to establish a foundation for evidence showing the statement was made as part of a fraudulent scheme and is false, statements offered to place in context other statements otherwise admissible made in a conversation, and statements offered to show that the listener conducted an adequate investigation.

**Characterizing act.** Also included in the group of statements comprising operative legal acts are assertions which relate to and characterize a particular act. Thus for example, where an instrument designating the executive's wife as his beneficiary was unclear as to whether she was to be the beneficiary of his insurance policy or of a six months gratuity payment, oral statements accompanying delivery of the instrument resolving the ambiguity were not hearsay.

**Effect on listener.** Another group falling outside the category of hearsay consists of statements made by one person which become known to another offered as a circumstance under which the latter acted and as bearing upon his conduct. For example when a law enforcement official explains his going to the scene of the crime by stating that he received a radio call to proceed to a given location or explains that as a result of a statement being made an investigation was undertaken or other subsequent conduct occurred, such testimony is not hearsay. However if he becomes more specific by repeating definite complaints of a particular crime by the accused, this is so likely to be misused by the jury as evidence of the fact asserted that the content of the statement should, absent special circumstances enhancing probative value, be excluded on the grounds that the probative value of the statement admitted for a non-hearsay purpose is substantially outweighed by the danger of unfair prejudice, Rule 403 Other illustrations of a statement being offered for the purpose of showing the probable state of mind of the listener include being placed on notice or having knowledge. Similarly threats made to the defendant bearing on the reasonableness of his apprehension of danger or conversely providing a motive for action are not hearsay when offered for such purpose. Instructions to an individual to do something are also not hearsay. Evidence relevant for its effect on the listener is subject to exclusion under Rule 403, after taking into consideration the giving of a limiting instruction.

A statement which is not hearsay when offered for its effect on listener is hearsay as defined in Rules 801(a)–(c) when offered to prove the truth of the matter asserted. The giving of a limiting instruction is appropriate. Thus a statement by Harry to John that Sam is the person who keyed John's car is not hearsay when offered as relevant to establish John's motive, and thus relevant to prove that John was the person who slashed Sam's tires, but hearsay when offered to prove that Sam in fact keyed John's car.

**Impeachment.** Prior statements of a witness inconsistent with the witness' in-court testimony offered solely to impeach, Rules 607 and 613, are not hearsay.

## § 801.6   Rule 801(c): Statements Offered Other Than to Prove the Truth of the Matter Asserted; Circumstantial Evidence

The employment of circumstantial evidence has occasionally over the years given rise to discussion of the application of the rule against hearsay. Such discussions have tended to be confusing and more often than not theoretically unsound. The reason for such inaccuracy may be attributed primarily to the fact that in most such instances while the evidence under consideration was highly probative, highly necessary and highly trustworthy, no applicable hearsay exception existed. Under such circumstances, it is not surprising that both the courts and commentators "squeezed" and thereby distorted the proper application of the definition of hearsay for the sake of admissibility of the evidence in the case at hand. With the enactment of the residual hearsay exception, Rule 807, resort to distortion of the hearsay definition in the interests of justice in the case at hand is no longer required. It should no longer be tolerated.

Hearsay questions arising with respect to evidence employed circumstantially, while varied, may for purpose of analysis conveniently be discussed in connection with certain relatively distinct and recurring situations. As will be developed, whether evidence is direct or circumstantial is irrelevant in determining whether the evidence falls within the rule against hearsay.

**Mechanical traces.** Presence of something upon a person or premises may constitute circumstantial evidence giving rise to an inference that a person did an act with which these circumstances are associated. Such items, referred to by 1A Wigmore, Evidence §§ 149–160 (Tillers rev.1983) as mechanical traces, include (1) the presence upon a person or premises of articles, fragments, stains, or tools, (2) brands on animals or timber, or (3) tags, signs and numbers on automobiles, railroad cars or other vehicles or premises and (4) postmarks, fingerprints and footmarks. Mechanical traces are frequently relevant as circumstantial evidence looking backwards to show that some act was or was not done. Hearsay questions arise only when the relevancy of the circumstantial evidence, such as a tag or sign, derives solely from the truth of the mechanical trace. Take for example the situation of a tag on a briefcase containing narcotics bearing the name "Bill Snow." Since the relevancy of the tag to identify the defendant whose name is Bill Snow with the briefcase to which the tag is attached derives from the truth of the assertion made on the tag, i.e., this briefcase belongs to Bill Snow, the tag is hearsay. To say that the tag is a mechanical trace admissible as "circumstantial evidence of ownership" improperly ignores the definition of hearsay. To say that the tag is extremely probative and trustworthy evidence of ownership is simply to say that hearsay evidence may be extremely probative and trustworthy.

To be distinguished is the situation where the relevancy of the mechanical trace does not derive from the truth of the statement itself. Consider a book of matches bearing the name Red Fox Inn found on the defendant accused of a murder committed at the Red Fox Inn. If authenticated solely as having been taken off the person of the defendant, the matchbook is hearsay since its relevancy depends on the acceptance of the assertive statement on the matchbook that its origin is the Red Fox Inn. Now assume that the owner of the Red Fox Inn testifies that the matchbook found on the defendant is identical to the matchbooks he places on tables for use by customers. At this juncture, the relevancy of the matchbook is no longer dependent on the truth of the matter asserted but is based upon personal knowledge and the process of comparison. This point can be more easily appreciated by changing the cover of the matchbook to a modern design bearing no lettering at all. When the owner of the Red Fox Inn testifies that this matchbook is identical to those distributed at his bar, the nonhearsay nature of the physical evidence is highlighted.

**Character of an establishment:** McCormick, Evidence § 249 at 102 (4th ed.1992) classifies as not hearsay situations where "the character of an establishment is sought to be proved by evidence of statements made in connection with activities taking place on the premises."

The classic illustration involves the placing of telephone calls to an establishment accused of gambling. To enhance the probative value and trustworthiness of the statements under consideration, assume 20 policemen accompanied by 20 clergy of various denominations place tape recorders on 40 telephones and record 100 calls each answered by a police officer or clergy and each proceeding something like, "This is Tom, put $2 to win on Acne Pimple in the third at Belmont." While occasionally considered not hearsay as either a statement characterizing an act or as circumstantial evidence not being offered for the truth of the matter asserted but solely for the fact said, the plain and simple fact is that such statements fall clearly within the definition of hearsay. As presented such statements also fall within the residual hearsay exception of Rule 807.

Notice that in the illustration the telephone calls were answered by the police officers and clergy. If a police officer had overheard a person working at the establishment respond to the statement, "This is Tom, put $2 to win on Acne Pimple in the third at Belmont," with, "You got it, settle up as usual," the situation would be entirely different. The statement of the out-of-court declarant need no longer be true to be relevant. Similarly, the statement of the person working at the establishment accepting the bet would be a verbal act possessing independent significance under applicable substantive criminal law.

**Personal knowledge of independently established facts.** On rare occasions, statements are offered into evidence to prove personal knowledge of the declarant as to the truth of the matter asserted when the truth of the matter asserted is firmly established by independent evidence. Personal knowledge of the declarant is relevant in such cases to establish the presence of the declarant at a particular location at a particular time. Consider, for example, the case of Bridges v. State (Wis. 1945). In *Bridges,* the defendant was convicted of taking indecent liberties with a seven year old girl named Sharon Schunk. She was abused by a man in an Army uniform at his house. The serious question was identification of the defendant as that person. This identification in part depended upon whether the house to which Sharon had been taken by her assaulter was the house at 125 East Johnson Street in which the defendant concededly resided at the relevant time. At trial, statements made by Sharon to her mother and police officers prior to discovery of the location of defendant's house as to the general appearance of the steps to the porch, the front door, and the room and articles therein of the house to which she had been taken by the perpetrator on February 26, 1945 were admitted. The Supreme Court of Wisconsin upheld admission of Sharon's statements as circumstantial evidence of personal knowledge not being offered to prove the truth of the matter asserted.

Notwithstanding the court's holding, Sharon's statements are hearsay. Her statements were offered for the inference that she acquired her memory in a manner consistent with the events described in her statement. As so offered, all four hearsay risks are present. It is certainly possible, albeit unlikely, that Sharon created a description of the house of the whole cloth. More likely, she may have in good faith provided a description of a house where she had been on an occasion not connected to the assault. Finally, she may have described a house that was suggested to her earlier by the police or someone else as being the house where she had been taken. Admittedly, the magnitude of the hearsay risks are small. Nevertheless, because the risks of perception, recordation and recollection, narration, and sincerity are present with respect to Sharon's statements, the statements fall within the definition of hearsay when offered to prove Sharon's personal knowledge of objects in the defendant's house to establish that the assault took place in that house. Relevancy of Sharon's statements involves hearsay risks located in the "Stickperson Hearsay" diagram on the right of the dotted line. Sharon's statements are, however, admissible under the residual hearsay exception of Rule 807.

**Circumstantial use of utterances to show state of mind.** McCormick asserts that while a direct declaration of the existence of a state of mind or feeling which it is offered to prove is hearsay, declarations which only impliedly, indirectly, or inferentially indicate the state of mind or feeling of the declarant are not hearsay. McCormick, Evidence § 249 at 590–91 (Cleary ed.1972) employed the following illustration:

In a contested will case the proponent might seek to support the validity of testator's bequest to his son Harold against the charge of undue influence by showing that long before the time when the alleged influence was exerted, the testator had shown a special fondness for Harold. For this purpose evidence might be offered (a) that the testator had paid the expenses of Harold, and for none other of his children, in completing a college course, (b) that the testator said, "Harold is the finest of my sons," and (c) that he said, "I care more for Harold than for any of my other children." When offered to show the testator's feelings toward his son, under the suggested definition item (a) would present no hearsay question, item (b) would be considered a nonhearsay declaration raising a circumstantial inference as to the testator's feelings, and (c) a direct statement offered to prove the fact stated, and hence dependent for its value upon the veracity of the declarant, would be considered hearsay.

For McCormick the distinction, as artificial as it is, itself breaks down when one considers statements offered to show a person's mental incompetency. McCormick concluded that even the direct assertion "I believe that I am King Henry the Eighth," undeniably falling squarely within the definition of hearsay, may nevertheless be classified as nonhearsay on the theory of "verbal conduct offered circumstantially." Many years ago Professor Hinton correctly exposed the errors of McCormick's ways:

> It has sometimes been argued by judges and writers that, where the issue is the sanity of the testator, and some absurd statement by him is proved, e.g., "I am the Emperor Napoleon", no hearsay use is involved because we are not seeking to prove that he really was Napoleon, and hence that we are making a purely circumstantial use of his words to prove his irrational belief. The difficulty is that this view ignores the implied assertion of belief. If the statement had taken the form, "I believe that I am Napoleon", and were offered to prove that the testator so believed, it would be generally conceded [but not by McCormick] that the statement was hearsay, and receivable only because of an exception to the rule. The former assertion is simply a short method of stating the speaker's opinion or belief. Implied assertions seem to fall within the hearsay category as well as express assertions.

Hinton, State of Mind and the Hearsay Rule, 1 U.Chi. L.Rev.394, 397–98 (1934).

If the declarant must believe the matter asserted to be true for any inference to logically flow, whether the statement is "Harold is the finest of my sons", "I believe I am King Henry the Eighth," or "I am the Emperor Napoleon," the hearsay risks of sincerity and narration are present. Such statements are thus properly classified as hearsay. It is sometimes asserted that determining whether such statements are or are not hearsay is "limited to the realm of theory" in that a hearsay exception exists for statements of a declarant's then existing, mental, emotional or physical condition, Rule 803(3). Nevertheless the confusion that broad use of the concept of circumstantial evidence creates in the overall analysis of hearsay versus not hearsay remains. Moreover mechanical traces and character of an establishment statements do not conveniently fall within a common law hearsay exception. Characterizing assertive statements as circumstantial is simply utterly irrelevant in addressing the definitional framework of hearsay set forth in Rules 801(a)-(c). The practice should be discontinued.

## § 801.7 Rule 801(c): Statements Offered Other Than to Prove the Truth of the Matter Asserted; Basis for Nonasserted Inference or "Implied Assertion"

If a statement, although assertive in form, is offered as a basis for inferring something other than the truth of the matter asserted, the Advisory Committee's Note to Rule 801(a) indicates that the statement is "excluded from the definition of hearsay by the language of subdivision (c)." The Advisory Committee's assertion as to the non-hearsay nature of statements offered for a different inference rests on the assumption of a reduced sincerity risk alleged to be similar to that associated with nonverbal conduct not intended as an assertion at all. Whether statements offered as a basis of inferring something other than the matter asserted possess a reduced sincerity risk, much less a reduced sincerity risk sufficient to warrant nonhearsay treatment, is extremely doubtful. More importantly whether such statements are in fact nonhearsay under Rules 801(a)–(c) is also extremely doubtful.

At early common law, such statements were treated as hearsay. The leading English case was Wright v. Doe d. Tatham (Eng.1838). In that case letters written to a testator and offered by the proponents of his will were of a kind that would not likely have been written to a mentally defective person. The inference suggested was that the writers believed him to be sane, which in turn justified the inference that he was sane. The House of Lords ruled the letters inadmissible hearsay on the basis that they were "implied assertions." Rejected was the notion that since the out of court declarant did not intend to assert the matter for which the statement was being offered, i.e., the competency of the testator, there existed a sufficient reduction in the likelihood of conscious fabrication to warrant non-hearsay treatment. Notice that in the situation under discussion the initial inference as to the declarant's state of mind is inferred from the statement not asserted by it. When the declarant necessarily intended to assert, although he did not directly assert, the inference for which the statement is offered, the statement is clearly hearsay. Matters that are implicitly being asserted are for hearsay analysis purposes tantamount to a direct assertion. Obviously, when the declarant also intends to assert the matter the

statement is used to infer, the argument of a reduced
risk of sincerity is a non sequitur. The closer the inference to be drawn is to the matter expressly asserted, the
more likely the declarant intended to assert the inference
the statement is offered to prove. Notice also that the
concept of a statement offered to infer something other
than the truth of the matter asserted, applies (if it ever
applies) solely to those situations where the actual statement of the declarant is used to infer the truth of an
"implied assertion" being made by the declarant and not
to inferences derived directly from assuming the truth of
the matter actually asserted.

The Advisory Committee's apparent attempted rejection of Wright v. Doe d. Tatham is as unfortunate as it is
incorrect. When a statement is offered to infer the declarant's state of mind from which a given fact is inferred in the form of an opinion or otherwise, since the
truth of the matter asserted must be assumed in order
for the nonasserted inference to be drawn, the statement
is properly classified as hearsay under the language of
Rules 801(a)–(c). Since the matter asserted in the statement must be true, a reduction in the risk of sincerity is
not present. The Advisory Committee's reliance on the
analogy to nonverbal nonassertive conduct where a reduction in the risk of fabrication is caused by a lack of
intent to assert anything is thus clearly misconceived. It
is further suggested that the fact that the practical
importance of the concept (even if assumed theoretically
sound) is so small in relation to the confusion in analysis
the concept causes in the minds of those attempting to
apply the hearsay rule argues strongly in favor of rejection of the concept that statements should be found to be
non-hearsay solely on the basis of being offered for the
truth of a different inference. With respect to those

statements possessing sufficient guarantees of trustworthiness, resort to the residual hearsay exception of Rule 807 is clearly preferable.

## § 801.8   Rules 801(a), (b) and (c): Statements Not Made in Presence of Opposite Party

Occasionally whether the party against whom a statement is offered was present when the statement was made has a bearing upon admissibility. Thus an oral statement relied upon as notice cannot have been effective as such unless made in the presence of the person sought to be charged with notice. Similarly, the presence of the party is essential if it is claimed that he admitted the truth of an oral statement by failing to deny it. In general, however, the presence or absence of the party against whom an extrajudicial statement is offered has no bearing upon either its status as hearsay or its admissibility, and an objection so phrased betrays a basic lack of understanding of the nature of hearsay. Accordingly, in a great majority of situations resort to the objections "not in the presence of the defendant," or the converse in support of admissibility, "in the presence of the defendant," simply fails to address questions relevant to determining admissibility under the hearsay rule.

## § 801.9   Rules 801(a), (b) and (c): Hearsay Admitted Without Objection

Under Rule 103, a party who does not make a timely objection cannot complain of the admission of hearsay. The question remains, however, of the weight and probative value of hearsay so admitted. The almost infinite variety which hearsay assumes precludes any answer except that hearsay will be considered and given its natural probative effect.

## § 801.10  Rules 801(a), (b) and (c): Interpreting the Definition of Hearsay

Courts and commentators have struggled with the definitional aspects of hearsay under the cloud that given the pigeonhole theory of class exceptions to the hearsay rule, many trustworthy and necessary statements if classified as hearsay would be excluded at trial. Attempts to expand admissibility through novel interpretations of the definition of hearsay naturally resulted. Such novel interpretations have taken the form, for example, of arguing that "I believe I am King Henry the Eighth" and statements offered to infer something other than the truth of the matter asserted are not hearsay. While novel, such interpretations are neither correct interpretations of the definition of hearsay nor do they comport with the analysis of risks the hearsay rule attempts to address. Such novel interpretations have at the same time greatly confused not only many practitioners and courts but thousands of law students each year. Whatever value these novel interpretations once had is no longer true today. With the availability of the residual hearsay exception of Rule 807, trustworthy and necessary hearsay will no longer be inadmissible simply because it fails to fit neatly into one of the pigeonhole hearsay exceptions.

It is therefor suggested that clarity would be fostered and confusion eliminated if once and for all the courts would declare that Rule 801(c) includes (1) a statement to the extent relevant only if the declarant believes the matter asserted to be true, whether that statement be "I am Napoleon" or "I believe I am King Henry the Eighth" and (2) a statement whose relevance depends upon the matter asserted being true without reference to whether a further inference is then going to be drawn.

Both of these novel approaches are in fact now recognized as hearsay by the text of Rule 801(c); any contrary suggestion in the Advisory Committee's Note with respect to statements forming the basis for a nonasserted inference is incorrect. What is needed is explicit court recognition thus putting the issue to rest. An alternative formulation of Rule 801(c), identical in content while highlighting the hearsay nature of statements offered as a basis for a nonasserted inference and all statements of state of mind, is as follows:

(c) Hearsay. "Hearsay" is a statement offered in evidence, other than one made by the declarant while testifying at the trial or hearing, to the extent relevance depends upon (1) the truth of the matter asserted or (2) the declarant's belief in the truth or falsity of the matter asserted.

## Rule 801(d)(1).

## STATEMENTS WHICH ARE NOT HEARSAY: PRIOR STATEMENT BY WITNESS

**The following definitions apply under this article:**

\* \* \*

**(d) Statements Which Are Not Hearsay. A statement is not hearsay if:**

**(1) Prior Statement by Witness. The declarant testifies at the trial or hearing and is subject to cross-examination concerning the statement, and the statement is (A) inconsistent with the declarant's testimony, and was given under oath**

subject to the penalty of perjury at a trial, hearing, or other proceeding, or in a deposition, or (B) consistent with the declarant's testimony and is offered to rebut an express or implied charge against the declarant of recent fabrication or improper influence or motive, or (C) one of identification of a person made after perceiving the person; or * * *

## § 801.11 Rule 801(d)(1)(A): Prior Inconsistent Statements

At common law a witness could be impeached on a non-collateral matter by extrinsic proof that he made a statement out of court inconsistent with his in court testimony. The prior statement had to be inconsistent, and a proper foundation had to be laid during cross-examination of the witness. The inconsistent statement was hearsay and hence was not admitted as substantive evidence but rather was limited solely to its impeaching effect upon the credibility of the witness. Of course, prior inconsistent statements of a witness are not to be confused with an admission of a party-opponent, which has always been and continues to be regarded as substantive evidence, Rule 801(d)(2), requiring no preliminary foundation on cross-examination, Rule 613(b).

Rule 801(d)(1)(A) alters the common law to the limited extent of exempting from the bar of the rule against hearsay, Rule 802, through definition as not hearsay a prior statement of a declarant who testifies at trial and is subject to cross-examination concerning the statement, if the statement is inconsistent with his testimony, and was given under oath, subject to the penalty of perjury at a trial, hearing, or other proceeding, or in a deposition. Thus those prior inconsistent statements made under oath at formal proceedings are now substantively admissible. Grand jury testimony is included within the concept of "other proceeding." However, statements, whether oral or written, even if given under oath and videotaped, made to law enforcement officials fall outside the concept of "other proceedings." The foundation requirement of Rule 613 applies to prior inconsistent statements admitted as substantive evidence solely under Rule 801(d)(1)(A). The rationale behind the limited departure from the common law represented by Rule 801(d)(1)(A) is that expressed by the House Committee on the Judiciary that (1) unlike most other situations involving unsworn or oral statements' including, for example, oral statements by an occurrence witness to a crime, there can be no dispute as to whether the prior statement was made, and (2) the context of a formal proceeding and an oath, provide firm additional assurances of the reliability of the prior statement.

Critics of the common law prohibition against substantive use of a prior inconsistent statement have long contended that the declarant at trial is under oath, his demeanor may be observed, his credibility tested by cross-examination and that the timing of cross-examination is not critical. Rule 801(d)(1)(A) accepts the arguments of such critics only to the extent that the non-contemporaneous cross-examination relates to a prior inconsistent statement made under oath at a formal proceeding; substantive admissibility is allowed only for those statements possessing the highest degree of certainty of making made under circumstances conducive to truth telling.

Of course prior inconsistent statements not falling within the scope of Rule 801(d)(1)(A) may still be employed for the limited purpose of impeachment in accordance with Rules 607 and 613.

## § 801.12  Rule  801(d)(1)(B):  Prior  Consistent Statements

Generally speaking, a witness cannot be corroborated on direct or redirect examination or rebuttal by proof of prior statements consistent with his in court testimony. Whatever inherent probative value such consistent statements may have is felt to be insufficient when viewed in light of trial concerns, Rule 403. However under certain circumstances the probative value of a prior consistent statement clearly warrants introduction. Rule 801(d)(1)(B) provides that a prior consistent statement of a declarant testifying at trial and subject to cross-examination concerning the statement is admissible when offered "to rebut an express or implied charge against him of recent fabrication, improper influence or motive." Thus to rebut an express or implied charge that the witness is motivated or has been influenced to testify falsely or that his testimony is a recent fabrication, evidence is admissible that he told the same story *before* the motive or influence came into existence or before the time of the alleged recent fabrication. The prior consistent statement is exempt from the bar of the rule against hearsay, Rule 802, through definition as not hearsay, Rule 801(d)(1)(B), and thus is admitted as substantive evidence.

To illustrate, assume that John, while standing on the sidewalk, witnessed an automobile accident involving a car driven by Mary and a truck driven by Bill. The factual issue in dispute is the color of the traffic light at the intersection facing both parties. At trial, John testifies that the light facing Mary was green. On cross-examination, Bill's attorney brings out that four weeks after the accident John met Mary for the first time at her lawyer's office, that they dated thereafter, and that they are now engaged to be married. On redirect examination, John may testify that one day after the accident, and thus *before* the alleged improper influence or motive arose, he told his best friend Tim that the light facing the car driven by the woman was green. However, John may not testify that two weeks after John and Mary were engaged he told his mother that the light facing Mary was green.

Where admissible, the prior consistent statement may be testified to by either the witness himself or any other person with personal knowledge of the statement. Rule 801(d)(1)(B) does require that the declarant testify at the trial and that he be subject to cross-examination concerning the prior statement, a requirement that is satisfied so long as the declarant is available to be recalled.

A prior statement that corroborates the witness may be admitted without reference to Rule 801(d)(1)(B) if it serves to explain or modify a fragment thereof introduced by the opposite party for purposes of impeachment, or if it is otherwise related to or supportive of a denial or explanation offered in response to impeachment of a witness by an alleged self-contradiction, whether an inconsistent statement or a failure to speak when natural to do so, Rule 613. Such prior consistent statements are admitted for corroborative purposes only and not as substantive evidence; the jury should be instructed accordingly.

The admissibility of prior consistent statements following impeachment of a witness is in fact an extremely complex subject. Unfortunately the terminology incorporated in Rule 801(d)(1)(B), in particular the terms "influence," "motive," and "recent fabrication," merely perpetuate the confusion present in the common law. To raise just one area of confusion, a charge of improper motive capable of being rebutted by introduction of a prior consistent statement must also be a charge of recent fabrication but a charge of recent fabrication need not be based upon an assertion of recently arising motive to falsify. The fortunate aspect is, however, that since the prior consistent statement is by its very nature consistent with in court testimony of the witness, introduction of reversible error through misinterpretation is very unlikely.

### § 801.13   Rule 801(d)(1)(C): Prior Identification of a Person After Perceiving Him; Police Officer Testimony

When a witness testifies and is subject to cross-examination, his prior statement identifying a person made after perceiving the person, usually at a lineup, a one on one viewing often called a showup, in a photograph or a sketch, or at a prior hearing, is exempt from the bar of the rule against hearsay, Rule 802, through definition as not hearsay, Rule 801(d)(1)(C). There is no requirement that the witness first be impeached. The theory is that courtroom identification is so unconvincing as practically to impeach itself thus justifying the corroboration. The purpose of the rule is to permit the introduction of more meaningful identifications made by a witness when memory was fresher and there had been less opportunity for influence to be exerted upon him. The circumstances of the prior identification may, of course, be considered by the trier of fact in determining the weight to be accorded.

Rule 801(d)(1)(C) requires by its terms only that the person who made the identification testify at the trial or hearing and be subject to cross-examination. It seems reasonable to assume that the rule also contemplates that the declarant will testify in court on the subject of identification and not simply be available to be recalled to the stand by the defendant for cross-examination. The rule does not limit testimony as to the statement of identification made after perception solely to that of the identifying witness; testimony of any person who was present, for example a police officer, is admissible. Of course overproof may unduly emphasize the prior identification to the extent of misleading the jury and consequently is subject to the court's discretionary control under Rule 403.

Rule 801(d)(1)(C) does not require on its face, nor has a requirement been imposed, that the identifying witness make a positive in court identification or identify the defendant in court at all. Similarly nothing in the text of the rule prohibits introduction of the out of court statement identifying the defendant made by a declarant who in court denies making or repudiates the identification and denies that the defendant is the person involved in the crime. Moreover while it has been asserted that a witness who lacks recollection as to the identity of the individual, whether such lack of recollection is real or feigned, is not "subject to cross-examination concerning the statement" as provided in Rule 801(d)(1), legislative history indicates substantial support for applicability of Rule 801(d)(1)(C) in this context. Judicial opinion is in accord. In short, the text, the legislative history, as well as judicial opinion interpreting Rule 801(d)(1)(C) place no restrictions upon admissibility other than having the alleged out of court declarant in court on the witness stand subject to cross-examination concerning the statement.

## Rule 801(d)(2).

## STATEMENTS WHICH ARE NOT HEARSAY: ADMISSION BY PARTY–OPPONENT

**The following definitions apply under this article:**

**\* \* \***

**(d) Statements Which Are Not Hearsay. A statement is not hearsay if—**

**\* \* \***

**(2) Admission by Party–Opponent. The statement is offered against a party and is (A) the party's own statement in either an individual or a representative capacity or (B) a statement of which the party has manifested an adoption or belief in its truth, or (C) a statement by a person authorized by the party to make a statement concerning the subject, or (D) a statement by the party's agent or servant concerning a matter within the scope of the agency or employment made during the existence of the relationship, or (E) a statement by a coconspirator of a party during the course and in furtherance of the conspiracy. The contents of the statement shall be considered but are not alone sufficient to establish the declarant's authority under subdivision (C), the agency or employment relationship and scope thereof under subdivision (D), or the existence of the conspiracy and the participation therein of the de-**

**clarant and the party against whom the statement is offered under subdivision (E).**

## § 801.14   Rule 801(d)(2): Admission by Party–Opponent; An Overview

Relevant admissions of a party, whether consisting of oral or written assertions or nonverbal conduct, are admissible when offered by an opponent. While formerly considered an exception to the hearsay rule, in recognition of its position in the adversary system, Rule 801(d)(2) exempts admissions of a party-opponent from the operation of the rule against hearsay, Rule 802, by defining admissions of a party-opponent as "not hearsay". Lack of opportunity to cross-examine is deprived of significance by the incongruity of the party objecting to his own statement on the ground that he was not subject to cross-examination by himself at the time.

In the nature of things, the statement is usually damaging to the party against whom offered, else it would not be offered. However neither Rule 801(d)(2) nor the common law cases lay down a requirement that the statement be against interest either when made or when offered, and the theory of the exception is not based thereon. The sometimes encountered label "admission against interest," is inaccurate, serves only to confuse, and should be abandoned.

Admissions are substantive evidence, as contrasted with mere impeaching statements, and no preliminary foundation need be laid by examining the declarant concerning the admission, Rule 613(b). Personal knowledge of the matter admitted is not required; nor is a requirement of mental capacity imposed. Admissions in the form of an opinion are competent, even if the opinion is a

conclusion of law. The opinion rule, designed to elicit
more concrete and informative answers, is a rule of
preference as to the form of testimony. Since out-of-court
statements are not made under circumstances in which
alternative forms of expressions may be secured, this
aspect of the opinion rule is inapplicable. Admissibility
does not depend upon whether the declarant is unavailable, available, or actually testifies. Whether the specific
requirements set forth in Rule 801(d)(2) not involving
conditional relevancy, Rule 104(b), have been satisfied,
such as whether a person is authorized to make a statement, Rule 801(d)(2)(C), or whether a statement concerns a matter within the scope of his agency or employment, Rule 801(d)(2)(D), are determined by the court,
Rule 104(a).

## § 801.15  Rule  801(d)(2)(A):  Admissions;  State-
### ments of Party Made in Individual Ca-
### pacity

A party's own statement made in his individual capacity when offered by an opposing party is defined as not
hearsay, Rule 801(d)(2)(A).

As with all admissions by a party-opponent, no requirement of mental capacity of the declarant is imposed;
the statement need not relate to a matter as to which the
party had personal knowledge; it need not be against
interest when made or when offered; it may contain
opinions or conclusions of law; and it may be offered
whether or not the party is unavailable, available, or
actually testifies. If the party does testify, no foundation
need be laid preliminary to its introduction in evidence,
Rule 613(b).

## § 801.16  Rule 801(d)(2)(A): Admissions; Plea of Guilty; Crimes Punishable in Excess of One Year, Minor Crimes Including Traffic Offenses

The introduction into evidence of a guilty plea not later withdrawn, differs in theory though perhaps not in result from the introduction of a judgment resulting from it. The judgment may constitute a hearsay exception under Rule 803(22) when offered to prove any fact essential to sustain the judgment. The plea of guilty is offered not to prove that essential facts have been previously found to exist but rather to prove that the offender admitted facts constituting guilt. Thus a plea of guilty may be admissible as an admission of a party under Rule 801(d)(2)(A) or as a statement against interest of a nonparty under Rule 804(b)(3).

Where evidence of a conviction on a plea of guilty is being offered against a party, the effect of proceeding pursuant to either Rule 803(22) or Rule 801(d)(2)(A) is identical. In both instances the facts admitted by the party by entering a plea of guilty, i.e., facts essential to sustain the conviction, may be admitted against him by a party-opponent as an evidentiary as distinguished from a judicial admission. The party's reason, if any, for pleading guilty may thus also be introduced.

A question is raised whether a plea of guilty may be introduced as either an admission of a party-opponent, Rule 801(d)(2)(A), or statement against interest, Rule 804(b)(3), in situations in which the judgment of conviction, Rule 803(22), could not be shown because the crime was not punishable by imprisonment in excess of one year. The question is not specifically addressed in either Rule 801(d)(2)(A) or 804(b)(3). Similarly, neither Rule

803(22) nor its Advisory Committee's Note contains a specific reference to the admissibility of a guilty plea to an offense punishable by imprisonment for no more than one year. However the rationale expressed by the Advisory Committee is excluding convictions for crimes punishable by imprisonment for no more than one year from the operation of Rule 803(22) is extremely telling:

> Practical considerations require exclusion of convictions of minor offenses, not because the administration of justice in its lower echelons must be inferior, but because motivation to defend at this level is often minimal or nonexistent.

The rationale for excluding a prior conviction after trial for a minor offense applies with even greater force to a guilty plea entered to a minor offense. Accordingly, a plea of guilty to an offense punishable by imprisonment for no more than one year should be declared to fall outside the breadth of both Rules 801(d)(2)(A) and 804(b)(3). Nevertheless, a majority of decisions admit the guilty plea under such circumstances with explanation.

## § 801.17  Rule 801(d)(2)(A): Admissions; Statements of Party Made in a Representative Capacity

Rule 801(d)(2)(A) provides that if an individual has a representative capacity such as an administrator, executor, trustee, guardian, or agent and the statement is offered against him in that capacity, the statement is admissible without reference to whether the individual was acting in a representative capacity in making the statement; all that is required is that the statement be relevant to representative affairs.

## § 801.18   Rule 801(d)(2): Admissions; Persons in Privity or Jointly Interested

At common law statements by a person in privity with a party were receivable in evidence as an admission of the party. An admission by one jointly interested was also receivable at common law against others similarly interested.

Rule 801(d)(2) alters prior law by omitting any provision declaring either a statement by a person in privity with another or by one of persons jointly interested to be an admission by the other or others. Thus Rule 801(d)(2) in excluding such statements from the definition of admissions adopts the position advocated by Professor Morgan and the Model Code of Evidence that considerations of privity and joint interest neither furnish criteria of credibility nor aid in the evaluation of testimony. Statements formerly treated as a separate category of admission will, however, frequently qualify as representative admissions, Rule 801(d)(2)(C), or as statements against interest, Rule 804(b)(3), or fall within another hearsay exception. Other such statements will meet the requirements of the residual hearsay exception contained in Rule 807.

## § 801.19   Rule   801(d)(2)(B):   Manifestation   of Adoption or Belief in Truth of Statement; Words or Conduct

Excluded from the definition of hearsay by Rule 801(d)(2)(B) are statements to which a party has manifested his adoption or belief in their truth. However the party's words or conduct asserted to be a manifestation of assent to the truth of the statement may be susceptible of more than one interpretation. Whether a party has manifested his assent to another person's statement is a question of conditional relevancy under Rule 104(b). The burden of proof is on the proponent to show that adoption was intended; a mere statement that another person had made a particular statement is insufficient.

## § 801.20 Rule 801(d)(2)(B): Admissions; Manifestation of Adoption or Belief in Truth of Statement; Silence

Manifestation of belief in the truth of a statement may occur by silence, that is, a failure to respond when natural to do so.

**Civil cases:** If an oral or written statement is communicated by another person to a party in the litigation containing assertions of fact which if untrue the party would under all the circumstances naturally be expected to deny, his failure to speak is receivable against him as an adoptive admission, Rule 801(d)(2)(B). With respect to a letter, while it is frequently stated that the general rule, subject to exception, is that failure to answer may not be introduced as an admission, McCormick asserts that the more acceptable view is that failure to reply to a letter containing statements which under all the circumstances one would expect the receiver to deny if felt untrue may be introduced in evidence as an admission by silence.

**Criminal cases:** Silence under circumstances naturally calling for a denial has also been recognized as an admission in criminal cases. Evidence must be introduced sufficient to support a finding, Rule 104(b), that in light of the totality of the circumstances, a statement was made which the defendant heard, understood, had an opportunity to deny or object and in which the defendant by his silence acquiesced. Mere possession of a document standing alone does not constitute a manifestation of adoption or belief in its truth. In addition the court must pursuant to Rule 104(a) determine that it is more probably true than not true that the statement was such that under the circumstances it would naturally be expected that an innocent person would deny in some form the truth of the statement if he believed it to be untrue.

Various considerations, however, raise doubts as to the propriety of applying the rule in criminal cases, especially when an accusation to the defendant is made under the auspices of law enforcement personnel. In addition to the inherently ambiguous nature of the inference itself, silence on the part of the defendant may be motivated by prior experience or prior advice of counsel. Treating silence as an admission also affords unusual opportunity to manufacture evidence. Moreover the accused would effectively be compelled to speak, either at the time or upon the trial by way of explaining his reasons for remaining silent, which, to say the least, crowds his privilege against self-incrimination uncomfortably. Nevertheless, silence of a witness, including the criminal defendant, that occurs postarrest but prior to the actual giving of *Miranda* warnings has been held admissible to impeach. Whether prearrest silence may constitutionally be admitted as substantive evidence is unclear. Obviously once the *Miranda* warnings have been given advising the defendant of his right to remain silent, the defendant's failure to speak may no longer possibly be considered an admission, nor may his silence be employed for purposes of impeachment.

## § 801.21 Rule 801(d)(2)(C): Admissions; Statements by Persons Authorized to Speak

Statements by a person authorized by a party to make a statement concerning the subject matter are admissions, Rule 801(d)(2)(C). The authority of the agent to speak as to a subject, which may be express or implied, must be established at trial.

As a matter of substantive agency law, neither the fact of authorization nor the scope of the subject matter of authority may be established by the agent's out of court statements. Nevertheless, Rule 801(d)(2) now provides that in determining whether a person was authorized at the time by the party to make a statement concerning the subject, the contents of the statement is to be considered but is not alone sufficient to establish the declarant's authority. Authorization to make a statement concerning the subject matter may, of course, be established by the acts or conduct of the principal or his statements to the agent or a third party.

Along with statements to other persons, statements by the authorized person to the principal himself are included in Rule 801(d)(2)(C). Accordingly a party's books or records are usable against him without regard to intent to disclose to third persons.

## § 801.22 Rule 801(d)(2)(D): Admissions; Statements by Agent or Servant Concerning Matter Within Scope of his Agency or Employment; Attorneys

A statement of an agent or servant concerning a matter within the scope of his employment, made during the existence of the relationship, is an admission of his employer, Rule 801(d)(2)(D). In determining whether an agency or employment relationship existed at the time of the statement and scope of such a relationship, the contents of the statement is to be considered but is not alone sufficient.

Prior to Rule 801(d)(2)(D) courts applied the traditional agency test in determining admissibility of statements by agents or servants, i.e., whether the particular statement was authorized by the principal. Courts generally decided that damaging statements were not within the scope of authority, even of relatively high level employees. The obvious difficulty with applying strict agency principles is that agents or servants are very rarely authorized to make damaging statements the truck driver is hired to drive, not to talk. However as a result of the fact that it also seemed unreasonable to deny admission to inculpatory statements by the driver about the driving he was hired to do in light of the probable reliability of such statements, courts often stretched to find a basis for admissibility.

In recognition of the reliability and reasonableness of admitting such statements, Rule 801(d)(2)(D) declares statements of an agent or servant concerning a matter within the scope of his agency or employment to be defined as not hearsay if made during the existence of the relationship. Authority to speak is thus no longer of concern; all that is required is that the statement concern a matter within the scope of the agency or employment, and that the agent or servant still be employed at the time of making the statement. A statement meeting the requirement of Rule 801(d)(2)(D) is not made inadmissible simply because the statement was made to the employer and not a third person. However in a criminal prosecution, government employees are apparently not considered agents or servants of a party-opponent for the purpose of the admissions rules.

An attorney may, of course, act as an ordinary agent and as such make evidentiary admissions admissible against his principal, Rule 801(d)(2)(C) and (D). In addition, an attorney has authority in general to make judicial admissions for the client in all matters relating to the progress and trial of an action.

## § 801.23 Rules 801(d)(2): The Requirement of Personal Knowledge

Admissions of a party-opponent are characterized by the Advisory Committee's Note to Rule 801(d)(2) as enjoying freedom from the restrictive influences of the rule requiring personal knowledge. However Weinstein's Evidence ¶ 801(d)(2)(C)[01] at 801-278-801-279 (1990) makes a strong argument that the rationale supporting elimination of the requirement of personal knowledge generally with respect to admissions fails to withstand analysis with respect to vicarious admissions, Rules 801(d)(2)(C) and (D). A similar argument can be made with respect to admissions by silence, Rule 801(d)(2)(B). Whatever the merits of requiring personal knowledge in connection with any of the foregoing rules, the fact remains that lack of personal knowledge on the part of the declarant does not bar introduction of a statement as an admission of a party-opponent under Rule 801(d)(2). On the other hand, lack of personal knowledge may appropriately be considered in determining whether admissibility should be denied under Rule 403.

## § 801.24 Rule 801(d)(2)(E): Admissions; Statements by Coconspirator

A statement of one coconspirator is admissible against the others as an admission of a party-opponent in both civil and criminal cases, if made during the course of and in furtherance of the common objectives of the conspiracy, Rule 801(d)(2)(E).

**Historical development.** When a statement is offered under Rule 801(d)(2)(E), a foundation must be laid establishing both the conspiracy and defendant's and declarant's participation in the conspiracy. Two questions of interpretation arose. First, whether in establishing the requisite foundation the content of the alleged coconspirator statement may itself be considered. A vast majority of federal decisions required that the foundation must be established solely by independent evidence, i.e., the content of the statement sought to be introduced could not be considered. The independent evidence could consist of the defendant's own statements or the in-court testimony of a coconspirator. The independent evidence could be circumstantial; hearsay evidence could be considered.

Second, whether the sufficiency of the foundation with respect to the existence of the conspiracy and defendant's and declarant's participation are questions solely for the court under Rule 104(a), or questions in which both the court and jury participate under Rule 104(b). Several commentators advocated Rule 104(b) treatment. Other commentators supported application of Rule 104(a). Reported federal decisions clearly favored application of Rule 104(a).

**Bourjaily v. United States.** The Supreme Court in Bourjaily v. United States (S.Ct.1987) declared that determining the admissibility of a statement of a coconspirator is solely a matter for the court, Rule 104(a), and that the court in making its determination must apply the more probably true than not true (preponderance) standard of proof. In *Bourjaily,* the court also held as a matter of statutory interpretation that in reaching a determination as to whether there is a conspiracy and that the defendant and the declarant participated in the conspiracy, the content of the coconspirator's statement itself *may* be considered. Whether the existence of the conspiracy and the defendant's and the declarant's participation therein can be established to be more probably true than not true *solely* based upon the content of the coconspirator's statement sought to be admitted was expressly left undecided. A negative answer was provided by the courts; some independent evidence was required. Rule 801(d)(2)(E) was subsequently amended to codify the holding in *Bourjaily* by stating expressly that a court shall consider the contents of a coconspirator's statement in determining "the existence of the conspiracy and the participation therein of the declarant and the party against whom the statement is offered." In addition amended Rule 801(d)(2)(E) now explicitly provides that the contents of the statement "are not alone sufficient to establish" "the existence of the conspiracy and the participation therein of the declarant and the party against whom the statement is offered." The independent evidence may consist of the circumstances surrounding the statement, such as the identity of the speaker, the context in which the statement was made, or evidence corroborating the contents of the statement.

**In furtherance.** The court must also decide under Rule 104(a) whether the statement was made by the declarant during the course of, and in furtherance of, the conspiracy. In making this determination it is also proper for the court to consider the content of the statement itself. The court applies the more probably true than not true burden of proof. Only if the court decides both of these issues in favor of the prosecution may the statement be admitted as a statement of a coconspirator, Rule 801(d)(2)(E). In reaching its decisions the court should take into account all relevant evidence, including evidence offered on behalf of the accused.

Statements made during the existence of the conspiracy must be more than casual statements. The statements must actually be in furtherance of the conspiracy. Statements in furtherance of the conspiracy include statements made to induce enlistment, induce further participation, prompt further action, reassure members, allay concerns or fears, keep conspirators abreast of ongoing activities, avoid detection, identify names and roles of conspiracy members while mere conversations or narrative declarations of past events are not in furtherance of the conspiracy.

The statement of the coconspirator is often made outside the defendant's presence. Similarly, it often does not refer to the defendant at all. Thus in a case of bank robbery, a statement by A to B to steal a car may be admissible against C even though C was neither present when the statement was made nor personally involved in stealing the car.

Statements made during the concealment phase fall within the scope of admissibility if in furtherance of the main objectives of the conspiracy, but not otherwise. Kidnappers in hiding waiting for ransom, or repainting a stolen car are illustrations of acts in furtherance of the main criminal objective of a conspiracy. Statements made in furtherance of these objectives are admissible. Statements made by a person after the objectives of the conspiracy have either failed or been achieved, or after the person against whom offered has withdrawn from the conspiracy, are not in furtherance of the conspiracy, and are thus not admissible under Rule 801(d)(2)(E).

**Order of proof.** With respect to the order of proof, the court has discretion to admit the coconspirator's statement subject to it being connected up later through introduction of sufficient evidence of the existence of the conspiracy and the declarant's or defendant's participation. Whenever it is reasonably practical, however, reported decisions prior to *Bourjaily* stressed that evidence of the conspiracy and the defendant's connection with it (at the time evidence independent of the coconspirator statement) should be admitted prior to the coconspirator's statement. At the conclusion of the presentation of evidence, the trial court on motion must determine on all the evidence including evidence offered by the defendant whether the government has established the requisite foundation to be more probably true than not true. The alternative of a "minihearing" in advance of trial has also been suggested. Either procedure avoids the danger of injecting into the record inadmissible hearsay in anticipation of proof of a conspiracy which never materializes.

The impact of *Bourjaily* on the order of proof is substantial. Consideration of the content of the coconspirator's statement in determining its admissibility, even with some undefined and probably undefinable quantum of independent evidence being required, significantly eases the government's burden in many of its more difficult cases, cases very often involving drug trafficking. Assume, for example, that an informant or coconspirator now cooperating with the prosecution testifies that A told him that cocaine was being shipped to X, the defendant, by truck. Such a statement, in context, would strongly support a finding by the court that is more probably true than not true that a conspiracy existed and that A and X were participants in the conspiracy. With respect to the provision in Rule 801(d)(2)(E) that the content of the statement is not alone sufficient, even the slightest additional evidence of X's participation in the conspiracy would cement the court's determination. Given the ease with which the prosecution will be able to satisfy the court as to the admissibility of the coconspirator's statement given that the content of the statement may now be considered, prior concern that the jury not be exposed to the content of the coconspirator's statement lest it ultimately be excluded because of the absence of an adequate evidentiary foundation has all but completely disappear.

The crime of conspiracy itself may be submitted to the jury only if the evidence, including the statement of a coconspirator once admitted, viewed in the light most favorable to the government, could be accepted by a reasonably-minded jury as adequate to support a conclusion that appellant was guilty of conspiracy beyond reasonable doubt.

**Jury instructions.** In the process of instructing the jury, the court should not refer to its preliminary determination of facts leading to the introduction of the statement of a coconspirator under Rule 801(d)(2)(E).

## § 801.25  Judicial and Evidentiary Admissions: Superseded and Alternative Pleadings; Testimony of a Party

Judicial admissions must be distinguished from ordinary evidentiary admissions. A judicial admission is binding upon the party making it; it may not be controverted at trial or on appeal of the same case. Judicial admissions are not evidence at all but rather have the effect of withdrawing a fact from contention. Included within this category are admissions in the pleadings in the case, admissions in open court, stipulations of fact, and admissions pursuant to requests to admit. Ordinary evidentiary admissions, on the other hand, may be controverted or explained by the party. Within this category fall the pleadings in another case, superseded or withdrawn pleadings in the same case, stipulations as to admissibility, as well as other statements admissible under Rule 801(d)(2).

Fed.R.Civ.Proc. 8(e)(2) permits a pleader who is in doubt as to which of two or more statements of fact is true to plead them alternatively or hypothetically, regardless of consistency. When this is done, an admission in one alternative in the pleadings in the case does not nullify a denial in another alternative as a matter of pleading. Since the purpose of alternative pleadings is to enable a party to meet the uncertainties of proof, policy considerations demand that alternative pleadings not be admitted either as an admission of a party-opponent or for the purpose of impeachment.

Unequivocal admissions made by counsel during the course of trial are judicial admissions binding on his client. The scope of a judicial admission by counsel is restricted to unequivocal statements as to matters of fact which otherwise would require evidentiary proof; it does not extend to counsel's statement of his conception of the legal theory of a case.

Occasionally a party while testifying at trial or during a deposition or in response to an interrogatory admits a fact which is adverse to his claim or defense. A question then arises as to whether such a statement may be treated as a judicial admission binding the party and if so what circumstances must be present to justify such treatment. Of the various approaches followed in answering the question, treating a party's testimony or response to an interrogatory on all occasions as solely an evidentiary admission is preferable.

The trial court possesses discretion to relieve a party from the consequences of a judicial admission.

## Rule 802.

## HEARSAY RULE

**Hearsay is not admissible except as provided by these rules or by other rules prescribed by the Supreme Court pursuant to statutory authority or by Act of Congress.**

### § 802.1 Rule 802: Hearsay Is Not Admissible

Rule 802 provides that hearsay is not admissible except as provided by these rules or by other rules prescribed by the Supreme Court pursuant to statutory authority or by Act of Congress. The effect is that unless provided otherwise by a non-evidence rule or by a statute, evidence classified as hearsay under Rules 801(a)–(c) is not admissible unless it is defined as not hearsay, Rule 801(d), or falls within a hearsay exception, Rule 803, Rule 804, or Rule 807. Illustrative of nonevidence rules of the Supreme Court prescribed pursuant to statutory authority are Fed.R.Civ.Proc. 56, affidavits in support of motions for summary judgment and Fed.R.Crim.Proc. 4(a), affidavits to show grounds for issuing warrants. The admissibility of depositions continues in part to be governed by

Fed.R.Civ.Proc. 32(a) and Fed.R.Crim.Proc. 15. Further illustrations of both other rules and Acts of Congress are contained in the Advisory Committee's Note.

Hearsay has been admitted against a party, including the criminal defendant, who wrongfully causes the hearsay declarant's unavailability.

While hearsay is not admissible except as provided, it is nevertheless incumbent upon the party opposing the introduction of an inadmissible hearsay statement to properly object, Rule 103(a). In the absence of an objection to hearsay, the jury may consider hearsay for whatever value it may have; such evidence is to be given its natural probative effect as if it were in law admissible.

## § 802.2 Rule 802: Hearsay Rule; Confrontation and Due Process

The Sixth Amendment provides in pertinent part that "[i]n all criminal prosecutions, the accused shall enjoy the right ... to be confronted with witnesses against him...." Confrontation clause cases fall into two broad categories: cases involving the admission of out-of-court statements and cases involving restrictions imposed by law or by the trial court on the scope or extent of cross-examination face to face with the accused which are discussed in §§ 611.10 and 611.11 supra and § 804.1 infra.

With respect to out-of-court statements, the Advisory Committee to the Federal Rules of Evidence, in drafting the proposed rules and Congress, during the legislative process, both evidenced a clear intention to draft rules in such a way as to eliminate, if possible, any tension between the hearsay rule as embodied in Article VIII of the Federal Rules of Evidence and the confrontation clause.

Under the confrontation clause as currently interpreted, substantive admissibility of prior inconsistent statements of an in-court witness testifying under oath subject to cross-examination is permissible even if the witness denies making the prior statements. Prior consistent statements admitted under similar circumstances also do not run afoul of the confrontation clause.

With respect to a witness who does not testify at trial under oath subject to cross-examination, the admissibility of the witness' hearsay statements is governed by Ohio v. Roberts (S.Ct.1980):

> The Court has applied this "indicia of reliability" requirement principally by concluding that certain hearsay exceptions rest upon such solid foundations that admission of virtually any evidence within them comports with the "substance of the constitutional protection." Mattox v. United States, 156 U.S. at 244 * * *. This reflects the truism "hearsay rules and the Confrontation Clause are generally designed to protect similar values," California v. Green, 399 U.S. at 155, * * * and "stem from the same roots," Dutton v. Evans, 400 U.S. 74, 86, * * * (1970). It also responds to the need for certainty in the workaday world of conducting criminal trials.

In sum, when a hearsay declarant is not present for cross-examination at trial, the Confrontation Clause normally requires a showing that he is unavailable. Even then, his statement is admissible only if it bears adequate "indicia of reliability." Reliability can be inferred without more in a case where the evidence falls within a firmly rooted hearsay exception. In other cases, the evidence must be excluded, at least absent a showing of particularized guarantees of trustworthiness.

In *Roberts*, although declining to "map out a theory of the Confrontation Clause that would determine the validity of all hearsay exceptions," the Supreme Court stated without qualification that sufficient trustworthiness of hearsay statements of witnesses not called at trial, whether or not the declarant must be shown to be unavailable, can be "inferred without more" with respect to evidence falling squarely within a "firmly rooted hearsay exception." The Supreme Court also provided for the admission of statements not falling within a "firmly rooted" hearsay exception if such statement possesses "particularized guarantees of trustworthiness." Notably, the court's language exactly fits the requirements of Rule 807. Pursuant to Rule 807, evidence can be admitted only if it possesses "equivalent circumstantial guarantees of trustworthiness" to the "firmly rooted" hearsay exceptions. Thus evidence properly admitted pursuant to Rule 807 also meets the requirements of the confrontation clause.

The quotation from *Roberts* presented above states that a hearsay statement falling within a hearsay exception contained in Rule 803 or an exemption through definition as "not hearsay" in Rule 801(d)(2) may be admitted against the criminal defendant in the normal case only if the government produces the declarant so he can be subjected to cross-examination at trial, or, if not produced, the government has made a sufficient showing that the declarant is not available to testify. Presumably, production would include making the declarant available to be called by the prosecution for direct examination at the option of the accused and subjected to cross-examination concerning the hearsay statement. In addition, if the declarant is not available for cross-examination at trial, the hearsay statement may be admitted only if it bears adequate "indicia of reliability." However, indicia of reliability "can be inferred without more in a case where the evidence falls within a firmly rooted hearsay exception." Taken literally, almost all hearsay exceptions in Rule 803 as well as statements defined as not hearsay in Rule 801(d)(2) could require a showing of unavailability or the production of an available declarant when a statement which is hearsay under Rules 801(a)–(c) is offered against the accused.

Several factors suggest that the Supreme Court had no such intention in mind. First, the foregoing indication in *Roberts* was made in the context of a discussion of the former testimony hearsay exception, Rule 804(b)(1), a hearsay exception which itself requires unavailability. Moreover, the casualness displayed in making the comment with respect to unavailability generally in the context of a hearsay exception requiring unavailability belied any intention to make a radical change in the law. As *Roberts* itself stated, while the confrontation clause "normally requires" a showing of unavailability, "competing interests" may warrant dispensing with confrontation at trial, and further relaxation of the hearsay rule in some cases depending on "considerations of public policy and the necessities of the case." The opinion also indicated that a demonstration of unavailability or production of the declarant is not required when the utility of confrontation is remote. In this context, it is interesting to note that generally speaking neither the state courts, the United States Courts of Appeals, nor the leading commentators on the Federal Rules of Evidence construed *Roberts* as ushering such a radical change. Finally, it is suggested that any reading of *Roberts* as mandating a requirement of unavailability or production with respect to almost all hearsay statements admissible pursuant to Rule 803 or Rule 801(d)(2) offered against the criminal defendant was completely out of character with other recent decisions of the Supreme Court, including Dutton v. Evans.

In United States v. Inadi (S.Ct.1986), the Supreme Court addressed the question whether the statement in *Roberts* that "the Confrontation Clause normally requires a showing that [the declarant] is unavailable" applies to coconspirator hearsay statements. The Supreme Court held that considerations of reliability and necessity, benefit, and burden all support its conclusion that the confrontation clause does not mandate an initial showing of unavailability of the declarant before a statement of a coconspirator may be received in evidence. In White v. Illinois (S.Ct.1992), the Supreme Court in the context of the "spontaneous declaration," see Rule 803(2), and the "medical examination," see Rule 803(4), hearsay exceptions being employed in a child sexual assault prosecution, went even further declaring that *Inadi* held that "*Roberts* stands for the proposition that unavailability analysis is a necessary part of Confrontation Clause inquiry only when the challenged out-of-court statements were made in the course of a prior judicial proceeding."

The second question raised by *Roberts* with respect to the admissibility of a statement of a coconspirator under the confrontation clause whether a statement of a coconspirator admitted as a representative admission of a party-opponent falls within the notion of a "firmly rooted hearsay exception," or conversely whether such an admission of a party-opponent requires a "showing of particularized guarantees of trustworthiness," was answered by the Supreme Court in Bourjaily v. United States (S.Ct.1987) in the affirmative: "We think the coconspirator exception to the hearsay rule is firmly enough rooted in our jurisprudence that, under this Court's holding in *Roberts*, a court need not independently inquire into the reliability of such statements." Interestingly, the majority opinion determines that the coconspirator hearsay exception satisfies the second prong of *Roberts*, not on the basis of an assessment of reliability, but rather on the basis that the coconspirator exception is of long standing tradition. The fact that an agency and adversary system plus necessity rationale are commonly asserted to support the common law coconspirator hearsay exception rather than an assessment of reliability was completely ignored. The fact that the adversary system rationale led the drafters of the Federal Rules of Evidence to provide that admissions of a party-opponent are not barred by application of the rule against hearsay by being defined in Rule 801(d)(2) as "not hearsay" rather than included as an exception in Rule 803 was completely overlooked. Thus in *Bourjaily*, the court answered the question posed by the second prong of *Roberts* as to whether a statement of a nonappearing declarant admissible under the rules of evidence under an exemption or exception for a statement of a coconspirator "bears adequate 'indicia of reliability' "without ever exploring the reliability of statements of a coconspirator. In fact the court in *Bourjaily* may fairly be said to have gone so far as to restate *Roberts'* second prong so as to remove the concept of "firmly rooted" from being a means to infer "indicia of reliability" and reintroduce "firmly rooted" as an alternative method of satisfying *Roberts'* second prong, i.e., any statement of a nonappearing declarant meeting the requirements of a "firmly rooted hearsay" exception does not run afoul of the confrontation clause. Under such a gloss, the court will not examine a "firmly rooted" hearsay exception to determine whether it in fact possesses "adequate 'indicia of reliability' ",—being of long standing tradition is all that is required. Other than with respect to statements against penal interest (Rule 804(b)(3)) discussed infra, all of the hearsay exceptions and exceptions specifically denominated in Rules 801(d)(2) and 804 are "firmly rooted."

In Lilly v. Virginia (S.Ct.1999), a case without a majority opinion, the Supreme Court indicated, more or less explicitly, that the admission of custodial statements to law enforcement personnel against penal interest, i.e., testimonial material, such as oral statements regardless of whether tape recorded or videotaped, written statements, and affidavits, whether or not constituting a confession, that incriminate another person should ordinarily be found to have violated the confrontation clause when admitted against such other person in a criminal case'; such evidence is "presumptively unreliable". It is clear that such a custodial statement to law enforcement personnel does not fall within a firmly rooted exception. However, because the various opinions employ different rationales and frequently refer to the facts surrounding the actual making of the statement, sometimes but not always mentioning that the declarant in the matter at hand was clearly attempting to shift blame to another, there appears to be ample wiggle room for lower courts to permit a custodial statement to law enforcement personnel into evidence if so inclined in spite of the clear tenor of the majority of the justices to the contrary. Thus applying *Lilly,* it is not be surprising to find some lower courts permitting a custodial statement to law enforcement personnel that incriminates another person to be admitted against such other person in a criminal case, not as a firmly rooted hearsay exception, but upon a finding of "particularized guarantees of trustworthiness".

Under *Lilly* it is clear that noncustodial incriminating collateral statements, while not firmly rooted, may be admitted against such other person in a criminal case pursuant to the confrontation clause if they satisfy the "particularized guarantees of trustworthiness" prong of *Roberts*

Determining under what circumstances, a noncustodial (or possibly even a custodial statement) incriminating collateral statement in fact satisfies the "particularized guarantees of trustworthiness" prong of *Roberts* is unclear as *Lilly* does not contain a majority opinion outlining the factors appropriately considered in making such a determination. The foregoing question should be of less concern in the federal court as Williamson v. United States (S.Ct.1994), discussed in § 804.3 infra, already declares non-self-inculpatory collateral statements inadmissible under Rule 804(b)(3). Former testimony, including depositions, meeting the requirements of Rules 804(a) and 804(b)(1) is unaffected by *Lilly* and continues to satisfy the requirements of the confrontation clause.

In short, *Inadi, White, Bourjaily and Lilly* interpret the confrontation clause to mean that statements falling within *any* traditional common law firmly rooted hearsay exception (i.e., all provided in the Federal Rules of Evidence except statements against penal interest under

Rule 804(b)(3) and statements offered under the residual exception of Rule 807) are sufficiently reliable on their face to be admitted against the accused and that the imposition of a requirement of unavailability by the confrontation clause exists only when the challenged out-of-court statement was made in the course of a prior judicial proceeding. If it's good enough for the Federal Rules of Evidence, it's good enough for the confrontation clause.

## Rule 803.

## HEARSAY EXCEPTIONS; AVAILABILITY OF DECLARANT IMMATERIAL

### Prelude

### § 803.0    Rule 803: Hearsay Exceptions; Availability of Declarant Immaterial

Exceptions to the general rule excluding hearsay, Rule 802, are separated into two categories: exceptions which are not affected by the availability, actual testimony or unavailability of the declarant, Rule 803, and exceptions which require that the declarant be unavailable before the hearsay statement may be admitted, Rule 804.

Each exception of Rules 803 and 804 specifies requirements considered to be sufficient guarantees of trustworthiness to justify introduction absent an opportunity to conduct contemporaneous cross-examination of the declarant before the trier of fact. Rule 803 includes those hearsay statements which have been considered so trustworthy as to be admissible without requiring imposition of the time and expense associated with production of a declarant if available or in spite of the fact that the declarant of the statement actually testifies at trial. The exceptions under Rule 804 require that the declarant be unavailable, thereby manifesting a recognition that in such instances the live testimony of the declarant is preferable, but that it is better to permit the evidence pursuant to one of those exceptions than to deprive the factfinder of the evidence altogether. The basis for distinguishing between Rule 803 and Rule 804 exceptions is also to a large degree historical.

Whether the requirements of a hearsay exception contained in Rule 803 have been satisfied is to be determined by the court, Rule 104(a). A statement qualifying as an exception to the hearsay rule must, of course, satisfy other provisions of the Federal Rules of Evidence before it may be admitted. As stated in the Advisory Committee's Note to Rule 803, "The exceptions are phrased in terms of nonapplication of the hearsay rule, rather than in positive terms of admissibility, in order to repel any implication that other possible grounds for exclusion are eliminated from consideration." Thus, for example, a statement that qualifies as an exception to the hearsay rule must be relevant, Rule 401; be based on personal knowledge, Rule 602; be properly authenticated, Rule 901; and meet the requirements of Rule 1002 where the content of a writing is being proved, before it can be admitted into evidence. On the other hand, statements of a declarant who is not competent to testify at trial for reasons not relating to personal knowledge, Rule 602, meeting the requirements of a hearsay exception are admissible.

Hearsay statements falling within an exception to Rule 803 are admissible whether or not selfserving when made or offered. Moreover, the opinion rule, Rules 701, 702 and 704, as it relates to the form of a witness' testimony, is not applicable to hearsay statements admitted pursuant to a Rule 803 hearsay exception. The opinion rule, designed to elicit more concrete and informative answers, is a rule of preference as to the form of testimony. Since out of court statements are not made under circumstances in which alternative forms of expressions may be secured, this aspect of the opinion rule is inapplicable.

Rule 403 is applicable to evidence offered as falling within a hearsay exception. Thus even though the evidence meets the requirement of an exception, the court may still exclude the evidence on the grounds that after considering where applicable the effectiveness of a limiting instruction, Rule 105, the incremental probative value of the evidence is substantially outweighed by the danger of unfair prejudice, confusion of the issues, or misleading the jury, or by considerations of undue delay, waste of time, or needless presentation of cumulative evidence.

Questions arising with respect to multiple level hearsay are addressed in Rule 805; attacking and supporting the credibility of the declarant is governed by Rule 806.

Rule 803 contains twenty-three hearsay exceptions. The text of each hearsay exception with accompanying commentary is presented in the sections that follow. Each hearsay exception is treated as a separate rule as a matter of convenience to the reader, with the exception of Rules 803(1) and (2) which are presented together to facilitate comparison.

## Rules 803(1) and (2).

## PRESENT SENSE IMPRESSION AND EXCITED UTTERANCE

The following are not excluded by the hearsay rule, even though the declarant is available as a witness:

(1) Present Sense Impression. A statement describing or explaining an event or condition made while the declarant was perceiving the event or condition, or immediately thereafter.

(2) Excited Utterance. A statement relating to a startling event or condition made while the declarant was under the stress of excitement caused by the event or condition.

## § 803.1 Rule 803(1): Present Sense Impression

A statement describing or explaining an event or condition made while the declarant was perceiving the event or condition, or immediately thereafter, is admissible as a hearsay exception, Rule 803(1). The theory underlying the exception is that substantial contemporaneity of event and statement negative the likelihood of deliberate or conscious misrepresentation. Accordingly the statement must either be made contemporaneously or immediately thereafter, i.e. following only a "slight lapse" of time. The person making the statement need not be a participant.

As an additional assurance of reliability, the Advisory Committee's Note states, "Moreover, if the witness is the declarant, he may be examined on the statement. If the witness is not the declarant, he may be examined as to the circumstances as an aid in evaluating the statement." However nothing in Rule 803(1) actually requires that the in court witness, in addition to the out of court declarant, have personal knowledge of the underlying event. Personal knowledge by the in court witness as to the making of the statement by the declarant is, of course, a necessity, Rule 602. Moreover the evidence establishing that the declarant actually made a statement describing or explaining an event or condition while perceiving the event or immediately thereafter may consist solely of the statement itself considered in light of surrounding circumstances, i.e., corroboration is not required, although hesitancy has been shown by courts in admitting such statements without more when the identity of the declarant is unknown. The subject matter of the statement is limited by the assurance of trustworthiness associated with the exception to a description or explanation of the event or condition.

## § 803.2 Rule 803(2): Excited Utterance; Abandonment of "Res Gestae"

A statement relating to a startling event or condition made while the declarant was under the stress of excitement caused by the event or condition is admissible as a hearsay exception, Rule 803(2). The exception is premised on the notion that the excitement caused by the event or condition temporarily stills the capacity for reflection thus producing statements free of conscious fabrication.

The requirements for admissibility under this exception are: (1) the occurrence of an event or condition sufficiently startling to produce a spontaneous and unreflecting statement; (2) absence of time to fabricate, i.e., the statement must be made while still under the influence of the startling event or condition; and (3) a statement relating to the startling event or condition. The statement may be made by a bystander; it need not be made by a participant as one may be startled by an event as to which one is not an actor.

If the statement relates to the startling event or condition, it matters not, for example, that the statement contains an opinion, provides details of the event or condition, accuses someone of committing a crime, or is self serving. A statement meeting the requirements of an excited utterance is admissible even if the witness denies making the statement at trial. The scope of subject matter covered by the concept of "relate" is illustrated by the Advisory Committee's Note:

> See Sanitary Grocery Co. v. Snood, 67 App.D.C. 129, 90 F.2d 374 (1937), cert. denied 302 U.S. 703, 58 S.Ct. 22, 82 L.Ed 543, slip-and-fall case sustaining admissibility of clerk's statement, "That has been on the floor for a couple of hours," and Murphy Auto Parts Co. v. Ball, 101 U.S.App.D.C. 416, 249 F.2d 508 (1957), cert. denied 355 U.S. 932, 78 S.Ct. 413, 2 L.Ed.2d 415, upholding admission, on issue of driver's agency, of his statement that he had to call on a customer and was in a hurry to get home.

With respect to the element of time, the standard of measurement is the duration of the state of excitement. The amount of time elapsed is but one factor to be considered by the court in reaching a determination in the particular case. Other factors include the nature of the condition or event, the age and condition of the declarant, the presence or absence of self-interest, and whether the statement was volunteered or in response to a question. Determining whether the statement was made while still under the influence of the startling event or condition has proved particularly troublesome with respect to statements by young alleged victims of sexual abuse.

The Advisory Committee's Note after stating that "[w]hether proof of the startling event may be made by the statement itself is largely an academic question, since in most cases there is present at least circumstantial evidence that something of a startling nature must have occurred," concludes that where the only evidence of the existence of the startling event or condition is in fact the content of the statement itself, the prevailing practice is to permit introduction. Personal knowledge of the declarant, Rule 602, may also be established by reference to the content and context of the statement. Where the declarant, however, happens to be an unidentified bystander, the Advisory Committee's Note's suggestion of hesitancy, better called reluctance, as to admission has much to commend it.

**Res gestae.** The term res gestae, i.e., things done, is carefully avoided in the Federal Rules of Evidence. As employed in the common law res gestae was so broadly and loosely defined that its main thrust was simply to forestall rational analysis as to the admissibility of a particular statement challenged as hearsay. Professor Morgan observed that seven distinct concepts were encompassed within the term res gestae. Several of these concepts are addressed in the Federal Rules of Evidence in the process of defining hearsay, Rules 801(a)-(c). The remaining are represented by hearsay exceptions contained in Rules 803 and 804 including in particular Rule 803(1), present sense expression, and Rule 803(2), excited utterance. Under the Federal Rules of Evidence reference to the common law concept of res gestae is improper and should be avoided.

## Rule 803(3).

## THEN EXISTING MENTAL, EMOTIONAL, OR PHYSICAL CONDITION; INTENT AS PROOF OF DOING ACT INTENDED; STATEMENT AS PROOF OF FACT REMEMBERED OR BELIEVED; WILL CASES

**The following are not excluded by the hearsay rule, even though the declarant is available as a witness:**

\* \* \*

**(3) Then Existing Mental, Emotional, or Physical Condition. A statement of the declarant's then existing state of mind, emotion, sensation, or physical condition (such as intent, plan, motive, design, mental feeling, pain, and bodily health), but not including a statement of memory or belief to prove the fact remembered or believed unless it relates to the execution, revocation, identification, or terms of declarant's will.**

**§ 803.3    Rule 803(3): Then Existing Mental, Emotional, or Physical Condition; Intent as Proof of Doing Act Intended; Statement as Proof of Fact Remembered or Believed; Will Cases**

A statement expressing the declarant's then existing state of mind, emotion, sensation, or physical condition such as intent, plan, motive, design, mental feeling, pain and bodily health is admissible as a hearsay exception, Rule 803(3). Where the then existing state of mind, emotion, sensation, or physical condition of the declarant is relevant, admissibility of statements of the declarant expressing such a fact of consequence to the litigation rests upon grounds of trustworthiness and necessity. Statements of memory or belief offered to prove the fact remembered or believed are not included within this hearsay exception, unless relating to the execution, revocation, identification of terms or declarant's will, Rule 803(3).

Under certain circumstances a statement meeting the requirements of this hearsay exception has been argued to properly be classified as not falling within the definition of hearsay, Rules 801(a)–(c), for example, as a statement offered for a different inference, as a statement relevant merely as circumstantial evidence, or as relating to or characterizing an otherwise ambiguous act. As previously developed, theoretical difficulties abound with respect to the first two such arguments advanced for classifying such statements as not hearsay, i.e., such arguments are unsound. Fortunately whether a particular statement disclosing a then existing state of mind, emotion, sensation, or physical condition is or is not classified as hearsay is of no practical importance, since declarations of this nature are admissible in any event pursuant to Rule 803(3).

While Rule 803(3) requires that the declarant describe a state of mind, emotion, sensation, or physical condition existing at the time of the statement, the evidentiary effect is broadened by the inference of continuity in time. Accordingly, the then existing mental state, emotion, sensation, or physical condition may be inferred to exist into the future and to have existed in the past. With respect to the length of time covered by the inference of continuity, McCormick, Evidence § 274 at 219–20 (5th ed.1999) suggests that "the duration of states of mind or emotion varies with the particular attitudes or feelings at issue and with the cause, and the court may require some reasonable indication that in light of all the circumstances, including the proximity in time, the state of mind was the same at the material time." Determining questions involving continuity of inference rests very much in the discretion of the court.

Where statements are admitted under Rule 803(3) to directly or circumstantially show the declarant's state of mind, emotion, sensation, or physical condition, the statement may also contain an assertion as to particular facts. Under such circumstances a limiting instruction, Rule 105, is required to insure that assertions as to particular facts contained in the statement will be considered by the jury solely as bearing upon the declarant's state of mind, etc., and not for the truth of the factual matter asserted. If the unfair prejudice to a party likely to result from the substantive consideration by the trier of fact of such factual assertion in spite of the giving of a limiting instruction substantially outweighs the probative value of the evidence as to declarant's state of mind, etc., considered in light of the need for such evidence, exclusion under Rule 403 is appropriate.

Every statement meeting the requirements of Rule 803(3) is subject to exclusion under Rule 403 if after considering the probable effectiveness of a limiting instruction, Rule 105, the incremental probative value of the statement is substantially outweighed by the danger of unfair prejudice or trial concerns. In reaching an assessment of incremental probative value, it has been suggested by Weinstein's Evidence ¶ 803(3)[04] at 803-121-803-122 (1984) that the presence of a motive on the part of the declarant to falsify, referred to a "bad faith," may properly be considered. Although whether "bad faith" may in fact properly be considered in applying Rule 403 has yet to be firmly decided by the courts, a negative answer is likely.

**Intent as proof of doing act intended.** A question arises whether a statement of current intent admissible under Rule 803(3) may be admitted for the inference that the intended act was done. The argument for admissibility is that persons who intend to do an act are more likely to do the act than are persons without the intent, and therefore the evidence of intent is relevant, Rule 401. At this point, however, some logical difficulty arises. The statement of intent as evidence is subject to two weaknesses: (1) the trustworthiness of the declarant and (2) the possibility of change of mind or supervening events to defeat the plan. A simple statement by the declarant that he had done the act would be subject only to weakness (1), yet it would be excluded by the hearsay rule, Rule 802. Consequently, if perception and recollection risks associated with recounting of the past event are held in proper perspective, to allow the declaration of intent as proof of the doing of the intended act is to admit evidence which is arguably inferior to that excluded by the hearsay rule. However notice that admissibility of a declaration of having done a past act, extended to its logical extent, would effectively destroy the hearsay rule.

Despite what may be a logical dilemma, at common law when the issue was squarely presented statements of intent to prove the doing of the intended act by the declarant were held admissible. Examination of the authorities discloses that the offered evidence usually possessed very substantial convincing power and often the necessity to resort to statements of intent was great. Rule 803(3) is in accord. As stated in the Advisory Committee's Note, "The rule of Mutual Life Ins. Co. v. Hillmon, * * *, allowing evidence of intention as tending to prove the doing of the act intended, is, of course, left undisturbed."

A related but much more difficult problem arises when the declarant's statement of intention is to do something with another person. Analysis must begin with Mutual Life Insurance Co. v. Hillmon (S.Ct.1892), where the Supreme Court approved introduction of a statement of intent of a declarant to infer not only the declarant's future act but the future act of another. The text of Rule 803(3) fails to address the question of admissibility of a statement of intent as evidence of the future actions of another. The Advisory Committee's Note implies admissibility in its statement that the doctrine of *Hillmon* is left undisturbed. On the other hand the Report of the House Committee on the Judiciary states an intention that Rule 803(3) be construed to limit the doctrine of *Hillmon,* so as to render statements of intent by a declarant admissible only to prove his future conduct, not the future conduct of another person. Neither the Report of the Senate Committee on the Judiciary nor the Conference Report speaks to the issue. The legislative history is thus inconclusive. Courts faced with deciding whether a statement of intent is admissible as evidence of actions of another under the Federal Rules of Evidence have opted in favor of admissibility.

**Statement as proof of fact remembered or believed, will cases.** Since a declaration of intent is admissible as proof of the doing of the act intended, it may be argued that a declaration of the happening of a past event discloses a current state of mind from which the happening of the event which produced the state of mind may be inferred. Such a result would accomplish the effective destruction of the hearsay rule, which generally excludes narratives of past events, and is rejected on the basis of the presence of hearsay risks, and the lack of circumstantial guarantees of trustworthiness with respect to such statements.

One exception based upon necessity and expediency is recognized in Rule 803(3): a statement of opinion or belief is admissible to prove the facts remembered or believed if it relates to the execution, revocation, identification, or terms of the declarant's will.

## Rule 803(4).

### STATEMENTS FOR PURPOSES OF MEDICAL DIAGNOSIS OR TREATMENT

**The following are not excluded by the hearsay rule, even though the declarant is available as a witness:**

\* \* \*

**(4) Statements for Purposes of Medical Diagnosis or Treatment. Statements made for purposes of medical diagnosis or treatment and describing medical history, or past or present symptoms, pain, or sensations, or the inception**

**or general character of the cause or external source thereof insofar as reasonably pertinent to diagnosis or treatment.**

## § 803.4　Rule 803(4): Statements for Purposes of Medical Diagnosis or Treatment

Statements describing present symptoms, pain, or sensations are admissible as an exception to the hearsay rule, if made by the declarant for purposes of medical diagnosis or treatment, Rule 803(4). The assumption underlying the exception is that the desire for proper diagnosis or treatment outweighs any motive to falsify. The same guarantee of trustworthiness extends under Rule 803(4) to statements of past conditions and medical history if made for the purposes of medical diagnosis or treatment. Finally, Rule 803(4) also provides for a hearsay exception for statements made for the purposes of medical diagnosis or treatment describing the inception or general character of the cause of external source of the symptoms, pain, or sensations. However any such statement made for the purposes of medical diagnosis or treatment falls within this hearsay exception *only* "insofar as reasonably pertinent to diagnosis or treatment", Rule 803(4). Thus it is not enough that the declarant made the statement with an intent to facilitate medical diagnosis or treatment; the statement must in addition in fact be reasonably pertinent to diagnosis or treatment.

Statements made for purposes of diagnosis or treatment may be made by either a patient or someone with an interest in his well being. If made for purposes of medical diagnosis or treatment, the statement may be addressed to anyone associated with providing such services, including a physician, nurse, ambulance attendant, or even family member. Statements made for purposes of medical diagnosis or treatment are admissible even if made after the filing of the action.

**Examining and treating physicians.** Under prior practice evidence of such statements, including those of pain, subjective symptoms, medical history, and physical demonstrations capable of simulation, were not admissible under this hearsay exception if made to a physician examining the patient solely for the purpose of being able to testify. A doctor hired solely to testify is often referred to as an examining physician. Statements to the examining physician were not given substantive effect because of an absence of a motive on the part of the patient to speak truthfully. The examining physician was limited to testifying to observable, purely objective conditions, even though the patient testified that the responses which he made to the physician were true. Of course, if proof of the facts contained in such statements was otherwise introduced into evidence, the examining physician was permitted to give his opinion in response to a hypothetical question incorporating those facts along with the physician's objective findings. In addition, while the patient's statements were not admissible as substantive evidence, the examining physician was frequently allowed to state the bases of his opinion, including what the patient told him to the extent pertinent to diagnosis.

Rule 803(4) eliminates the distinction between examining and treating physicians: an examining physician may now testify to statements made for the purpose of medical diagnosis to the same extent as the treating physician, even though the only purpose of the examination was to enable him to testify. Such statements are admitted as substantive evidence. As the Advisory Committee's Note states, "This position is consistent with the provision of Rule 703 that the facts on which expert testimony is based need not be admissible in evidence if of a kind ordinarily relied upon by experts in the field." Moreover Rule 803(4) recognizes that realistically the jury can not distinguish between facts admitted for the truth and those admitted solely as forming the bases of an expert witness's opinion.

**Statements of causation.** While statements to physicians as to the cause of an injury or condition were originally excluded, recent common law decisions sensibly recognize that cause may be a factor in medical diagnosis or treatment and accordingly that such statements are admissible as falling within the guarantee of truthfulness. Under Rule 803(4), the admissibility of statements as to causation is specifically limited to those of inception or general character of the cause or external source of the injury insofar as reasonably pertinent to medical diagnosis or treatment. Statements of fault would not qualify. Thus a patient's statement that he was struck by an automobile would be admissible but not his statement that the car was driven through a red light.

**Child sexual abuse.** In child sexual abuse prosecutions, statements of the alleged child victim to a physician identifying the defendant as the perpetrator, when a member of the child's family or household, are admitted as pertinent to diagnosis or treatment of emotional and psychological injuries and pertinent to preventing a recurrence of the injury.

**Statement to lay witnesses.** Statements of medical history, or past or present symptoms, pain or sensations, made to lay witnesses, are not admissible under Rule 803(4) unless made for purposes of medical diagnosis or treatment. To illustrate, a statement by a wife to her husband advising what the husband should tell a physician concerning a sick child is a statement for purposes of medical diagnosis or treatment, while a statement by the wife simply informing her husband that the child has a cold would not qualify. Evidence concerning the cold the child was suffering may, of course, if relevant, be introduced in other ways. For example, if the condition was expressed by the child himself, the child's statement concerning his then existing physical or mental condition would qualify as a hearsay exception under Rule 803(3). Alternatively, a parent could testify as to his opinion as to the state of health of the child.

## Rule 803(5).

## RECORDED RECOLLECTION

**The following are not excluded by the hearsay rule, even though the declarant is available as a witness:**

* * *

**(5) Recorded Recollection. A memorandum or record concerning a matter about which a witness once had knowledge but now has insufficient recollection to enable the witness to testify fully and accurately, shown to have been made or adopted by the witness when the matter was fresh in the witness' memory and to reflect that knowledge correctly. If admitted, the memorandum or record may be read into evidence but may not itself be received as an exhibit unless offered by an adverse party.**

## § 803.5 Rule 803(5): Recorded Recollection

A record or memorandum is admissible as an exception to the hearsay rule if the proponent can show that the witness once had personal knowledge of the matter, Rule 602, that the record or memorandum was prepared or adopted by him when it was fresh in his memory, that it accurately reflected his knowledge, and that the witness currently has insufficient recollection to enable him to testify fully and accurately, Rule 803(5). The witness may testify either that he remembers making an accurate recording of the event in question which he now no longer sufficiently remembers, that he routinely makes accurate records of this kind, or, if the witness has entirely forgotten the exact situation in which the recording was made, that he is confident from the circumstances that he would not have written or adopted such description of the facts unless that description truly described his observations at the time. Multiple person involvement in the process of observation and recording is permitted, though on this point the rule is less clear than might be desired. This hearsay exception is commonly referred to as past recollection recorded.

It is not necessary to establish that the witness lacks *any* independent recollection; the requirement of absence of recollection is satisfied if the witness lacks sufficient present recollection to testify fully and accurately. This determination is to be made by the court, Rule 104(a). One method of satisfying the requirement is to show that the record or memorandum fails to refresh the witness' recollection.

If admitted, the record or memorandum may be read into evidence but may not itself be received as an exhibit unless offered by an adverse party. This provision is designed to keep the record or memorandum from going to the jury room during deliberation. Records or memoranda satisfying the requirements of recorded recollection are subject to application of the Original Writing Rule, Rule 1002.

## Rule 803(6).

## RECORDS OF REGULARLY CONDUCTED ACTIVITY

**The following are not excluded by the hearsay rule, even though the declarant is available as a witness:**

\* \* \*

**(6) Records of Regularly Conducted Activity. A memorandum, report, record, or data compilation, in any form, of acts, events, conditions, opinions, or diagnoses, made at or near the time by, or from information transmitted by, a person with knowledge, if kept in the course of a regularly conducted activity, and if it was the regular practice of that business activity to make the memorandum, report, record, or data compilation, all as shown by the testimony of the custodian or other qualified witness, or by certification that complies with Rule 902(11), Rule 902(12), or a statute permitting certification, unless the source of information or the method of circumstances of preparation indicate lack of trustworthiness. The term "business" as used in this paragraph includes business, institution, association, profession, occupation, and callings of every kind, whether or not conducted for profit.**

## § 803.6 Rule 803(6): Records of Regularly Conducted Activity; Business Records

**Overview.** A memorandum, report, record, or data compilation, in any form, of acts, events, conditions, opinions, or diagnoses, made at or near the time by, or from information transmitted by, a person with knowledge, if kept in the course of a regularly conducted business activity, and if it was the regular practice of that business activity to make the memorandum, report, record, or data compilation, all as shown by the testimony of the custodian or other qualified witness is admissible as an exception to the hearsay rule unless the source of information or the method or circumstances of preparation indicate lack of trustworthiness, Rule 803(6). The term "business" as used in Rule 803(6) includes business, institution, association, profession, occupation, and calling of every kind, whether or not conducted for profit. The form which the "record" of a regularly conducted business activity may assume is described broadly as a "memorandum, report, record, or data compilation, in any form"; it is not limited in any manner to books of account. The expression "data compilation" is used as broadly descriptive of any means of storing information other than the conventional words and figures in written or documentary form. It includes, but is by no means limited to, electronic computer storage.

The hearsay exception for records of regularly conducted business activities, widely referred to as the business records hearsay exception, rests upon considerations of both reliability and necessity. Records of regularly conducted activities cannot fulfill the function of aiding the proper transaction of business unless accurate. The motive for following a routine of accuracy is great and the motive to falsify largely non-existent. More specifically, the reliability of business records is supplied by systematic checking, by regularity and continuity which produce habits of precision, by actual experience of business in relying upon them, and/or by a duty to make an accurate record as part of a continuing job or occupation. Given the nature of the reliability of business records, it makes no difference whether the records are those of a party or of a third person.

As to necessity, the common law requirement that all participants in the process of gathering, transmitting and recording information be produced or their unavailability be accounted for proved to be burdensome in practice if not insurmountable. Accordingly Rule 803(6) adopts the sensible position of permitting the requisite foundation testimony to be provided by the "custodian or other qualified witness". Rule 803(6) is based upon the realization that the dependability of regular entries rests upon proof of a routine of making accurate records, rather than upon the testimony of each participant that he himself was accurate. Lack of personal knowledge of the entrant or maker may be shown to affect the weight to be given to the record, but does not affect its admissibility. Nor is admissibility affected by the fact that the person furnishing the information upon personal knowledge did not participate in the matter recorded.

The Original Writing Rule, Rule 1002, is applicable to writings and records admitted pursuant to Rule 803(6). Provided an exhibit has been shown to comply with both rules it may be admitted into evidence and, in the court's discretion, be either read to or handed to the jury. A witness, however, over proper objection should not be permitted to testify as to the contents of the document or provide a summary thereof; the document "speaks for itself."

**Regularly conducted activity; at or near the time.** In order for any business record made to memorialize an act, event, condition, opinion or diagnosis to be admissible under Rule 803(6), it is necessary that the record be made at or near the time by, or from information transmitted by, a person within the business with firsthand knowledge. More than one person within the business may be involved in the transmission of the information. In addition, the gathering of the information, its transmission, and its memorialization must all occur (1) in the course of a regularly conducted business activity and (2) it must be the regular practice of that business activity to make the memorandum, report, record, or data compilation in the form in which it was made. Thus the familiar questions: "Was it the regular course of business to make this record?" and "Was this record kept in the regular course of business?" An alternative form of question gaining popularity is "Was this record kept in the regular course of a regularly conducted business activity?" With respect to either alternative, the following questions are added: "Was this record made at or near the time of the matter recorded?" and "Was the record made by a person within the business with knowledge of, or made from information transmitted by a person within the business with knowledge of, the acts, events, conditions, opinions or diagnosis appearing in it?"

**Business duty to record; multiple level hearsay.** Since the guarantee of accuracy of regular entries rests upon a duty to make an accurate record, all persons who participate in the initial furnishing of information must

possess personal knowledge of matters related, Rule 602.
Thus the records must be made by a person with knowledge or from information transmitted by a person with
knowledge. In addition all persons furnishing and recording information must be under a duty to do so. If the
supplier of the information does not act in the regular
course, an essential link is broken; the assurance of
accuracy does not extend to the information itself, and
the fact that it may be recorded with scrupulous accuracy
is of no avail. Consider the report of an ambulance driver
incorporating information obtained from a bystander: the
driver qualifies as acting in the regular course but the
bystander does not. Of course, if the statement by one
not under a duty to report, i.e., one not acting in the
regular course of business, is not hearsay, is defined as
not hearsay or meets the requirements of a hearsay
exception, and if the person recording the information is
under a duty to do so, the statement, if it meets the other
requirements of Rule 803(6), is admissible under Rule
805. Thus if the statement of the bystander meets the
requirements of Rule 803(2), excited utterance, and if the
ambulance driver was under a business duty to record a
statement of that kind, the ambulance report would be
admissible.

A statement made by someone not within the business
duty that is either not hearsay, is defined as "not hearsay" under Rule 801(d)(2), or meets the requirement of a
hearsay exception contained in Rule 803 or 804, is admissible only if the person within the business perceiving
the statement is under a business duty to record such a
statement. The fact that the statement was in fact recorded is insufficient. To illustrate, assume at the scene
of an accident, an ambulance driver is told by an occurrence witness, "The boy was hit by that car. It went

through the light." Assuming the occurrence witness' statement meets the requirements for an excited utterance, Rule 803(2), only that part of the statement relating to the car striking the boy is admissible under Rule 803(2), 803(6) and 805. Since the ambulance driver's duty to record does not extend to statements clearly not pertinent to medical diagnosis or treatment, that part of the occurrence witness' statement relating to the car going through a red light is inadmissible even though the ambulance driver included that segment of the statement in his report. Note that if the same statement had been overheard by a police officer, the entire excited utterance would be admissible under Rules 803(2), 803((8) and 805 in a civil case by virtue of the fact that the policeman was under a business duty to record all statements relating to the cause and circumstances of the accident being investigated.

To illustrate further:

(1) If a security guard at Universal Studios observed an accident and filed an accident report, because he was under a business duty to observe and record, if the report was also made in the regular course of business by following proper procedures at the proper times, Rule 803(6) is satisfied.

(2) Assume that the security guard, instead of preparing the report, transmitted his observations over his car radio to headquarters, and the person at headquarters took notes of the radio transmission. The notes were then typed into a formal report by a third person. Provided each person was performing his assigned duty in the regular course of a regularly conducted business activity, Rule 803(6) is satisfied.

(3) Now assume that ten minutes after the accident, the security guard spoke to a nonparty eyewitness who calmly described how the accident occurred. Although the security guard was under a business duty to record the statement, the matter reported was not transmitted by an individual with a business duty to report. Under such circumstances, Rule 803(6) extends only to the point of admitting the statement of the occurrence witness for the fact the statement was said, but not as proof of the truth of the facts stated. Because the statement of the occurrence witness is only relevant when offered for the truth of the matter asserted, the statement will be excluded as hearsay. If the security guard was not under a business duty to record the particular statement made by the occurrence witness, the record prepared containing the statement would not be admissible even to establish that the statement was made.

(4) Finally, if the occurrence witness's statement as to which there was a business duty to record is not hearsay, Rules 801(a)–(c), is defined as "not hearsay" under Rule 801(d)(2), or satisfies the requirements of any hearsay exception contained in Rule 803, 804, or 807, then the statement of the occurrence witness will be admitted, if relevant, under Rule 805. Rule 803(6) permits introduction of the occurrence witness' statement for the fact it was said, while either Rule 801(d)(2), or a hearsay exception would provide for admissibility of such a statement for the truth of the matter stated.

**Opinions and diagnosis.** Entries in the form of opinions were not encountered in traditional business records in view of the purely factual nature of the items recorded, but they are now commonly encountered with respect to medical diagnoses, prognoses, and test results, as well as occasionally in other areas. The limitation in the prior federal business records statute, the Commonwealth Fund Act, to "act, transaction, occurrence or event" probably accounted for the reluctance of some, but not all, federal courts to admit diagnostic entries. Admissibility is no longer in doubt for Rule 803(6) specifically includes both diagnoses and opinions, in addition to acts, events, and conditions, as proper subjects of admissible entries. Whether the qualifications of an expert witness whose opinion is contained in the record must be affirmatively established depends upon the circumstances of the particular case. A critical factor is whether the expert opinion was incident to or part of factual reports of contemporaneous events or transactions or conversely whether the expert opinion was specifically prepared for the purpose of being included in a record setting forth the expert's opinion.

**Custodian or other qualified witness.** A sufficient foundation for the admission of records of regularly conducted activities may be established through the testimony of the custodian of the record or other person familiar with the business and its mode of operation identifying the record and establishing that it is a record in fact made at or near the time in the regular course of a regularly conducted business activity, made by or from information transmitted by a person within the business with knowledge; neither the original entrant nor the individual possessing personal knowledge of the event itself need be produced nor identified.

**Personal knowledge.** In laying a foundation establishing that the record offered was made at or near the time by or from information transmitted by a person with firsthand knowledge, it is not necessary that the party seeking to introduce the record be able to produce, or even identify, the specific individual upon whose first-hand knowledge the record was based. "A sufficient foundation for the introduction of such evidence will be laid if the party seeking to introduce the evidence is able to show that it was the regular practice of the activity to base such memorandums, reports, records, or data compilations upon a transmission from a person with knowledge, e.g., in the case of the content of a shipment of goods, upon a report from the company's receiving agent or in the case of a computer printout, upon a report from the company's computer programmer or one who has knowledge of the particular record system." While the custodian of the record will usually be able to so testify, on some occasions testimony from another witness and/or resort to reliance upon the content of the statement itself as evidence of personal knowledge, Rule 602, may be necessary.

**Lack of trustworthiness.** The modern trend necessarily tends to be liberal as to the admission of business records as business gets more complicated and transactions are broken down into various operations so that no particular person can identify any particular operation. Admissibility is greatly facilitated by the fact that lack of personal knowledge of the entrant or maker of a record goes only to weight and not admissibility. While admissibility is favored, nevertheless where the "source of information or the method or circumstances of preparation indicate lack of trustworthiness," the record will not be received, Rule 803(6). Of particular importance is the extent to which the business record was prepared for purposes of litigation.

**Review on appeal.** Determining whether an adequate foundation has been presented as well as whether the circumstances surrounding preparation of the record indicate lack of trustworthiness rests in the discretion of the court.

**Sample foundation.**

Elements:

a.   Record is relevant.

b.   Record is a "memorandum, report, record or data compilation in any form."

c.   Witness is the "custodian or other qualified witness."

d.   Record was "made by a person with knowledge" of the facts or was "made from information transmitted by a person with knowledge" of the facts.

e.   Record was "made at or near the time" of the "acts, events, conditions, opinions, or diagnoses" appearing on it.

f.   Record was made as part of "the regular practice of that business activity."

g.   Record was "kept in the course of a regularly conducted business activity."

The following example shows how easily the required technical elements of FRE 803(6) can be met.

Example:

Q.   Mr. Doe, please state your occupation.

A.   I'm the records keeper of the XYZ Corporation.

Q.   What does your job involve?

A. I collect, keep, and maintain all the company records according to our indexing system.

Step 1. Have exhibit marked.

Step 2. Show exhibit to opposing counsel.

Step 3. Ask permission to approach witness.

Step 4. Show exhibit to witness.

Step 5. Establish foundation:

Q. Mr. Doe, I am showing you what has been marked Plaintiff's Exhibit #1. Do you recognize it?

A. Yes, it's one of our records.

Q. Was that record made by a person with knowledge of, or made from information transmitted by a person with knowledge of, the acts and events appearing on it?

A. Yes.

Q. Was the record made at or near the time of the acts and events appearing on it?

A. Yes.

Q. Is it the regular practice of the XYZ Corporation to make such a record?

A. Yes.

Q. Was that record kept in the course of a regularly conducted business activity?

A. Yes.

Step 6. Offer exhibit in evidence.

Step 7. Have exhibit marked in evidence.

Step 8. Have witness mark/explain exhibit.

Step 9. Ask permission to show/read exhibit to jury.

Step 10. Show/read exhibit to jury.

Mauet, Fundamentals of Trial Techniques 189–90 (3rd ed.1992).

**Certification alternative.** Rule 803(6) also provides that the foundation requirements can be satisfied under certain circumstances without the expense and inconvenience of producing time-consuming foundation witnesses by certification that complies with Rule 902(11) for domestic records, Rule 902(12) for foreign records in civil cases, or a statute permitting certification, e.g., 18 U.S.C. § 3505 dealing with foreign records in criminal cases.

**Records generated by outside agents; incorporated or verified records.** A custodian or other qualified witness may also lay an adequate foundation for the admissibility of business records now in the possession of a successor entity. Similarly, two businesses may be operated as one and thus be considered as one for business record purposes. The records of regularly conducted activity of a business also include computer and other records prepared by outside agents of the business such as a payroll service bureau. An adequate foundation may be laid by the custodian or other qualified witness of the contracting business. In addition, records of regularly conducted activities containing information presented by someone not under a business duty is admissible when a proper foundation is laid by the custodian or other qualified witness which in this context includes a requirement that a person within the business acting pursuant to a business duty adequately verifies the information furnished by a third party, such as might occur with respect to identity at the time of a hotel guest registration.

The person presenting the foundation for a business record must be testifying as to the procedures of the appropriate business. Accordingly, a person receiving a document from an unaffiliated business could not solely by virtue thereof lay a sufficient foundation for the record as a business record of the issuing business. A different situation exists when the business receiving the information in the regular course of business integrates the information received into its business' records, relies upon it in its day-to-day operations, and surrounding circumstances indicate trustworthiness. Under such limited circumstances admissibility through the testimony of the receiving custodian or other qualified witness is permitted, but not otherwise.

**Relationship to other rules.** The breadth of Rule 803(6) overlaps the hearsay exception for public records contained in Rule 803(8). Where a conflict exists, a public record not meeting the requirements of the more specific rule, in particular Rules 803(8)(B) and (C), should *not* ordinarily be admitted under Rule 803(6), although such public record may be admissible under another hearsay exception such as Rule 803(5), Rule 803(10), or Rule 807. Any other construction would frustrate the intent of Congress with respect to limitations on admissibility imposed in Rules 803(8)(B) and (C).

### Rule 803(7).

### ABSENCE OF ENTRY IN RECORDS OF REGULARLY CONDUCTED ACTIVITY

**The following are not excluded by the hearsay rule, even though the declarant is available as a witness:**

\* \* \*

**(7) Absence of Entry in Records Kept in Accordance With the Provisions of Paragraph (6). Evidence that a matter is not included in the memoranda reports, records, or data compilations, in any form, kept in accordance with the provisions of paragraph (6), to prove the nonoccurrence or nonexistence of the matter, if the matter was of a kind of which a memorandum, report, record, or data compilation was regularly made and preserved, unless the sources of information or other circumstances indicate lack of trustworthiness.**

## § 803.7  Rule 803(7): Absence of Entry in Records of Regularly Conducted Activity

Failure to record or include a matter which would ordinarily be included in a record of a regularly conducted business activity offered to prove the nonoccurrence or nonexistence of the matter constitutes a hearsay exception, Rule 803(7). While in many instances such a failure might not be classified as hearsay, in order to assure uniform admissibility a hearsay exception is provided. The memoranda, reports, record or data compilation must, of course, have been kept in accordance with the provisions of Rule 803(6), and the matter itself must be shown to be of a kind of which a memorandum, report, record or data compilation was regularly made and preserved. If the sources of information or other circumstances indicate lack of trustworthiness, admission will be denied, Rule 803(7).

The testimony of the custodian of the record or other qualified person is necessary in order to lay the proper foundation. In addition either the record from which the matter is absent must be introduced in evidence or someone with personal knowledge must testify that a diligent search failed to disclose the matter in the memorandum, report, record or data compilation. The Original Writing Rule, Rule 1002, does *not* apply to testimony that a record has been examined and found not to contain any reference to a designated matter but does apply if the record itself is offered into evidence.

## Rule 803(8).

## PUBLIC RECORDS AND REPORTS

**The following are not excluded by the hearsay rule, even though the declarant is available as a witness:**

* * *

**(8) Public Records and Reports. Records, reports, statements, or data compilations, in any form, of public offices or agencies, setting forth (A) the activities of the office or agency, or (B) matters observed pursuant to duty imposed by law as to which matters there was a duty to report, excluding, however, in criminal cases matters observed by police officers and other law enforcement personnel, or (C) in civil actions and proceedings and against the Government in criminal cases, factual findings resulting from an investigation made pursuant to authority granted by law, unless the sources of information or other circumstances indicate lack of trustworthiness.**

## § 803.8   Rule 803(8): Public Records and Reports

**Overview.** Records, reports, statements, or data compilations, in any form, of public offices or agencies, setting forth (A) the activities of the office or agency, or (B) matters observed pursuant to duty imposed by law as to which matters there was a duty to report, excluding, however, in criminal cases matters observed by police officers and other law enforcement personnel, or (C) in civil actions and proceedings and against the Government in criminal cases, factual findings resulting from an investigation made pursuant to authority granted by law, unless the sources of information or other circumstances indicate lack of trustworthiness are admissible as an exception to the hearsay rule, Rule 803(8).

The exception is based upon the assumption that public officers will perform their duties, that they lack motive to falsify, and that public inspection to which many such records are subject will disclose inaccuracies. In addition the disruptive effect of bringing public officials into court to testify about matters that have generally been accurately reported and recorded is avoided. Use of the record also serves the public convenience by saving time and the expenditure of public money. Moreover, the record is likely to be much more reliable than the official's often hazy recollection. If the source of information or the method or circumstances of preparation indicates lack of trustworthiness, the court may bar admissibility.

Rule 803(8) does not provide a blanket hearsay exception for reports or statements made by nonpublic officials to public offices even when made pursuant to statutory duty. Admissibility for some such reports concerning vital statistics is provided in Rule 803(9). Rule 803(14) provides a hearsay exception for recorded documents affecting an interest in real property. Since the guarantee of accuracy of public records admissible under Rules 803(8)(A) and (B) rests upon an official duty, i.e., a duty imposed by law upon a public official, to make an accurate record, all persons who participate in the initial furnishing of information must possess personal knowledge of matters related, Rule 602. In addition the records must be made by a person with knowledge or from information transmitted by a person with knowledge. Finally all persons furnishing and recording information must be under an official duty to do so. If the supplier of the information is not under such a duty to do so, an essential link is broken; the assurance of accuracy does not extend to the information itself, and the fact that it may be recorded with scrupulous accuracy is of no avail. An illustration is the report of a police officer incorporating information obtained from a bystander: the police officer qualifies as acting pursuant to an official duty but the bystander does not. Of course, if the statement by one not under an official duty to report is not hearsay, Rules 801(a)–(c), is defined as not hearsay, Rules 801(d)(2), or meets the requirements of a hearsay exception, Rules 803, 804, or 807, and if the person recording the information is under a duty to do so, the statement, if it meets the other requirements of Rule 803(8), is admissible under Rule 805. Thus if the statement of the bystander meets the requirements of Rule 803(2), excited utterance, and if the police officer was under an official duty to record a statement of that kind, the police report would be admissible.

**Rule 803(8)(A).** Rule 803(8)(A) provides a hearsay exception for records prepared by public offices or agencies dealing with official activities of the office or agency reasonably necessary for the performance of the duties of the office. Records of official activities of the office or agency prepared for purposes independent of specific litigation are encompassed. Official reports of a statistical nature are also included within the exception.

**Rule 803(8)(B).** Records in any form setting forth matters observed pursuant to duty imposed by law as to which matters there was a duty to report, excluding, however, in criminal cases matters observed by police officers and other law enforcement personnel, are admissible as a hearsay exception under Rule 803(8)(B). The exclusion in Rule 803(8)(B) applies to observations made by police officers and other law enforcement personnel made at the scene of the crime, at the apprehension of the accused, or otherwise in connection with an investigation but not to records of routine, ministerial, objective nonevaluative matters made in nonadversarial settings. The Report of the Senate Committee on the Judiciary states that "the reason for this exclusion is that observations by police officers at the scene of the crime or the apprehension of the defendant are not as reliable as observations by public officials in other cases because of the adversarial nature of the confrontation between the police and the defendant in criminal cases." The limitation applies only to the introduction of a public record or report when offered by the prosecution in a criminal case; thus public records or reports containing statements of matters observed first-hand pursuant to duty imposed by law as to which there was a duty to report by police officers or other law enforcement personnel are admissible when offered by the criminal defendant or any party in a civil case.

**Rule 803(8)(C).** Rule 803(8)(C) provides for the admission in civil actions and proceedings and against the government in criminal cases of "factual findings" resulting from an investigation made pursuant to authority granted by law. Disagreement existed at common law as to admissibility. The approach taken in Rule 803(8)(C) is to provide for admissibility unless the sources of information or other circumstances indicate lack of trustworthiness. Factors which may be of assistance in passing upon the admissibility of evaluative reports include: (1) the timeliness of the investigation, (2) the special skill or experience of the official, (3) whether a hearing was held and the level at which conducted, and (4) possible motivation problems. Public records otherwise admissible under Rule 803(9)(C) are subject to exclusion under Rule 403.

A partial list of some evaluative reports made admissible by federal statute is contained in the Advisory Committee's Note. Of course, as provided in Rule 802, these statutory exceptions remain. If either the sources of information or circumstances of preparation of such an evaluative report offered pursuant to statutory authority indicate lack of trustworthiness, Rule 403 would support exclusion. Some federal statutes themselves provide for inadmissibility of the government report.

With respect to a factual finding resulting from an investigation made pursuant to authority granted by law, Rule 803(8)(C), the underlying factual bases for such "factual finding" may itself in whole or in part be either not admissible or not admitted in evidence. The "factual finding" is nevertheless admissible if the investigative report is judged reliable. The question to be asked in making this determination is whether the facts, data, or opinions taken as a whole are "of a type reasonably relied upon by experts in the particular field in forming opinions or inference upon the subject", Rule 703. Policy considerations underlying Rules 703, 705 and in particular 403 require that where the investigative report is found reliable whether the bases may be disclosed by the party offering the evaluative report depends upon whether the particular fact had otherwise been admitted in evidence or had been reasonably relied upon by an expert in preparation of the evaluative report in accordance with Rule 703 and if so whether the disclosure provision of Rule 703 itself has been complied with. For example, if a statement of an occurrence witness not itself admitted and not reasonably relied upon was considered, prohibiting disclosure of such factual basis could be appropriate. However exclusion of the factual finding contained in the evaluative report solely on this ground would unduly curtail the applicability of Rule 803(8)(C). This is not to say that substantial reliance upon hearsay information of this kind may not itself constitute a sufficient showing of lack of trustworthiness to bar admissibility. Similar considerations govern objections based upon the qualifications of the expert witness, Rule 702, and disclosure of the bases of the factual finding on cross-examination, Rule 705.

With respect to scope of the phrase "factual finding", the Report of the House Committee on the Judiciary stated that it intended the phrase be strictly construed and that evaluations in the form of conclusions or opinions contained in public reports should not be admissible. However the Report of the Senate Committee on the Judiciary stated:

> The committee takes strong exception to this limiting understanding of the application of the rule. We do not think it reflects an understanding of the intended

operation of the rule as explained in the Advisory Committee notes to this subsection. The Advisory Committee notes on subsection (c) of this subdivision point out that various kinds of evaluative reports are now admissible under Federal statutes. \* \* \* These statutory exceptions to the hearsay rule are preserved. Rule 802. The willingness of Congress to recognize these and other such evaluative reports provides a helpful guide in determining the kind of reports which are intended to be admissible under this rule. We think the restrictive interpretation of the House overlooks the fact that while the Advisory Committee assumes admissibility in the first instance of evaluative reports, they are not admissible if, as the rule states, "the sources of information or other circumstances indicate lack of trustworthiness."

The Report of the Senate Committee advocating the admissibility of conclusions and opinions was accepted by the Supreme Court as advancing the correct position in Beech Aircraft Corp. v. Rainey (S.Ct.1988). Accordingly "factual finding" includes not only what happened, but how it happened, why it happened, and who caused it to happen.

**Against the criminal defendant.** Rule 803(8)(B) specifically excludes public records and reports setting forth matters observed pursuant to a duty imposed by law by police officers or other law enforcement personnel when offered against the criminal defendant. Rule 803(8)(C) similarly excludes factual finding from a government investigation when offered against the criminal defendant. Such public records may, however, be admissible when offered under another hearsay exception such as Rule 803(5), Rule 803(10), or Rule 807.

A particular problem arises with respect to forensic laboratory reports. The plain meaning of the exclusions in Rule 803(8) incorporates such reports, i.e., makes them inadmissible when offered by the government. However, where the laboratory technician who personally conducted the tests testifies on personal knowledge, subject to cross-examination, it seems reasonable to also permit introduction of the forensic laboratory report itself. A much more difficult situation arises when the person actually conducting the test is unavailable. A proposal to admit forensic laboratory reports under such circumstances was made as part of the legislative process leading up to the enactment of the Federal Rules of Evidence but not included in the final version. Faced with such circumstances, some courts have sanctioned admissibility upon the testimony of the supervisor of the unavailable laboratory technician as an "other qualified witness" pursuant to Rule 803(6).

## Rule 803(9).

## RECORDS OF VITAL STATISTICS

**The following are not excluded by the hearsay rule, even though the declarant is available as a witness:**

\* \* \*

**(9) Records of Vital Statistics. Records or data compilations in any form, of births, fetal deaths, deaths, or marriages, if the report thereof was made to a public office pursuant to requirements of law.**

## § 803.9 Rule 803(9): Records of Vital Statistics

Records or data compilations in any form, of births, fetal deaths, death, or marriages, if the report thereof was made to a public office pursuant to requirements of law, constitute a hearsay exception, Rule 803(9). The informant required to report the matter need not be a public officer. Reports of births, marriages, or deaths are usually made by doctors, ministers, or undertakers, or by parents or children with reference to the birth or death of their child or parent. The public officer creating the record or data compilation in any form must be required by law to record the matter reported. The exception is thus based upon the notion that such records are commonly made by disinterested professionals with no motive to misrepresent or by a parent or child under circumstances which bespeaks reliability. Necessity also supports the exception, since there may be so long a time between the event and the lawsuit in which such a fact is in issue that other proof would be difficult to obtain.

With respect to the question of the admissibility of "factual findings" contained in records of vital statistics, such as cause of death, resort should be had to the principles underlying Rules 803(8)(B) and (C). Thus admissibility of a statement as to cause of death appearing in a record of vital statistics and the identical statement appearing otherwise in a public record should be judged by the same criteria. If the statement as to cause of death is being offered against the criminal defendant, it should not be received. In all other cases, the statement as to cause of death, being a "factual finding," is admissible unless sources of information or other circumstances indicate lack of trustworthiness, Rule 803(8)(C).

Authentication of a record of a vital statistic as to a matter reported pursuant to requirements of law is usually accomplished by means of the offering of a certified copy of the public record, Rule 902(4).

## Rule 803(10).

## ABSENCE OF PUBLIC RECORD OR ENTRY

**The following are not excluded by the hearsay rule, even though the declarant is available as a witness:**

* * *

**(10) Absence of Public Record or Entry. To prove the absence of a record, report, statement, or data compilation, in any form, or the nonoccurrence or nonexistence of a matter of which a record, report, statement, or data compilation, in any form, was regularly made and preserved by a public office or agency, evidence in the form of a certification in accordance with Rule 902, or testimony, that diligent search failed to disclose the record, report, statement, or data compilation, or entry.**

## § 803.10   Rule 803(10): Absence of Public Record or Entry

Evidence in the form of a certification in accordance with Rule 902, or testimony, that diligent search failed to disclose the record, report, statement, or data compilation, or entry, is admissible as a hearsay exception to prove the absence of a record, report, statement, or data compilation in any form, or the nonoccurrence or nonexistence of a matter of which a record, report, statement, or data compilation, in any form, was regularly made and preserved by a public office or agency, Rule 803(10).

Public records included are those specified in Rules 803(8) and 803(9). Rule 803(10) provides for proof of the absence of a record where the existence of the record itself is in issue as well as for proof of the nonoccurrence or nonexistence of the event by showing the absence of the public record which would regularly have been made recording its happening.

## Rule 803(11).

## RECORDS OF RELIGIOUS ORGANIZATIONS

**The following are not excluded by the hearsay rule, even though the declarant is available as a witness:**

\* \* \*

**(11) Records of Religious Organizations. Statements of births, marriages, divorces, deaths, legitimacy, ancestry, relationship by blood or marriage, or other similar facts of personal or family history, contained in a regularly kept record of a religious organization.**

### § 803.11 Rule 803(11): Records of Religious Organizations

Statements contained in regularly kept records of a religious organization concerning matters such as birth, marriage, divorce, death, legitimacy, ancestry, relationship by blood or marriage, or similar facts of personal or family history constitute a hearsay exception, Rule 803(11).

Since such facts will usually be recorded in connection with a solemn religious ceremony, the likelihood of fabricating information furnished on such an occasion is remote, although arguably less so with respect to the mother's designation of the father offered in a paternity suit. In the later situation, the probative value of such evidence could normally be explored during cross-examination of the mother. Additional guarantees of trustworthiness of records of religious organizations are found in the solemn nature of the sacrament, lack of personal interest of the church official, the duty under church law or usage to make the record, and the moral nature of the act.

Facts provable under this exception include both relevant dates and relationships. Thus a regularly kept church record of baptism is admissible to prove the age of the child and his parentage as well as the fact that the ceremony took place at a certain time and place. Moreover, unlike the hearsay exceptions for public records, Rule 803(8), vital statistics, Rule 803(9), and records of regularly conducted business activity, Rule 803(6), this hearsay exception contains no requirement that the person providing the information be under a business duty or legal obligation to do so.

## Rule 803(12).

## MARRIAGE, BAPTISMAL, AND SIMILAR CERTIFICATES

**The following are not excluded by the hearsay rule, even though the declarant is available as a witness:**

\* \* \*

**(12) Marriage, Baptismal, and Similar Certificates. Statements of fact contained in a certificate that the maker performed a marriage or other ceremony or administered a sacrament, made by a clergyman, public official, or other person authorized by the rules or practices of a religious organization or by law to perform the act certified, and purporting to have been issued at the time of the act or within a reasonable time thereafter.**

## § 803.12 Rule 803(12): Marriage, Baptismal and Similar Certificates

Statements of fact contained in a certificate that the maker performed a marriage or other ceremony or administered a sacrament are admissible under a hearsay exception, provided the clergyman, public official, or other person making the statement is authorized by the rules or practice of a religious organization or by law to perform the act certified, Rule 803(12). The certificate must also purport to be issued at the time of the act or a reasonable time thereafter, Rule 803(12). Thus a recital of date created upon the certificate itself would satisfy the foundation requirement with respect to time of issuing. The basis of the hearsay exception is that the maker being authorized by a religious organization or by law to make the certificate is very unlikely to fabricate on such an occasion.

When the record is one of a vital statistic, Rule 803(9), instead of procuring a certified copy of the record, Rule 902(4), a party under Rule 803(12) may simply introduce in evidence a properly authenticated certificate given to a participant by the person performing the ceremony. When the certificate is offered, it must be accompanied by proof that the act which the certificate relates is one which the maker of the certificate was authorized to perform. Rule 803(12) also extends to certain acts not covered by Rule 803(9); certification of such matters as baptism and confirmation are included, even though they are not required to be recorded in a public office.

## Rule 803(13).

## FAMILY RECORDS

**The following are not excluded by the hearsay rule, even though the declarant is available as a witness:**

\* \* \*

**(13) Family Records. Statements of fact concerning personal or family history contained in family Bibles, genealogies, charts, engravings on rings, inscriptions on family portraits, engravings on urns, crypts, or tombstones, or the like.**

## § 803.13   Rule 803(13): Family Records

Statements of fact concerning personal or family history contained in family Bibles, genealogies, charts, engravings on rings, inscriptions on family portraits, engravings on urns, crypts, or tombstones, or the like, constitute a hearsay exception, Rule 803(13). Statements admissible as concerning personal or family history include statements of births, marriages, divorces, deaths, legitimacy, ancestry, relationship by blood or marriage.

The basis of the exception is that the family would not allow an untruthful entry or inscription to be made or to remain without protest. Thus a family record shown to have been given recognition by the family is sufficiently authenticated. Under such circumstances, the author of the statement need not be identified, the author need not be a member of the family, nor must the author be shown to have had personal knowledge. Alternatively, the family record may be authenticated by establishing the handwriting or signature of a specific family member. However in such cases the absence of proof of general family recognition would seem to require that personal knowledge of the declarant be established.

Rule 803(13) is more liberal than the common law approach in that it does not require that the declarant be unavailable, that the statement be made before the controversy or a motive to misrepresent arose, or that the declarant be related by blood or marriage to the family, each apparently required at common law.

## Rule 803(14).

## RECORDS OF DOCUMENTS AFFECTING AN INTEREST IN PROPERTY

**The following are not excluded by the hearsay rule, even though the declarant is available as a witness:**

\* \* \*

**(14) Records of Documents Affecting an Interest in Property. The record of a document purporting to establish or affect an interest in property, as proof of the content of the original recorded document and its execution and deliv-**

ery by each person by whom it purports to have been executed, if the record is a record of a public office and an applicable statute authorizes the recording of documents of that kind in that office.

## § 803.14    Rule 803(14): Records of Documents Affecting an Interest in Property

The record of a document purporting to establish or affect an interest in property is admissible under an exception to the hearsay rule as proof of the content of the original recorded document and its execution and delivery by each person by whom it purports to have been executed, if the record is a record of a public office and an applicable statute authorizes the recording of documents of that kind in that office, Rule 803(14). This relatively minor hearsay exception allows admission of a record of a title document to prove not only the contents of the document but also its due execution and delivery by each person by whom it purports to have been executed. The record must be of a public office and an applicable statute must authorize the recording of documents of that kind in that office. The effect of introduction of the record is that provided by local law. Thus whether the record is in fact admissible to prove execution and delivery remains a question of local law. Notice that local statutory provisions relating to recording of documents affecting interest in property seemingly all require proof of execution either by form of probate or the requirement that the person taking an acknowledgment of any person executing a document satisfy himself that the person is who he purports to be. In addition, either affidavits of delivery are required or a presumption exists as to delivery of an executed and recorded document.

## Rule 803(15).

## STATEMENTS IN DOCUMENTS AFFECTING AN INTEREST IN PROPERTY

**The following are not excluded by the hearsay rule, even though the declarant is available as a witness:**

\* \* \*

**(15) Statements in Documents Affecting an Interest in Property. A statement contained in a document purporting to establish or affect an interest in property if the matter stated was relevant to the purpose of the document, unless dealings with the property since the document was made have been inconsistent with the truth of the statement or the purport of the document.**

## § 803.15 Rule 803(15): Statements in Documents Affecting an Interest in Property

The circumstances under which documents purporting to establish or affect an interest in property are executed will normally guarantee the trustworthiness of recitals of fact relevant to the purpose of the document. Accordingly Rule 803(15) provides that a statement contained in a document purporting to establish or affect an interest in property if the matter stated was relevant to the purpose of the document constitutes a hearsay exception, unless dealings with the property since the document was made are inconsistent with the truth of the statement or the purport of the document. Statements included within Rule 803(15) may, for example, concern the existence of a power of attorney to execute the document or that the grantors of a deed are all the heirs of the last record owner. While there is no requirement that the document be of a certain age, one may expect that many such documents would also qualify as an ancient document under Rule 803(16).

### Rule 803(16).

## STATEMENTS IN ANCIENT DOCUMENTS

**The following are not excluded by the hearsay rule, even though the declarant is available as a witness:**

\* \* \*

**(16) Statements in Ancient Documents. Statements in a document in existence twenty years or more the authenticity of which is established.**

### § 803.16　Rule 803(16): Statements in Ancient Documents

Statements in a document in existence 20 years or more whose authenticity is established constitute a hearsay exception, Rule 803(16). Authenticity is established pursuant to Rule 901(b)(8), by showing that (a) its condition creates no suspicion concerning its authenticity, (b) it was in a place where it would be likely to be if authentic, and (c) it has been in existence 20 years or more at the time it is offered. In both Rules 803(16) and 901(b)(8) the common law time period of 30 years is reduced to 20 years.

Sufficient assurance of trustworthiness for the hearsay exception is provided by the fact that the document was almost invariably created prior to the existence of any motive to falsify arising from the instant litigation. The written form of the assertion reduces the possibility of error in transmission. In addition, it will frequently occur that a person with personal knowledge is not available or that the testimony of such a witness concerning a matter occurring so long ago would be less probative than statements contained in the document.

The ancient document exception contained in Rule 803(16) is not limited as it was often said to be under the common law to documents affecting an interest in property. It now clearly applies to any document including letters, records, contracts, maps, newspapers and certificates. No requirement is imposed that dealings with the subject of the statement have been consistent with the document.

## Rule 803(17).

## MARKET REPORTS, COMMERCIAL PUBLICATIONS

**The following are not excluded by the hearsay rule, even though the declarant is available as a witness:**

\* \* \*

**(17) Market Reports, Commercial Publications. Market quotations, tabulations, lists, directories, or other published compilations, generally used and relied upon by the public or by persons in particular occupations.**

### § 803.17   Rule 803(17): Market Reports, Commercial Publications; Mortality Tables

A hearsay exception is provided in Rule 803(17) for market quotations, tabulations, lists, directories, or other published compilations generally used and relied upon by the public or by persons in particular occupations. The basis of this exception is the high degree of reliability of items of this nature. General reliance by the public or a particular segment thereof upon the contents of the publication reinforces the motivation of the compiler to be accurate. Moreover no reason exists for the compiler to deceive. Necessity also plays a part in that in many instances it would be virtually impossible to produce the many people each having personal knowledge of a part of the matter compiled.

Telephone or city directories, weather reports, and printed pedigree registers begin to illustrate the diversity of the types of published compilations included within the hearsay exception provided in Rule 803(17). Also included are reports in official publications or trade journals or in newspapers or periodicals of general circulation published as the reports of such established commodity market. Mortality and annuity tables, shown to be or recognized as standard authorities, may be introduced under Rule 803(17) to show expectancy of life.

Certain compilations raise unique problems. For example, credit reports, if published as a compilation, would seem to meet the requirement of Rule 803(17) on its face. However credit reports being evaluative in nature should be subjected to the same criteria for trustworthiness associated with admissibility under Rules 803(6) and 803(8) and in particular Rule 803(8)(C). Since information relied upon in compiling a credit report will generally extend well beyond objective facts furnished by a person under a business duty to transmit, automatic inclusion in Rule 803(17) of such evaluative reports is unwarranted. Similar problems relating to trustworthi-

ness are associated with the admission of safety codes
and public opinion polls.

## Rule 803(18).

## LEARNED TREATISES

**The following are not excluded by the hearsay
rule, even though the declarant is available as a
witness:**

* * *

**(18) Learned Treatises. To the extent called to
the attention of an expert witness upon cross-
examination or relied upon by the expert witness in direct examination, statements contained in published treatises, periodicals, or
pamphlets on a subject of history, medicine, or
other science or art, established as a reliable
authority by the testimony or admission of the
witness or by other expert testimony or by judicial notice. If admitted, the statements may be
read into evidence but may not be received as
exhibits.**

### § 803.18   Rule 803(18): Learned Treatises

To the extent called to the attention of an expert
witness upon cross-examination or reasonably relied
upon by an expert witness on direct examination, statements contained in published treatises, periodicals, or
pamphlets on a subject of history, medicine, or other
science or art, established as a reliable authority by the
testimony or admission of the witness or by other expert
testimony or by judicial notice, are admissible as an
exception to the hearsay rule, Rule 803(18). However the

statement may only be read into evidence; the published authority may not be received as an exhibit.

Views of recognized authorities, expressed in treatises, pamphlets or periodicals written for professional colleagues, may be employed on cross-examination of an expert witness to impeach provided the author's competency is established by an admission of the expert witness, by other expert testimony, by judicial notice, or possibly otherwise determined to be reliable by the court. Moreover, under Rule 803(18) such statements employed to impeach may also be received as substantive evidence. Statements in established reliable authorities may also be admitted for the truth of their content when relied upon by an expert witness upon direct examination.

Whether a particular published authority has been sufficiently established as reliable is a decision for the court, Rule 104(a). Rule 803(18) provides that statements contained in a learned treatise, periodical, or pamphlet may be established as a reliable authority by the testimony of a witness expert in the profession, art, or trade of the author testifying that the learned treatise is a reliable authority or by judicial notice. The burden of establishing that the authority is reliable is upon the party offering the item. The burden is easily satisfied in that even if the expert being cross-examined denies that the learned treatise is a reliable authority, an expert called by the cross-examining party can so testify. A safeguard against jury misuse of the published authority is found in the final sentence of Rule 803(18) which provides that statements may be read into evidence but shall not be taken to the jury room. This provision attempts to prevent jurors from overvaluing the written word and from roaming at large through the treatise thereby forming conclusions not subjected to expert explanation and assistance. In addition, statements in published authorities are admissible only under circumstances in which an expert is testifying. Whether relied upon in support of direct examination or raised on cross-examination, an expert witness will have an opportunity to evaluate and explain to the trier of fact how the statement contained in the learned treatise relates to the issues that they are to decide.

## Rule 803(19).

## REPUTATION CONCERNING PERSONAL OR FAMILY HISTORY

**The following are not excluded by the hearsay rule, even though the declarant is available as a witness:**

\* \* \*

**(19) Reputation Concerning Personal or Family History. Reputation among members of a person's family by blood, adoption, or marriage, or among a person's associates, or in the community, concerning a person's birth, adoption, marriage, divorce, death, legitimacy, relationship by blood, adoption, or marriage, ancestry, or other similar fact of his personal or family history.**

## § 803.19 Rule 803(19): Reputation Concerning Personal or Family History

Rule 803(19) broadens the hearsay exception for reputation concerning personal or family history. It includes within the hearsay exception reputation among members of his family by blood, adoption, or marriage, or among his associates, or in the community, concerning a person's birth, adoption, marriage, divorce, death, legitimacy, or relationship by blood, adoption, or marriage, ancestry, or other similar fact of his personal or family history.

Reputation generally accepted among the family based upon more than occasional and casual conversation had previously been accepted as a means of proving family history. Reputation in the community or among the person's associates was permitted to establish marriage and in some instances other aspects of family history. Rule 803(19) clarifies the breadth of the exception for reputation by declaring it to be among members of the person's family, his associates, or community with respect to all aspects of personal and family history. As stated in the Advisory Committee's Note, the world in which the reputation may exist "has proved capable of expanding with changing times from the single uncomplicated neighborhood, in which all activities take place, to the multiple and unrelated worlds of work, religious affiliation, and social activity, in each of which a reputation may be generated."

The witness called to testify to such reputation must be shown to be among the particular group and to be familiar with the reputation. The common law requirement that the reputation must have arisen prior to the controversy is eliminated. Trustworthiness in reputation evidence is found when the topic is such that the facts are likely to have been inquired about and that persons having personal knowledge have disclosed facts which have thus been discussed in the community; and thus the community's conclusion, if any has been formed, is likely to be a trustworthy one. Moreover introduction of reputation testimony may be necessary when considered in light of the difficulty or even impossibility of obtaining other evidence as to the matter for which offered.

## Rule 803(20).

## REPUTATION CONCERNING BOUNDARIES OR GENERAL HISTORY

**The following are not excluded by the hearsay rule, even though the declarant is available as a witness:**

\* \* \*

**(20) Reputation Concerning Boundaries or General History. Reputation in a community, arising before the controversy, as to boundaries of or customs affecting lands in the community, and reputation as to events of general history important to the community or State or nation in which located.**

## § 803.20 Rule 803(20): Reputation Concerning Boundaries or General History

Reputation in a community, arising before the controversy, as to boundaries of or customs affecting lands in the community, both public and private, and reputation as to events of general history important to the community or State or nation in which located is admissible under a hearsay exception, Rule 803(20). While reputation concerning boundaries must have arisen prior to the controversy, this requirement is not applied to reputation testimony of matters of general history since the historical character of the subject matter dispenses with any need that the reputation antedate the controversy with respect to which it is offered.

## Rule 803(21).

## REPUTATION AS TO CHARACTER

**The following are not excluded by the hearsay rule, even though the declarant is available as a witness:**

* * *

**(21) Reputation as to Character. Reputation of a person's character among associates or in the community.**

### § 803.21   Rule 803(21): Reputation as to Character

A hearsay exception is provided for evidence of reputa tion of a person's character among his associates or in the community, Rule 803(21). The hearsay exception is merely a restatement in the hearsay context of Rules 405(a) and 608(a), which outline the methods of proving character when evidence as to character is admissible, and does not mean that reputation as to character is admissible without limit.

Reputation testimony as to character may be employed to prove a fact of consequence when character is in issue, Rule 405(b), or to establish a pertinent trait of character of the accused, Rule 404(a)(1), or victim, Rule 404(a)(2). In addition reputation testimony as to character is admissible to support or attack the credibility of a witness as provided in Rule 608(a).

## Rule 803(22).

## JUDGMENT OF PREVIOUS CONVICTION

**The following are not excluded by the hearsay rule, even though the declarant is available as a witness:**

\* \* \*

**(22) Judgment of Previous Conviction. Evidence of a final judgment, entered after a trial or upon a plea of guilty (but not upon a plea of nolo contendere), adjudging a person guilty of a crime punishable by death or imprisonment in excess of one year, to prove any fact essential to sustain the judgment, but not including, when offered by the Government in a criminal prosecution for purposes other than impeachment, judgments against persons other than the accused. The pendency of an appeal may be shown but does not affect admissibility.**

### § 803.22   Rule 803(22): Judgment of Previous Conviction; Other Adjudications

Evidence of a final judgment, entered after trial or upon a plea of guilty (but not upon a plea of nolo contendere), adjudging a person guilty of a crime punishable by death or imprisonment in excess of one year, is admissible as a hearsay exception to prove any fact essential to sustain the judgment, but not including, when offered by the prosecution in a criminal case for purposes other than impeachment, judgments against persons other than the accused, Rule 803(22). The pendency of an appeal may be shown but does not affect admissibility. Neither a judgment of acquittal nor a dismissal is included within this exception. The exception does not apply to the use of civil judgments in a subsequent litigation.

The judgment of conviction must be for a crime punishable by death or imprisonment in excess of one year. The purpose of this limitation is to exclude lesser offenses where the motivation to defend vigorously may be lacking. The judgment of conviction may be after trial or entered upon a plea of guilty. A judgment based upon a plea of nolo contendere is not admissible, Rule 803(22). Although judgments of convictions conforming to the rule are admissible in both civil and criminal proceedings to prove any fact essential to sustain the judgment, because of considerations of confrontation, a judgment of conviction of a third person offered by the prosecution against the accused in a criminal case for purposes other than impeachment is inadmissible.

The party against whom the evidence is offered, who frequently will but need not be the person against whom the judgment of conviction was entered, may attempt to rebut such evidence by offering whatever explanation there may be concerning either the circumstances surrounding the conviction or the underlying event. Introduction of evidence to rebut may be curtailed, if required, under Rule 403. The ultimate weight to be afforded to evidence of conviction is for the trier of fact to determine.

## Rule 803(23).

## JUDGMENT AS TO PERSONAL, FAMILY, OR GENERAL HISTORY, OR BOUNDARIES

**The following are not excluded by the hearsay rule, even though the declarant is available as a witness:**

\* \* \*

**(23) Judgment as to Personal, Family, or General History, or Boundaries. Judgments as proof of matters of personal, family or general history, or boundaries, essential to the judgment, if the same would be provable by evidence of reputation.**

## § 803.23   Rule 803(23): Judgment as to Personal, Family or General History, or Boundaries

Rule 803(23) provides a hearsay exception for a prior judgment as proof of matters of personal, family or general history, or boundaries, essential to the judgment to the extent the foregoing would be provable by reputation evidence, Rules 803(19) and 803(20). A prior judgment is thought to be at least as trustworthy as reputation evidence, since the process of inquiry and scrutiny relied upon as the basis for admitting evidence of reputation occurs to an even greater degree in the process of litigation. While the employment of judgments for such a purpose has long been recognized, the matter arises infrequently in practice.

## Rule 803(24).

## OTHER EXCEPTIONS

## [Transferred to Rule 807]

### § 803.24   Rule 803(24): Other Exceptions

[Author's Note: The Advisory Committee's Notes to Rules 803(24), Rule 804(b)(5) and new Rule 807 enacted in 1997 indicate that the contents of Rule 803(24) and Rule 804(b)(5) have been combined and transferred to a new Rule 807 re-titled "Residual Exception". The purpose was stated to be to facilitate additions to Rule 803 and 804 and that no change in meaning was intended.]

## Rule 804.

## HEARSAY EXCEPTIONS, DECLARANT UNAVAILABLE

## Prelude

### § 804.0   Rule 804: Hearsay Exceptions, Declarant Unavailable

Rule 804 provides for certain hearsay exceptions each sharing the requirement that the declarant be "unavailable as a witness" as defined in Rule 804(a). Unlike the hearsay exceptions contained in Rule 803 which are based on the assumption that each contains certain indicia of trustworthiness justifying the conclusion that the availability or unavailability of the declarant is not a relevant factor in determining admissibility, the hearsay exceptions contained in Rule 804 recognize that a statement meeting the requirements of the particular exception is not equal in quality to the testimony of the declarant at trial. Accordingly Rule 804 provides for admissibility only if the declarant is unavailable. As the Advisory Committee's Note to Rule 804(b) states, "The rule expresses preferences: testimony given on the stand in person is preferred over hearsay, and hearsay if of a specified quality, is preferred over complete loss of the evidence of the declarant."

Unavailability is treated as a single concept applicable to each exception, a departure from the approach of the common law in which distinctions were made as to what satisfied the unavailability requirement for the different exceptions. An exception to this unified approach exists only with respect to imposition of a requirement with respect to procurement of testimony of a witness absent from the hearing, applicable solely to Rules 804(b)(2), (3) and (4), where the proponent of the hearsay statement is unable to compel the witness' attendance by process or other reasonable means, Rule 804(a)(5). Rule 804(a) is based upon the premise that the essential factor in determining unavailability is the unavailability of the testimony rather than the unavailability of the witness. Thus physical presence on the witness stand does not make a witness available within the meaning of the rule if the witness exercises a privilege, simply refuses to or is unable to answer, or testifies to a lack of memory as to the subject matter of his prior statement.

Whether the requirements of a hearsay exception contained in Rule 804 have been satisfied is to be determined by the court, Rule 104(a). A statement meeting the requirements of the hearsay exception must, of course, satisfy other provisions of the rules of evidence before it may be admitted. As stated in the Advisory Committee's Note to Rule 803, "The exceptions [contained in Rules 803 and 804] are phrased in terms of nonapplication of the hearsay rule, rather than in positive terms of admissibility, in order to repel any implication that other possible grounds for exclusion are eliminated from consideration." Thus for example, a statement that qualifies as an exception to the hearsay rule must be relevant, Rule 401; be properly authenticated, Rules 901 and 902; be based upon personal knowledge, Rule 602, with the exception of statements by the declarant as to his own personal or family history, Rule 804(b)(4) ; and meet the requirements of the Original Writing Rule, Rule 1002, where the content of a writing is in issue, before it can be admitted into evidence. On the other hand, statements of a declarant who is not competent to testify at trial for reasons not related to personal knowledge, Rule 602, meeting the requirements of a hearsay exception are admissible. Questions arising with respect to multiple level hearsay are addressed in Rule 805; attacking and supporting the credibility of the declarant is governed by Rule 806.

With the exception of a statement against interest, Rule 804(b)(3), hearsay statements falling within an exception are admissible whether or not self-serving when made or offered. Moreover the opinion rule, Rules 701, 702 and 704, as it relates to the form of the witness' testimony, is not applicable to hearsay statements admitted pursuant to Rule 804 hearsay exceptions. The opinion rule, designed to elicit more concrete and informative answers, is a rule of preference concerning the form of testimony. Since out of court statements are not made under circumstances in which alternative forms of expressions may be secured, this aspect of the opinion rule is inapplicable.

Rule 403 is applicable to evidence offered as falling within a hearsay exception. Thus even though the evidence meets the requirement of an exception, the court may still exclude the evidence on the grounds that its probative value is substantially outweighed by the danger of unfair prejudice, confusion of the issues, or misleading the jury, or by considerations of undue delay, waste of time, or needless presentation of cumulative evidence.

The requirement of unavailability applicable to the hearsay exceptions of Rule 804(b) is defined in Rule 804(a). The requirement of unavailability is applied to the five hearsay exceptions contained in Rule 804(b). They are former testimony, Rule 804(b)(1); statement under belief of impending death, Rule 804(b)(2); statement against interest, Rule 804(b)(3); statement of personal or family history, Rule 804(b)(4); and forfeiture by wrongdoing, Rule 804(b)(6). The text of Rule 804(a) and that of the five exceptions contained in Rule 804(b), together with the accompanying Advisory Committee's Note, legislative history and commentary, are presented in the sections that follow. Rule 804(a) and each of the exceptions in Rule 804(b) are treated separately for the convenience of the reader.

### Rule 804(a).

## DEFINITION OF UNAVAILABILITY

**(a) Definition of Unavailability. "Unavailability as a witness" includes situations in which the declarant—**

**(1) is exempted by ruling of the court on the ground of privilege from testifying concerning**

the subject matter of the declarant's statement; or

(2) persists in refusing to testify concerning the subject matter of the declarant's statement despite an order of the court to do so; or

(3) testifies to a lack of memory of the subject matter of the declarant's statement; or

(4) is unable to be present or to testify at the hearing because of death or then existing physical or mental illness or infirmity; or

(5) is absent from the hearing and the proponent of a statement has been unable to procure the declarant's attendance (or in the case of a hearsay exception under subdivision (b)(2), (3), or (4), the declarant's attendance or testimony) by process or other reasonable means.

A declarant is not unavailable as a witness if exemption, refusal, claim of lack of memory, inability, or absence is due to the procurement or wrongdoing of the proponent of a statement for the purpose of preventing the witness from attending or testifying.

## § 804.00    Rule 804(a): Definition of Unavailability

The definition of unavailability contained in Rule 804(a) provides that unavailability "includes" five alternatives, each alone sufficient to meet the requirement. The thrust of the alternative definitions of unavailability is upon the unavailability of the testimony of the witness which includes but is not limited to situations in which the witness is not physically present in court. Thus to illustrate, although not falling within any of the five

illustrative alternatives, a child witness who is too frightened of the defendant, defense counsel, or the courtroom
to be able and willing to testify, or who is found to be
incompetent to testify, is similarly unavailable.

Rule 804(a)(1) provides that a witness exempt from
testifying concerning the subject matter of his statement
on the grounds of privilege is unavailable. An actual
claim of privilege must be made by the witness and
allowed by the court before the witness will be considered unavailable on the basis of privilege.

Rule 804(a)(2) provides that one who persists in refusing to testify concerning the subject matter of his statement despite an order of the court that he do so is
unavailable. Silence resulting from misplaced reliance
upon a privilege without making a claim, or in spite of a
court denial of an asserted claim of privilege, constitutes
unavailability under this subsection.

Rule 804(a)(3) provides that a witness who testifies to
a lack of memory of the subject matter of his statement
is unavailable. A witness may either truly lack recollection or for a variety of reasons, including concern of a
possible perjury prosecution, feign lack of recollection. In
either event, the witness is unavailable to the extent that
he asserts lack of recollection of the subject matter of the
prior statement, even if the witness recalls other events.

Rule 804(a)(4) provides that a witness unable to be
present or to testify at the hearing because of death or
then existing physical or mental illness or infirmity is
unavailable. Death is the most obvious basis; mental
illness or physical disability of a serious nature are
equally compelling. In criminal matters, if the reason for
the government's witness' unavailability is only tempo-
rary, considerations underlying the confrontation clause

may require resort to a continuance. In both civil and criminal cases, where the testimony of the witness is critical, the trial court should consider carefully the option of granting a continuance.

Rule 804(a)(5) provides that in both civil and criminal cases, a declarant is unavailable if his presence cannot be secured by process or other reasonable means. In criminal cases the confrontation clause also requires that the government make a good faith effort to obtain the presence of the witness at trial going beyond the mere showing of an inability to compel appearance by subpoena before prior testimony may be introduced as a substitute for testimony. Whether the government has shown good faith in attempting to first locate and second procure the witness' attendance by process or voluntarily by reasonable means must be determined on a case-by-case basis after careful review of the particular facts and circumstances. In addition Rule 804(a)(5) requires that it be shown that the testimony of the witness cannot be procured by process or other reasonable means before a hearsay statement may be admitted as a hearsay exception pursuant to Rule 804(b)(2), (3) or (4). The requirement of an attempt to obtain the testimony of the witness by deposition or otherwise as a prerequisite to a finding of unavailability imposed by Rule 804(a)(5) is not applicable to either Rule 804(b)(1), former testimony, or Rule 804(b)(6), forfeiture by wrongdoing.

Determination of unavailability is a matter for the court, Rule 104(a). The burden of showing unavailability is upon the party offering the statement. A witness is not "unavailable" under any of the subdivisions of Rule 804(a) if the circumstances which would otherwise constitute unavailability are due to the procurement or other wrongdoing of the proponent of the statement, Rule 804(a).

## Rule 804(b)(1).

## FORMER TESTIMONY

\* \* \*

**(b) Hearsay Exceptions. The following are not excluded by the hearsay rule if the declarant is unavailable as a witness:**

**(1) Former Testimony. Testimony given as a witness at another hearing of the same or a different proceeding, or in a deposition taken in compliance with law in the course of the same or another proceeding, if the party against whom the testimony is now offered, or, in a civil action or proceeding, a predecessor in interest, had an opportunity and similar motive to develop the testimony by direct, cross, or redirect examination.**

### § 804.1 Rule 804(b)(1): Former Testimony

Testimony given as a witness at another hearing of the same or a different proceeding, or in a deposition taken in compliance with law in the course of the same or another proceeding, is admissible as a hearsay exception under Rule 804(b)(1) if (1) the witness is unavailable as defined in Rule 804(a) and (2) the party against whom the testimony is being offered, or, in a civil action or proceeding a predecessor in interest, had an opportunity and similar motive to develop the testimony by direct, cross or redirect examination. Identity of counsel in both proceedings is not a condition of admissibility.

The exception for former testimony involves the admission of testimony taken under oath and subject to cross-examination. Obviously, however, the demeanor of the witness was not and normally will not be observed by the trier of fact. Thus the imposition of the requirement of unavailability represents a strong preference for the personal appearance of the witness as an aid in evaluating his testimony. The additional requirement of the same party, or predecessor in interest in a civil case, possessing an opportunity and a similar motive to develop the testimony is designed to insure the presence of an adequate opportunity to develop the witness' testimony when it was given. An adequate opportunity to develop the witness' testimony at the earlier hearing may be either the opportunity to conduct direct and redirect examination, or to cross-examine fully which are treated as equivalent for purposes of Rule 804(b)(1). Moreover, the adequacy of the opportunity is apparently not affected by counsel's tactical decision not to inquire. Thus a decision not to cross-examine or to cross-examine fully at a preliminary hearing, before a grand jury, at a deposition, etc., assumes the risk that the witness will not be available at trial. Similarly, when the opponent takes a deposition, counsel who refrains from laying bare the full story of his client or of a favorable witness assumes the risk that the deponent will be unavailable at trial so that his onesided deposition becomes admissible.

**Same party or in civil action predecessor in interest.** Early cases interpreting the common law requirement of identity of parties imposed the concept of mutuality, i.e., both the party offering and the party against whom the former testimony was offered had to have been parties to the former suit. Under the guidance of Wigmore, the requirement of mutuality was abandoned at common law in favor of admissibility of former testimony against a party to the prior hearing in criminal cases and against a party to the former suit or someone in privity in civil actions.

Rule 804(b)(1) as proposed by the Supreme Court would have completely eliminated any requirement with respect to identity of parties in favor of permitting the introduction against a party whenever a party in the former action possessing a motive and interest similar to that of the party against whom now offered had an opportunity to develop the prior testimony of the witness by direct and redirect or cross-examination. Congress rejected this proposal reasoning that it is "generally unfair to impose upon the party against whom the hearsay evidence is being offered [in particular the criminal defendant] responsibility for the manner in which the witness was previously handled by another party." The sole exception to this principle was felt to be where in a civil case the party's predecessor in interest had an opportunity and similar motive to examine the witness. While the term predecessor in interest is not defined in either the rule itself or the legislative history, arguably a meaning consistent with the common law concept of privity as stated in Metropolitan St. Ry. Co. v. Gumby (2d Cir.1900) was intended:

> The term "privity" denotes mutual or successive relationships to the same rights of property, and privies are distributed into several classes, according to the manner of this relationship. Thus, there are privies in estate, as donor and donee, lessor and lessee, and joint tenants; privies in blood, as heir and ancestor 'and coparceners; privies in representation, as executor and testator, administrator and intestate; privies in law,

where the law, without privity of blood or estate casts the land upon another, as by escheat.

In any event, courts have interpreted the phrase predecessor in interest to extend beyond privity to encompass parties sharing a "community of interest", such as a husband and wife or a corporation and its sole shareholder. In fact it has been asserted, albeit incorrectly, by some courts that predecessor in interest is coterminous with opportunity and similar motive.

**Similar motive to develop the testimony.** With respect to the party or predecessor in interest in civil cases, and a party to the prior hearing in a criminal case who had an opportunity to develop the witness' testimony by direct and redirect or cross-examination, the former testimony will be admitted against the party only if the party, or predecessor in civil cases, had a similar motive to develop the testimony at the prior hearing. Generally speaking, a similar motive would have existed at the prior hearing when the issue at the prior hearing and at the current hearing are substantially identical. All the issues at the earlier hearing need not be the same; only the particular issue as to which the testimony was first offered must be substantially identical to the issue upon which offered in the current action. Accordingly it follows that neither the form of the proceeding, the theory of the case, nor the nature of the relief sought need be the same.

At common law the requirement was couched in terms of substantial identity of issues rather than in terms of similar motive. Rule 804(b)(1) employs the term similar motive in recognition that "identity of issues is significant only in that it bears on motive and interest in developing fully the testimony of the witness." Conversely in determining when the motive to develop was "similar", looking at the relationship of the issues in controversy will be of assistance.

**Adequacy of opportunity to cross-examine; preliminary hearing; deposition; suppression hearing.** Adequacy of opportunity to cross-examine at a prior hearing is best illustrated by reference to the preliminary hearing. Under Rule 804(b)(1), testimony given by the witness at the preliminary hearing may be offered by the government against the same criminal defendant if the witness becomes unavailable. If the defendant had been afforded a full and fair opportunity to conduct a meaningful cross-examination of the witness, the preliminary hearing testimony is admissible. The question, of course, is given the circumstances surrounding the preliminary hearing, when can it be said that the defendant has, in fact, been afforded such opportunity.

Analysis is complicated by the nature of the preliminary hearing itself, tactical questions faced by counsel, as well as whether discovery to a meaningful extent is available prior to the preliminary hearing. A preliminary hearing is ordinarily a much less searching exploration of the merits of a case than a trial, simply because the function is the more limited one of determining whether probable cause exists to hold the accused for trial. Defense counsel faced with the testimony of a witness realizes that to the extent his interrogation attempts to discredit the witness by attacking, for example, powers of observation or showing bias, the effort is extremely unlikely to affect the result. Moreover, counsel tactically might prefer to spring such matters for the first time at trial. Finally in practice discovery to which the defendant is ultimately entitled will frequently be incomplete or even nonexistent at the time of the preliminary hearing.

Nevertheless, determination of the adequacy of opportunity to conduct meaningful cross-examination focuses primarily not on the practical realities facing counsel at the preliminary hearing or any other hearing but rather upon the scope and nature of the opportunity for cross-examination permitted by the court. Accordingly a decision by counsel not to cross-examine at any prior hearing or to do so only to a limited extent, no matter how much practical sense the decision makes, does not appear to affect adequacy of opportunity. The same principle is applicable with respect to a deposition. Thus even though the potential benefits derived from developing the witness' testimony on cross-examination or direct and redirect may clearly be overshadowed by the attendant disadvantages, an adequate opportunity nevertheless existed. A failure to cross-examine or to do so fully may under very unusual circumstances lead to exclusion on the grounds of misleading the jury or unfair prejudice under Rule 403.

Since the purpose of a suppression hearing with respect to a confession is to determine voluntariness and not truth or falsity, and adequate opportunity and similar motive is not present.

**Offense against a child.** In a proceeding involving an alleged offense against a child, the child's testimony may be taken in a room outside the courtroom and be televised by 2–way closed circuit television or the child's testimony may be taken by deposition recorded and preserved on videotape provided that the court first finds that the child is unable to testify in open court in the presence of the defendant, because (1) the child is unable to testify because of fear, (2) there is a substantial likelihood, established by expert testimony, that the child would suffer emotional trauma from testifying because of the presence of the defendant, or (3) the child suffers a mental or other infirmity, or (4) conduct by defendant or defense counsel causes the child to be unable to continue testifying.

## Rule 804(b)(2).

## STATEMENT UNDER BELIEF OF IMPENDING DEATH

\* \* \*

**(b) Hearsay Exceptions. The following are not excluded by the hearsay rule if the declarant is unavailable as a witness:**

\* \* \*

**(2) Statement Under Belief of Impending Death. In a prosecution for homicide or in a civil action or proceeding, a statement made by a declarant while believing that the declarant's death was imminent, concerning the cause or circumstances of what the declarant believed to be impending death.**

## § 804.2 Rule 804(b)(2): Statement Under Belief of Impending Death

The hearsay exception for a statement made under belief of impending death, known in the common law as a dying declaration, Rule 804(b)(2), finds its guarantee of trustworthiness in the assumption that belief of impending death substantially curtails the possibility of falsification by the declarant. A statement under belief of impending death is a statement made by a declarant, while believing that his death was imminent, concerning the cause and circumstances of what he believed to be his impending death, Rule 804(b)(2). Whether the requirements of the hearsay exception have been satisfied, including whether the declarant believed himself in extremis when the statement was made, is to be determined by the court, Rule 104(a). Belief in the imminence of his death may be shown by the declarant's own statements or from circumstantial evidence, such as the nature of his wounds, statements made in his presence, or by opinion of his physician. At the same time a sufficient foundation establishing personal knowledge must be laid, which in this context may require evidence sufficient to establish that the declarant possessed adequate mental and physical facilities after the injury to perceive, record and recollect, and narrate the cause or circumstances surrounding his death. Any adequate means of communication including words or signs will suffice so long as the indication is positive and definite. Statements in the form of an opinion are admissible.

Statements under belief of impending death are admissible generally in civil actions or proceedings but in criminal proceedings only if for homicide, Rule 804(b)(2). In prosecutions for homicide, such statements are admissible when offered either by or against the accused. The common law required that the declarant be the victim of the homicide for which the accused is being prosecuted. Rule 804(b)(2) does not by its terms incorporate such a requirement. Whether restricting application of the exception to the hearsay rule to homicide implies an intent to so limit application of Rule 804(b)(2) is as unclear as the rationale for limiting application to homicide prosecutions in the first place.

## Rule 804(b)(3).

## STATEMENT AGAINST INTEREST

\* \* \*

**(b) Hearsay Exceptions. The following are not excluded by the hearsay rule if the declarant is unavailable as a witness:**

\* \* \*

**(3) Statement Against Interest. A statement which was at the time of its making so far contrary to the declarant's pecuniary or proprietary interest, or so far tended to subject the declarant to civil or criminal liability, or to render invalid a claim by the declarant against another, that a reasonable person in the declarant's position would not have made the statement unless he believed it to be true. A statement tending to expose the declarant to criminal liability and offered to exculpate the accused is not admissible unless corroborating circumstances clearly indicate the trustworthiness of the statement.**

## § 804.3 Rule 804(b)(3): Statement Against Interest

A statement which was at the time of its making so far contrary to the declarant's pecuniary or proprietary interest, or so far tended to subject him to civil or criminal liability, or to render invalid a claim by him against another, that a reasonable man in his position would not have made the statement unless he believed it to be true is admissible as a hearsay exception, Rule 804(b)(3). However a statement tending to expose the declarant to criminal liability and offered to exculpate the accused is not admissible unless corroborating circumstances clearly indicate the trustworthiness of the statement, Rule 804(b)(3).

The assumption that people do not make false statements damaging to themselves furnishes the basis for the hearsay exception admitting statements against interest contained in Rule 804(b)(3). Such a statement will be that of a nonparty, for if the statement is that of a party, offered by his opponent, it comes in as an admission, Rule 801(d)(2). There is under the latter circumstance no occasion to inquire whether the statement was against interest, this not being a condition precedent to admissibility of an admission by a party-opponent.

The common law requirements of this hearsay exception, referred to as a declaration against interest, were (1) the declarant be unavailable; (2) the declaration was against his proprietary or pecuniary interest when made; (3) the declarant had personal knowledge of the fact declared; and (4) the declarant had no probable motive to falsify. Since conventional doctrine required that the statement be contrary to the pecuniary or proprietary interest of the declarant, confessions of third persons were excluded in criminal cases.

The nature of declarations of unavailable witnesses felt sufficiently trustworthy to be admitted as a statement against interest is expanded in Rule 804(b)(3) to include any statement which was at the time of its making so far contrary to the declarant's pecuniary or proprietary interest, or so far tended to subject him to civil liability, or to render invalid a claim by him against another, that a reasonable man in his position would not have made the statement unless he believed it to be true.

Rule 804(b)(3) also provides a hearsay exception in both civil and criminal actions for statements tending to subject the declarant to criminal liability. The statement need not be a confession of guilt; all that is required is that the statement "tend" to expose the declarant to criminal liability to such an extent that a reasonable person would not have made such a statement unless he believed it to be true. Statements tending to expose the declarant to criminal liability may be offered in a criminal matter to inculpate or exculpate the accused. Whether statements collateral to the declarant's interest that inculpate or exculpate are also admissible was the subject of substantial dispute.

In Williamson v. United States (S.Ct.1994), the Supreme Court decided that non-self-inculpatory collateral statements are not admissible under Rule 804(b)(3). The fact that a portion of a statement inculpates another, however, does not mean that that portion, when viewed in context, is not against the penal interest of the declarant.

In Lilly v. Virginia (S.Ct.1999), a case without a majority opinion, the Supreme Court indicated, more or less explicitly, that the admission of custodial statements to law enforcement personnel against penal interest, i.e., testimonial material, such as oral statements regardless of whether tape recorded or videotaped, written statements, and affidavits, whether or not constituting a confession, that incriminate another person should ordinarily be found to have violated the confrontation clause when admitted against such other person in a criminal case; such evidence is "presumptively unreliable". It is clear that such a custodial statement to law enforcement personnel does not fall within a firmly rooted hearsay exception. However, because the various opinions employ different rationales and frequently refer to the facts surrounding the actual making of the statement, sometimes but not always mentioning that the declarant in the matter at hand was clearly attempting to shift blame to another, there appears to be ample wiggle room for lower courts to permit a custodial statement to law enforcement personnel into evidence if so inclined in spite of the clear tenor of the majority of the justices to the contrary. Thus applying *Lilly,* it is not surprising to find some lower courts permitting a custodial statement to law enforcement personnel that incriminates another person to be admitted against such other person in a criminal case, not as a firmly rooted hearsay exception, but upon a finding of "particularized guarantees of trustworthiness".

Under *Lilly,* it is clear that noncustodial incriminating collateral statements, while not firmly rooted, may be admitted against such other person in a criminal case pursuant to the confrontation clause if they satisfy the "particularized guarantees of trustworthiness" prong of *Roberts.*

Determining under what circumstances, a noncustodial (or possibly even a custodial statement) incriminating collateral statement in fact satisfies the "particularized guarantees of trustworthiness" prong of *Roberts* is unclear as *Lilly* does not contain a majority opinion outlining the factors appropriately considered in making such a determination. The foregoing question should be of little concern in the federal court as *Williamson* supra already declares non-self-inculpatory collateral statements inadmissible under Rule 804(b)(3).

A statement offered to exculpate the accused is not admissible unless corroborating circumstances clearly indicate the trustworthiness of the statement. The additional requirement that the court pursuant to Rule 104(a) find the presence of corroborative circumstances clearly indicating the trustworthiness of the statement against penal interest when offered to exculpate an accused was imposed in response to an awareness of both the suspect nature of such statements and the impact such a statement would have upon a jury applying a standard of proof of guilt beyond a reasonable doubt.

Although not required by the terms of Rule 804(b)(3), the requirement that corroborating circumstances be shown has been applied to inculpating statements as well.

## Rule 804(b)(4).

## STATEMENT OF PERSONAL
## OR FAMILY HISTORY

\* \* \*

**(b) Hearsay Exceptions. The following are not excluded by the hearsay rule if the declarant is unavailable as a witness:**

\* \* \*

**(4) Statement of Personal or Family History. (A) A statement concerning the declarant's own birth, adoption, marriage, divorce, legitimacy, relationship by blood, adoption, or marriage, ancestry, or other similar fact of personal or family history, even though declarant had no means of acquiring personal knowledge of the matter stat-**

ed; or (B) a statement concerning the foregoing matters, and death also, of another person, if the declarant was related to the other by blood, adoption, or marriage or was so intimately associated with the other's family as to be likely to have accurate information concerning the matter declared.

## § 804.4　Rule 804(b)(4): Statement of Personal or Family History

A hearsay exception is provided by Rule 804(b)(4) for (A) statements concerning the declarant's own birth, adoption, marriage, divorce, legitimacy, relationship by blood, adoption, or marriage, ancestry, or other similar fact of personal or family history, even though the declarant had no means of acquiring personal knowledge of the matter stated, and (B) for statements concerning any of the foregoing matters, and death also, of another person, if the declarant was related to the other by blood, adoption, or marriage, or was so intimately associated with the other's family as to be likely to have accurate information concerning the matter declared.

Unavailability under Rule 804(a) is not limited to death. The common law requirement that when the subject of the statement is the relationship between two other persons the declarant must qualify as to both, is no longer followed. Also eliminated is the requirement that the statement be made before the controversy arose. Such a fact is now to be considered on the question of weight rather than admissibility. The traditional insistence that the declaration come only from a member of the family is relaxed in favor of admission, in addition, of statements by a person intimately associated with the family.

The requirement of personal knowledge in Rule 602 is explicitly dispensed with in relation to statements concerning the declarant's own personal or family history, Rule 804(b)(4)(A). With respect to such statements concerning another person, the requirement of personal knowledge is satisfied if the unavailable declarant is shown to be a member of the family and thus in a position to be familiar with the matter, or so intimately associated with the other family as to be likely to have accurate information upon the matter addressed, Rule 804(b)(4)(B). Moreover, as provided in Rule 602, evidence of personal knowledge may consist of the statement of the declarant himself.

## Rule 804(b)(5).

## OTHER EXCEPTIONS

## [Transferred to Rule 807]

### § 804.5   Rule 804(b)(5): Other Expenses

[Author's Note: The Advisory Committee's Notes to Rules 803(24), Rule 804(b)(5) and new Rule 807 enacted in 1997 indicate that the contents of Rule 803(24) and Rule 804(b)(5) have been combined and transferred to a new Rule 807 retitled "Residual Exception". The purpose was stated to be to facilitate additions to Rule 803 and 804 and that no change in meaning was intended.]

## Rule 804(b)(6).

## FORFEITURE BY WRONGDOING

\* \* \*

**(b) Hearsay Exceptions. The following are not excluded by the hearsay rule if the declarant is unavailable as a witness:**

\* \* \*

**(6) Forfeiture By Wrongdoing. A statement offered against a party that has engaged or acquiesced in wrongdoing that was intended to, and did, procure the unavailability of the declarant as a witness.**

### § 804.6   Rule 804(b)(6): Forfeiture By Wrongdoing

A statement offered against a party that has engaged or acquiesced in wrongdoing that was intended to, and did, procure the unavailability of the declarant as a witness is admissible as an exception to the rule against hearsay pursuant to Rule 804(b)(6). Every party, including parties in civil cases and the government in criminal cases in addition to the criminal defendant, forfeits the right to object on hearsay and confrontation clause grounds when the party's deliberate wrongdoing or acquiescence therein, i.e., actions taken after the event to prevent a witness from testifying, procured the unavailability of the declarant of the statement as a witness. The wrongdoing or acquiescence need not consist of a criminal act.

The determination is governed by Rule 104(a). Thus the more probably true than not true standard of proof is applied.

Rule 804(b)(6) is an attempt to respond to the problem of witness intimidation whereby the criminal defendant, his associates, or friends through one means or another, often a simple telephone call, procures the unavailability of the witness at trial and thereby benefits from the wrongdoing by depriving the trier of fact of relevant testimony of a potential witness. While the principle of forfeiture of the right to object on hearsay grounds and confrontation clause grounds as well had been previously recognized by the circuit courts, Rule 804(b)(6) is an attempt to encourage both prosecutorial resort to forfeiture and judicial acceptance of the doctrine by specifically recognizing the concept in the federal rules of evidence. Nevertheless, difficulties of proof make it unlikely that codification will bring about a significant increase in application of the forfeiture principle.

## Rule 805.

## HEARSAY WITHIN HEARSAY

**Hearsay included within hearsay is not excluded under the hearsay rule if each part of the combined statements conforms with an exception to the hearsay rule provided in these rules.**

### § 805.1   Rule 805: Hearsay Within Hearsay

Hearsay within hearsay, often referred to as double level or multiple hearsay, is addressed in Rule 805, which provides that if each of two or more statements falls within an exception to the hearsay rule, multiple hearsay is admissible. An illustration is the business record coming within the hearsay exception provided in Rule 803(6), which includes within it information supplied by an informant not himself under a duty to provide such information. If the informant's statement itself qualifies as a hearsay exception, for example, an excited utterance, Rule 803(2), the record containing it is admissible provided among others that the person recording the excited utterance was under a business duty to do so. Similarly, if either the original statement or the statement within which the second level statement appears is admissible as not hearsay as defined in Rule 801(d), provided that the remaining statement is so defined or qualifies as a hearsay exception, the two statements are admissible.

## Rule 806.

## ATTACKING AND SUPPORTING CREDIBILITY OF DECLARANT

When a hearsay statement, or a statement defined in Rule 801(d)(2), (C), (D), or (E), has been admitted in evidence, the credibility of the declarant may be attacked, and if attacked may be supported, by any evidence which would be admissible for those purposes if declarant had testified as a witness. Evidence of a statement or conduct by the declarant at any time, inconsistent with the declarant's hearsay statement, is not subject to any requirement that the declarant may have been afforded an opportunity to deny or explain. If the party against whom a hearsay statement has been admitted calls the declarant as a witness, the party is entitled to examine the declarant on the statement as if under cross-examination.

## § 806.1 Rule 806: Attacking and Supporting Credibility of Declarant

The credibility of a declarant of a hearsay statement or of a statement defined as not hearsay under either Rule 801(d)(2), (A), (B), (C), (D), or (E) may be attacked by any evidence which would be admissible for that purpose if the declarant had testified as a witness, Rule 806. Thus a declarant's bias, interest, coercion, or corruption, his prior conviction of a crime (Rule 609), evidence of character and conduct bearing on truthfulness (Rule 608), or his inconsistent statements (Rule 613) may be shown. Similarly if the declarant's credibility has been attacked, it may be rehabilitated to the same extent as if he were a witness.

Rule 806 also makes clear that evidence of an inconsistent statement or conduct of the declarant is not subject to any requirement that the witness be afforded an opportunity to deny or explain. Accordingly the requirements of Rule 613(b), including that the witness be given an opportunity to explain or deny, do not apply to impeachment by prior inconsistent statement when a statement of a declarant not testifying as a witness is introduced into evidence. Moreover, evidence of such prior inconsistent statement or conduct may be introduced to attack the credibility of the declarant without reference to (1) whether the prior inconsistent statement or conduct occurred prior to or after the statement admitted into evidence or (2) whether the prior statement admitted into evidence was made at a prior hearing or deposition. Prior law was not always in accord.

The last sentence of Rule 806 allows a party against whom an out of court statement has been admitted to call the declarant and examine him as if under cross-examination. Such a witness is hostile in law and may be interrogated by leading questions, Rule 611(c).

## Rule 807.

## RESIDUAL EXCEPTION

A statement not specifically covered by Rule 803 or 804 but having equivalent circumstantial guarantees of trustworthiness, is not excluded by the hearsay rule, if the court determines that (A) the statement is offered as evidence of a material fact; (B) the statement is more probative on the point for which it is offered than any other evidence which the proponent can procure through reasonable efforts; and (C) the general purposes of these rules and the interests of justice will best be served by admission of the statement into evidence. However, a statement may not be admitted under this exception unless the proponent of it makes known to the adverse party sufficiently in advance of the trial or hearing to provide the adverse party with a fair opportunity to prepare to meet it, the proponent's intention to offer the statement and the particulars of it, including the name and address of the declarant.

[Author's Note: The Advisory Committee's Notes to Rules 803(24), Rule 804(b)(5) and new Rule 807 enacted in 1997 indicate that the contents of Rule 803(24) and Rule 804(b)(5) have been combined and transferred to a new Rule 807 re-titled "Residual Exception". The purpose was stated to be to facilitate additions to Rules 803 and 804 and that no change in meaning was intended. The legislative history of Rule 803(24) and Rule 804(b)(5) follows.]

## § 807.1 Residual Exception

In order to provide the flexibility needed to carry out the goals set forth in Rule 102, including the encouragement of growth and development of the law of evidence, Rule 807 provides a hearsay exception permitting introduction of hearsay statements possessing circumstantial guarantees of trustworthiness equivalent to those present with respect to the twenty-three specific exceptions contained in Rule 803 and the five hearsay exceptions contained in Rule 804 but failing to meet the specific requirements of any of said exceptions. A statement possessing such equivalent circumstantial guarantees of trustworthiness is admissible if, in addition, the court determines that (A) the statement is offered as evidence of a material fact, (B) the statement is more probative on the point for which it is offered than any other evidence the proponent can procure through reasonable efforts, and (C) the general purposes of these rules and the interests of justice will best be served by admission of the statement into evidence. Moreover, a party intending to request the court to admit a statement under this provision must notify any adverse party of this intention as well as the particulars of the statement, including the name and address of the declarant. This notice must be given sufficiently in advance of the trial or hearing to provide any adverse party with a fair opportunity to prepare to meet or contest the use of the statement, Rule 807.

Rule 807 is the successor to former Rule 803(24) and Rule 804(b)(5) which where combined together and transferred to Rule 807 in 1997. According to the Advisory Committee's Note, the purpose was to "facilitate additions to Rules 803 and 804" and that "no change in meaning is intended." Decisions interpreting either Rule 803(24) or Rule 804(b)(5) are thus authority with respect to Rule 807 as well. Rule 804(b)(5) specifically required that the declarant of the hearsay statement be unavailable as defined in Rule 804(a); Rule 803(24) did not so require.

Rule 807 is not intended to operate to destroy the hearsay rule. The Advisory Committee's Note cautioned, "[Rule 803(24) and Rule 804(b)(5)] do not contemplate an unfettered exercise of judicial discretion, but they do provide for treating new and presently unanticipated situations which demonstrate a trustworthiness within the spirit of the specifically stated exceptions." Congress went further to insure against excessive resort to the then two open ended rules by adding the three lettered provisions and the requirement of notice. Moreover, the Report of the Senate Committee on the Judiciary states that it "is intended that the residual hearsay exceptions will be used very rarely, and only in exceptional circumstances" and that the "committee does not intend to establish a broad license for trial judges to admit hearsay statements that do not fall within one of the other exceptions contained in rules 803 and 804(b)." Overall, reported decisions have interpreted the express requirements of Rule 803(24) and Rule 804(b)(5), and now Rule 807, with awareness of the "very rarely" and "exceptional circumstances" gloss contained in the Senate Committee's Report so as to prevent the exception from swallowing the rule.

As structured what is now Rule 807 contains five express requirements, all of which must be determined by the court to have been satisfied, Rule 104(a), before the statement may be admitted:

1. **Equivalent Trustworthiness.** The most significant requirement is that the statement possess "circumstantial guarantees of trustworthiness" equivalent to that of statements admitted under the specific exceptions. The focus is upon the circumstances that "surround the making of the statement and that render the declarant particularly worthy of belief." Courts will look to several criteria: certainty that the statement was made which should include an evaluation of the credibility of the in court witness; whether the statement was under oath; assurance of personal knowledge of the declarant of the underlying event; practical availability of the declarant at trial for meaningful cross-examination concerning the underlying event; and finally, an ad hoc assessment of reliability based upon the totality of the surrounding circumstances including an assessment of credibility of the out of court declarant, considered in light of the class-type exceptions to the hearsay rule supposed to demonstrate such characteristics. Relevant factors bearing upon the ascertainment of trustworthiness include (1) the declarant's partiality, i.e., interest, bias, corruption, or coercion, (2) the presence or absence of time to fabricate, (3) suggestiveness brought on by the use of leading questions, and (4) whether the declarant has ever recanted or reaffirmed the statement.

Corroborating evidence establishing the truth of the matter asserted by the declarant in the statement may *not* be considered.

2. **Necessity.** Introduction of the hearsay statement must be necessary in the sense of being more probative on the point for which offered than any other evidence which the proponent may reasonably procure. Whether a particular effort to obtain alternative proof of a matter

may reasonably be demanded must, of course, depend upon the fact at issue considered in light of its posture in the total litigation.

3. **Material fact.** The requirement that the statement be offered as evidence of a material fact probably means that not only must the fact the statement is offered to prove be relevant, Rule 401, but that the fact to be proved be of substantial importance in determining the outcome of the litigation.

4. **Satisfaction of purpose of rules.** The requirement that the general purposes of the rules of evidence and the interests of justice be best served by admission of the statement into evidence is largely a restatement of Rule 102 and as such is of little practical importance in determining admissibility.

5. **Notice.** The notice in advance of trial requirement, while generally enforced, may be dispensed with when the need for the hearsay statement arises on the eve of trial or in the course of trial, if no prejudice to the opponent is apparent. One method used to avoid prejudice is to grant a continuance to the opponent to prepare to meet or contest introduction of the hearsay statement.

Rules 803(24) and 804(b)(5), and now Rule 807, have been employed on a case-by-case basis to admit reliable and necessary hearsay. No pattern indicating the creation of new specific exceptions is apparent in the decisions. What is apparent, however, is that on certain occasions statements narrowly failing to meet the requirement of a specific exception or of the definition of not hearsay such as prior inconsistent statements, former testimony, prior consistent statements, judgment for a nonfelony conviction, or records of regularly conducted activities, have been admitted under what is now Rule

807, but not always. Such statements are sometimes referred to as a near miss.

An area of particular controversy emerged under then Rule 804(b)(5) having to do with the admissibility of grand jury testimony of a witness unavailable for any of the reasons specified in Rule 804(a). The most difficult cases involved situations where it appears that direct or indirect pressure has been brought to bear upon the witness not to testify at trial consistently with his grand jury testimony. If perceived by the court, there arises a natural inclination to admit the prior grand jury testimony in the hope that admissibility will serve to deter the placing of pressure upon other witnesses not to testify in the future. It is, of course, impossible to determine from reported decisions how significant a factor that desire to shield witnesses from such pressure and thus obtain witness testimony at future trials is in explaining the divergent results evidenced in the cases.

In Lilly v. Virginia (S.Ct.1999), a case without a majority opinion, all nine justices of the Supreme Court indicated, more or less explicitly, that the admission of custodial statements to law enforcement personnel against penal interest that also incriminate another person should ordinarily be held to violate the confrontation clause when admitted against such other person in a criminal case; such evidence is "presumptively unreliable". Grand jury testimony of the same sort argued to be admissible under Rule 807 may ultimately be held inadmissible under the confrontation clause as well.

With respect to statements neither falling within a near miss category or being grand jury testimony, as could be anticipated from the nature of the requirements for admissibility, no clear pattern has emerged. Moreover, given the importance of the factual context surrounding the making of the statement and the hearsay statements relationship to the litigation, precedent can be expected to play an extremely small role in determining admissibility in the future.

# ARTICLE IX

# AUTHENTICATION AND IDENTIFICATION

*Table of Rules*

## Rules 901(a) and (b).

## REQUIREMENT OF AUTHENTICATION OR IDENTIFICATION

**(a) General Provision. The requirement of authentication or identification as a condition precedent to admissibility is satisfied by evidence sufficient to support a finding that the matter in question is what its proponent claims.**

**(b) Illustrations. By way of illustration only, and not by way of limitation, the following are examples of authentication or identification conforming with the requirements of this rule:**

\* \* \*

### Prelude

### § 901.0  Rules 901(a) and (b): Authentication and Identification: General Provision

Authentication of things and identification of people represent a special aspect of relevancy, Rule 401. To illustrate, a telephone conversation offered to show knowledge on the part of a speaker is not relevant unless the person speaking is sufficiently identified, nor is a purported letter of the defendant relevant unless it is properly shown that the defendant actually wrote the letter. Proof of authenticity or identification may be by either direct or circumstantial evidence.

Satisfaction of the requirement of authentication or identification is a matter to be approached in accordance with Rule 104(b). Accordingly once the court finds that evidence has been introduced sufficient to permit a reasonable juror to find that the matter in question is what its proponent claims, a sufficient foundation for introduction in evidence has been laid, Rule 104(b). When an item is offered into evidence, the court may permit counsel to conduct a limited cross-examination, referred to as voir dire, on the foundation offered. In reaching its determination, the court must view all the evidence introduced as to authentication or identification, including issues of credibility, most favorably to the proponent. The ultimate decision as to whether a person, document, or item of real or demonstrative evidence is as purported is for the trier of fact. Of course, the party who opposed introduction of the evidence may still offer contradictory evidence before the trier of fact or challenge the credibility of the supporting proof in the same way that he can dispute any other testimony. However upon consideration of the evidence as a whole, if a sufficient foundation has been laid in support of introduction, contradictory evidence goes to the weight to be assigned by the trier of fact and not to admissibility.

Primarily in civil proceedings the time and uncertainty incident to authenticating documents and items of real or demonstrative evidence at trial may often be avoided by the use of procedures available before trial. Authentication may be accomplished through a pleading, by a request to admit, by stipulation, by deposition, by interrogatory, or as a result of an agreement reached at the pretrial conference.

Documents and real evidence once properly authenticated must be offered into evidence.

Compliance with the requirement of Rule 901 does not guarantee that the documentary, real, demonstrative or testimonial evidence subsequently offered is admissible, for the offered evidence may still be excluded because of some other bar to admission, such as the rule against hearsay, lack of relevancy, or Rule 403.

Rule 901(b) provides a list of ten illustrations of authentication or identification conforming to the requirements of the rule. The illustrations are not exclusive but serve only as examples, leaving room for growth and development in this area of the law, Rule 102. While ordinarily the authentication of a writing is satisfied by the introduction of evidence, in some instances the writing alone is treated as sufficient to support a finding of its authentication, Rule 902.

The text of each of the ten illustrations provided in Rule 901(b), together with commentary is presented in the sections which follow. Each of the illustrations is treated as a separate rule for the convenience of the reader. A similar pattern is followed with respect to the twelve subdivisions relating to self-authentication contained in Rule 902.

## Rule 901(b)(1).

### TESTIMONY OF WITNESS
### WITH KNOWLEDGE

**(a) General Provision. The requirement of authentication or identification as a condition precedent to admissibility is satisfied by evidence sufficient to support a finding that the matter in question is what its proponent claims.**

**(b) Illustrations. By way of illustration only, and not by way of limitation, the following are examples of authentication or identification conforming with the requirements of this rule:**

**(1) Testimony of Witness With Knowledge. Testimony that a matter is what it is claimed to be.**

## § 901.1 Rule 901(b)(1): Testimony of Witness With Knowledge; Chain of Custody

An obvious method of identification or authentication is the testimony of a witness with personal knowledge, Rule 602, that a matter is what it is claimed to be, Rule 901(b)(1).

Personal knowledge acquired from any of the five senses may form the basis for the testimony of the witness. A witness may testify, for example, that the person who made a particular statement is the plaintiff, that the writing bears his signature, that he observed someone write the letter, or that the exhibit is a piece of the bottle found on the floor immediately after it exploded. In addition if an object is involved, and if relevancy requires, evidence must be introduced sufficient to support a finding not only that the object offered is *the* object involved but also that the object is in substantially the same condition now as it was at the time relevant in the litigation. If changes have occurred, the object may still be admitted provided that after the changes have been explained, the jury will not be confused or misled, Rule 403. In order to assist identification of a particular object in court it is common for the person, especially a police officer, to place identifying marks or labels on the object.

Where the object is unique and thus identifiable in court on the basis of its distinctive appearance, evidence that the object is the same object and is in substantially the same condition can often be offered by one individual. Where the item is not readily identifiable, such as where narcotics are involved, the object must be authenticated by means of a chain of custody. Chain of custody requires testimony of continuous possession by each individual having possession, together with testimony by each that the object remained in substantially the same condition during its presence in his possession. All possibility of alteration, substitution or change of condition need not be eliminated. For example, normally an object may be placed in a safe to which more than one person had access without each such person being produced. Similarly an actual break in the chain of custody will not result in exclusion of the evidence when the chain of custody established to have occurred viewed as a whole supports the improbability of alteration, substitution or change of condition. Overall the more authentication is genuinely in issue, the greater the need to negate the possibility of alteration, change in condition, or substitution. Thus if the accused's defense is that the substance was sugar, a court might require the production of all available persons in the chain of custody as well as all available persons with access to the safe before ruling that a sufficient foundation has been introduced to admit the narcotics into evidence. The requirements of a chain of custody has been more rigorously applied in criminal than in civil cases.

Where a sample is offered, it is also necessary to establish that the sample is representative of the mass.

## Rule 901(b)(2).

## NONEXPERT OPINION
## ON HANDWRITING

**(a) General Provision. The requirement of authentication or identification as a condition pre-**

cedent to admissibility is satisfied by evidence sufficient to support a finding that the matter in
question is what its proponent claims.

(b) **Illustrations.** By way of illustration only, and
not by way of limitation, the following are examples of authentication or identification conforming with the requirements of this rule:

\* \* \*

(2) **Nonexpert Opinion on Handwriting.** Nonexpert opinion as to the genuineness of handwriting, based upon familiarity not acquired for
purposes of the litigation.

## § 901.2   Rule 901(b)(2): Nonexpert Opinion on Handwriting

A witness who is not an expert can give his opinion
authenticating a writing or signature if he is sufficiently
familiar with the handwriting of the putative writer,
provided the familiarity was not acquired for purposes of
the litigation, Rule 901(b)(2). The witness' familiarity
may be acquired by seeing the person write. In addition,
familiarity with writings purporting to be those of the
person acquired under circumstances indicating their
genuineness such as by conducting a correspondence, or
as in the case of a bank employee by handling his checks
or deposits, may also be sufficient.

Whether the witness' familiarity however acquired is
sufficient to allow him to give an opinion is a question
governed by Rules 602 and 104(b); the court must decide
whether a reasonable jury viewing the evidence most
favorably to the proponent could believe that the witness
has sufficient familiarity to identify the handwriting and
thus that the purported identification is accurate. An

assertion by the witness of familiarity coupled with a description of circumstances from which knowledge might reasonably be acquired will ordinarily be held sufficient. Remarkably little familiarity has been found sufficient. The witness may testify in less than absolute terms such as "I believe", "I can't be positive but", or "the writing is similar to." A showing of limited opportunity to become familiar with the handwriting is normally treated as going to the weight to be given the witness' testimony by the trier of fact rather than to the admissibility of the document.

Rule 901(b)(2) provides specifically that a nonexpert witness cannot rely upon familiarity acquired for the purpose of litigation; only an expert may testify to familiarity obtained for that purpose. Moreover a lay witness will not be permitted to point out the similarities or differences between a disputed specimen and an exemplar or otherwise base his testimony on examination of an exemplar; comparisons with specimens can be made only by an expert witness and/or the trier of fact, Rule 901(b)(3). A lay witness may, of course, be cross-examined as to the basis of his opinion and in the court's discretion may be asked to pick out a genuine writing from false copies prepared for such purposes.

Since a lay person's ability to distinguish between a genuine and skilled forgery is minimal at best, where a genuine issue is raised as to authenticity, employment of an expert witness should be considered.

## Rule 901(b)(3).

## COMPARISON BY TRIER OR
## EXPERT WITNESS

(a) **General Provision.** The requirement of authentication or identification as a condition precedent to admissibility is satisfied by evidence sufficient to support a finding that the matter in question is what its proponent claims.

(b) **Illustrations.** By way of illustration only, and not by way of limitation, the following are examples of authentication or identification conforming with the requirements of this rule:

\* \* \*

(3) **Comparison by Trier or Expert Witness.** Comparison by the trier of fact or by expert witnesses with specimens which have been authenticated.

## § 901.3   Rule 901(b)(3): Comparison by Trier or Expert Witness

An expert witness and/or the trier of fact may base an opinion as to authenticity upon a comparison between the questioned piece of evidence and an exemplar the authenticity of which has been sufficiently established, Rule 901(b)(3). The process of authentication by comparison rests upon the notion that with respect to a particular item there are so many common identifying characteristics that it is possible by this means to establish that the exemplar and the item in question have the same origin. Comparison is frequently used in connection with ballistics, handwriting, fingerprints, and typewriting. The same technique has also been used to authenticate tire tread marks, shoe prints, and other items where the presence of sufficient common characteristics is shown.

Rule 901(b)(3) which deals with all comparisons, not just handwriting, liberalizes the requirements for authentication by comparison by the trier of fact alone, or by the trier of fact aided by expert testimony. At common law the court alone determined whether a handwriting exemplar was authentic; the expert and/or jury was concerned only with comparing the exemplar once admitted with the disputed item. The genuineness of any exemplar is now a matter of conditional relevancy which pursuant to Rule 104(b) is ultimately to be decided by the trier of fact. The court will admit the exemplar into evidence for purposes of comparison if evidence sufficient to support a finding by a reasonable jury of genuineness has been introduced The exemplar itself may be authenticated by use of any of the methods available prior to trial or by one of the methods outlined in Rule 901(b) or 902. Evidence authenticating the exemplar may be either direct or circumstantial. Where the comparison is to be made by the trier of fact, it may be conducted in the jury room and/or in open court.

Once the exemplar has been authenticated, the expert, whether for example testifying as to handwriting, typewriting, fingerprints or ballistics, will commonly demonstrate the validity of his comparison by using blown-up photographic copies or similar evidence of both the exemplar and the questioned writing or item so as to be able to demonstrate graphically the similarities or differences leading to his opinion as to the origin of the questioned exhibit.

The cross-examiner is afforded wide scope in examination of such expert witnesses. Where it is fair to do so, the cross-examiner should be permitted to require the expert witness to pick a genuine item from among false samples.

### Rule 901(b)(4).

## DISTINCTIVE CHARACTERISTICS AND THE LIKE

**(a) General Provision. The requirement of authentication or identification as a condition precedent to admissibility is satisfied by evidence sufficient to support a finding that the matter in question is what its proponent claims.**

**(b) Illustrations. By way of illustration only, and not by way of limitation, the following are examples of authentication or identification conforming with the requirements of this rule:**

\* \* \*

**(4) Distinctive Characteristics and the Like. Appearance, contents, substance, internal patterns, or other distinctive characteristics, taken in conjunction with circumstances.**

### § 901.4  Rule 901(b)(4): Distinctive Characteristics and the Like

Appearance, contents, substance, internal patterns, or other distinctive characteristics may be sufficient to support a finding when taken in conjunction with surrounding circumstances that the matter in question is what its proponent claims, Rule 901(b)(4). Thus a letter may be authenticated by its contents with or without the aid of physical characteristics if the letter is shown to contain information that persons other than the purported sender are not likely to possess. A common aspect of authentication permissible under Rule 901(b)(4) is the reply doctrine which provides that once a letter, e-mail, fax, telegram, or telephone call is shown to have been mailed, sent or made, a letter, e-mail, fax, telegram or telephone call shown by its contents to be in reply is authenticated without more.

### Rule 901(b)(5).

## VOICE IDENTIFICATION

**(a) General Provision. The requirement of authentication or identification as a condition precedent to admissibility is satisfied by evidence sufficient to support a finding that the matter in question is what its proponent claims.**

**(b) Illustrations. By way of illustration only, and not by way of limitation, the following are examples of authentication or identification conforming with the requirements of this rule:**

\* \* \*

**(5) Voice Identification. Identification of a voice, whether heard firsthand or through mechanical or electronic transmission or recording, by opinion based upon hearing the voice at any time under circumstances connecting it with the alleged speaker.**

## § 901.5　Rule　901(b)(5):　Voice　Identification; Sound Recordings; Transcripts of Recordings

Voice identification is adequate if made by a witness having sufficient familiarity with the speaker's voice.

Accordingly Rule 901(b)(5) provides that a witness may testify in the form of an opinion identifying a voice, whether heard firsthand or through mechanical or electronic transmission or recording, based upon hearing the voice at any time under circumstances connecting it with the alleged speaker. Familiarity may be gained either before or after hearing the voice to be identified. A voice heard firsthand may be authenticated by hearing it over the telephone or on a recording and vice versa. Moreover where circumstances exist connecting the voice with the alleged speaker, a witness who has never heard the voice in person may nevertheless lay a sufficient foundation of identification of the speaker.

Whether the witness' familiarity, however and whenever acquired, is sufficient to allow him to give an opinion is a question governed by Rules 602 and 104(b); the court must decide whether a reasonable jury viewing the evidence most favorable to the proponent could believe that the witness has sufficient familiarity to identify the voice and thus that the purported identification is accurate. An assertion by the witness of familiarity coupled with a description of circumstances from which knowledge might reasonably be acquired will ordinarily suffice. Thus a showing of limited opportunity to become familiar with the voice generally is treated as going to the weight given the witness' testimony by the trier of fact rather than to admissibility.

A defendant may be compelled to speak before a witness without violating his privilege against self-incrimination, even if he is asked to use words purportedly uttered by the person committing the crime of which he is suspected. A defendant may also be compelled to speak into a tape recorder. Where a voice exemplar is taken, a witness may compare the exemplar taken from the speaker to a voice heard on another occasion and render an opinion as to whether the two speakers were one and the same.

A sound recording of voices is authenticated if a proper foundation is laid, including identification of the speakers. The specific requirements for authentication of sound recordings vary depending upon the circumstances. Thus for example a person who overheard or participated in the entire conversation and can identify the speakers may lay a proper foundation by testifying that the sound recording fully, fairly, and accurately reflects the conversation. In other instances depending upon the circumstances a mechanical capability plus chain of custody foundation, including testimony as to (1) capability of the device for recording, (2) competency of the operator, (3) proper operation of the device, (4) preservation of the recording with no changes, additions or deletions, along with (5) identification of the speakers, may be necessary. The recording to be admissible must not be barred by the eavesdropping statute. A sound recording that is inaudible, incomprehensible, incomplete, or of questionable authenticity may be excluded under Rule 403. Sound recordings are to be played only in open court in the presence of both judge and jury.

Accurate transcripts of the sound recording may be admitted to assist the jury in listening to the tapes. Transcripts of sound recordings may be sent to the jury room.

## Rule 901(b)(6).

## TELEPHONE CONVERSATIONS

**(a) General Provision. The requirement of authentication or identification as a condition precedent to admissibility is satisfied by evidence sufficient to support a finding that the matter in question is what its proponent claims.**

**(b) Illustrations. By way of illustration only, and not by way of limitation, the following are examples of authentication or identification conforming with the requirements of this rule:**

**\* \* \***

**(6) Telephone Conversations. Telephone conversations, by evidence that a call was made to the number assigned at the time by the telephone company to a particular person or business, if (A) in the case of a person, circumstances, including self-identification, show the person answering to be the one called, or (B) in the case of a business, the call was made to a place of business and the conversation related to business reasonably transacted over the telephone.**

### § 901.6    Rule 901(b)(6): Telephone Conversations

Communications by telephone do not authenticate themselves. A mere assertion by the speaker as to his identity, being hearsay, cannot be taken as a sufficient showing of his identity. Testimony that the witness was familiar with and recognized the speaker's voice is obviously sufficient, Rule 901(b)(5). The familiarity may be acquired prior to the conversation, or afterward. Authenticating evidence may also be circumstantial such as the contents of the statement or the reply doctrine, Rule 901(b)(4). Calls made or received by the witness may be authenticated in any of the foregoing ways.

Rule 901(b)(6) provides an additional means of authentication with respect to outgoing calls made to a particular number assigned at the time by the telephone company to a particular person or business. It prescribes that a sufficient foundation is laid identifying the person reached by such a call if (a) in the case of a person, circumstances, including self-identification, show the person answering to be the one called or (b) in the case of a business, the call was made to a place of business and the conversation related to business reasonably transacted over the telephone.

With respect to incoming telephone calls, caller identification technology provides an additional method of authentication.

### Rule 901(b)(7).

### PUBLIC RECORDS OR REPORTS

**(a) General Provision. The requirement of authentication or identification as a condition precedent to admissibility is satisfied by evidence sufficient to support a finding that the matter in question is what its proponent claims.**

**(b) Illustrations. By way of illustration only, and not by way of limitation, the following are examples of authentication or identification conforming with the requirements of this rule:**

\* \* \*

**(7) Public Records or Reports. Evidence that a writing authorized by law to be recorded or filed and in fact recorded or filed in a public office, or a purported public record, report, statement, or data compilation, in any form, is from the public office where items of this nature are kept.**

## § 901.7　Rule 901(b)(7): Public Records or Reports

Evidence that a writing authorized by law to be recorded or filed and in fact recorded or filed in a public office, or a purported public record, report, statement, or data compilation, in any form, is from the public office where items of this nature are kept is sufficient to support a finding that the writing or record is what it purports to be, Rule 901(b)(7). This provision applies to local, state, federal and foreign writings or records. Any writing or record meeting the requirements of Rule 901(b)(7) may be authenticated without reference to whether such writing or record is available for public inspection.

The party authenticating the writing or public record pursuant to Rule 901(b)(7) must introduce evidence sufficient to support a finding that the writing or public record is from the public office where such items are kept. All writings authorized by law to be recorded or filed in a public office, such as tax returns, safety inspection reports, or documents affecting real property, are included, as are purported public records, reports, statements, or data compilations in any form prepared by the public office itself. A writing or public record may be shown to be from the public office where such items are kept by the testimony of a person from the office or other person with knowledge.

Production of the original record pursuant to Rule 901(b)(7), coupled with testimony as to its being from the public office, is clearly not the only means of authenticating a public record or recorded or filed writing. A duplicate of the public record or recorded or filed writing authorized by law to be recorded or filed may be employed in place of the original in accordance with Rule 1003. Rules 902(1), (2), and (4) provide for self-authentication of public records and certified copies of public records and writings authorized to be recorded or filed. Rule 1005 provides for admissibility of certified copies under the Original Writing Rule. In addition Rule 1005 provides for authentication of a public record and a recorded or filed writing by testimony of a person that he has compared a copy with the original and that it is correct.

Rule 803(8) provides a hearsay exception for records, reports, statements and data compilations of public offices and agencies. It does not, however, apply to writings authorized by law to be recorded or filed in a public office or agency. Rule 803(9) does contain a hearsay exception for recorded or filed writings relating to vital statistics made to a public office pursuant to requirements of law and Rule 803(14) provides a hearsay exception for records of documents affecting an interest in property recorded in a public office pursuant to a statute authorizing the recording of such documents in such public office.

## Rule 901(b)(8).

## ANCIENT DOCUMENTS OR DATA COMPILATION

**(a) General Provision. The requirement of authentication or identification as a condition pre-**

cedent to admissibility is satisfied by evidence sufficient to support a finding that the matter in question is what its proponent claims.

(b) **Illustrations.** By way of illustration only, and not by way of limitation, the following are examples of authentication or identification conforming with the requirements of this rule:

* * *

(8) **Ancient Documents or Data Compilation.** Evidence that a document or data compilation, in any form, (A) is in such condition as to create no suspicion concerning its authenticity, (B) was in a place where it, if authentic, would likely be, and (C) has been in existence 20 years or more at the time it is offered.

## § 901.8 Rule 901(b)(8): Ancient Documents or Data Compilation

A document or data compilation, in any form, is authenticated by evidence that the exhibit (A) is in such condition as to create no suspicion concerning its authenticity, (B) was in a place where it, if authentic, would likely be, and (C) has been in existence 20 years or more at the time it is offered, Rule 901(b)(8). Thus the common law ancient document rule limitation solely to documents affecting an interest in real property is abrogated. In addition the 30–year period is reduced to 20 years for all documents. If a document has been recorded, the recording is evidence of age. There is no requirement that possession in the case of documents such as deeds, have been consistent with the documents. Possession where it does occur is however a circumstance corroborating authenticity of the document.

## Rule 901(b)(9).

## PROCESS OR SYSTEM

(a) **General Provision.** The requirement of authentication or identification as a condition precedent to admissibility is satisfied by evidence sufficient to support a finding that the matter in question is what its proponent claims.

(b) **Illustrations.** By way of illustration only, and not by way of limitation, the following are examples of authentication or identification conforming with the requirements of this rule:

＊ ＊ ＊

(9) **Process or System.** Evidence describing a process or system used to produce a result and showing that the process or system produces an accurate result.

## § 901.9   Rule 901(b)(9): Process or System; Computer Records, Faxed Documents, E–Mail

Evidence describing a process or system used to produce a result and showing that the process or system produces an accurate result, is sufficient to authenticate the result when offered at trial, Rule 901(b)(9). Thus evidence describing, for example, the process of creating x-rays, photographs, tape recordings, computer generated records, radar records, or scientific surveys when coupled with evidence showing that a particular process or system produces an accurate result when correctly employed and properly operated and that the process or system was in fact so employed and operated, constitutes sufficient evidence that the result is what it purports to be.

Underlying mechanical equipment, data, computer programs, etc., need not be introduced under Rule 901(b)(9), but where available must be made available to the opposing party, usually far in advance of trial.

Evidence as to the process or system and its accuracy may come either from an expert witness or be judicially noticed, Rule 201. In still other instances authentication is provided by statute, Rule 901(b)(10).

It is probably fair to say that in most instances evidence of the results of a process or system is simply admitted without evidence ever being introduced either as to the capability of the process or system properly employed to produce an accurate result, or as to the actual employment and operation of the process or system in the matter at hand. This is almost always the case, for example, where a physician testifies to the results of a test such as an electroencephalogram.

**Computer records.** Computer generated records may be put into evidence as business records, Rules 803(6) and (8), if evidence sufficient to support a finding is introduced that the electronic computing equipment is recognized as standard, that the entries were made in the regular course of a regularly conducted business activity at or reasonably near the happening of the event recorded by or from someone within the business possessing personal knowledge, that the computer process produces an accurate result when correctly employed and properly operated, and that the computer process was so employed and operated with respect to the matter at hand, unless the court determines that the sources of information, method, or time of preparation indicate lack of trustworthiness. Data placed into a computer in accordance with the foregoing requirement may be admitted when presented in a different form provided a sufficient foundation is laid with respect to the mechanical equipment, program, etc. When the underlying data itself does not comply with any hearsay exception, employment of the results of computer analysis may nevertheless be presented to the trier of fact if reasonably relied upon by an expert witness, Rule 703.

**Faxed documents.** Authentication of a faxed document varies depending upon whether the proponent is seeking to establish that a particular document was sent by the proponent or another and received by a particular person or entity or whether the faxed document was sent by a particular person or entity and received by the proponent or another.

**E-mail.** An E-mail message may be authenticated through various traditional common law methods such as the reply doctrine, distinctive characteristics, chain of custody, or process or system similar to the foundation presented above with respect to faxed documents. To further insure the accuracy of the message and the identity of the sender a digital signature, created and verified by cryptography, may be utilized.

## Rule 901(b)(10).

## METHODS PROVIDED BY
## STATUTE OR RULE

**(a) General Provision. The requirement of authentication or identification as a condition precedent to admissibility is satisfied by evidence sufficient to support a finding that the matter in question is what its proponent claims.**

**(b) Illustrations. By way of illustration only, and not by way of limitation, the following are examples of authentication or identification conforming with the requirements of this rule:**

\* \* \*

**(10) Methods Provided by Statute or Rule. Any method of authentication or identification provided by Act of Congress or by other rules prescribed by the Supreme Court pursuant to statutory authority.**

## § 901.10   Rule 901(b)(10): Methods Provided by Statute or Rule

Authentication or identification is sufficient if made in compliance with any Act of Congress or by other rules prescribed by the Supreme Court pursuant to statutory authority, Rule 901(b)(10). The purpose of the rule is to make clear that methods of authentication provided by Act of Congress and by the Rules of Civil and Criminal Procedure or by Bankruptcy Rules are not intended to be superseded.

## Rule 902.

## SELF-AUTHENTICATION

### Prelude

## § 902.0   Rule 902: Self–Authentication

Certain kinds of evidence possess on their face indicia of authenticity sufficient alone to support a finding by a reasonable jury that the item is what it purports to be. Thus evidence satisfying any one of the ten subdivisions of Rule 902 is self-authenticating; extrinsic evidence as to authentication is not required. The rationale underlying the notion of self-authentication is that the likelihood of fabrication or honest error is so slight in comparison with the time and expense involved in authentication that extrinsic evidence is not required. Evidence of non-authenticity may, of course, be introduced. Although an item of evidence is made self-authenticating by Rule 902, the contents of the item may still have to meet other requirements such as the rule against hearsay, Rule 802, and the Original Writing Rule, Rule 1002, in order to be admitted.

Out of court statements admitted under Rule 902 for the purpose of establishing that the exhibit offered into evidence is as purported to be are received in evidence to establish the truth of the matter stated, Rules 801(a)-(c). Rule 802 provides that "hearsay is not admissible except as provided by these rules * * *." Rule 902 thus operates as a hearsay exception on the limited question of authenticity. Rule 902 does not, however, purport to create a hearsay exception for matters asserted to be true in the self-authenticated exhibit itself.

With respect to each of twelve subdivisions of Rule 902, the writing itself is self-authenticating when presented in court. A writing is not self-authenticating when a witness in court testifies that a given document she observed out of court was, for example, a newspaper. The rational of sufficient indicia of reliability requires actual production in court of the item claimed to be self-authenticating. If the actual item is not produced, authentication should proceed under Rule 901 rather than Rule 902. The requirement of actual production of the item under Rule 902 operates independently of the Original Writing Rule, Rule 1002.

The text of each of the twelve subdivisions of Rule 902, together with commentary is presented in the sections which follow. Each subdivision of Rule 902 is treated as a separate rule for the convenience of the reader.

## Rule 902(1).

## DOMESTIC PUBLIC DOCUMENTS UNDER SEAL

**Extrinsic evidence of authenticity as a condition precedent to admissibility is not required with respect to the following:**

**(1) Domestic Public Documents Under Seal. A document bearing a seal purporting to be that of the United States, or of any State, district, Commonwealth, territory, or insular possession thereof, or the Panama Canal Zone, or the Trust Territory of the Pacific Islands, or of a political subdivision, department, officer, or agency thereof, and a signature purporting to be an attestation or execution.**

## § 902.1 Rule 902(1): Domestic Public Documents Under Seal; Attestation

A document bearing a seal purporting to be that of the United States, or of any State, district, Commonwealth, territory, or insular possession thereof, or the Panama Canal Zone, or the Trust Territory of the Pacific Islands, or of a political subdivision, department, officer, or agency thereof, and a signature purporting to be an attestation or execution is self-authenticating, Rule 902(1). There is no requirement imposed with respect to authentication of either the seal or the signature. Attestation in this context means that the signer has examined the document and found it to be a genuine public document. The underlying justification is that forgery is a crime and that detection is fairly easy and certain.

Documents acknowledged before notaries public are separately covered in Rule 902(8) and are not governed by the rule here under discussion.

## Rule 902(2).

## DOMESTIC PUBLIC DOCUMENTS NOT UNDER SEAL

**Extrinsic evidence of authenticity as a condition precedent to admissibility is not required with respect to the following:**

**\* \* \***

**(2) Domestic Public Documents Not Under Seal. A document purporting to bear the signature in the official capacity of an officer or employee of any entity included in paragraph (1) hereof, having no seal, if a public officer having a seal and having official duties in the district or political subdivision of the officer or employee certifies under seal that the signer has the official capacity and that the signature is genuine.**

## § 902.2　Rule 902(2): Domestic Public Documents Not Under Seal

A document purporting to bear the signature in his official capacity of an officer or employee of any entity included in Rule 902(1), having no seal, if a public officer having a seal and having official duties in the district or political subdivision of the officer or employee certifies under seal that the signer has the official capacity and that the signature is genuine is self-authenticating, Rule 902(2). This provision restricts self-authentication to those persons possessing a seal as an attribute of office and is believed thus to reduce the risk of fabrication.

Notaries public are not included within 902(2).

### Rule 902(3).

## FOREIGN PUBLIC DOCUMENTS

**Extrinsic evidence of authenticity as a condition precedent to admissibility is not required with respect to the following:**

\* \* \*

**(3) Foreign Public Documents. A document purporting to be executed or attested in an official capacity by a person authorized by the laws of a foreign country to make the execution or attestation, and accompanied by a final certification as to the genuineness of the signature and official position (A) of the executing or attesting person, or (B) of any foreign official whose certificate of genuineness of signature and official position relates to the execution or attestation or is in a chain of certificates of genuineness of signature and official position relating to the execution or attestation. A final certification may be made by a secretary of embassy or legation, consul general, consul, vice consul, or consular agent of the United States, or a diplomatic or consular official of the foreign country assigned or accredited to the United States. If reasonable opportunity has been**

given to all parties to investigate the authenticity and accuracy of official documents, the court may, for good cause shown, order that they be treated as presumptively authentic without final certification or permit them to be evidenced by an attested summary with or without final certification.

## § 902.3   Rule 902(3): Foreign Public Documents

Rule 902(3) deals with documents executed or attested to by a person in an official capacity in a foreign country. It is designed to meet the practical problems in obtaining properly authenticated documents from abroad by abolishing all unnecessary procedural requirements.

A document purporting to be executed or attested in his official capacity by a person authorized by the laws of a foreign country to make the execution or attestation, and accompanied by a final certification as to the genuineness of the signature and official position (A) of the executing or attesting person, or (B) of any foreign official whose certificate of genuineness of signature and official position relates to the execution or attestation or is in a chain of certificates of genuineness of signature and official position relating to the execution or attestation is self-authenticating. A final certification may be made by a secretary of embassy or legation, consul general, consul, vice consul, or consular agent of the United States, or a diplomatic or consular official of the foreign country assigned or accredited to the United States. If reasonable opportunity has been given to all parties to investigate the authenticity and accuracy of official documents, the court may, for good cause shown, order that they be treated as presumptively authentic without final certification or permit them to be evidenced by an attest-

ed summary with or without final certification, Rule
902(3).

## Rule 902(4).

## CERTIFIED COPIES OF
## PUBLIC RECORDS

**Extrinsic evidence of authenticity as a condition
precedent to admissibility is not required with
respect to the following:**

\* \* \*

**(4) Certified Copies of Public Records. A copy
of an official record or report or entry therein,
or of a document authorized by law to be recorded or filed and actually recorded or filed in a
public office, including data compilations in any
form, certified as correct by the custodian or
other person authorized to make the certification, by certificate complying with paragraph
(1), (2), or (3) of this rule or complying with any
Act of Congress or rule prescribed by the Supreme Court pursuant to statutory authority.**

## § 902.4  Rule 902(4): Certified Copies of Public
Records

Considerations of inconvenience and danger of loss or
damage in removing a public record from its usual place
of keeping led to the common law rule that a public
record may be proved by a copy certified by the custodian
and bearing an official seal.

Under Rule 902(4) a copy of an official record or report
or entry therein, or of a document authorized by law to
be recorded or filed and actually recorded or filed in a

public office, including data compilations in any form, certified as correct by the custodian or other person authorized to make the certification, by certificate complying with Rule 902(1), (2), or (3) or complying with any Act of Congress or rule presented by the Supreme Court pursuant to statutory authority is self-authenticating. The custodian prepares a certificate stating that he has custody of the original record, report, entry or recorded or filed document and that the copy annexed is true and correct; nothing further is required nor permitted. The certificate itself qualifies as a public document receivable as self-authenticating when in conformity with Rule 902(1), (2) or (3). No additional certification as to the fact of custody, the custodian's authority, the authenticity of the seal or signature is required other than with respect to foreign documents. The phrase "other person authorized to make the certification" applies to deputy custodians or others in public offices authorized to make copies of records in their keeping.

The certification procedure provided in Rule 902(4) extends only to *official* records, reports, entries and to recorded or filed documents, including data compilations; it does not apply to documents of the public office or agency generally. Hence certain public documents provable when presented in original form under Rule 902(1), (2), or (3) may not be provable by certified copy under Rule 902(4). No reason for this limitation is provided in the Advisory Committee's Note. Documents authorized to be recorded or filed and actually recorded or filed may also be self-authenticated by means of a certified copy, Rule 902(4).

A certified copy of a public record, Rule 902(4), complies with the requirements of the Original Writing Rule,

Rule 1002, by virtue of Rule 1005. A hearsay exception for most official public records is provided in Rule 803(8); it does not apply to filed or recorded documents.

Evidence in the form of an affidavit certified in accordance with Rule 902(1), (2), or (3) is admissible as an exception to the hearsay rule to prove absence of a record, report, statement, or data compilation, in any form, or the nonoccurrence or nonexistence of a matter of which a record, report, statement, or data compilation, in any form, was regularly made and preserved by a public office or agency, Rule 803(10). When a copy of the public record is itself annexed to the affidavit Rule 902(4) is called into play but not otherwise.

## Rule 902(5).

## OFFICIAL PUBLICATIONS

**Extrinsic evidence of authenticity as a condition precedent to admissibility is not required with respect to the following:**

\* \* \*

**(5) Official Publications. Books, pamphlets, or other publications purporting to be issued by public authority.**

### § 902.5   Rule 902(5): Official Publications

Books, pamphlets, or other publications purporting to be issued by public authority, are self-authenticating, Rule 902(5).

Dispensing with preliminary proof of the genuineness of purported official publications, most commonly encountered in connection with statutes, court reports, rules, and regulations, had to a very large extent been previously accomplished by statutes and court decisions. Consistent with other rules dealing with authentication, Rule 902(5) does not confer admissibility upon all official publications; it merely provides a means whereby their authenticity may be taken as established for purposes of admissibility.

### Rule 902(6).

### NEWSPAPERS AND PERIODICALS

**Extrinsic evidence of authenticity as a condition precedent to admissibility is not required with respect to the following:**

\* \* \*

**(6) Newspapers and Periodicals. Printed materials purporting to be newspapers or periodicals.**

### § 902.6  Rule 902(6): Newspapers and Periodicals

Printed materials purporting to be newspapers or periodicals are self-authenticating, Rule 902(6). The realities of newspaper and periodical publication make the risk of forgery extremely low. The Advisory Committee's Note states that "[e]stablishing the authenticity of the publication may, of course, leave still open questions of authority and responsibility for items therein contained". While the issue is clearly "still open", notices and advertisements appearing in newspapers and periodicals should be considered self-authenticating with respect to the fact that they were inserted by authority of the person purporting to have inserted them. Contrary evidence would, of course, be admissible.

## Rule 902(7).

## TRADE INSCRIPTIONS AND THE LIKE

**Extrinsic evidence of authenticity as a condition precedent to admissibility is not required with respect to the following:**

\* \* \*

**(7) Trade Inscriptions and the Like. Inscriptions, signs, tags, or labels purporting to have been affixed in the course of business and indicating ownership, control, or origin.**

## § 902.7  Rule 902(7): Trade Inscriptions and the Like

Inscriptions, signs, tags, or labels purporting to have been affixed in the course of business and indicating ownership, control, or origin, are self-authenticating, Rule 902(7). The basis for self-authentication of these items is the day-to-day reliance by members of the public on their correctness and the unlikelihood of fabrication. Moreover many cases will involve trademarks and brand names registered under federal and state laws prohibiting others from using them.

## Rule 902(8).

## ACKNOWLEDGED DOCUMENTS

**Extrinsic evidence of authenticity as a condition precedent to admissibility is not required with respect to the following:**

\* \* \*

**(8) Acknowledged Documents. Documents accompanied by a certificate of acknowledgment**

**executed in the manner provided by law by a notary public or other officer authorized by law to take acknowledgments.**

## § 902.8    Rule 902(8): Acknowledged Documents

Documents accompanied by a certificate of acknowledgment executed in a manner provided by law by a notary public or other officer authorized to take acknowledgments are self-authenticating, Rule 902(8). Statutory provisions with respect to title documents are in accord.

The certificate of acknowledgment should provide in one form or another that the person executing the particular document in question has (1) come before a public official or a notary public authorized to take an acknowledgment, (2) that his identity was known to the said official or notary or he produced sufficient documents of identification, and (3) that he stated to the official or notary that he executed the document of his own free will. If a partnership, the person should indicate that he acknowledged the document on behalf of the partnership. If a corporation, the person should indicate that he executed the document or affixed the corporation seal, if so affixed, or both, by authorization of the corporation. Notice that the mere execution of a jurat by the notary public, i.e., "sworn to before me this 10th day of January 2001", does not establish the identity of the person being sworn.

## Rule 902(9).

## COMMERCIAL PAPER AND RELATED DOCUMENTS

**Extrinsic evidence of authenticity as a condition precedent to admissibility is not required with respect to the following:**

\* \* \*

**(9) Commercial Paper and Related Documents. Commercial paper, signatures thereon, and documents relating thereto to the extent provided by general commercial law.**

### § 902.9   Rule 902(9): Commercial Paper and Related Documents

Commercial paper, signatures thereon, and documents relating thereto, to the extent provided by general commercial law, are self-authenticating, Rule 902(9). The general commercial law referred to is the Uniform Commercial Code. For example, Uniform Commercial Code § 1–202 makes certain documents required by an existing contract "prima facie evidence" of their own authenticity and § 3–505 provides that a formal certificate of protest, a stamp by the drawee that payment was refused, or bank records are all admissible in evidence and create a presumption of dishonor.

## Rule 902(10).

## PRESUMPTIONS UNDER ACTS OF CONGRESS

**Extrinsic evidence of authenticity as a condition precedent to admissibility is not required with respect to the following:**

* * *

**(10) Presumptions Under Acts of Congress. Any signature, document, or other matter declared by Act of Congress to be presumptively or prima facie genuine or authentic.**

## § 902.10 Rule 902(10): Presumptions Under Acts of Congress

Any signature, document, or other matter declared by Act of Congress to be presumptively or prima facie genuine or authentic is self-authenticating, Rule 902(10). Statutory provisions often employ the terms presumption or prima facie evidence in reference to authentication.

## Rule 902(11).

### CERTIFIED DOMESTIC RECORDS OF REGULARLY CONDUCTED ACTIVITY

**Extrinsic evidence of authenticity as a condition precedent to admissibility is not required with respect to the following:**

* * *

**(11) Certified Domestic Records of Regularly Conducted Activity. The original or a duplicate of a domestic record of regularly conducted activity, that would be admissible under Rule 803(6), if accompanied by a written declaration of its custodian or other qualified person, in a manner complying with any Act of Congress or rule prescribed by the Supreme Court pursuant to statutory authority, certifying that the record**

(A) was made at or near the time of the occurrence of the matters set forth by, or from information transmitted by, a person with knowledge of those matters;

(B) was kept in the course of the regularly conducted activity; and

(C) was made by the regularly conducted activity as a regular practice.

A party intending to offer a record into evidence under this paragraph must provide written notice of that intention to all adverse parties, and must make the record and declaration available for inspection sufficiently in advance of their offer into evidence to provide an adverse party with a fair opportunity to challenge them.

## § 902.11 Rule 902(11): Certified Domestic Records of Regularly Conducted Activity

In both civil and criminal cases, Rule 902(11) provides that the original or a duplicate of a domestic record of regularly conducted activity, that would be admissible under Rule 803(6), if accompanied by a written declaration of its custodian or other qualified person, in a manner complying with any Act of Congress or rule prescribed by the Supreme Court pursuant to statutory authority, certifying that the record, (A) was made at or near the time of the occurrence of the matters set forth by, or from information transmitted by, a person with knowledge of those matters; (B) was kept in the course of the regularly conducted activity; and (C) was made by the regularly conducted activity as a regular practice, is self-authenticating.

A party intending to offer a record into evidence under Rule 902(11) must provide written notice of that intention to all adverse parties, and must make the record and declaration available for inspection sufficiently in advance of their offer into evidence to provide an adverse party with a fair opportunity to challenge them, Rule 902(11).

## Rule 902(12).

### CERTIFIED FOREIGN RECORDS OF REGULARLY CONDUCTED ACTIVITY

**Extrinsic evidence of authenticity as a condition precedent to admissibility is not required with respect to the following:**

\* \* \*

**(12) Certified foreign records of regularly conducted activity. In a civil case, the original or a duplicate of a foreign record of regularly conducted activity that would be admissible under Rule 803(6) if accompanied by a written declaration by its custodian or other qualified person certifying that the record**

**(A) was made at or near the time of the occurrence of the matters set forth by, or from information transmitted by, a person with knowledge of those matters;**

**(B) was kept in the course of the regularly conducted activity; and**

**(C) was made by the regularly conducted activity as a regular practice.**

**The declaration must be signed in a manner that, if falsely made, would subject the maker to criminal penalty under the laws of the country where the declaration is signed. A party intending to offer a record into evidence under this paragraph must provide written notice of that intention to all adverse parties, and must make the record and declaration available for inspection sufficiently in advance of their offer into evidence to provide an adverse party with a fair opportunity to challenge them.**

## § 902.12    Rule 902(12): Certified Foreign Records of Regularly Conducted Activity

In a civil case, Rule 902(12) provides that the original or a duplicate of a foreign record of regularly conducted activity that would be admissible under Rule 803(6), if accompanied by a written declaration by its custodian or other qualified person certifying that the record (A) was made at or near the time of the occurrence of the matters set forth by, or from information transmitted by, a person with knowledge of those matters; (B) was kept in the course of the regularly conducted activity; and (C) was made by the regularly conducted activity as a regular practice, is self-authenticating.

The declaration must be signed in a manner that, if falsely made, would subject the maker to criminal penalty under the laws of the country where the declaration is signed.

A party intending to offer a record into evidence under Rule 902(12) must provide written notice of that intention to all adverse parties, and must make the record and declaration available for inspection sufficiently in advance of their offer into evidence to provide an adverse party with a fair opportunity to challenge them.

In a criminal case, 18 USCA § 3505 provides for self-authentication of the original or duplicate of a foreign record of regularly conducted activity upon certification by the custodian:

(a)(1) In a criminal proceeding in a court of the United States, a foreign record of regularly conducted activity, or a copy of such record, shall not be excluded as evidence by the hearsay rule if a foreign certification attests that—

(A) such record was made, at or near the time of the occurrence of the matters set forth, by (or from information transmitted by) a person with knowledge of those matters;

(B) such record was kept in the course of a regularly conducted business activity;

(C) the business activity made such a record as a regular practice; and

(D) if such record is not the original, such record is a duplicate of the original; unless the source of information or the method or circumstances of preparation indicate lack of trustworthiness.

(2) A foreign certification under this section shall authenticate such record or duplicate.

(b) At the arraignment or as soon after the arraignment as practicable, a party intending to offer in evidence under this section shall provide written notice of that intention to each other party. A motion opposing admission in evidence of such record shall be made by the opposing party and determined by the court before trial. Failure by a party to file such motion before trial shall constitute a waiver of objection to such record or duplicate, but the court for cause shown may grant relief from the waiver.

(c) As used in this section, the term-

(1) "foreign record of regularly conducted activity" means a memorandum, report, record, or data compilation, in any form, of acts, events, conditions, opinions, or diagnoses, maintained in a foreign county;

(2) "foreign certification" means a written declaration made and signed in a foreign country by the custodian of a foreign record of regularly conducted, activity or another qualified person that, if falsely made, would subject the maker to criminal penalty under the laws of that country; and

(3) "business" includes business, institution, association, profession, occupation, and calling of every kind, whether or not conducted for profit.

## Rule 903.

## SUBSCRIBING WITNESS' TESTIMONY UNNECESSARY

**The testimony of a subscribing witness is not necessary to authenticate a writing unless required by the laws of the jurisdiction whose laws govern the validity of the writing.**

### § 903.1   Rule 903: Subscribing Witness' Testimony Unnecessary

The testimony of a subscribing witness is not necessary to authenticate a writing unless the law of the jurisdiction whose law governs the validity of the writing specifically so requires, Rule 903. A subscribing witness, referred to in the Advisory Committee's Note as an attesting witness, is a person who at the request or with the consent of the maker places his name on the document for the purpose of making thereby an implied or expressed statement that the document was then known by him to have been executed by the purported maker.

The early common law rule required in the case of all attested documents either the production of each attesting witness or a satisfactory accounting for his absence.

# ARTICLE X

# CONTENTS OF WRITINGS, RECORDINGS, AND PHOTOGRAPHS

*Table of Rules*

## Rules 1001–1008.

## THE ORIGINAL WRITING (BEST EVIDENCE) RULE

### Prelude

### § 1001.0 The Original Writing (Best Evidence) Rule

Article X codifies what has misleadingly been named the "Best Evidence Rule", a rule of preference for the production of the original of a writing, recording or photograph when the contents of the item are sought to be proved. Secondary evidence establishing the content of the item is admissible only if the absence of all originals is adequately explained. Better described as the "Original Writing Rule", the rule is limited to writings, recordings, and photographs, Rule 1002; there is no general rule of evidence that a party must produce the best evidence which the nature of the case permits.

The rule developed at common law to provide a guarantee against inaccuracy and fraud by insistence upon production at trial of original documents. The emphasis is upon assuring accuracy as to the terms of the writing, recording, or photograph by avoiding the uncertainties of recollection which are inherent in oral testimony, avoiding the chances of mistake which may be present in the handmade copy, and reducing the risk of inaccuracy associated with lack of sincerity. Over time the scope of the rule was broadened to reflect modern reliance on photographic, mechanical, and electronic recording devices and sophisticated methods of data compilation, storage, and retrieval, Rule 1001. While the great expansion of pretrial discovery has measurably reduced the need for the rule, it still has significant application in criminal cases where a greater limitation on discovery exists, as well as in unanticipated situations.

Appellate consideration of issues concerning application of the Original Writing Rule must be made in light of the purpose of the rule to secure the most reliable information as to the contents of a writing, recording, or photograph. Thus before any technical violation of the Original Writing Rule will be held reversible error, counsel must at least be in a position to assert that there is a good faith dispute as to the existence or content of the writing, recording or photograph. Absent such representation, any error is clearly harmless.

The requirement of production of the original when the contents are in issue is contained in Rule 1002; Rule 1003 provides for admissibility of a duplicate under most circumstances. Definitions of both the terms original and duplicate, along with that of writings, recordings, and photographs, are provided in Rule 1001. Rule 1004 states the circumstances under which the original is not required. The functions of the court and jury with respect to the Original Writing Rule are addressed in Rule 1008. Rules 1005, 1006 and 1007 concern related issues involving public records, summaries and admissions of a party-opponent respectively.

## Rule 1001.

## DEFINITIONS

**For purposes of this article the following definitions are applicable:**

**(1) Writings and Recordings. "Writings" and "recordings" consist of letters, words, or numbers, or their equivalent, set down by handwriting, typewriting, printing, photostating, photographing, magnetic impulse, mechanical or electronic recording, or other form of data compilation.**

**(2) Photographs. "Photographs" include still photographs, X-ray films, video tapes, and motion pictures.**

**(3) Original. An "original" of a writing or recording is the writing or recording itself or any**

counterpart intended to have the same effect by a person executing or issuing it. An "original" of a photograph includes the negative or any print therefrom. If data are stored in a computer or similar device, any printout or other output readable by sight, shown to reflect the data accurately, is an "original".

(4) **Duplicate.** A "duplicate" is a counterpart produced by the same impression as the original, or from the same matrix, or by means of photography, including enlargements and miniatures, or by mechanical or electronic re-recording, or by chemical reproduction, or by other equivalent techniques which accurately reproduces the original.

## § 1001.1   Rules 1001(1), (2) and (3): Nature of an Original; An Overview

A "writing" and "recording" consists of letters, words, or numbers, or their equivalent, set down by handwriting, typewriting, printing, photostating, photographing, magnetic impulse, mechanical or electronic recording, or other form of data compilation, Rule 1001(1). "Photographs" include still photographs, X-ray films, video tapes, and motion pictures, Rule 1001(2). An "original" of a writing or recording is the writing or recording itself or any counterpart intended to have the same effect by a person executing or issuing it. An "original" of a photograph includes the negative or any print therefrom. If data are stored in a computer or similar device, any printout or other output readable by sight, shown to reflect the data accurately, is an "original", Rule 1001(3).

Whether a particular writing, recording or photograph is an original depends upon the intent of the parties. Whether the writing, recording or photograph being offered is in fact an original thus depends upon the circumstances under consideration. The mere fact of identicalness does not turn a copy into an original. However if the party executing or issuing intends that a writing, recording or photograph have the same effect as the original, the writing, recording or photograph then is an original, Rule 1001(3). Thus with respect to instruments executed in multiple copies, each is an original without regard to whether each party executed only one or all copies, for it is the intent of the parties that controls. Similarly counterparts of writings, recordings, or photographs usually but not necessarily produced by the same impression as the original, or from the same matrix, or by means of photography or equivalent measures, if intended to be regarded by the party as originals, are also originals. To illustrate handwritten or photostatic copies of a contract and carbon copies of a sales receipt each constitute an original if so intended by the parties. Finally a party by his conduct may confer the status of an original upon a writing, recording, or photograph originally produced as a copy, for what is a copy for one purpose may be an original for another.

## § 1001.2   Rule 1001(3): Nature of an Original; Business and Public Records; Telegrams; Faxed Documents; E–Mail

Retained copies, however produced, may qualify as the originals of business or public records. What is of importance is the intent of the issuer in creating the copy. Thus a carbon copy of a contract executed in duplicate becomes an original as does a sales ticket carbon copy given to a customer. Since the retained copy of the sales ticket, like the duplicate copy of the contract, is intended by the issuer to have the same effect as the original, the retained copy is also treated as an original. Any writing, record, or photograph created by a business or public entity for use in the operations of the business or public entity, whether or not derived from records such as sales tickets or invoices, may constitute an original. A copy of a copy of a copy may thus be an original depending upon use of the copy within the business or public entity itself in relation to the fact for which offered to prove in the given litigation.

The original of a telegram is determined by analogy to contract rules governing risk of error in transmission. If the party sending the message selects the telegraph as the means of transmission, the original is the writing delivered to the addressee, but if the addressee makes the selection, then the original is the writing delivered to the telegraph company. If what would be the original if written is instead telephoned, the Original Writing Rule is inapplicable.

The original of a faxed document or an e-mail should be determined by the same principles that would apply if the transmission was a letter, i.e., the transmission received would ordinarily be the original with the document that was faxed or the file that was e-mailed being a duplicate, Rule 1001(4).

## § 1001.3 Rule 1001(4): Duplicates

A duplicate is a counterpart produced by the same impression as the original, or from the same matrix, or by means of photography, including enlargements and miniatures, or by mechanical or electronic re-recording, or by chemical reproduction, or by other equivalent technique which accurately reproduces the original, Rule 1001(4). A duplicate differs from a counterpart treated as an original in that a duplicate is not intended by the person executing or issuing it to have the same effect. Thus a copy of an original produced for the purpose of litigation is a duplicate.

Of course hand produced copies are not originals unless so intended. Moreover, the likelihood of mistake, plus inadequacies with regard to establishing authenticity, supports the position taken in Rule 1001(4) that a copy made by hand is not a duplicate for purpose of introduction pursuant to Rule 1003.

## Rule 1002.

## REQUIREMENT OF ORIGINAL

**To prove the content of a writing, recording, or photograph, the original writing, recording, or photograph is required, except as otherwise provided in these rules or by Act of Congress.**

### § 1002.1   Rule 1002: Requirement of Original: An Overview

To prove the content of a writing, recording, or photograph, the original writing, recording, or photograph is required, except as otherwise provided by the Federal Rules of Evidence or by Act of Congress, Rule 1002. Thus in order for the Original Writing Rule to apply, the contents of a writing, recording, or photograph must be sought to be proved. If the contents are not sought to be proved, then evidence other than the original writing, recording, or photograph is admissible without reference to Rule 1002. The Original Writing Rule does not apply when evidence is presented that a memorandum, report, record or data compilation in any form does *not* contain a particular matter.

When a happening or transaction itself assumes the form of a writing, recording, or photograph, as with a deed or a written contract, proof of the happening or transaction necessarily involves the contents of the writing, recording, or photograph and calls for application of the Original Writing Rule. If however the happening or transaction does not take the form of a writing, recording, or photograph, it may be proved by other evidence even though a writing, recording, or photograph was made. The proof is directed to the occurrence of the happening or transaction and not to the contents of the writing, recording, or photograph. The Original Writing Rule, Rule 1002, applies in this situation only when the happening or transaction is sought to be proved by the writing, recording, or photograph, not when it is sought to be proved by other evidence. Thus for example payment may be proved without producing the written receipt which was given. Similarly reference to a writing, recording or photograph to prove its existence, execution or delivery does not call for application of the Original Writing Rule. To illustrate further assume an accused makes an oral confession to a police officer that is tape recorded and taken down by a stenographer. The stenographer types up her notes. The typed confession is then signed by the defendant. The police officer may testify to the oral confession without accounting for either the tape recording or the signed confession. If the police officer, however, attempts to testify as to the content of the tape recording or the content of the independently relevant signed confession, because the content of a writing, re-

cording or photograph is being sought to be proved, the
Original Writing Rule requires that such evidence be
introduced by having the tape recording or signed confession authenticated and admitted into evidence prior to
publication of its content to the jury. Naturally enough
there is often difficulty determining when the contents
are sought to be proved and when the writing, recording
or photograph is being referred to for some other purpose.

Rule 1002 is limited in its application by Rule 703
which permits an expert to give an opinion based on
matters not in evidence to the extent such matters are
reasonably relied upon by experts in the field. For example, the Advisory Committee Note states that "hospital
records which may be admitted as business records under Rule 803(6) commonly contain reports interpreting X
rays by the staff radiologist, who qualifies as an expert,
and these reports need not be excluded from the records
by [Rule 1002]."

## § 1002.2  Rule 1002: Requirement of Original; For-
mer Testimony; Depositions

Testimony which was given on another occasion is a
proper subject for the testimony of any witness who
heard it, despite the fact that it was taken down in
shorthand or otherwise contemporaneously recorded,
thereby affording a means of proof far more accurate
than the recollection of the witness. The Original Writing
Rule does not apply for it is the occurrence of the
happening rather than the contents of the transcript
which is sought to be proved. Several different avenues
of proof of the prior testimony are potentially available:
(1) by the testimony of a firsthand observer of the former
proceedings who can satisfy the court that he is able to

remember the purport of all the witness said even if he cannot remember the exact words; (2) by the testimony of a firsthand observer who has refreshed his present recollection with a memorandum, such as the stenographer's notes or transcript; (3) by the official stenographer's notes or transcript which qualifies as a public record, Rule 803(8), or (4) by the notes of an observer at the trial if they meet the requirements of a memorandum of recorded recollection, Rule 803(5). In addition a transcript of testimony given at a hearing, certified by an official court reporter, is by statute admissible to prove that the statements transcribed were said, Rule 802. With respect to depositions, Rule 30(f)(1) of the Federal Rules of Civil Procedure provides:

> The officer shall certify that the witness was duly sworn by the officer and that the deposition is a true record of the testimony given by the witness. This certificate shall be in writing and accompany the record of the deposition. Unless otherwise ordered by the court, the officer shall securely seal the deposition in an envelope or package indorsed with the title of the action and marked "Deposition of [here insert name of witness]" and shall promptly file it with the court in which the action is pending or send it to the attorney who arranged for the transcript or recording, who shall store it under conditions that will protect it against loss, destruction, tampering, or deterioration. * * * *

Depositions in criminal actions are also subject to the foregoing provision. Together with a reasonable construction of Rule 902(10), the effect of the rule is to make transcripts of testimony given at a deposition, if filed in the same courthouse, also admissible to prove that the statements transcribed were said, Rule 802. With respect to transcripts certified and filed in another courthouse, while probably unnecessary, resort to either Rule 901(b)(7), 902(4) or 1005 in combination with Rule 803(8) would certainly suffice to admit the transcript as a true record of the witness' testimony.

## § 1002.3  Rule 1002: Document Speaks for Itself; Cross–Examination on Writing

After a writing, recording or photograph whose content is in issue is admitted into evidence, the exhibit may be published to the jury. This can be accomplished in several ways including the passing of the exhibit from one juror to another. Another method of publication is for either counsel or the witness to read the exhibit to the jury. When a witness is so requested, opposing counsel may object, "Your Honor, the document speaks for itself." When raised in this context, the opposing party is objecting to the undue emphasis the exhibit may receive from being read in a particular fashion by the witness. Provided the witness is not attempting to characterize the content of the exhibit which is improper, whether the document may be read to the jury by the witness rests in the discretion of the court.

Occasionally an objection is interposed that a witness who admits having written or signed a writing cannot then be cross-examined as to its contents, the writing being the best evidence thereof. If the writing is desired as evidence of contradiction, it may, of course, be necessary to introduce or account for it in due course. However the purpose of the questioning is not to establish the contents but to test the memory and veracity of the witness, which does not call for application of the Original Writing Rule at all.

## § 1002.4    Rules 1002 and 1001(2): Photographs

Photographs, including still photographs, X-ray films, video tapes, and motion pictures, Rule 1001(2), are subject to the Original Writing Rule when their contents are in issue. The original of a photograph includes the negative or any print therefrom, Rule 1001(3).

The Original Writing Rule applies to photographs only when the contents of the photograph possess independent probative value rather than being merely illustrative of a witness' testimony as to matters observed. Photographic defamation, invasion of privacy, and charges of photographic pornography provide illustrations of instances where the contents of the photograph are sought to be proved. As the Advisory Committee's Note states, introduction into evidence of a surveillance photograph taken of a bank robber requires that the contents of the photograph be proved since there is presumably no one whose testimony the photograph may be said to illustrate. X-rays also fall into the latter category, although the presence of Rule 703 permitting an expert witness to rely upon facts or data not admitted into evidence if reasonably relied upon by experts in the field substantially reduces the frequency with which the original X-ray will have to be produced.

In a majority of instances the witness testifies that the photograph is a correct representation at the relevant time of events which he saw or of a scene with which he is familiar. Since the photograph itself is produced at trial and is in effect adopted by the witness as his testimony, no problem under the Original Writing Rule arises; the original is in fact in evidence.

## § 1002.5   Rule 1002: Chattels Bearing Inscription

Whether the Original Writing Rule should be applied with respect to chattels bearing inscriptions, such as the name on the side of a truck or a policeman's badge, is not specifically addressed in Article X of the Federal Rules of Evidence. Both McCormick and Wigmore advance the position that requiring application of the Original Writing Rule should rest in the court's discretion. On balance, application of the Original Writing Rule to inscribed chattels, coupled with a liberal and flexible interpretation of the original not obtainable and collateral matters inapplicability provisions of Rule 1004, would appear to be a sensible solution. Secondary evidence of the contents of an inscribed chattel can often be conveniently presented in the form of a photograph.

## Rule 1003.

## ADMISSIBILITY OF DUPLICATES

**A duplicate is admissible to the same extent as an original unless (1) a genuine question is raised as to the authenticity of the original or (2) in the circumstances it would be unfair to admit the duplicate in lieu of the original.**

## § 1003.1   Rule 1003: Admissibility of Duplicates

A duplicate, Rule 1001(4), is admissible to the same extent as an original, Rule 1001(3), unless (1) a genuine question is raised as to the authenticity of the original or (2) in the circumstances it would be unfair to admit the duplicate in lieu of the original, Rule 1003. A duplicate, being a counterpart produced by a method providing assurance of accuracy and precision, provides a convenient substitute for an original under most circumstances. Thus under normal circumstances the convenience of placing into the record a photostatic copy of an original document is provided.

Where, however, there is some reason for the original itself to be required, such as where a genuine question is raised as to its authenticity, the original will be required and duplicate may not be used, Rule 1003(1); production of the original will facilitate resolution of the issue. A genuine question as to the accuracy of the duplicate as reflecting the original, i.e., the proferred duplicate is not an accurate copy as it contains different content, or that while it is a correct copy the copy masks the color of ink used or the original was a cut and paste creation, etc., would also call for production of the original, Rule 1003(2). The reason need not be "persuasive," because the question of persuasiveness is one for the jury once the original is produced or its unavailability accounted for. The question raised, however, must be genuine, not spurious. If the original is unavailable as provided in Rule 1004, the duplicate may be received as secondary evidence.

The admissibility of a duplicate of a business record, Rule 803(6), is provided for upon certification in accordance with Rules 902(11) and 902(12) and § 18 USCA § 3505. The admissibility of duplicates of public records is governed by Rule 1005.

## Rule 1004.

# ADMISSIBILITY OF OTHER EVIDENCE OF CONTENTS

The original is not required, and other evidence of the contents of a writing, recording, or photograph is admissible if

**(1) Originals Lost or Destroyed.** All originals are lost or have been destroyed, unless the proponent lost or destroyed them in bad faith; or

**(2) Original not Obtainable.** No original can be obtained by any available judicial process or procedure; or

**(3) Original in Possession of Opponent.** At a time when an original was under the control of the party against whom offered, that party was put on notice, by the pleadings or otherwise, that the contents would be a subject of proof at the hearing, and that party does not produce the original at the hearing; or

**(4) Collateral Matters.** The writing, recording, or photograph is not closely related to a controlling issue.

## § 1004.1   Rule 1004: Admissibility of Other Evidence of Contents; No Degrees of Secondary Evidence

When the contents of a writing, recording, or photograph are sought to be proved, production of the original will be excused, Rule 1004, if *all* of the originals are either (1) lost or destroyed, (2) not obtainable, (3) in the possession of an opponent, or (4) relate to a collateral matter. Under such circumstances, other evidence, referred to as secondary evidence, of the contents of the writing, recording, or photograph is admissible. Whether an excuse provided by Rule 1004 for failure to produce the original has been shown is a preliminary matter for the court, Rule 104(a). The rules of evidence, except with respect to privilege, do not apply.

Rule 1004 recognizes no degrees of secondary evidence. If failure to produce the original is excused by virtue of any of the provisions of Rule 1004, relevant evidence of any kind as to the contents of the original may be introduced. Thus if it appears that a copy was made, its nonproduction does not have to be accounted for before parol evidence of the contents of the writing, record, or photograph is admissible. As a practical matter, tactical considerations will almost always, however, result in the party introducing the most convincing evidence available. Contrary evidence is of course admissible.

If parol evidence is given as to the contents, the witness must state the substance of the language, though not necessarily its exact terms, so that the effect of the writing or recording may be determined from its language and not by the judgment of the witness.

## § 1004.2    Rule 1004(1): Original Lost or Destroyed

An original is not required, and other evidence of content is admissible if all originals are lost or have been destroyed, unless the proponent lost or destroyed them in bad faith, Rule 1004(1). Proof of loss or destruction, a determination to be made by the court pursuant to Rule 104(a), will ordinarily consist of testimony in open court of a failure to locate after diligent search or personal knowledge of destruction. Under Rule 104(a) the rules of evidence, except those with respect to privilege, do not apply to the determination of the preliminary question. Thus in appropriate cases deposition testimony and proof by affidavit will be accepted. Whether a given search is in fact diligent depends upon what is reasonable under the circumstances.

Destruction of the original in bad faith by the party or another person at his instigation precludes introduction of secondary evidence of the contents by the guilty party, Rule 1004(1); voluntary destruction must be proved not to have been of fraudulent design.

## § 1004.3   Rule 1004(2): Original in Possession of Third Person Not Obtainable

Secondary evidence as to the contents of a writing, recording, or photograph may be introduced if no original can be obtained by any available judicial process or procedure, Rule 1004(2). When an original is traced to the possession of a third party, it must be shown that the third party for whatever reason cannot be subpoenaed to produce the original at trial or at a deposition, and that no other judicial procedure compelling production is available. Resort to the foregoing is compelled even where the original is located in another jurisdiction. However that is all that is required; it is not necessary to show further that reasonable efforts to secure the original from its possessor have been or would be fruitless.

## § 1004.4   Rule 1004(3): Original in Possession of Opponent; Notice to Produce

If during the time an original of the writing, recording, or photograph is in the possession of the opponent reasonable notice is given that the contents will be the subject of proof at a hearing and he fails to produce the original at the hearing, secondary evidence of its contents may be introduced, Rule 1004(3). Notice may be provided by the pleadings or be given otherwise, including by service of a notice to produce the writing, recording, or photograph at trial. If from the nature of the case or the prior actions of the parties, it is clear that the opponent must be aware that his adversary will rely upon a writing, recording, or photograph alleged to be in the opponent's possession, formal notice of any kind is not required; Rule 1004(3) states "pleadings or otherwise". However, customary practice is to give formal written notice, denominated a notice to produce, in advance of the hearing, describing the particular exhibit and calling upon the opposing party to produce the writing, recording or photograph at the hearing without regard to whether notice had previously been given in the pleadings or otherwise.

## § 1004.5   Rule 1004(4): Collateral Matters

Writings, recordings, or photographs may enter into a case only incidentally, with their significance being merely that an item of that general character exists or existed. Under these circumstances, while the content of the writing, recording, or photograph is in issue, Rule 1002, it is unlikely that the precise terms of the item can become a center of controversy of real significance in the litigation. Hence the original is not required when not closely related to a controlling issue, Rule 1004(4). The purposes for which reference may be made to writings, recordings, or photographs are so varied that precise definition of when an exhibit is collateral is impossible. However three factors appear critical in making this determination: (1) the centrality of the exhibit to the principal issues of the litigation; (2) the complexity of the relevant features of the writing, recording, or photograph; and (3) the existence of a genuine dispute as to its contents. Evaluation of these factors in the particular instance is left to the discretion of the court, Rule 104(a).

## Rule 1005.

## PUBLIC RECORDS

**The contents of an official record, or of a document authorized to be recorded or filed and actually recorded or filed, including data compilations in any form, if otherwise admissible, may be proved by copy, certified as correct in accordance with rule 902 or testified to be correct by a witness who has compared it with the original. If a copy which complies with the foregoing cannot be obtained by the exercise of reasonable diligence, then other evidence of the contents may be given.**

### § 1005.1  Rule 1005: Public Records

The same policy which permits authentication of official records and documents authorized to be recorded or filed including data compilations in any form by certified copy, Rule 902(4), also exempts the certified copy from the requirements of the Original Writing Rule; there is no need to account for failure to produce the original, Rule 1005. In addition the contents of an official record, or of a document authorized to be recorded or filed and actually recorded or filed, including data compilations in any form, may be proved by a copy testified to be correct by a witness who has compared it with the original, Rule 1005.

With respect to public records, a preference is expressed in Rule 1005 for a certified or compared copy in comparison to recollection testimony. In the normal situation, the compared copy will meet the definition of a duplicate, Rule 1001(4). As provided in Rule 1005, the certified or compared copy of a public record is admissible; the requirements of admissibility for a duplicate contained in Rule 1003 do not apply. Thus while evidence disputing the accuracy of the certified or compared copy is admissible, such evidence does not require that the original public record be introduced in evidence at the hearing.

Other secondary evidence of the contents of a public record may be introduced only if neither a certified nor compared copy can be obtained by the exercise of reasonable diligence. In the event of loss or destruction of the public record, its contents may be established by secondary evidence upon proof that the record was in fact made.

The purpose of Rule 1005 is to encourage use of a certified or compared copy to avoid the serious inconvenience attendant upon removing the public record from its place of keeping and to avoid the risk of loss or damage naturally associated with any requirement for the production of the original; thus no showing need be made excusing failure to produce the original public record.

## Rule 1006.

### SUMMARIES

**The contents of voluminous writings, recordings, or photographs which cannot conveniently be examined in court may be presented in the form of a chart, summary, or calculation. The originals, or**

**duplicates, shall be made available for examination or copying, or both, by other parties at reasonable time and place. The court may order that they be produced in court.**

## § 1006.1   Rule 1006: Summaries

The results of examinations of masses of figures, or of other voluminous writings, recordings, or photographs which cannot conveniently be examined in court may be presented in the form of a chart, summary, or calculation as constituting the only method of intelligible presentation, Rule 1006. A proper foundation must of course be laid establishing the correctness of the exhibit and otherwise authenticating the writings, recordings, or photographs forming the basis of the chart, summary or calculation. The originals of the records thus summarized must be made available to the opposite party for examination or copying, or both, in advance of trial at a reasonable time and place, Rule 1006. The original records need not be introduced into evidence, although the court may require that they be produced in court, Rule 1006. Charts, summaries, or calculations are not admissible if any of the originals on which they are based are inadmissible because they are hearsay not falling within an exception or for some other reason except to the extent that they have been reasonably relied upon by an expert pursuant to Rule 703.

If adequate supporting data are presented, the coincidence of final computation or other presentation with the ultimate issue is of no moment, Rule 704. On the other hand, Rule 1006 may not be employed as a guise for placing before the jury an argumentative synopsis of oral testimony or documentary evidence.

While Rule 1006 does not on its face require that an individual responsible for the preparation of the summary, chart, or calculation testify and thus become subject to cross-examination, it is unlikely that a sufficient foundation for accuracy of the exhibit can be laid other than by such a person. Even if possible in theory, introduction of a summary absent the opportunity to cross-examine with regard to its preparation should be prohibited under Rule 403 if not by operation of the rule against hearsay, Rule 802. All persons involved in preparation are not required; a sufficient foundation may be laid as to accuracy by one in a supervisory position.

Charts, summaries, or calculations of testimony, writings, recordings, or photographs actually admitted in evidence and those reasonably relied upon by an expert pursuant to Rule 703 will also be received when such testimony, writings, recordings, or photographs are too voluminous to be conveniently examined in court.

## Rule 1007.

## TESTIMONY OR WRITTEN ADMISSION OF PARTY

**Contents of writings, recordings, or photographs may be proved by the testimony or deposition of the party against whom offered or that party's written admission, without accounting for the nonproduction of the original.**

### § 1007.1 Rule 1007: Testimony or Written Admission of Party

The contents of a writing, recording, or photograph may be proved without accounting for the nonproduction of the original by the testimony or deposition of the party against whom offered or by his written admission, Rule 1007. Use of a party-opponent's testimony, deposition, or written admission to prove the content of a writing, recording, or photograph does not require any preliminary showing as to unavailability of the original.

Oral admissions are not included within Rule 1007. The risk of inaccuracy with oral admissions is substantial; permitting proof by oral admission would be at odds with the purpose of the Original Writing Rule's preference for the original. Oral admissions as to the contents of a writing, recording, or photograph by a party-opponent are of course admissible where nonproduction of the original has been accounted for, Rule 1004, and secondary evidence generally has become admissible.

## Rule 1008.

## FUNCTIONS OF COURT AND JURY

**When the admissibility of other evidence of contents of writings, recordings, or photographs under these rules depends upon the fulfillment of a condition of fact, the question whether the condition has been fulfilled is ordinarily for the court to determine in accordance with the provisions of rule 104. However, when an issue is raised (a) whether the asserted writing ever existed, or (b) whether another writing, recording, or photograph produced at the trial is the original, or (c) whether other evidence of contents correctly reflects the contents, the issue is for the trier of fact to determine as in the case of other issues of fact.**

## § 1008.1   Rule 1008: Functions of Court and Jury

The allocation of responsibility between judge and jury provided in Rule 1008 for determining preliminary questions of fact with respect to the Original Writing Rule is a specialized application of Rule 104. The court decides pursuant to Rule 104(a) whether production of the original is excused under Rule 1004; whether a writing, recording or photograph is a duplicate, Rule 1001(4); and whether a genuine issue of fact has been raised as to the authenticity of the original or duplicate so as to make a duplicate inadmissible without accounting for failure to produce the original, Rule 1003. These matters involving administration of a protective policy are solely for the court, Rule 104(a).

Where, however, relevancy depends upon satisfaction of a condition of fact, the issue relating to the condition of fact is ultimately for the jury. The court determines only whether evidence has been introduced sufficient to support a finding by a reasonable juror of the fulfillment of the condition of fact, Rule 104(b). Thus if an issue is raised (a) whether the asserted writing ever existed, (b) whether another writing, recording, or photograph produced at the trial is the original, or (c) whether other evidence of contents correctly reflects the contents, the issue is for the trier of fact to determine, Rule 1008.

Rule 1008 thus provides that factual determinations concerning the merits of the controversy are to be made by the trier of fact while those concerning merely the administration of the Original Writing Rule are to be decided solely by the court. To illustrate, assume plaintiff desires to offer secondary evidence of the content of an alleged contract after first introducing evidence as to loss of the original. Assume further that defendant counters with evidence that no such contract was ever executed. If the court were to decide that the contract was never executed and exclude the secondary evidence, the case would be at an end without ever going to the jury on the central issue. Accordingly under Rule 1008 the court would alone decide only (1) whether plaintiff has established loss of the original, Rule 1004(1), to be more probably true than not true thereby permitting the introduction of secondary evidence and (2) whether evidence has been introduced sufficient to support a finding by a reasonable juror that the secondary evidence accurately reflects the original. Whether or not the contract was in fact ever executed and if so whether the secondary evidence correctly reflects the contents of the original would be decided by the jury.

In reaching its determination as to whether the proponent had established that the original was lost, it is not necessary for the court to first decide whether the original ever existed, a determination reserved for the jury, Rule 1008(a). The jury will be permitted to decide whether a contract was entered provided evidence has been introduced sufficient to support a finding by a reasonable juror of its one time existence, Rule 104(b). Once such evidence has been introduced, the court simply assumes the existence of the original in determining whether the proponent of secondary evidence has established its loss to be more probably true than not true.

# ARTICLE XI

# MISCELLANEOUS RULES

*Table of Rules*

## Rule 1101.

## APPLICABILITY OF RULES

**(a) Courts and Judges. These rules apply to the United States district courts, the District Court of Guam, the District Court of the Virgin Islands, the District Court for the Northern Mariana Islands, the United States courts of appeals, the United States Claims Court, and to United States bankruptcy judges and United States magistrate judges, in the actions, cases, and proceedings and to the extent hereinafter set forth. The terms "judge" and "court" in these rules include United States bankruptcy judges and United States magistrate judges.**

597

(b) **Proceedings Generally.** These rules apply generally to civil actions and proceedings, including admiralty and maritime cases, to criminal cases and proceedings, to contempt proceedings except those in which the court may act summarily, and to proceedings and cases under title 11, United States Code.

(c) **Rule of Privilege.** The rule with respect to privileges applies at all stages of all actions, cases, and proceedings.

(d) **Rules Inapplicable.** The rules (other than with respect to privileges) do not apply in the following situations:

(1) **Preliminary Questions of Fact.** The determination of questions of fact preliminary to admissibility of evidence when the issue is to be determined by the court under rule 104.

(2) **Grand Jury.** Proceedings before grand juries.

(3) **Miscellaneous Proceedings.** Proceedings for extradition or rendition; preliminary examinations in criminal cases; sentencing, or granting or revoking probation; issuance of warrants for arrest, criminal summonses, and search warrants; and proceedings with respect to release on bail or otherwise.

(e) **Rules Applicable in Part.** In the following proceedings these rules apply to the extent that matters of evidence are not provided for in the statutes which govern procedure therein or in other rules prescribed by the Supreme Court pursuant to statutory authority: the trial of misdemeanors and other petty offenses before United States magistrate judges; review of agency actions when the facts are subject to trial de novo under section 706(2)(F) of title 5, United States Code; review of orders of the Secretary of Agriculture under section 2 of the Act entitled "An Act to authorize association of producers of agricultural products" approved February 18, 1922 (7 U.S.C. 292), and under sections 6 and 7(c) of the Perishable Agricultural Commodities Act, 1930 (7 U.S.C. 499f, 499g(c)); naturalization and revocation of naturalization under sections 310–318 of the Immigration and Nationality Act (8 U.S.C. 1421–1429); prize proceedings in admiralty under sections 7651–7681 of title 10, United States Code; review of orders of the Secretary of the Interior under section 2 of the Act entitled "An Act authorizing associations of producers of aquatic products" approved June 25, 1934 (15 U.S.C. 522); review of orders of petroleum control boards under section 5 of the Act entitled "An Act to regulate interstate and foreign commerce in petroleum and its products by prohibiting the shipment in such commerce of petroleum and its products produced in violation of State law, and for other purposes", approved February 22, 1935 (15 U.S.C. 715d); actions for fines, penalties, or forfeitures under part V of title IV of the Tariff Act of 1930 (19 U.S.C. 1581–1624), or under the Anti–Smuggling Act (19 U.S.C. 1701–1711); criminal libel for condemnation, exclusion of imports, or other proceedings under the Federal Food, Drug, and Cosmetic Act (21 U.S.C. 301–392); disputes between seamen under sections 4079, 4080, and 4081 of the Revised Statutes (22 U.S.C.

256–258); **habeas corpus under sections 2241–2254 of title 28, United States Code; motions to vacate, set aside or correct sentence under section 2255 of title 28, United States Code; actions for penalties for refusal to transport destitute seamen under section 4578 of the Revised Statutes (46 U.S.C. 679); actions against the United States under the Act entitled "An Act authorizing suits against the United States in admiralty for damage caused by and salvage service rendered to public vessels belonging to the United States, and for other purposes", approved March 3, 1925 (46 U.S.C. 781–790), as implemented by section 7730 of title 10, United States Code.**

## § 1101.1   Rule 1101: Applicability of Rules

The Federal Rules of Evidence apply generally to civil actions and proceedings, including admiralty and maritime cases, to criminal cases and proceedings, to contempt proceedings except those in which the court may act summarily and to proceedings and cases under the Bankruptcy Code, Rule 1101(b), in the United States district courts, the District Court of Guam, the District Court of the Virgin Islands, the District Court for the Northern Mariana Islands, the United States courts of appeals, the United States Claims Court, as well with respect to such actions, cases, and proceedings before United States bankruptcy judges and United States magistrate judges. The terms "judge" and "court" in the rules include United States bankruptcy judges and United States magistrate judges, Rule 1101(a).

The Federal Rules of Evidence (other than those with respect to privilege) do not apply in the following situations, Rule 1101(d):

(1) Preliminary questions of fact under Rule 104.

(2) Proceedings before grand juries.

(3) Proceedings for extradition or rendition; preliminary examinations in criminal cases; sentencing, or granting or revoking probation; issuance of warrants for arrest, criminal summonses, and search warrants; proceedings with respect to release on bail or otherwise.

With respect to those proceedings outlined in Rule 1101(e), the Federal Rules of Evidence apply only to the extent that matters of evidence are not provided for in the statutes that govern procedure therein or in other rules prescribed by the Supreme Court.

The rule with respect to privilege, Rule 501, applies at all stages of all actions, cases, and proceedings, Rule 1101(c).

## Rule 1102.

## AMENDMENTS

**Amendments to the Federal Rules of Evidence may be made as provided in section 2072 of title 28 of the United States Code.**

## Rule 1103.

## TITLE

**These rules may be known and cited as the Federal Rules of Evidence.**

\*

# INDEX

**JUDGE ONLY DETERMINATION**
Generally, § 104.1
Original Writing Rule, § 1008.1

**JUDGMENT AS TO PERSONAL, FAMILY OR GENERAL HISTORY OR BOUNDARIES,** § 803.23

**JUDGMENT OF PREVIOUS CONVICTION**
Hearsay exception, § 803.22
Impeachment, § 609.1

**JUDICIAL ADMISSION,** § 801.25

**JUDICIAL NOTICE**
Accurate and ready determination, § 201.3
Adjudication facts, §§ 201.1, 201.2, 201.3
Applicability of rules, § 201.7
Ascertaining the law, § 201.4
Authoritative treatise, §§ 201.3, 803.18
Contrary evidence, § 201.7
Court records, § 201.3
Criminal cases, § 201.7
Discretionary, § 201.7
Disputability, § 201.7
Factual aspects of legislation, § 201.6
Factual basis of judicial rules, § 201.5
Foreign law, § 201.4
Instructing jury, § 201.7
Learned treatises, §§ 201.3, 803.18
Legislative facts, §§ 201.1, 201.5, 201.6
Mandatory, § 201.7
Matters generally known, § 201.2
Nature, § 201.1
On appeal, §§ 201.1, 201.7
Opportunity to be heard, § 201.7
Preliminary questions of fact, § 201.7
Procedural aspects, § 201.7
Public records, § 201.3
Scientific principles, § 201.3
Time of taking, § 201.7
Unconstitutionality of legislation, § 201.6

**JURORS**
As witness, § 606.1
Attacking validity of verdict or indictment, § 606.2

**JURY VERDICT**
Attack by juror, § 606.2
Extraneous information or influence, § 606.2

**NOLO CONTENDERE,** § 410.1

**NONDISPUTED FACTS,** § 401.1

**NONVERBAL CONDUCT**
Intended as an assertion, § 801.2
Not intended as an assertion, § 801.3

**NOT HEARSAY**
Admission by party-opponent, §§ 801.14–801.25
Prior statement of witness, §§ 801.11–801.13

**NOTICE TO PRODUCE, ORIGINAL WRITING RULE,** § 1004.4

**OATH,** § 603.1

**OBJECTIONS**
In general, § 103.2
Continuing, § 103.2
Door opening, § 103.4
General, § 103.2
Grounds for, § 103.2
Harmless error, § 103.1
Hearing of jury, § 103.6
"Irrelevant, immaterial and incompetent," § 103.2
Motion to strike, § 103.3
Nonjury case, § 103.5
Offer of proof, § 103.6
Plain error, § 103.8
Presentation, § 103.2
Reliance on ruling, § 103.4
Specific, § 103.2
Specificity required, § 103.2
Time of objecting, § 103.3
Waiver, §§ 103.2, 103.4

**OFFENSE AGAINST CHILD,** §§ 414.1, 415.1, 804.1

**OFFER OF PROOF,** § 103.5

**OFFERS OF PLEAS,** § 410.1

**OFFERS TO COMPROMISE,** § 408.1

**OPINION OF LAY WITNESS,** §§ 701.1, 704.1

**OPINION TESTIMONY**
Character, § 405.1
Truthfulness, §§ 608.2, 608.3

**OPINIONS**
See also Expert Witness; Opinion of Lay Witness

†